Herschel Island
Qikiqtaryuk

Wildlife Management Advisory Council
North Slope

© 2012 Wildlife Management Advisory Council (North Slope)

Library and Archives Canada Cataloguing in Publication
Herschel Island: a natural and cultural history of Yukon's Arctic island = Qikiqtaryuk / Christopher R. Burn, editor.

Includes index.
ISBN 978-0-9880009-0-2 (bound) ISBN 978-0-9880009-1-9 (paperback)

1. Herschel Island (Yukon).
2. Herschel Island (Yukon)—History.
3. Natural history—Yukon—Herschel Island.
4. Herschel Island Territorial Park (Yukon).
I. Burn, Christopher Robert, 1959–
II. Wildlife Management Advisory Council (North Slope) (Canada)
III. Title: Qikiqtaryuk.

FC4045 H47 H47 2012   971.9'1   C2012-980069-4

To order copies of this book, contact:
University of Calgary Press
2500 University Drive NW
Calgary, Alberta T2N 1N4
uofcpress.com

Design and production: Aasman Brand Communications, Whitehorse
Printing: McCallum Printing, Edmonton

Cover photo by Fritz Mueller: Pauline Cove, Herschel Island, and the Beaufort Sea.

Herschel Island
Qikiqtaryuk

a natural and cultural history
of Yukon's Arctic island

Christopher R. Burn, editor

This book was made possible with financial support from

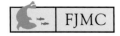 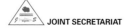 

This book is dedicated to the memory of all Inuvialuit elders who lived on and near Herschel Island.

In particular we remember the lives and families of

Neil and Annie Allen
Sam and Lucy Arey
Bob and Margaret Cockney
Charlie and Thea Gordon
Alex and Hope Gordon
George and Martha Harry
Harry and Minnie Inukutlak
Joe and Annie Inglangasuk
Luke and James Inukuk
Paul and Mary Kayotuk
Old Irish and Lucy Kegoyook
Diamond and Christina Klengenberg
William and Sarah Kuptana
Daniel and Clara Kupuk
Jonas and Sarah Meyook
Garrett and Emma Nutik
Kenneth and Rosie Peelolook
David and Olga Roland
Roland and Kitty Saʔuaq
Isaac and Emily Simon
Alex and Mabel Stefansson
Gus and Jean Tardiff
Allan and Aileen Uqpik

TABLE OF CONTENTS

PREFACE

Qikiqtaryuk or Herschel Island has a rich natural and cultural history, so much so that it was proposed for nomination in 2004 as a World Heritage Site along with adjacent Ivvavik and Vuntut national parks. It has been a Yukon territorial park since 1987, established as a result of the Inuvialuit Final Agreement, giving it a land claim settlement status that infuses modern governance with Inuvialuit tradition. The common name for the park is Herschel Island–Qikiqtaruk Territorial Park, but the transliteration of the Inuvialuktun pronounciation in the Siglitun dialect is **Qikiqtaryuk**.

The island has been central to the history of Canada's western Arctic. The oral history of the island and the Yukon North Slope were carefully documented and published in 1994, but it is remarkable that other aspects of the island's story are scattered through the scientific and technical literature, government reports, scholarly books, and the stories of travellers and traders. This book is the first comprehensive publication on Qikiqtaryuk–Herschel Island, drawing on recent research, indigenous knowledge, and historical material to provide a many-sided portrait of this vibrant and complex place.

Today, most visitors walk around the settlement buildings at Pauline Cove or hike up onto the tundra surrounding the settlement. Caribou wander nearby, and occasionally a visiting grizzly bear. The buildings and the abandoned RCMP dog kennels are prominent reminders of the Inuvialuit, whalemen, missionaries, fur traders, scientists, and police who occupied Herschel Island in the late nineteenth and twentieth centuries. The sturdy community house, built by the Pacific Steam Whaling Company in 1893 and now the oldest frame building in the Yukon, has served at one time or another as a church, hospital, recreation centre, police station, home, post office, mining recorder's office, and museum. Smaller workshops, sheds, and houses still stand, while the whalemen's warehouse, where the infamous trials of 1923 were held, is filled with bones, artifacts, and other relics from the whaling period. The continuous presence of indigenous people is recorded in the oral history of the island, archaeological remains at Avadlek Spit and near Pauline Cove, and mounds that mark the position of sod houses at Pauline Cove, some from before the whaling period. A log cabin is still in use by the Mackenzie family, and a cabin has been erected by the Yukon government for use by hunters, travellers, and official visitors throughout the year.

Visitors also hike around the ponds of the long sandspit on which these buildings sit to watch the abundant shorebirds—the sandpipers, plovers, guillemots, eider ducks, and Lapland longspurs that make Pauline Cove their summer home. The spit separates the shelter of the cove from the open Beaufort Sea, creating a safe harbour during the summer for the small boats that anchor there. Seals and whales chase their prey into the cove, where they feed on char, cisco, and other fish before continuing on their journeys along the western Arctic coast. Throughout the summer the blowing of belugas draws people to the sea, and often fishnets are set for char that are eaten fresh or preserved in a smokehouse. There are warm days with a gentle breeze when the place feels like an arctic paradise, remote from the pressures and stress of our society. Other days bring fierce winter storms or storm surges that flood the spit and damage the makeshift landing strip, forcing changes and delays to the well-made plans of human beings.

The settlement at Pauline Cove. *Photo by Cameron Eckert.*

Rolling hills of sand and mud, thrust out of the coastal plain during the Ice Age, form the backdrop to the settlement. They now rise gently about 60 metres above the ocean. The hills are underlain by massive sheets of ground ice, exposed in many places by the eroding coastline, that testify to the ubiquitous presence of permafrost, or perennially frozen ground. The whalemen recognized the potential of the permafrost to provide storehouses for frozen food. One of these cellars is still intact and allows an unusual glimpse of the ice within the ground. Near the cellar are four graveyards, two of which are for Inuvialuit, many of whom perished when diseases were brought into the region a hundred years ago. A pair of solitary graves holds the bodies of two Royal Northwest Mounted Police who died at Herschel Island, and a line of twenty-two wooden tablets marks the resting places of whalemen who never returned to their families.

It is difficult to separate human and natural history at Herschel Island because the economy and way of life have always been tied to natural resources. As a result, relations between people and their natural environment are emphasized throughout this book. Initially, the indigenous people lived off the land and sea. Later, both whalemen and traders sought animal products on an industrial scale. The short period of petroleum exploration between 1975 and 1985 was followed by designation of the park in 1987, a status that should allow conservation and preservation of the environment and wildlife for generations.

When the park was established, the Government of Yukon made a considerable effort to document the history and terrain conditions, especially the vegetation, on the island. These records now form a basis against which we may determine the effects of climate change in the western Canadian Arctic. Current research at Qikiqtaryuk focuses not only on developing a foundational understanding of the Arctic environmental system on the island, but also on how it has changed over the last century, is changing now, and how future conditions may affect it further. The research is possible because of the logistical support at Pauline Cove, especially the seasonal landing strips on the ice and the beach, and the shelter provided by the buildings. Much of this research was stimulated by the Government of Canada's support for the 2007–09 International Polar Year (IPY). At Herschel Island, IPY research was able to capitalize on a maturing series of environmental monitoring programs initiated by Yukon government biologists and conducted in collaboration with Park staff. Similarly, resource management in the region has come of age, with the agencies established under the Inuvialuit Final Agreement now being full, active, and experienced partners in decisions regarding the region. As a result, this book both

integrates a dispersed literature and presents a fresh perspective, founded in the experience of a changing environment.

Each chapter of this book was written by a person who has spent considerable time in professional study or practice in his or her field, and who has a direct connection to Herschel Island. Most of the authors are northerners based in the Mackenzie Delta, Whitehorse, or Yellowknife, who visit the island regularly as active research specialists. Others are academics who have spent considerable time at Herschel and have subsequently published their work. All have contributed enthusiastically and have opened a perspective on the island that is both wide and detailed. At the end of the book, you will find brief portraits of these contributors and their suggestions for further reading if you would like to learn more about a particular topic.

The work of putting together this book has been a collaborative effort, supported throughout by agencies and key individuals. I would especially like to thank Cameron Eckert, Richard Gordon, Jeff Hunston, Don Reid, Clint Sawicki, Pippa Seccombe-Hett, and Norm Snow for their unfailing encouragement of this project. I am most grateful to the reviewers who examined each chapter, especially Mark O'Donoghue, who read most of the Flora and Fauna section, as well as Frances Abele, John Bockstoce, Jeff Bond, Cameron Eckert, Jeff Hunston, Murray Humphries, Jill Johnstone, Steve Kokelj, Dave Ladret, Gita Laidler, Bill Morrison, Don Murphy, Isla Myers-Smith, Murielle Nagy, Taryn Parker, Brent Riley, Vicki Sahentien, Patricia Sutherland, Linda Thistle, Peter Usher, and Stephen Wolfe. Several people have taken time to answer questions of detail, particularly Cathy Cockney of the Inuvialuit Cultural Resource Centre and elders Rosie Albert and Esther McLeod of Inuvik; Ronald Lowe of Université Laval; Laurel Parson at the General Synod Archives of the Anglican Church of Canada; Dr. J. Ross Mackay of the University of British Columbia; Shannon Allen at Environment Canada; Bruce Bennett at Environment Yukon; Christine Cleghorn and Jennifer Smith at the Wildlife Management Advisory Council (North Slope); and staff at Yukon Archives. Patricia Robertson, an exemplary copy editor, has provided her eagle-eyed skill and been a literary sounding board. The handiwork of Christine Earl, a gifted cartographer, appears in many chapters. The design and production is by Aasman Brand Communications in Whitehorse. Photographs contributed by Fritz Mueller, Mary Beattie, Bruce Bennett, Alistair Blachford, Michelle Christensen, Luke Copland, Bharat Dixit, Colin Gallagher, Graham Gilbert, Colin Gordon, Chuck Gruben, Nancy Halliday, Jeff Hunston, Chris Hunter, Jutta Jantunen, Michael Kawerninski, Doug Larsen, J. Ross Mackay, Frank Pokiak, Clara Reid, Morley Riske, Louis Schilder, Michelle Sicotte, Jennifer Smith, John Snell, and Guillaume Szor have enhanced this book.

The following have all contributed to the preparation of this book: the Natural Sciences and Engineering Research Council of Canada; Yukon Parks, Heritage Resources Unit, and the

The landscape at Pauline Cove. *Panorama by Cameron Eckert.*

Inuvialuit Final Agreement Implementation Office, Government of Yukon; the Fisheries Joint Management Committee, an Inuvialuit agency, and the Inuvialuit Joint Secretariat; the Aurora Research Institute, Aurora College; the Yukon Research Centre, Yukon College; Aboriginal Affairs and Northern Development Canada; the Government of Canada's Program for the International Polar Year; and Carleton University. Much of the information presented here resulted from research programs supported by the Polar Continental Shelf Project of Natural Resources Canada, and, of course, Herschel Island–Qikiqtaruk Territorial Park.

I would like to thank various libraries and archives for their permission to reproduce images held in their collections: Yukon Archives, Government of Yukon; the General Synod Archives of the Anglican Church of Canada; New Bedford Whaling Museum; Climate Services of Environment Canada; the National Archives of Canada; the Canadian Museum of Civilization; Mystic Seaport; the Peabody Museum of Archaeology and Ethnology, Harvard University; Martha's Vineyard Museum; the Mariners' Museum; the National Library of Norway; the National Portrait Gallery, London; the Naval War College Museum, Newport, RI; the Master and Fellows of St. John's College, Cambridge; the Royal Geographical Society with the Institute of British Geographers; Parks Canada; the Vancouver Maritime Museum; and John Herschel-Shorland.

The images in this book are reproduced with permission of the photographers, or of the collection where the original photographs are held. Almost all of the photographs were taken at Herschel Island. Unexpired copyrights of photographs remain with the photographers and/or their agencies. Copyright of the text remains with the authors, but the copyright for the layout of the pages and presentation of this book is with the publisher.

The park rangers of Herschel Island always provide a warm welcome to itinerant travellers and researchers. In recent years Senior Park Ranger Richard Gordon and Rangers Lee John Meyook, Pierre Foisy, and Edward McLeod have given first-class field support to research at Herschel Island. My own research program on the island has been assisted throughout by Douglas Esagok, to whom I am indebted for fresh meat and fish, valuable observations, an encyclopaedic knowledge of the western Arctic coastlands, considered judgment of our travel plans, and unfailing good humour.

Joan Ramsay Burn has been with this project from beginning to end, and has been with me since my second summer in the Yukon in 1983. I am grateful to her for everything.

—*Christopher Burn*
  Carleton University, Ottawa, February 2012

FOREWORD

The story of our people and Herschel Island begins in Alaska. I was born on Barter Island, Alaska, then went to Point Barrow with my dad by schooner. Later, when I was eight years old in 1946, my dad said we were going to Canada.

Dad moved to Canada because his two brothers were already there—Alec and Donald. Fred was the other one and the first to go to Aklavik. He travelled on a snow machine from Alaska in 1950. We had heard that the Delta was plentiful with wildlife. In Alaska when caribou didn't come, there was no food, and if there was no open water then people can't get seals and people would go hungry.

We started walking—eight of us with six dogs—in April from Point Barrow and arrived at Barter Island in June. It was slow. The dogs had to be rested. We needed to stop and fatten them up for a few days at a time. People who could walk had to walk and they walked over long distances. I don't remember complaining—maybe I was too small. We never think anything about it.

The intent was to stay in Canada at Ptarmigan Bay and trap. But one of my sisters burned herself and we had to get her by plane and take her to Aklavik. So they left for Aklavik and we stayed at Ptarmigan Bay until April 1947. We made our final journey to Aklavik in April of that year.

At that time and a little earlier in the 1950s there were about 15 or 20 families living on Herschel Island. My wife Annie's grandfather and grandmother were at Herschel. Annie's grandmother is buried here. Eight families were over there at Ptarmigan Bay. Old Roland Saruk was always there. He was in this area all of his life and never went to Aklavik.

When we lived at Ptarmigan Bay in 1946 we knew all the families here and on the mainland. Most were from Alaska. The ones on Herschel used to come inland to hunt caribou. They used dog teams to go back and forth often and hunted caribou inland.

When I think of Herschel today I think of our connection to Alaska and Aklavik.

There has always been an Alaskan presence on the island. For years we have moved back and forth between Alaska and Aklavik by boat and plane. We still travel by boat and we still stop at Herschel on the way.

In the last ten years, I'm seeing less people here compared to long ago due to the price of gas. Still, it is important that our young people and elders have an opportunity to get to Herschel. It is such an important part of our history and who we are.

We remain connected to Herschel in many ways. Since the signing of the Inuvialuit Final Agreement, our people work here as park rangers. In the last 30 years, I've brought students here about six times. On one trip we called "Retrieving Inuvialuit footprints," we took young people to Alaska—all the way to Barter Island by boat with the support of our Inuvialuit Regional Corporation.

Danny Gordon on Herschel Island. *Photo by Jennifer Smith*

The partnership between our people and the Yukon government has made it possible for us to be an important part of the management of Herschel. This is the way it should be. We have a history here.

We know much about Herschel, but we are still seeing and learning new things. Weather is different now and the land has changed a lot. There is more slumping of the coast and it is eroding into the ocean. The harbours and land spits change every year. In the last 10 years, things are changing really rapidly. The weather is more extreme and unpredictable. East wind is unusual, but it happens all the time now. We can't plan our trips anymore. We just have to travel when conditions are right—often in the middle of the night. And we are seeing plants we have never seen before and others are disappearing.

Now that the Herschel Island book is coming out, other people can read about some of the things that are important to me and that I am talking about. I have been a part of some of the research on Herschel. Now I am reading some facts about it in this book. I have always wondered why researchers study flowers and plants and permafrost and other things so much. Now I know and this book explains a lot of this to me. I am supportive of research as long as it is properly explained. This book does that. It brings together a lot of information about Herschel. And it brings together the work of a lot of people who have worked on Herschel. It also helps us to remember those who are no longer with us. All of this is important.

Herschel should be a place people can continue to come and use. The management of the place is good. When I am on the land I always feel that this land is my land. That's the way I feel about it. I know where the shallow spots are, the shoals, and the harbours for safety. This book will help all of us share Herschel—those of us who are fortunate enough to make the trip here and those who can't. I hope you enjoy this book.

—*Danny C. Gordon*
  Herschel Island, July 27, 2011

Herschel Island
Qikiqtaryuk

INTRODUCTION

introduction

YUKON'S ARCTIC ISLAND

Christopher Burn

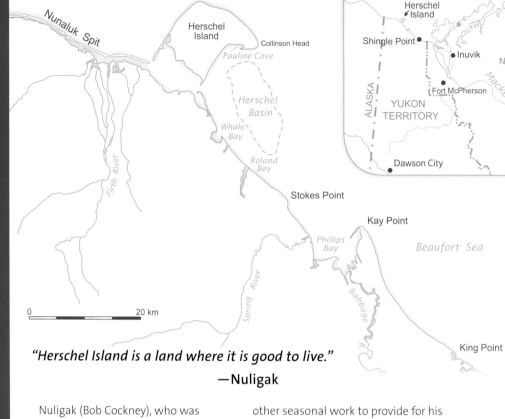

"Herschel Island is a land where it is good to live."
—Nuligak

Nuligak (Bob Cockney), who was born about 1895 and died in 1966, described life at Herschel Island in his autobiographical memoir, *I, Nuligak*. He recorded his delight at the buildings and amenities of Herschel, which he called "the big town." His well-known remark above is a reflection on the preparations for winter 1912–13 after his adoptive parents had harvested many seals at Pauline Cove. Nuligak spent over fifty years living intermittently on Herschel Island as he travelled back and forth along the western Arctic coast, hunting, trapping, and finding other seasonal work to provide for his family. His story not only emphasizes the traditional cycles of Inuvialuit life but also recognizes the changes and adjustments that followed the arrival of industrial society in Canada's western Arctic. Nuligak left us a unique description from an aboriginal perspective of cultural conditions during the transition from a subsistence to a mercantile economy between 1890, when the first whaling ships were frozen in at Pauline Cove, and the mid-1960s. Today, Herschel Island straddles, and at times integrates, two cultures.

The community house, built at Herschel Island by the Pacific Steam Whaling Company, and used as a mission and police barracks, is the oldest standing frame structure in the Yukon Territory. *Photo by Christopher Burn.*

Fig. 1 *Map* The Yukon coast of the southeastern Beaufort Sea, showing Herschel Island (Qikiqtaryuk). *Cartography by Christine Earl.*

Fig. 2 Alec Irish and his father, Old Irish Kegoyook, at their fish camp in Workboat Passage, 1957. *Photo by J. Ross Mackay.*

Fig. 3 Pauline Cove, Thetis Bay, and the Yukon mainland from Collinson Head in August 2005. The Steel Drilling Caisson (SDC), formerly the Semi-submersible Drilling Caisson (SSDC), berthed in Thetis Bay was then awaiting deployment by Devon Canada Corporation.
Photo by Christopher Burn.

Herschel Island is the northernmost part of the Yukon Territory and the westernmost of Canada's Arctic islands (Fig. 1). The whole island is included in Herschel Island Territorial Park, which was established in 1987 under the 1984 Inuvialuit Final Agreement (the western Arctic land claim) to recognize its unique natural and cultural heritage. The primary intention was, and remains, to conserve and preserve the lands and waters of the area so that the flora and fauna of the region may thrive and continue to sustain the cultural and subsistence activities of Inuvialuit (Fig. 2). Its designation as a park also recognizes the historical significance of the island to western Arctic Canada.

Qikiqtaryuk has a long history of aboriginal occupation and has been significant for both economic development and Canada's sovereignty in the Arctic ever since its functional recognition by the American whaling fleet in 1889. The island is fundamental to the social history of northern Canada because of the continuous documentation of the encounter and subsequent contact between Euro-American and aboriginal cultures. The documents, both written and photographic, are Euro-American (journals, books, and reports) and aboriginal (for example, *I, Nuligak*). A brief examination of some of these sources, especially the annual police reports to the Parliament of Canada,

shows that the interest of the federal government in the Arctic, centered on considerations of sovereignty, resource development, and the cost of northern operations, has hardly changed in a century.

The ecosystem at Qikiqtaryuk has sustained human life for hundreds of years and likely much longer. The people Capt. John Franklin met on the island on July 17, 1826, told him it was a good place to hunt "deer," and in fact one group had been chasing caribou into the water when they first saw his boats. Workboat Passage, between the island and the mainland, was similarly recognized for good fishing, while the sea to the east of the island was known to be excellent for seal hunting.

Today the island maintains its reputation for traditional harvesting, but it also acts as a scientific laboratory. The island's ecosystem is semi-isolated because Workboat Passage is a moat that prevents the casual movement of animals between the mainland and the island in summer. Birds, of course, are uninhibited by the water, and in spring and winter animals may cross the ice, but the island's partial separation, moderate size, and relatively uniform tundra landscape make possible comprehensive surveys of animal populations and quantitative tracking of the island's biodiversity and ecosystem health. The designation of

the island as a park provides habitat protection to sustain the ecosystem, while its size and lack of infrastructure mean that many parts of the island are still wild places, even though they may be monitored.

QIKIQTARYUK

Herschel Island is called **Qikiqtaryuk** in Siglitun, the Inuvialuktun dialect spoken in the eastern Mackenzie Delta, and **Qikiqtarr̂uk** in Uummarmiutun, the dialect of the western Delta. (The "r̂" is sounded like an English "r;" without the diacritic, "r" is sounded similarly to a French "r.") In both dialects the name means "big island." It is commonly written as Qikiqtaruk.

Siglitun is the surviving dialect closest to that of the Tuyurmiat, the inhabitants of **Qikiqtaryuk** before the arrival of Europeans in the western Arctic. Uummarmiutun is a dialect of Iñupiaq, an Alaskan language spoken by the Nunatarmiut, people from Alaska who migrated into the Canadian Arctic between the end of the nineteenth century and the 1960s.

Fig. 4 CCGS *Sir Wilfrid Laurier* and MV *Hanseatic* in Thetis Bay, July 2002.
Photo by Cameron Eckert.

Fig. 5 Flooding of the spit at Pauline Cove, August 2010. A similar flood on August 19–21, 1910, was reported by Insp. G.L. Jennings, RNWMP. "Never in the memory of the oldest native did the water come so high over the sandspit," he wrote. *Photo by Nicole Couture.*

Fig. 6 Retrogressive thaw slumps on the coast of Thetis Bay. *Photo by Nicole Couture.*

Human occupation and activities at Herschel Island have never been successful without respect for the Arctic environment. Even today, Thetis Bay provides one of the few sheltered anchorages on the western Arctic coast of North America (Fig. 3). The Arctic ecosystem, occupation by Inuvialuit, resource development, inter-cultural contact, and the establishment of sovereignty present continuous threads of the island's story, but in the last twenty years the growing effects of climate change have included the acceleration of rising sea level and the prospect of thawing permafrost, both of which threaten the historic infrastructure in the park. A longer ice-free season and increased storm intensity may destroy the offshore realm of the polar bear. Warmer summers slowly but noticeably affect the vegetation on the island, the first step in significant adjustments to the terrestrial ecosystem.

The chapters that follow this introduction, which provides an overview of the island's story, present systematic summaries of physical, biological, and cultural aspects of that story. As a collection they provide a variety of perspectives on a single place. The chapters are grouped into five sections. The first section explores the names of places at and near Herschel Island, because place names are commonly associated with foundational histories that may now be obscure. The next three sections concern the physical environment, the ecosystem, and human occupation and use of the land. The last section describes the territorial park and its operation. At the end of the book are suggestions for further reading about each topic, and brief biographies of the contributing authors.

Glacial Origin

Herschel Island was formed during the advance of the great ice sheets that covered most of Canada between 110,000 and 10,000 years ago. The ice reached its maximum extent along the Yukon coast toward the end of the glaciation, and in the process pushed up a mass of frozen sediments from what is now the continental shelf of the Beaufort Sea. This excavation left a large depression in the coastal plain, Herschel Basin (Fig. 1), which is a favoured feeding ground for bowhead whales. The depth of Herschel Basin made it attractive as a potential deep-water harbour for tankers when offshore development of oil reserves beneath the Canadian Beaufort Sea was proposed in the 1960s. However, the passage into Herschel Basin is only 14 metres deep and insufficient for the largest vessels. The depth is quite sufficient for small and medium-sized ships that may visit the Arctic more frequently in future (Fig. 4).

The ridge built by the glaciation must have been a prominent landmark for millennia, for only recently has the Beaufort Sea risen sufficiently to flood Workboat Passage, the strait between the island and the mainland (Fig. 1). Sea level has risen continuously since the last glaciation, but the island was probably only separated from the mainland in the last 1,600 years, possibly as recently as 600 years ago. In fact, the late Inuvialuit elder Jean Tardiff of Aklavik related that the people who lived on what is now the island were called Nuvuuyaqmiut, meaning "People of the Point," but later were known as Qikiqtaryungmiut, meaning "People of the Island." At the moment, sea level in the southeastern Beaufort Sea is rising at 3.3 millimetres per year—an important issue for the territorial park over the next century as water level rises to meet the structures and cover the landing strip at Pauline Cove, which are all less than a metre above mean sea level. Flooding is already a serious concern during storms or when strong easterly winds raise the water level (Fig. 5). Flooding is mentioned only once in the police reports for 1903–20.

The ground that forms Herschel Island was permafrost when it was pushed up from the coastal plain. It is mostly marine and beach sediments, now covered by a layer of glacial deposits left from the Ice Age. Masses of ice are deeply buried in these ocean sediments, which are exposed in coastal bluffs, and which testify to the hundreds of millennia that permafrost has existed in the region. Close to the surface, the ground on the island is in many places almost pure ice to a depth of 15 metres or so. These ice masses create extensive thaw slumps where the permafrost is exposed (Fig. 6). The rapid erosion of exposed melting ground ice in these features is sometimes taken to demonstrate the effect of climate change on permafrost, but really they are each local disturbances. They only develop where there is considerable ice in the ground.

Coastal erosion, on the other hand, continues steadily. Undercutting of the cliffs occurs in the open-water season, removing about half a metre of the northern cliffs on average each year. The rate of erosion may well increase as the climate changes because the open-water season is expected to lengthen in future. Coastal erosion is one important factor responsible for the relatively short archaeological record on the island. People lived close to the coast, as marine mammals were their principal source of food. Indeed, one of the key archaeological sites near Pauline Cove (the Washout site) was excavated in the late 1970s as it was being washed away. It is no accident that the oldest domestic site left on the island is on Avadlek Spit, at the western end of Workboat Passage, a land surface that is protected from erosion by gravel beaches. Older sites, as at Pauline Cove, have probably been washed away.

Aboriginal Occupation

The documented occupation of Herschel Island extends back eight hundred years to a time close to the opening of Workboat Passage and the formation of the island. The archaeology of the Washout site tells us that people lived off the ocean, especially on bowhead whales and seals. In contrast, archaeologists excavating at Avadlek Spit found larger amounts of fish and bird bones but hardly any traces of seal. The Avadlek Spit site is unique in Inuit archaeology for its paucity of seal, likely because Workboat Passage has always been too shallow to be good seal habitat, and the ice in the open ocean on the other side of the spit too rough for seal hunting.

The physical setting of the island has changed over time as sea level has risen, affecting the resources available locally for harvesting. The island extends across almost all of the continental shelf, acting as a wall that diverts westward drifting water from the Mackenzie Delta off the shelf. To the east of the island the ocean water is diluted by the Mackenzie's outflow, attracting numbers of migrating anadromous fish (species that spend part of the year in freshwater and part in coastal waters) to Pauline Cove. Herschel Island is also close to Mackenzie Trough, a submarine canyon in the continental shelf that is an efficient conduit for upwelling of cold, nutrient-rich, deep ocean water onto the shelf. As a result, the ocean near the island supports a full and healthy food chain, from microscopic plankton up to the polar bear, and is close to favoured feeding grounds for bowhead whales. Critically, the island protects Herschel Basin from the full force of northwesterly storms in autumn and early winter, so that the landfast ice extending over this deep water is relatively smooth, and excellent habitat for ringed seals.

Fig. 7 Inuvialuit fish camp on the southern shore of Workboat Passage in 1957. *Photo by J. Ross Mackay.*

These physical conditions and the particular habitat they create led to a coastal marine ecosystem in which ancestors of the Inuvialuit could sustain human culture. Estimates of the coastal population suggest that at least 2,500 people lived in western Arctic Canada, between what is now Alaska and Cape Bathurst, during the nineteenth century. The people of the Yukon coast were a distinct linguistic group known as the Tuyurmiat, of whom there may have been 300 to 400 people. When John Franklin travelled along the coast in 1826, he met three groups of Tuyurmiat at Herschel Island. The Tuyurmiat were largely a dispersed community, but their journeys along the coast ranged at least as far west as Kaktovik, in Alaska, and as far east as Kitigaaryuit, at the mouth of the East Channel of the Mackenzie River. Franklin found them living in small family groups, but at times they gathered as a larger community.

The Tuyurmiat were part of various trading networks among both Inuit and First Nations people. They travelled along the coast to trade, but they also received visitors from the interior who descended via the Babbage or Firth rivers, the latter initially named Mountain Indian River by Franklin. Russian trade goods made their way to the area by the late eighteenth century through these networks.

Firearms arrived in the second half of the nineteenth century, after the Hudson's Bay Company (HBC) established posts in the Yukon and at Fort McPherson.

Inuvialuit oral traditions indicate that people along the coast gathered for feasts and celebrations, especially around the winter solstice. Archaeologists have recovered drum hoops and a beautifully carved seal-head toggle from Herschel Island, although the majority of recovered artifacts are tools associated with hunting, preparing food, and making clothes. In the early twentieth century, anthropologists and missionaries described the culture and world view of the aboriginal people they met in the western Arctic. The people believed in spirits that moved in and out of their lives, and numerous practices and taboos developed accordingly. Individuals with special spiritual power were recognized as shamans and held positions of prominence, but were not necessarily community leaders.

Indigenous subsistence activities and trapping continued at and near Herschel Island for two-thirds of the twentieth century (Fig. 7). A few people worked as Special Constables for the police at Herschel Island, ensuring a food supply for the detachment's dog teams, assisting with patrols along the western Arctic coast, and maintaining the police infrastructure. The population dwindled after the

detachment closed in 1964, with the last year-round residents being Bob and Elizabeth Mackenzie. Mrs. Mackenzie still owns a cabin at Pauline Cove to which she returns each summer with her children and grandchildren. The Yukon government has built a cabin for visitors who come to hunt polar bears in spring and caribou year-round. Twenty to thirty caribou are harvested annually on the island by Inuvialuit.

Since the Tuyurmiat initially had no firearms, the search for food must have been a constant activity, but its effects on fish and wildlife populations would have been small. Fishnets made from baleen were used from about 1500 AD. The arrival of firearms, particularly rifles brought by the whalemen, made caribou hunting easier and, to the south, moose, which were harvested in considerable numbers to supply the whaling crews and other residents at Pauline Cove. This meat was traded for western food such as coffee, flour, or syrup, and for cloth, guns and ammunition, and liquor. Although the local effects of this hunting on caribou and moose populations may have been significant, the Porcupine Caribou Herd, whose calving grounds are on the Yukon coast and in adjacent Alaska, remained strong. This herd continues to be a critically important food supply on the western side of the Inuvialuit Settlement Region, and is hunted along the coast mostly by Inuvialuit from Aklavik.

Encounter with Modernity

Herschel Island was "discovered" and named by Capt. John Franklin on July 15, 1826, in honour of the foremost scientific family of his time. It was associated with a significant economy for about fifty years, initiated by the whaling industry when the potential to winter over safely at Herschel Island opened up the southeastern Beaufort Sea whaling grounds (Fig. 8). There are no natural harbours on the north coast of Alaska suitable for ocean-going vessels, and whaling ships, caught in the ice, had been wrecked throughout the history of the industry. The whalemen moved eastward as the fleet hunted out the bowhead population of the Alaskan Beaufort Sea, but they were reluctant to enter the "forbidden sea" east of the 141st meridian. Such hesitation was driven by fear of being stranded and unable to make a safe exit from the Arctic at the end of the season. Once the ability to winter safely in Pauline Cove was established, a flurry of attention, not unlike the boom and bust of the Klondike gold rush, followed for about five years. Fifteen ships overwintered at Herschel Island in 1894–95 and thirteen in 1895–96, but only three in 1896–97 and two in 1897–98 as the whale stock declined. The last season that several ships stayed over at Pauline Cove was 1905–06, when the fleet was caught out by an unexpected freeze-up in early September, and the last overwintering by a whaler, *Belvedere*, was in 1911–12. In total, over 1,200 whales were taken commercially in the Canadian Beaufort Sea, the last in 1921.

The whalemen introduced Euro-American culture and economy to the western Arctic coast. Before the whalemen, the HBC post and Archdeacon Robert McDonald of the Church Missionary Society at Fort McPherson were the northwestern limit of southern Canadian influence. The whaling station was established at Herschel Island in 1890, a mission in 1897, the police detachment in 1904, and the HBC post in 1915. Aboriginal people travelled to the island to find work and to trade for supplies (Fig. 9). The Tuyurmiat were overwhelmed in numbers by Nunatarmiut from Alaska who quickly arrived to take advantage of the opportunities brought by the whaling fleet. The whalemen brought their own workforce, including aboriginal people from Alaska, Siberia, and Hawaii, to join the people on the island, while Gwich'in regularly travelled from Old Crow Flats to trade meat for goods brought in from San Francisco. By 1908, the anthropologist and explorer Vilhjalmur Stefansson referred to the indigenous population of Herschel Island as simply Kigirktarugmiut (the current transliteration would be Qikiqtaryungmiut), indicating that there was a significant community of aboriginal people on the island.

Fig. 8 The steam bark *Thrasher* at Pauline Cove, Herschel Island. *Thrasher* overwintered twice at Herschel Island, in 1894–95 and involuntarily in 1905–06. *Photo courtesy of the New Bedford Whaling Museum, New Bedford, MA.*

Fig. 9 *Left* Gareth (Garrett) and Emma Notik (Nutik) and family at Pauline Cove. *Photo courtesy of Yukon Archives, Anglican Church of Canada, General Synod Archives fonds, 78/67, #175.*

The material goods brought to Herschel Island by the whaling fleet had previously been introduced to the western Arctic by the HBC. However, the whalemen traded the goods at San Francisco prices and heavily undercut the Company. Ultimately this competition became an issue that concerned the Government of Canada, though Ottawa more or less ignored the whaling fleet's activities throughout the 1890s. Inspector Constantine of the North-West Mounted Police (NWMP) and William Bompas, Bishop of Selkirk (Yukon), petitioned the federal government to mitigate some of the social consequences of the arrival of the whalemen, especially those associated with an abundant supply of alcohol, and to establish the rule of law on the frontier. In 1895 Constantine also relayed stories of child abuse, but these pleas had little effect on the authorities in Ottawa. The same year, the whaling captains signed a pledge, initiated by the church and the HBC, to restrict the availability of alcohol. Aboriginal people traded meat, furs, and even the services of their children for liquor. Nuligak wrote that "(t)here were drinking bouts almost every day. People would drink anything; the Alaskan Inuit are renowned for that." Several serious incidents were recorded, including the killing of family members after drinking.

Still, the appeals to the authorities for police-enforced moderation fell on deaf ears. Even as late as October 1903, Comptroller Frederick White of the NWMP wrote to A.E. Forget, Lieutenant Governor of the Northwest Territories: "[I]t is so difficult to convince the goody-goody people that in the development and settlement of a new country allowances must be made for the excesses of human nature."

Some whaling captains brought their wives and children to winter over at Herschel Island, but the rest of the crews were single men. Various arrangements were made between these men and women living at Herschel Island. In some cases aboriginal women moved temporarily onto the ships, in others crewmen moved on shore. Most of these arrangements seem to have been mutually beneficial, for the annual return of the ships was greeted enthusiastically. Numerous children were born of unions between aboriginal women and the whalemen. Children were also conceived between aboriginal women and men who came from the south to live for several years in the western Arctic. The most well-known among northerners was Alex, son of Fanny Pannigabluk and Vilhjalmur Stefansson. The whalemen also brought syphilis and gonorrhea to the western Arctic, which spread

into the local population, but in the 1890s they do not seem to have brought infections that developed into epidemics.

The first major epidemic to sweep across the western Arctic was measles, introduced to the region in 1902 by people travelling from Dawson City. Sixty aboriginal people along the coast died, as well as 70 from a group of 80 Qikiqtaryungmiut who were then visiting Fort McPherson. A series of diseases, often brought down the Mackenzie River, subsequently devastated the coastal population— most notably influenza (especially in 1916 and 1928), but also typhus, pneumonia, and tuberculosis (Fig. 10). Of all external influences in the early twentieth century, the epidemics had the most direct consequences for local people. Inuvialuit had no resistance to these new diseases and no one had knowledge of effective treatment. Many people hastened death by going

Fig. 10 The Inuvialuit graveyard at Pauline Cove, July 2010. Recent growth of willow bushes partially obscures some of the graves. *Photo by Christopher Burn.*

Fig. 11 The settlement at Herschel Island early in the twentieth century. *Photo courtesy of Library and Archives Canada, Royal Canadian Mounted Police fonds, e10836726.*

Fig. 12 *Right* The *Herman*, Capt. C.T. Pedersen, at Herschel Island in 1914. *Photo courtesy of Library and Archives Canada, Royal Canadian Mounted Police fonds, e10836740.*

outside and removing their clothes in order to cool down when they developed a fever, rather than resting in a sheltered environment. By 1905, according to police estimates, residents born in the area were reduced to only 10 percent, i.e., 250, of the initial population, with 100 Nunatarmiut and a few Inuit from Bering Strait also on the western Arctic coast. Five years later, there were only 260 aboriginal people in the region, half of whom were Nunatarmiut. The aboriginal population of Herschel Island was 55. In time, Nunatarmiut replenished the population, leading to the strong ties today between the Iñupiat of Arctic Alaska and the Inuvialuit. Iñupiat and Inuvialuit travelling on family visits between Aklavik in the Mackenzie Delta and Kaktovik in Alaska often stop in at Qikiqtaryuk to break their journey or shelter from bad weather.

The arrival of whalemen and the sudden growth of the population at Herschel Island had prompted Rev. Isaac Stringer to visit the island in 1893 and then to establish a mission at Pauline Cove in 1897. He was invited to live in and use the community house previously built by the Pacific Steam Whaling Company (PSWC) in 1893, a tacit recognition by the company that the fishery was in decline. Stringer campaigned against the free availability of alcohol, even smashing a still he bought from a resident. Both he and his wife, Sadie, were well respected by whalemen and aboriginal people, but in the short term they made no converts. Instead, their tangible success was in education and health care. They provided a rudimentary clinic and started a day school for aboriginal people. Sadie Stringer also taught whalemen secretarial skills to improve their prospects when the sailors returned south. The value of such education was recognized by the aboriginal population, who petitioned the government in 1926 to establish a residential school at Shingle Point. The school was started in 1929, with Rev. Thomas Umaok, the first Inuvialuit catechist, as one of the staff. Umaok was one of many Inuvialuit who converted to Christianity from 1909 on, some of whom fully embraced and experienced their new faith.

The economic contact between indigenous people and the whalemen, primarily for meat, but also for furs on the side, was as important for the PSWC as for the people. However, the greatest impression on Nuligak was the infrastructure built at Herschel Island (Fig. 11), and the improved access to food and material goods, both brought from San Francisco. As the whaling industry declined, fur trading assumed a greater importance, and dominated at Herschel after 1908. The collapse of the baleen price, and the resulting absence of ships overwintering in 1906–07, brought great hardship to Inuvialuit, but refocused economic activity on furs, particularly that of white fox. The HBC established a post on Herschel Island in 1915 in response to competition from the ship-based traders, particularly Capt. C.T. Pedersen of San Francisco. Pedersen operated the *Herman* (Fig. 12) and then the *Nanuk* as floating trading posts until government regulations prohibited such enterprises in the late 1920s. (He then designated his ship differently in order to circumvent the regulations.) Until 1936 trading vessels visited the coast each year.

The HBC intended to develop a substantial coastal fur trade extending as far east as King William Island. They, too, brought their supplies from the west coast, but it proved impossible to establish a viable operation on the scale the investment demanded in the long run. Problems included the variability in the fox harvest, over-extension of credit to local trappers, competition from itinerant traders carrying low overhead costs, the profit required by the company, and the state of the wider economy, especially during the Great Depression. However, for several years during the 1920s, when white fox pelts were fetching up to $50 each, the fur trade brought great material prosperity to the western Arctic coast, and Herschel Island was central to the trade. By the time the HBC post closed in 1938, Aklavik had replaced Herschel Island as the regional centre.

Inclusion in Canada

The naming of Herschel Island by Franklin was an act of establishing sovereignty over the island. Its "discovery" occurred during an expedition specifically dispatched in 1825 to map the western Arctic coast of British North America in order to counter Russian ambitions in the region. The boundary between Russian and British territories was agreed that year along the 141st meridian, which later became a basis for the purchase of Alaska by the United States. Word reached Franklin of the Anglo-Russian agreement before he left Fort Franklin (now Deline) for the Arctic coast in June 1826, because he named Demarcation Point as he passed 141° W.

The Canadian government had shown little interest when the whaling fleet arrived at Herschel Island, and were not even alarmed that the first map of the island was published by the United States Hydrographic Office. The government had neither the funds nor the inclination to deal with the Arctic in the 1890s. Throughout the decade it was more concerned with applying the rule of Canadian law to the miners arriving in the Yukon, especially during the Klondike gold rush.

The government's attitude changed at the turn of the century, however, partly as a consequence of the boundary dispute with the United States over the Alaskan "panhandle," which was settled in 1903. J.A. Smart, Deputy Minister of the Department of the Interior, stated in an internal government memorandum that "if American citizens are permitted to land and pursue the industries of whaling, fishing, and trading with the Indians without complying with the revenue laws of Canada and without any assertion of sovereignty on the part of Canada, unfounded and troublesome claims may hereafter be set up." Sensitized by the HBC to the duty-free trading the whalemen were carrying on at Herschel Island, the government recognized that a royalty should be assessed on whales caught in Canadian territorial waters. No explicit concern for the welfare of the aboriginal people was expressed in the justification for establishing the NWMP detachment at Herschel Island in 1904 (Fig. 13). The Americans did not contest this exercise of sovereignty.

Initially, at least, the police at the Herschel Island detachment reinforced the official indifference to aboriginal welfare. Stefansson's diary for August 10, 1906, indicates that Major Howard (Insp. D. M. Howard, RNWMP) exonerated a whaling captain of child abuse when the evidence suggested otherwise. Roald Amundsen, then waiting with his ship *Gjøa* at Herschel Island for a clear passage to the west, alludes to similar events in his account of the first transit of the Northwest Passage. As time passed, the police responded to the social needs of local residents, especially when food was scarce after the departure of the whalemen, or when disease required treatment or control.

There were, of course, a myriad of relationships at the human level. When Isaac Stringer, by then Bishop of the Yukon, officiated at the first weddings on the island in 1909, the first couple married was ex-Cst. Samuel Carter and Mabel Rauchenna. Carter had just retired from the RNWMP. This was the first legal marriage of a white man and an Inuit woman in the Canadian Arctic. Cohabitation continued both before and after this marriage, as with Sgt. Francis Fitzgerald, who lived for several years with Lena Unalina at Herschel Island. When Fitzgerald asked permission to marry her, Insp. Howard, who would not contemplate the formal union of a serving police

POLICE REACH THE ARCTIC

The North-West Mounted Police (NWMP) was established in 1873 to bring Canadian authority to the North-West Territories (present-day Alberta and Saskatchewan). The first detachment in the Yukon was established in 1895, and in the Mackenzie River District in 1903 (at Fort McPherson). In 1904 the force became the Royal North-West Mounted Police (RNWMP), and was renamed the Royal Canadian Mounted Police in 1919. (From 1906 RNWMP was written as Royal Northwest Mounted Police.)

Fig. 13 The police detachment at Herschel Island. The whaling and trading vessel anchored in Pauline Cove is probably the *Nanuk*. *Photo courtesy of Library and Archives Canada, Royal Canadian Mounted Police fonds, e10836724.*

Fig. 14 RCMP schooner *St. Roch* at Herschel Island in October 1947. *Photo courtesy of Library and Archives Canada, Royal Canadian Mounted Police fonds, e10836735.*

Fig. 15 The North Warning radar station at Stokes Point, often visible in the distance from Pauline Cove, 28 kilometres away. *Photo by John Snell, Parks Canada, 2007.*

Fig. 16 The Canadian Coast Guard ship *Sir Wilfrid Laurier* anchored off Simpson Point in 2005. *Photo by Cameron Eckert.*

officer with an aboriginal woman, refused. Howard was replaced by Insp. A.M. Jarvis in 1907, who was more liberal, and reported obliquely in 1908 that he had given Fitzgerald permission to sleep out of barracks. Fitzgerald had opened the detachment on the island but is most remembered for his death as leader of the Lost Patrol in 1911, along with ex-Cst. Carter, who had joined the patrol as guide.

The clearest assertion of Canadian force involved the case of Tatamigana and Alikomiak, Inuit from near Tree River in the central Arctic. They were arrested for the murder of Pugnana, an Inuk, but while being held at the Tree River detachment in April 1922, Alikomiak shot and killed RCMP Cpl. W.A. Doak, who had earlier been stationed at Herschel Island, and Otto Binder of the HBC. Tatamigama and Alikomiak were taken to Herschel Island and held for trial in order to demonstrate the judicial process. A court was assembled at Pauline Cove in July 1923 under Justice Lucien Dubuc of Edmonton. Ominously, the court party included a hangman and portable gallows. The judge's one-sided summation made clear that the intention of the trials was to bring the Arctic under Canadian law. Tatamigana and Alikomiak were convicted of murder and sentenced to death. Seven months later, on February 1, 1924, after considerable discussion of the case in the newspapers, they were denied clemency on appeal and

hanged in the warehouse next to the community house. The beam that served as the gallows has since been replaced.

During the trial and judgement of Alikomiak, the killing of a policeman was a significant factor. The authorities wanted to impress upon aboriginal people the seriousness with which they regarded this offence. Three other Inuit were also tried in the same court in connection with the death of an Inuk named Ahkak. Two of them were acquitted, but the third, named Ekootokone, was convicted of manslaughter and sentenced to one year of imprisonment at Herschel Island. Earlier, in 1919, two Inuit named Sinnisiak and Uluksuk, who were convicted of murdering two Catholic priests, and who had been detained at Herschel Island after their arrest, had their sentences commuted after public appeals urging recognition of the culturally constructed nature of the justice system, to which the accused were not party.

Across Arctic Canada in the early twentieth century, the police were the only direct representatives of the government. Education and health care were made available through the churches. At Herschel Island, the police detachment acted as a general government agent, including post office, for several years until it was closed in 1933. The police vessel *St. Roch* overwintered in 1947–48 (Fig. 14), when the detachment was reopened.

In its last years (1962–64), a principal activity was the breeding of police sled dogs. The detachment formally closed in 1964 when the threat to sovereignty came from the Soviet Union, and military forces represented by the Distant Early Warning (DEW) Line of radar stations were called for rather than civilian police. The DEW Line itself was replaced by the North Warning System in the 1990s (Fig. 15). Today the island represents the formalization of a new northern sovereignty. A range of federal agencies rely on the island for its logistical capacity and on occasion for its shelter (Fig. 16). Herschel Island Territorial Park is a territorial responsibility, but is co-managed with the Inuvialuit.

Fig. 17 The flags of Canada, the Yukon Territory, and the Inuvialuit fly above the community house at Pauline Cove. *Photo by Louis Schilder.*

Fig. 18 A polar bear wanders amongst the fractured ice on the north side of Herschel Island. The ice north and west of the island is rough and exposed to the movements of the pack. *Photo by Lee John Meyook.*

Fig. 19 Blue ice, likely from an ice shelf in the High Arctic, stranded on the northwest coast of Herschel Island in April 2009. *Photo by Mary Beattie.*

The flags that normally fly on the island above the main community house (built by the whalemen but occupied as a mission and then a police barracks) demonstrate the three-fold interest in managing and asserting Canadian sovereignty, not as a remote frontier outpost of an empire ruled from Ottawa, but through the evolving governance of an Arctic homeland (Fig. 17).

A Warmer Arctic

Herschel Island Territorial Park, along with Ivvavik National Park and Vuntut National Park on the mainland, are protected ecosystems that may soon be nominated together as a World Heritage Site. The fundamental purpose of this designation is to protect the Porcupine Caribou Herd, which has sustained residents in the region for millennia. The coast, and especially Herschel Island, also provides a significant number of denning sites for the southern Beaufort polar bear population (Fig. 18), a species that is beginning to show signs of stress as sea-ice conditions change.

Herschel Island provides us with some of the few early records of freeze-up and break-up of the sea ice in the western Arctic, events of great significance to whalemen and traders at the turn of the century. The ocean is open in autumn now for a month or more longer than it was then. As this period lengthens and the ice cover contracts, polar bears will be forced

either to become a terrestrial species, or their habitat will shrink to the High Arctic islands. The stranding of icebergs from the High Arctic off the north and west coasts of Herschel Island in the winter of 2008–09 (Fig. 19), unseen before by Inuvialuit travellers, is local evidence of the break-up of the Arctic ice shelves. The arrival of these icebergs also indicates their relatively rapid passage from the High Arctic during the few months of extensive ice-free ocean in 2007 and 2008.

The logistical facilities at Herschel Island, principally the landing strip (Fig. 20), buildings, and harbour (Fig. 21), have turned the island into one of the most important locations for scientific research in the western Arctic. Such activity, beginning with Capt. John Franklin (1826) and ethnologist Frank Russell (1894), has been almost continuous since the 1950s, including research offshore during the hydrocarbon exploration of the 1970s and 80s,

Fig. 20 A Twin Otter that has just brought scientists and equipment to Herschel Island prepares to depart. *Photo by Christopher Burn.*

Fig. 21 Pauline Cove, the natural harbour on Herschel Island named in 1889 by Lt. Cdr. Charles Stockton, with the settlement buildings on the sandspit. *Photo by Fritz Mueller.*

and the Herschel Island and Yukon North Slope Inuvialuit Oral History Project in the 1990s. For Stefansson and Anderson (1908–12) and then the Canadian Arctic Expedition (1913–18), Herschel Island was a support station but not a place to investigate. A century later, during the International Polar Year (IPY) 2007–09, research was conducted on the island by biologists and paleontologists, geologists, permafrost scientists, and geophysicists. Most of these projects were based near Pauline Cove, but several ranged over the island. For both permafrost science and research on the terrestrial food web, the island has become an observatory for detecting and monitoring the effects of climate change in the Arctic. For example, the ground temperature profile indicates that permafrost on the island has warmed to a depth of about 120 metres over the twentieth century, and the climate and permafrost are about 3°C warmer than when Rev. Isaac Stringer faithfully made weather observations during his years of residence between 1897 and 1901.

The changes in ground conditions and climate are beginning to affect vegetation on the island. An increase in the extent of plant cover has been noticed since the late 1980s, along with a deepening of the seasonally thawed "active layer" above permafrost. Woody shrubs and grasses seem to be spreading the most, and the small rodents that eat these and use them for cover may benefit greatly. However, there are fewer lichens, likely due to competition from more vigorous plant species, so caribou, who eat a great deal of lichen in winter, may suffer. As temperatures have risen, butterflies and birds not previously seen on the island have also been observed.

Unfortunately, climate change affects not only temperature but also precipitation, and is most likely to create problems for wildlife in winter. If snowfall becomes rainfall and the snow pack turns to ice, then access to the underlying vegetation is limited and starvation of animals more likely. The dynamics of the ecosystem depend on these physical factors and

on the interrelations between species in the food web, central to which are the lemmings and voles that convert vegetation into meat and sustain the carnivores and raptors on the island (Fig. 22). Potential benefits to animal populations of a warming climate may be counter-balanced by other changes to the ecosystem.

Herschel Island presents a remote, protected ecosystem where tiny shorebirds (Fig. 23), foxes, raptors, caribou, bears, and humans intermingle (Fig. 24). The chapters that follow paint a portrait of a place that has been home to people for at least eight hundred years. Perhaps the most important issue facing Qikiqtaryuk is the development of a management strategy that will allow it to remain a protected ecosystem in the next hundred years as Canada's sovereignty over the Northwest Passage is challenged, marine traffic in the Arctic increases, resource development proceeds offshore, and climate change alters the conditions to which the present wildlife populations are adapted.

Fig. 22 A Snowy Owl or Ukpik (*Bubo scandiaca*), resident at Herschel Island in some summers, but which wanders in autumn and winter when breeding is over. *Photo by Cameron Eckert.*

Fig. 23 Semipalmated Plover or Taliviak (*Charadrius semipalmatus*), a common and conspicuous shorebird at Pauline Cove. *Photo by Cameron Eckert.*

Fig. 24 Caribou or tuktu (*Rangifer tarandus*) in early summer, while shedding its winter hair. *Photo by Fritz Mueller.*

THE HERSCHEL FAMILY

Michael Hoskin

William Herschel's 40-foot (12-metre) telescope, built in 1785–89 near Windsor Castle, west of London. The telescope became a famous landmark and was included on the 1830 Ordnance Survey (government) map of the area. It was the subject of the first photograph ever taken on glass (by John Herschel in 1839). *This watercolour image is reproduced with the kind permission of John Herschel-Shorland.*

On July 15, 1826, Captain John Franklin of the Royal Navy landed at Kay Point on a journey westward along the coast of the Beaufort Sea (Figs. 1 and 2). The British government wanted Franklin to chart the northern coast of Alaska and pre-empt Russian intentions of claiming this land. From Kay Point he could see an island "about fifteen miles distant" to which he gave "the distinguished name of Herschell" (Fig. 3), spelling it here with two l's. Franklin and his second-in-command, Lieutenant George Back, took their two small boats into Workboat Passage on July 17 (Fig. 4) and camped that night on the island, probably at Lopez Point. They met three groups of people. They then travelled on into Alaska, intending to reach the Bering Sea, but turned back on August 18 after they recognized they were unlikely to reach it that year. They returned to Herschel Island on August 26 and Franklin again referred to reaching the island "that has been distinguished by the name of Herschel."

Although Franklin's party included Augustus, an interpreter who was able to talk with the people of the western Arctic, there is no record in Franklin's journal of any indigenous name for Herschel Island. (Augustus was from the west coast of Hudson's Bay and had travelled with Franklin on his first, disastrous, journey to the central Arctic coast in 1819–21.) Unlike the other features Franklin named along the coast, the name of Herschel Island doesn't honour one particular individual. Instead, it seems that Franklin wished to celebrate the entire Herschel family, the most distinguished scientific family of the time.

Fig. 1 Capt. Sir John Franklin, F.R.S. (1786–1847), replica by Thomas Phillips, oil on canvas, 1828. *Courtesy of the National Portrait Gallery, London.*

William Herschel and his sister Caroline had originally come to England from Germany to earn a living through music, but had found fame in astronomy. Three years before his voyage along the western Arctic coast, Franklin had been elected a Fellow of the Royal Society of London, and would have known of William Herschel's outstanding reputation as an astronomer. Franklin would also have been aware of Caroline Herschel's fame as a comet hunter, which had led to popular accounts and cartoons in the newspapers. In London Franklin lived next door to William's son John, a scientific prodigy who had won the top prize of the Royal Society (the Copley Medal) in 1821 and was Secretary of the Society when Franklin left for Canada in 1825. John was known for his mathematical skills and for his ability in chemistry, with which he laid the foundations for photography. He was also becoming known as a gifted astronomer, following in his father's footsteps.

Beginnings

Isaac Herschel (1707–67), the father of William and Caroline, was a largely self-taught German musician who joined the band of the Hanoverian Guards in 1731. His marriage to Anna Moritzen the following year produced ten children, six of whom survived infancy. At the age of fourteen, their third son William (1738–1822) (Fig. 5) joined his father in the band of the Guards. In 1757, when the Hanoverians were defeated by the French at the battle of Hastenbeck, William deserted and took refuge in England. There he made a career in music, eventually settling in the fashionable town of Bath in the southwest. In 1772 William rescued his sister Caroline (1750–1848) (Fig. 6) from a life of drudgery in the family home in Hanover by inviting her to Bath to run his household and sing in the performances he promoted there.

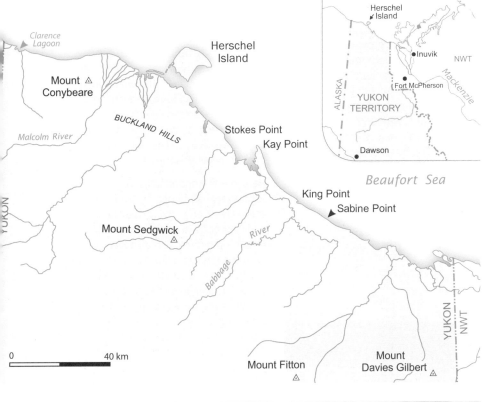

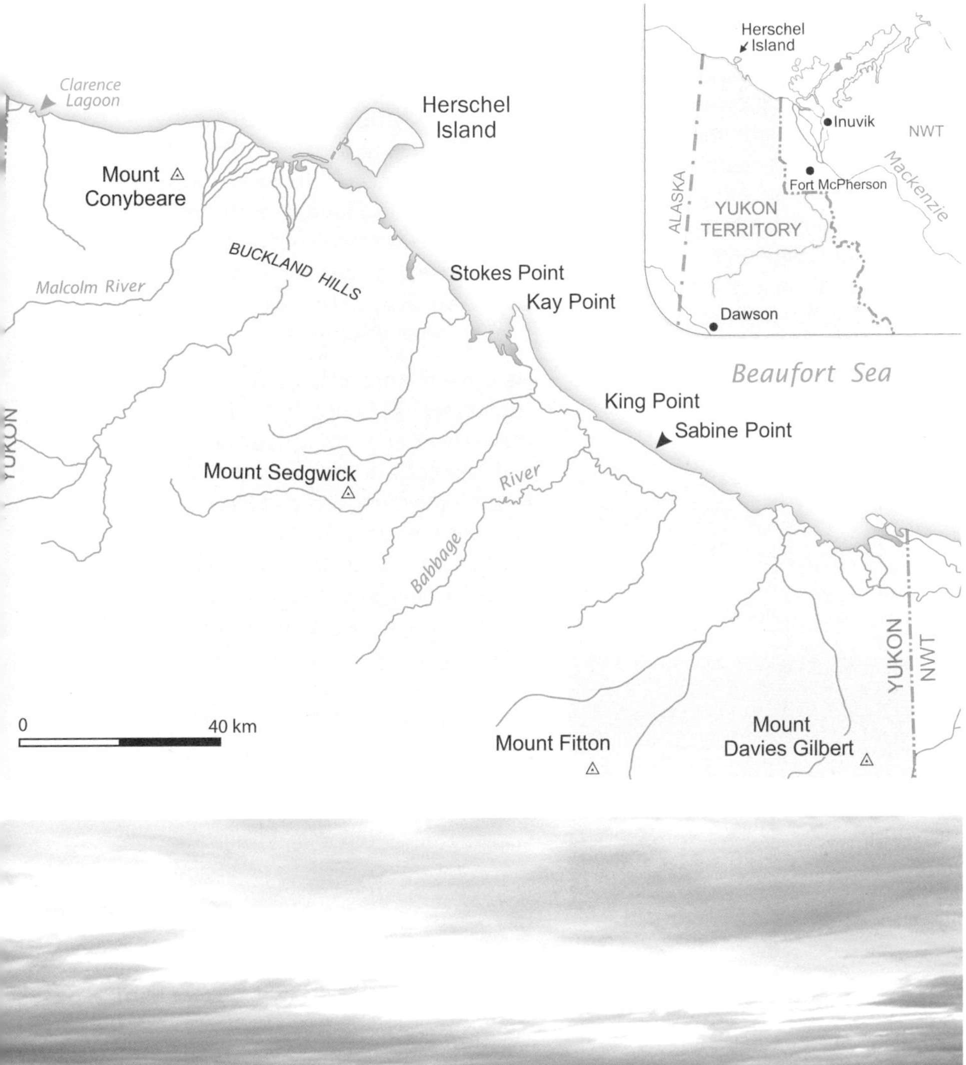

Fig. 2 Herschel Island and other features near the Yukon coast named after eminent scientists by Capt. John Franklin in 1826:
• Capt. Edward Sabine R.A., F.R.S. (1788–1883), geophysicist
• Charles Babbage, F.R.S. (1791–1871), mathematician
• Rev. William Buckland, F.R.S. (1784–1856), geologist
• Dr. William Fitton, F.R.S. (1780–1861), geologist
• Rev. Adam Sedgwick, F.R.S. (1785–1873), geologist
• Rev. William Conybeare, F.R.S. (1787–1857), geologist
• Davies Gilbert, F.R.S. (1767–1839), engineer

Franklin named other physiographic features along the coast after:
• his friends Capt. P.P. King, R.N. (1791–1856) and Charles Stokes, a businessman and amateur naturalist
• the Lord High Admiral the Duke of Clarence (1765–1837), who became King William IV
• Vice-Admiral Sir Pulteney Malcolm (1768–1838), a leading naval officer of the time
• his relatives, the Kay family

He also marked Demarcation Point, "the boundary between the British and Russian dominions on the northern coast of America."
Cartography by Christine Earl.

Fig. 3 View of Herschel Island from the sea near Stokes Point. This view is probably similar to that seen by Franklin through his telescope from Kay Point on July 15, 1826.
Photo by Christopher Burn.

William Herschel

Unfortunately for Caroline's future musical career, William was even then becoming obsessed with astronomy. Before long he was constructing his own telescopes, and in 1778 he ground and polished a mirror for his seven-foot (two-metre) reflecting telescope that—although he did not know it—was the finest of its kind in the world (Fig. 7). He soon decided to familiarize himself with the brighter stars by examining them one by one. He kept a particular lookout for any that were, in fact, double stars—two separate stars that at first glance appeared to be one, presumably because by chance they lay in the same direction from Earth. Unknown to William, the Cambridge geologist John Michell had argued that the number of double stars was so great they could not occur by chance and must in fact be companions in space. When William returned to his double stars a quarter of a century later, he found that Michell was right and that in some instances the two stars orbited around each other, demonstrating that gravity (or some similar force) was at work in the starry heavens.

Whatever the reason for the double stars, whether a star was a double was itself interesting, and one of the very first that William identified was Polaris, the Pole Star, with its much weaker companion, Polaris B. It was weeks before any other astronomer was able to confirm his discovery, making it clear to William's growing circle of admirers that the Bath musician was an amateur astronomer of exceptional talent. He was persevering, too; before long he published his first catalogue of double stars, with 269 entries. But how could he be relieved of his need to earn his living by teaching music for as much as 40 hours a week and dedicate himself full time to astronomy?

The answer came in March 1781. William turned his telescope to what he expected to be yet another bright star and found that it had a strange appearance: "a curious either Nebulous Star or perhaps a Comet," he wrote in his journal. He returned to it four nights later and found that it had altered position, which meant that it must be within the solar system. No one had discovered a planet since the dawn of history, so William thought it must be a comet. Word spread, but both the Astronomer Royal at Greenwich, Nevil Maskelyne, and the Professor of Astronomy at Oxford, Thomas Hornsby, had great difficulty in finding it, since all the objects in that region of sky looked much the same in their telescopes. Eventually the strange body was shown to be the planet we now call Uranus, orbiting the Sun beyond Saturn.

Here was the opportunity William's supporters had hoped for. William was a Hanoverian living in Britain, and George III, in addition to being Britain's monarch, was also Elector of Hanover. If he allowed William to name his planet the Georgian Star, the king would be obliged by the customs of patronage to show his appreciation by providing financial support for William, which would allow him to give up music for astronomy. In fact, this is exactly what happened. William, now 43 years old, was appointed personal astronomer to King George (William was not the Astronomer Royal), and in the autumn of 1782 he and Caroline, now 32, left Bath and settled near Windsor Castle, just west of London. (Ironically, the name Georgian Star did not stick, and by 1850 the name Uranus was accepted everywhere.)

Fig. 4 The south coast of Herschel Island across Workboat Passage. Franklin and his party camped on this coast on July 17, 1826. Franklin's two small boats, HMS *Lion* and HMS *Reliance*, encountered considerable ice when they sailed through this strait. *Photo by Cameron Eckert.*

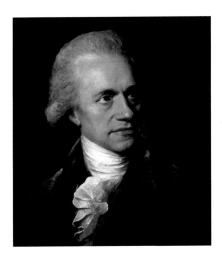

Fig. 5 Sir William Herschel, F.R.S. (1738–1822) by L.F. Abbott, oil on canvas, 1785. *Courtesy of the National Portrait Gallery, London. Reproduced by kind permission of John Herschel-Shorland.*

Fig. 6 Caroline Herschel (1750–1848) by M.F. Tieleman, 1829. *Courtesy of the Bridgman Art Library. Reproduced by kind permission of John Herschel-Shorland.*

Astronomers could distinguish themselves in the construction of telescopes, or as observers, or in developing theories about the universe. William excelled in all three. The king encouraged him to add to his salary by making telescopes for sale, and he soon became recognized throughout Europe as the top constructor of reflectors great and small. Kings and emperors vied for his services. A replica has recently been constructed in Spain of the 25-foot (7.6-metre) telescope that William built for the Spanish king.

William and Caroline Study the Nebulae

As an observer, William had already shown his skill with his catalogues of double stars. However, he left his mark on history in the study of the milky patches in the sky known as nebulae. Clearly, a star cluster so distant that the individual stars could not be seen would appear nebulous, but were all nebulae simply star clusters disguised by distance, or were some truly nebulous (or gaseous, as we would say)? While William lived

in Bath, he had come across only a handful of nebulae, but late in 1781 a friend sent him a catalogue of nebulae assembled by the French astronomer Charles Messier, who found them a distraction in his search for comets. To keep Caroline occupied, once the move from Bath meant her career as a singer had ended, William gave her a small refracting telescope in the autumn of 1782 and suggested she go out and look for anything interesting. Before long, she was finding nebulae unknown to Messier.

A year later, William finished building a more powerful telescope with a focal length of 20 feet (6 metres) and mirrors of 18 inches (46 centimetres) in diameter. He decided to use it to sweep the entire sky visible from Windsor for nebulae. At first he tried to do the job single-handedly, but when he used artificial light to record his observations, his eyes lost their adaptation to the dark, and it was minutes before he could resume his search. He then arranged for Caroline to be seated at a nearby window, ready to copy down the observations he shouted from his telescope and

to record the position of each nebula relative to a nearby star. Meanwhile, he remained outside at the eyepiece of the reflector as it faced south, keeping watch for nebulae as the heavens slowly turned in front of him. In 20 years, the partnership of William and Caroline added some 2,500 nebulae to the hundred or so known to Messier.

THE ELECTOR OF HANOVER

Elector was the title of each of the princes and bishops in Germany who chose the Emperor of the Holy Roman Empire, a federation that governed central Europe for a millennium until 1806. In 1714 the Elector of Hanover became King George I of Great Britain. The House of Hanover then ruled Great Britain, Ireland, and Hanover in personal union until 1837.

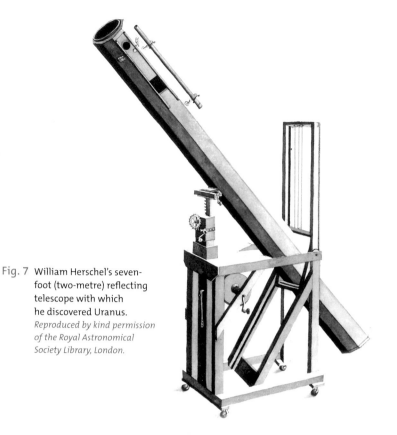

Fig. 7 William Herschel's seven-foot (two-metre) reflecting telescope with which he discovered Uranus.
Reproduced by kind permission of the Royal Astronomical Society Library, London.

When William lived in Bath, as yet unaware of the extent to which viewing conditions can affect the appearance of a nebula, he believed that the Orion Nebula had changed from one year to the next. If so, it could not be a vast and distant star system, but must be truly nebulous. How, then, was he to distinguish a star system from a genuine nebula? The answer, he thought, was that a star system would look mottled, while a genuine nebula would look milky. But in 1784 he came across nebulae that (so it seemed to him) contained both mottled and milky nebulosity. He therefore changed his mind: all nebulae were star systems, and mottled nebulosity revealed the presence of stars in the middle distance, while milky nebulosity revealed their presence at a greater distance.

This simple picture of the universe made it possible for him to think about what he termed "the construction of the heavens." The existence of star clusters showed that gravitational attraction (or a similar attractive force) was at work among the stars. Some clusters were scattered, others tightly packed. Evidently, as time passed, the outlying stars in a scattered cluster would be pulled more and more into the centre and the cluster would become increasingly dense. Therefore, scattered clusters were youthful and tightly packed clusters were elderly. This theory was the seed that began to transform astronomers' views of the universe from a fixed, mechanical construction to the "biological" universe of modern astronomy, in which even the cosmos itself has a life story.

To reach out further into space and study ever more distant nebulae, William persuaded the king to fund a 40-foot (12-metre) reflecting telescope with 4-foot (1.2-metre) mirrors, the like of which the world had never seen. It was a monumental instrument and prompted the king, when showing off the tube of the telescope to the Archbishop of Canterbury in 1787, to say "Come, my Lord Bishop, I will show you the way to Heaven." Unfortunately, it proved cumbersome and never fulfilled its promise as a telescope. Worse still, shortly after it was finished in 1789 it lost its primary purpose—to contribute to the debate about the nature of nebulae. In November 1790, William came across a star with a halo that could not be stellar in nature, but was condensing out of the nebulosity that surrounded it. True nebulosity therefore existed after all, and was not simply the appearance of many stars at a very great distance.

William made many other contributions to astronomy. He discovered infra-red rays, two of the moons of Uranus, two additional moons of Saturn, and the direction in which the solar system is travelling through space—and all of this in spite of becoming a professional astronomer when he was already halfway through his life. Caroline's help was indispensable. In 1787 she became the first professional female astronomer in history when the king awarded her a salary as William's assistant.

Caroline Herschel's Later Career

In 1788, at the age of 49, William married Mary Pitt, a wealthy neighbour who had been widowed two years earlier. Caroline thus ceased to be mistress of her brother's household, as she had been for many years, and she moved into the cottage attached to the Herschel home. However, William had secured the salary for Caroline before his marriage, allowing her the leisure to search for comets on her own. In all she was to discover eight comets and may have seen a ninth on two separate occasions, but mistook it each time for a nebula. In 1787, she became the first woman to publish a scientific paper in the journal of the Royal Society.

Astronomers throughout Europe were amazed and competed in the extravagant tributes they paid her. Her most significant work at Windsor was to revise the existing British catalogue of stars. She found hundreds of errors and added 561 stars, bringing the total to over 3,500. The Royal Society published her revised catalogue in 1798.

John Herschel

William's only son, John, was born in 1792 (Fig. 8). After a sheltered schooling he went to Cambridge University, where he was the best student of his time. On leaving Cambridge, he initially went into law, against his parents' wishes, but before long was back in Cambridge teaching mathematics. William, however, was now getting old, and his work was unfinished. In particular, he had never seen the skies below the horizon of Windsor. In 1816, therefore, he persuaded John to abandon his university career and return home to learn from his father how to build telescopes and observe with them.

William died in 1822, and Caroline—in a decision she would bitterly regret—returned to Hanover to live with her brother Dietrich. She was, she knew, abandoning John to complete William's work single-handedly. But John was by then much involved with the Royal Society and the infant Royal Astronomical Society, and was also working with his friend and fellow astronomer James South on bright double stars. These two friends had no need of an assistant as William had done.

Before long John dedicated himself to his "sacred duty" of revising his father's catalogues of nebulae. William had listed them by class and by date of discovery. John could not hope to re-examine them until the catalogues had been completely reorganized so

that he could determine in advance what he might expect to see on a given night. Caroline carried out this vast job at her desk in Hanover, and partly for it was awarded the Gold Medal of the Royal Astronomical Society in 1828. (This medal was next awarded to a woman in 1996!)

Eleven years after his father's death, in 1833, John published the resulting catalogue of the nebulae and star clusters visible from his observatory. The need for the revision was evident: over 700 of his father's nebulae were omitted, and there were over 500 additions.

It was now time to extend his father's work to the planet's southern skies. John's mother Mary had died in 1832, freeing him from emotional ties to England and making him wealthy enough to plan and pay for an expedition exactly as he thought best. From 1834–38 he lived at the Cape of Good Hope in South Africa, conducting one of the most concentrated observing campaigns in history. On his return Queen Victoria granted him the hereditary title of baronet.

It took John a very long time to prepare his Cape observations for publication. At last, in 1847, he was able to send the 97-year-old Caroline what he called "the completion of my father's work." Caroline died only a few months later. John, for his part, gave up active observing after his return from the Cape and became a central figure in British scientific life. When he died in 1871, he was buried next to Isaac Newton in Westminster Abbey.

Fig. 8 Sir John Herschel, F.R.S. (1792–1871) by H.W. Pickersgill, oil on canvas, 1833. *Reproduced by kind permission of the Master and Fellows of St. John's College, Cambridge.*

JOHN HERSCHEL'S OBSERVATIONS OF ICE

In 1833 John published a short paper on ice growth out of plant stems during a sharp frost. He reported the ice growing as a series of thin columns. This is one of the earliest scientific reports about the growth of ice out of natural materials. We call such ice "needle ice," and on cold mornings in the autumn it can sometimes be seen on muddy surfaces at Herschel Island. This is an example of the wide range in John Herschel's observational powers.

PLACE NAMES

Christopher Burn
and John B. Hattendorf

The names we use today for the physical features of the area near Herschel Island come from three main sources. Many places have Inuvialuktun names, which came into use at different times depending on local circumstances, and some places have more than one Inuvialuktun name. A few of these names and English translations of others were adopted in the twentieth century as official names by the Government of Canada, and are printed on maps issued by the federal government. Other place names along the Yukon coast, especially for bays and points, were given by Capt. John Franklin (1786–1847) of Britain's Royal Navy during his second journey to the Arctic in the summer of 1826. At the time, naming of features was part of the process of claiming the land for Britain. Since most of the people Franklin chose to honour in this way were well known in the British Isles and Europe, this remote landscape was introduced to Europe in familiar terms.

Fig. 1 Capt. Charles H. Stockton, USN (1845–1924) in about 1899, during his Presidency of the Naval War College, 1898–1900. *Photo courtesy of the Naval War College Museum, Newport, RI.*

Pauline Cove and the cliffs leading up to Collinson Head. *Photo by Fritz Mueller.*

USS *Thetis* in 1884, while on the Greely Relief expedition. *U.S. Navy photograph.*

Most of the official names for features on Herschel Island were given by Lt. Cdr. Charles H. Stockton (1845–1924) (Fig. 1), commanding USS *Thetis*, when he visited and surveyed the island on August 15 and 16, 1889. These places also have Inuvialuktun names. Following Stockton's survey, the first chart of the entire island and its adjacent waters was published in March 1890 by the Hydrographic Office of the United States Navy (Fig. 2).

Aboriginal people who met Franklin on Herschel Island told him that it was difficult for them to understand the language spoken by the people who lived to the west, on the coast of what is now Alaska. The people at Herschel Island were Tuyurmiat, whose dialect was close to Siglitun (S), now spoken by Inuvialuit living in Inuvik, Tuktoyaktuk, Sachs Harbour, and Paulatuk. The dialect spoken to the west was close to Uummarmiutun (U),

now spoken by Inuvialuit living in Aklavik and Inuvik. Uummarmiutun was brought to Herschel Island by Nunatarmiut, who had begun to arrive from Alaska by 1893, largely associated with the whaling industry.

The following paragraphs describe the origin of official place names for features on Herschel Island or in its vicinity (Fig. 3), and provide Inuvialuktun names for the same features (Fig. 4).

Fig. 2 Sketch of the Herschel Island area by the officers of USS *Thetis* from field measurements on August 15–16, 1889, published in March 1890 by the Hydrographic Office of the United States Navy. The small squares in the inset map on Simpson Point and at the head of Pauline Cove mark the locations of the first Pacific Steam Whaling Company warehouse and the ice cellar constructed in October 1890 and March 1891, respectively. The positions were marked by whaling captain Hartson Bodfish. *Courtesy of the New Bedford Whaling Museum, New Bedford, MA.*

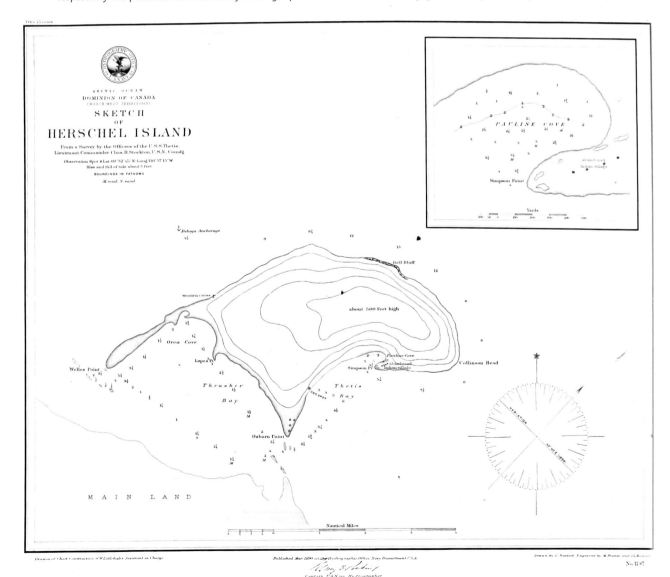

Herschel Island was named by Franklin on July 15, 1826. Looking out from Kay Point (Fig. 3), he saw an island "the Centre of which bears about 15 Miles distant." It is, in fact, 25 miles (42 kilometres) between Kay Point and Herschel Island, but Franklin estimated the distance before travelling to the island. He named it after the astronomers William, Caroline, and John Herschel, the most distinguished scientific family of his time. An early transliteration of the Inuvialuktun name for the island, published in the report of the Canadian Arctic Expedition (1924), is **Kikiaktaryuak**, meaning big island, but **Qikiqtaruk** is the spelling that is part of the working name for the territorial park. In Uummarmiutun a transliteration of the current pronounciation is **Qikiqtarr̂uk**, and in Siglitun, **Qikiqtaryuk**. In this book we use the Siglitun transliteration (Fig. 4).

The name of **Avadlek Spit** comes from the Inuvialuktun (S) word *avalliq*, meaning furthest away. It is also called **Avaliq**, meaning wall, **Ualiq**, meaning farther place, farther over there, and, in Uummarmiutun, **Nuvugr̂uaq**, which means big point.

Babbage River was named by John Franklin on July 15, 1826, after Charles Babbage (1791–1871), a very able mathematician whose greatest contribution was the invention of the modern computer. Babbage was a close friend of John Herschel, and lived at 5 Devonshire Street in London when Franklin and Herschel lived at numbers 55 and 56. Franklin noted that the Tuyurmiatun name for the river was **Cooghkiaktak**, meaning rocky river.

Beaufort Sea was named after Rear-Admiral Sir Francis Beaufort (1774–1857), one of the Royal Navy's best surveyors. Beaufort was partly responsible for developing the first high-quality tide tables as hydrographer to the Admiralty from 1829 to 1846, and is best known for inventing the wind speed scale. Franklin originally named a bay just west of the Alaska border after Beaufort on August 3, 1826, and this name was adopted for the sea early in the twentieth century. The Inuvialuktun (S & U) word for the ocean is **Tariuq**, which also means salt.

Bell Bluff, a series of cliffs on the north side of Herschel Island, was named by Lt. Cdr. Stockton during his visit to the island in August 1889 after Ensign John A. Bell, one of his junior officers. The bluff is marked on the chart of Herschel Island published in 1890 (Fig. 2). The area is called

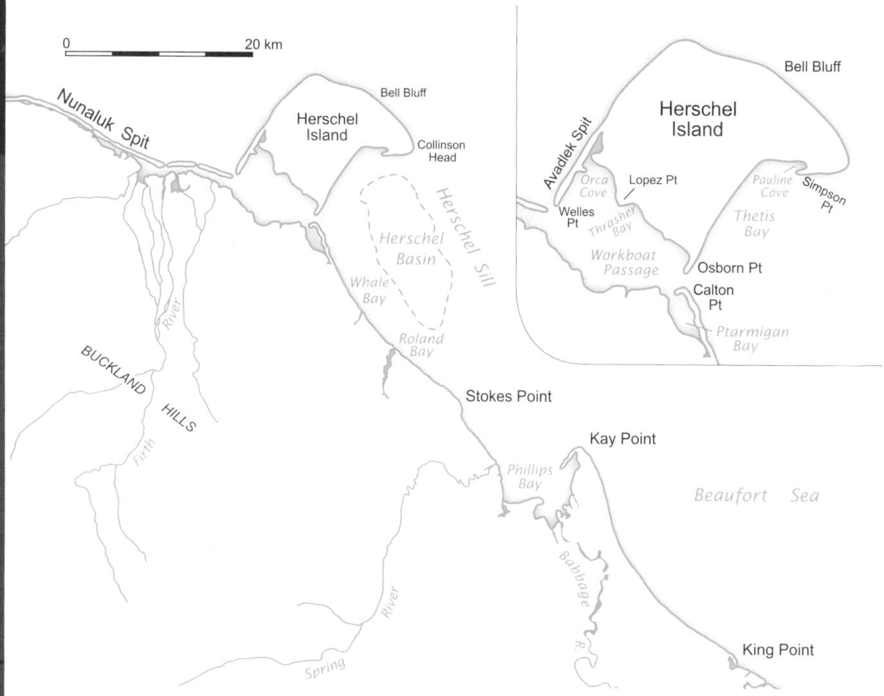

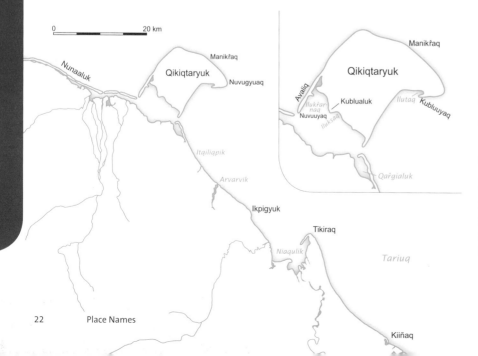

Fig. 3 Part of the coast of the Yukon Territory in the southeastern Beaufort Sea, with official names of places and features. *Cartography by Christine Earl.*

Fig. 4 Inuvialuktun place names for sites on Herschel Island and nearby on the Yukon coast. The names are from maps published by Yukon Parks and the Wildlife Management Advisory Council (North Slope). *Cartography by Christine Earl.*

Fig. 5 Bell Bluff with blocks that have fallen off the cliffs. *Photo by Mary Beattie.*

Fig. 6 *Right* Capt. Sir Richard Collinson (1811–1883), by James Stephens, 1855. *Courtesy of the National Portrait Gallery, London.*

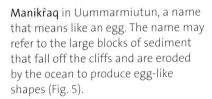

Manikr̂aq in Uummarmiutun, a name that means like an egg. The name may refer to the large blocks of sediment that fall off the cliffs and are eroded by the ocean to produce egg-like shapes (Fig. 5).

Calton (or Catton) Point was named by Franklin on July 17, 1826, but unfortunately neither his journal nor his published narrative identify the person after whom he chose to name the point. The text of his published account of the journey calls the point "Catton Point," but on the map of the coast included with the book, the spelling is "Calton Point." As a result, the point was labeled "Calton" on British Admiralty chart 2435, dated 1881, and on the charts of the Canadian Hydrographic Service, most recently nautical chart 7661. However, the point was named "Catton" on National Topographic Series Map 117D, although it has been corrected to "Calton" on the most recent edition. The difference between the two spellings in Franklin's original account is almost certainly due to a typographical error. In 1849, Lt. W.H. Hooper of the Royal Navy noted in his diary that the party of three boats under the command of Lt. W.J.S. Pullen camped to the east of what he called Calton Point, probably because it was the name on Franklin's map. However, in Pullen's diary it was called Catton Point. At the time, Hooper and Pullen were searching for Franklin's third expedition by travelling east from the

Bering Sea in small boats. The official name is Calton Point.

Collinson Head was named after Capt. Sir Richard Collinson (1811–1883) (Fig. 6), who commanded HMS *Enterprise* during the search for the ships of the third Franklin expedition, HMS *Erebus* and HMS *Terror*. *Enterprise* entered the Beaufort Sea through Bering Strait in 1851 and spent two winters near Victoria Island. The ship was delayed near Herschel Island for a few days on each of her journeys past the island. The name of Collinson Head first appears on the chart of Herschel Island published in March 1890 (Fig. 2), and was probably chosen by Stockton. He considered it unfortunate that Collinson's record was overshadowed by his junior officer, Robert M'Clure (1807–1873), who commanded HMS *Investigator*, the wreck that was surveyed in July 2010 in Mercy Bay, northern Banks Island. The Inuvialuktun (S) name is **Nuvugyuaq**, which means big point (Fig. 4). In 1905, the annual report of Royal North-West Mounted Police Inspector D.M. Howard referred to Collinson Head as Cape Point.

Firth River is named after John Firth (1855–1939), a trader for the Hudson's Bay Company, who was based at Fort McPherson for nearly 50 years. The river was sometimes called Herschel Island River or Herschel River early in the twentieth century, and had been

named Mountain Indian River by Franklin, because people at Herschel Island told him that First Nations people used the river as their route through the mountains when they visited the coast to trade.

Herschel is the official name given in 1959 to the unincorporated settlement at Pauline Cove (Fig. 7). On the 1890 chart, the settlement is marked as an "abandoned Indian village," but the discovery of Pauline Cove by the American whaling industry in 1889 led to its prominence in the history of the Canadian Arctic during the first few decades of the twentieth century.

Herschel Basin is the depression in the coastal plain of the Beaufort Sea between Herschel Island and Kay Point. The geographer J. Ross Mackay identified the basin as the place from which glacial ice pushed up land to create the ridge that later became Herschel Island. The basin is over 70 metres deep.

TRANSLATIONS

English meanings of the Inuvialuktun place names were kindly provided by Rosie (Ruth) Albert and Cathy Cockney, both of Inuvik, in August 2010.

Fig. 8 View westward along Workboat Passage, with Osborn Point in the foreground and Nunaluk Spit in the background.
Photo by Sara Nielsen.

Fig. 7 *Left* Simpson Point and Pauline Cove, Herschel Island.
Photo by Fritz Mueller.

Herschel Sill is the underwater ridge that runs between Collinson Head and Kay Point, separating Herschel Basin from the continental shelf of the Beaufort Sea. The deepest point on the sill is 14 metres below sea level. The name was made official in 1982.

Kay Point was named by John Franklin on July 15, 1826, after some "much esteemed relatives." One of the Kay women later married E.N. Kendall, who accompanied Franklin to the outer Mackenzie Delta as midshipman and surveyor in 1825, and after whom Franklin named Kendall Island. The Inuvialuktun (S) name for Kay Point is **Tikiraq**, which comes from *tikiq*, meaning index finger.

King Point was named by Franklin on July 15, 1826, after his friend the hydrographic surveyor Capt. Philip Parker King (1791–1856) of the Royal Navy. The Inuvialuktun (S) name for King Point is **Kiiñaq**, from the word *kiinaq*, meaning face.

Lopez Point appears on the first chart of Herschel Island, published in March 1890, but is not mentioned in earlier accounts. Stockton named it after Ensign Robert F. Lopez, who was a junior officer of *Thetis* at the time. Stockton's log for August 16, 1889 states that he sent Lopez in a boat to relieve Ensign Rogers Wells, Jr., whom he had earlier sent to sound the water (now named Workboat Passage) between the island and the mainland.

The point's Inuvialuktun names are **Kublualuk** (S), or **Kuvlualuk** (U), which mean old thumb. The name of the last shaman to live on Qikiqtaryuk was also Kublualuk. Franklin camped near this point or on Avadlek Spit on July 17, 1826.

Nunaluk Spit. *Nunaaluk* means old ground or ground in Inuvialuktun (S & U).

Orca Cove was named by Stockton after the steam bark *Orca* during his 1889 survey of Herschel Island. *Orca* was one of the seven whaling ships that arrived at Herschel Island on August 11, 1889. The flotilla had left the Colville River delta area after hearing about the potential harvest of bowhead whales in Canadian waters. Most of the vessels returned almost immediately after the *Jesse H. Freeman* found a shoal because they feared the consequences of being stranded so far from home. *Orca* and *Thrasher* remained and were found in Thetis Bay by Stockton. Each vessel caught two bowhead whales and left before winter. *Orca* returned each summer to Herschel Island and the southeastern Beaufort Sea from San Francisco until she was crushed by ice off Alaska in 1897. The Uummarmiutun name for this cove is **Ilukr̂arnaq**, which means inside a bay or cove.

Osborn Point (Fig. 8) was named on the 1890 chart of Herschel Island. The suggestion that the name was

given by Stockton to commemorate Rear-Admiral Sherard Osborn (1822–1875) of the Royal Navy, who edited the journal of Capt. Robert M'Clure of HMS *Investigator* for publication in 1856, is possibly true. However, it is unlikely because, unlike Collinson, Sherard Osborn had no personal connection to the island. Furthermore, one of Stockton's officers on board *Thetis* was Lt. Arthur P. Osborn. Since several other points on the island were named after his officers, it is almost certain that this point bears Lt. Osborn's name. When Vilhjalmur Stefansson camped here in 1908, he called it Flanders Point. The place is also called **Nuvugyuaq**, meaning big point in Inuvialuktun (S).

Pauline Cove was named by Stockton for his second wife, Pauline Lethilhon King, after he visited the island in 1889 (Fig. 7). Stockton sent Ensign Edward Simpson to sound the harbour, and the survey is published as an inset on the 1890 chart (Fig. 2). The Inuvialuktun (S) name is **Ilutaq**, which means inside a bay (Fig. 4).

Phillips Bay was named by Franklin on July 15, 1826, after Thomas Phillips (1770–1845), Professor of Painting at the Royal Academy in London. The Inuvialuktun (S) name is **Niaqulik**, after Archie "Headpoint" Erigaktuak, who raised his family there. *Niaquq* means head.

Fig. 10 The eastern entrance to Workboat Passage, near Osborn Point. The entrance was nearly blocked by ice when Franklin's boats entered the passage on July 17, 1826. *Photo courtesy of Dorothy Cooley.*

Fig. 9 *Right* Cst. "Frenchy" Chartrand, Special Cst. Roland Sar̂uaq, and Cst. Derek Parkes at Herschel Island, 1933. *Photo courtesy of Yukon Archives, Derek Parkes fonds, 95/53, #1.*

Ptarmigan Bay is a local name for the bay, reported by a field party of the Geographical Branch of the federal government led by J. Ross Mackay in 1957. The Inuvialuktun (U) name is **Qar̂gialuk**, from the Uummarmiutun *qar̂giq*, a general word for ptarmigan.

Roland Bay is a local name for this bay. Roland Sar̂uaq and his wife Kitty Kuttuq lived near the bay for many years in the first half of the twentieth century. Roland Sar̂uaq was a Special Constable for the RCMP detachment at Herschel Island for several years (Fig. 9). Kitty's daughter Jean Tardiff contributed extensively to the Inuvialuit Oral History of the Yukon North Slope published in 1994. The Inuvialuktun (S) name for the bay is **Arvarvik**, meaning the place to find bowhead whales. *Arviq* is an Inuvialuktun word for bowhead whale.

Simpson Point, named by Stockton for Ensign Edward Simpson, was included on the 1890 chart of Herschel Island (Fig. 2). Most of the settlement at Herschel was built on the sandspit leading to Simpson Point. The Inuvialuktun names for the sandspit are **Kubluuyaq** (S) or **Kuvluur̂aq** (U), which mean like a thumb (Fig. 7).

Spring River is a local name, recognizing that the river flows through an area which is a good place to hunt caribou in the spring.

Stokes Point was named by Franklin on July 16, 1826, after his friend Charles Stokes, naturalist and amateur geologist. The Inuvialuktun (S) name is **Ikpigyuk**.

Thetis Bay was named by Stockton for the USS *Thetis*, a steam bark of the United States Navy, sent to patrol the Beaufort Sea as a revenue cutter and survey vessel, and to give assistance to the whaling fleet. *Thetis* was built by Alexander Stephen and Sons of Dundee, Scotland, in 1881 and acquired by the United States Navy on February 2, 1884. *Thetis* arrived at Herschel Island under Stockton's command on August 15, 1889.

Thrasher Bay was named by Stockton after the steam bark *Thrasher*, owned by the Pacific Steam Whaling Company of San Francisco. *Thrasher* was part of the whaling fleet that entered the Canadian Beaufort Sea in 1889 and, like *Orca*, remained to cruise for whales after the *Jesse H. Freeman* encountered a reef and most of the fleet departed. *Thrasher* caught two bowhead whales and left before freeze-up, but returned to winter at Pauline Cove in 1894–95 and 1905–06. The Inuvialuktun names for the bay are **Iluksaq** (S) and **Ilukr̂aq** (U), which mean inside a bay.

Welles Point is the official name for the southern tip of Avadlek Spit. The name was given by Stockton and is printed on the first chart of

Herschel Island (Fig. 2). On August 16, 1889, Stockton sent Ensign Rogers Wells, Jr. in a boat to sound the water between Herschel Island and the mainland. According to the U.S. Navy Registers, Ensign Wells was one of five ensigns on board USS *Thetis*. It is likely that "Welles" is a misprint for "Wells," as the second "e" is missing from the name in both Stockton's log and the Navy Registers. The Inuvialuktun names for the point are **Nuvuuyaq** (S) or **Nuvuur̂aq** (U), which mean like a point.

Whale Bay is a local name. The Inuvialuktun (S) name is **Itqiliqpik**, which is derived from the word *itqiliq*, meaning the one with lice, also used as a derogatory term for a First Nations person. This bay is a place where Gwich'in, travelling via Babbage River from the Old Crow Flats to trade at Herschel Island, reached the coast.

Workboat Passage (Fig. 8 and 10) was named after a tender of CSS *Richardson*, a vessel of the Canadian Hydrographic Service used for coastal surveys of the Beaufort Sea in the 1960s and 70s. Workboat Passage is mostly less than two metres deep, so a tender, or "workboat," of the *Richardson* was used to chart the bathymetry (depth) of the water that separates Herschel Island from the mainland. The survey of Workboat Passage took place in 1963.

FORGET-ME-NOTS

Ensign Edward Simpson (1860–1930) was a junior officer on the Arctic voyage of USS *Thetis* in 1889. *Thetis* arrived at Herschel Island on August 15, closely followed by the *Beluga*, and found *Orca* and *Thrasher* already there. On the morning of August 16, Simpson was asked by his captain, Lt. Cdr. Charles Stockton, to survey the harbour now known as Pauline Cove. Stockton named Simpson Point at the entrance to the harbour after him. Subsequently, Simpson had a distinguished career, reaching the rank of rear admiral. A book of short prose pieces he wrote about his naval service, *Yarnlets: The Human Side of the Navy*, was published posthumously in 1934 by G.P. Putnam's Sons of New York. One of these pieces, "Forget-Me-Nots," is based on his visit to Herschel Island.

About midnight, with the sun shining brightly, one day in August, 1889, we anchored in the Arctic Ocean, in open water off the mouth of the Mackenzie River, near three steam whaling ships. Never before had vessels sailed those waters. The shore line of the chart was inaccurate and based on reconnaissances of hardy explorers on shore and information from nomad Esquimaux, and the soundings were unknown. Truly it was a lonely part of the world. An unusually long continuous and severe southerly gale had started a northerly movement of the Arctic pack ice, which had broken off from the shore ice, and through the leads of open water, water holes, and cracks made thereby, these three of about a dozen of the steam whaling fleet had succeeded in twisting, ramming, cutting, and

butting their way hundreds of miles to the eastward from Point Barrow along the entire northern coast of Alaska, past the boundary line at Demarcation Point, along the northern Canadian coast, and had at last attained that long-dreamed-of, and hitherto impossible, goal of the whalemen—the open water known to exist off the mouth of the Mackenzie River in summer by reason of its flow. This the whalemen believed to be the breeding place of the bowhead whale, and this was the haven of fortune they hoped they could some lucky day fight their way to, but which day had never before dawned. At last they had attained their goal, but it had proved a myth. No whales in sight. To the eastward, open water; to the northward, ice; to the westward, ice, with the reflected ice blink in the sky marked by the dark lines

Alpine forget-me-nots (*Myosotis alpestris* spp. *asiatica*) and arctic lupines (*Lupinus arcticus*) at Herschel Island. The forget-me-nots are the lighter blue flowers. *Photo by Maria Leung.*

Rear-Admiral Edward Simpson (1860–1930).
Frontispiece from Yarnlets:The Human Side of the Navy,
published in 1934 by G.P. Putnam's Sons, New York.

Alpine forget-me-nots near the Babbage River.
Photo by Bruce Bennett.

and patches showing the leads and water holes in the ice through which they had fought their way; and to the southward on the horizon a faint outline of the uninhabited shore; and near where we were anchored was Herschel Island, a small patch of land a few miles square and about forty feet high, uninhabited, bleak, with no trees or bushes, only the scant Arctic vegetation of the Arctic tundra which thaws down an inch or so in midsummer. My, but it was a lonely piece of ground; and what must it be in winter!

Our stay could only be for a few hours, as the ice blink to the westward warned us that leads were closing; but the opportunity to add to the geographical knowledge of the world by making a quick running survey of the island could not be lost. So down went the boats and ashore we pulled. As we approached the land, we noticed how white the beach looked, and found it

was caused by logs which had been carried down the Mackenzie River and had been ground and barked and battered and broken in the Arctic ice, and finally been thrown ashore here where they had been weather-beaten and bleached for ages. On landing, our attention was attracted to what appeared to be a tent or structure of some sort farther down the beach. Could it be possible that there were any natives on this forsaken spot? Drawing nearer, it showed itself to be a shelter, built, teepee fashion, of the smaller of the white drift logs, with the opening toward the south; and the tundra of the gently sloping hill behind it began to take on more and more definitely, as we approached it, a bluish tint, until when we reached the shelter the whole background was quite blue. Inside the shelter lay the bones of a human skeleton; just outside was a broken dog sledge. Nothing more.

What was the story? Had he been lost alone, his sledge broken down, deserted by his dogs, and perished alone in the rude shelter he had erected? Or, had his friend erected the shelter, stayed with the sick man until he died, abandoned the broken sledge, and completed his journey alone with a double team of dogs? Who knows? But it was a lonely spot.

We walked around the shelter and up the gently sloping hill which had furnished the bluish background to our approach. The ground was completely covered with Forget-Me-Nots.

—Edward Simpson

LAND
AND WATER

land and water

PHYSICAL SETTING

Christopher Burn

Qikiqtaryuk (69° 35' 20" N, 139° 05' 20" W), Canada's westernmost Arctic island, lies about 60 kilometres east of Alaska in the southeastern Beaufort Sea. Roughly 116 square kilometres in area, the island sits three kilometres north of the mainland on the Yukon–Alaskan Beaufort continental shelf (Fig. 1). The present landscape began to form about 110 million years ago when the rock masses in what are now the Canadian Arctic islands moved away from the Yukon coast to open up the depression that, over time, became the Beaufort Sea. The British Mountains, which rise to over 1,600 metres (5,000 feet), are often clearly visible 30 kilometres to the south. These peaks are the northernmost part of the great western mountains of Canada. They took on their present form between 70 and 45 million years ago when they were pushed up by the collision between northern Yukon and Alaska and by other tectonic forces on the Pacific side. The edge of the Pacific Ocean was then only 200 kilometres south of the location that would become Herschel Island.

The rising British Mountains were eroded by streams that spread their deposits in the nearshore waters of the ancestral Beaufort Sea. These deposits accumulated to a thickness of between three and 13 kilometres at the foot of the mountains, covering the continental shelf and the Yukon Coastal Plain, the shelf's continuation on land. The coastal plain extends for 20 kilometres inland to the Buckland Hills at the foot of the British Mountains, and the continental shelf stretches 25 kilometres offshore from the coast to the shelf break. This break happens at a depth of 80 metres, where the sea floor plunges toward the ocean depths (Fig. 1).

Both the continental shelf and the coastal plain are almost flat, reflecting the millions of years during which streams on the plain have deposited and reworked the sedimentary ground. The uppermost hundred metres of these sediments have also been deposited and redistributed by glacial ice. In the last two million years, coastal erosion has further redistributed sediments as sea level has risen and fallen with the ice ages.

Herschel Basin and the Continental Shelf

Southeast of Herschel Island, Herschel Basin is an oval-shaped depression in the continental shelf, with water depths to 73 metres (Fig. 1). On the island itself, steep cliffs rise 20 to 60 metres to a gently rolling land surface with an elevation, at its highest point, of 182 metres. In fact, as geographer J. Ross Mackay showed, the surface gradient is continuous

View of Pauline Cove, looking south over Thetis Bay. *Photo by Fritz Mueller.*

Fig. 1 Bathymetric chart of the southeastern Beaufort Sea. *Cartography by Christine Earl.*

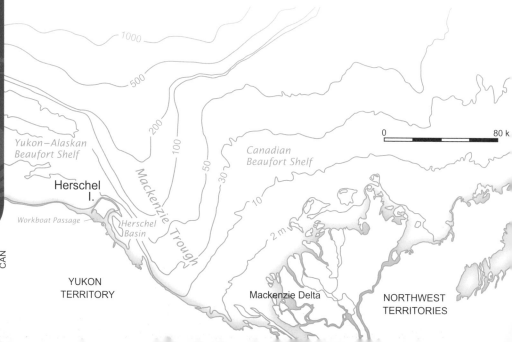

from the height of land down to the coast and eastward into Herschel Basin, apart from the cliffs (Fig. 2). This discovery helps demonstrate, as Mackay proposed, that the island was formed from sediments that were pushed up out of Herschel Basin during the last ice age. The volume of the island is similar to the volume of Herschel Basin—another key piece of evidence.

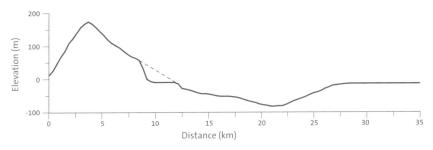

Fig. 2 Cross-section of Herschel Basin and Herschel Island.
Modified from a profile published by J.R. Mackay in 1959.

Fig. 3 Infrared satellite image of Herschel Island and the nearby Yukon Coastal Plain taken on September 13, 2006. The darker blue colours of the ocean represent progressively colder water.
Image available from Natural Resources Canada at geogratis.ca, and processed by Blair Kennedy.

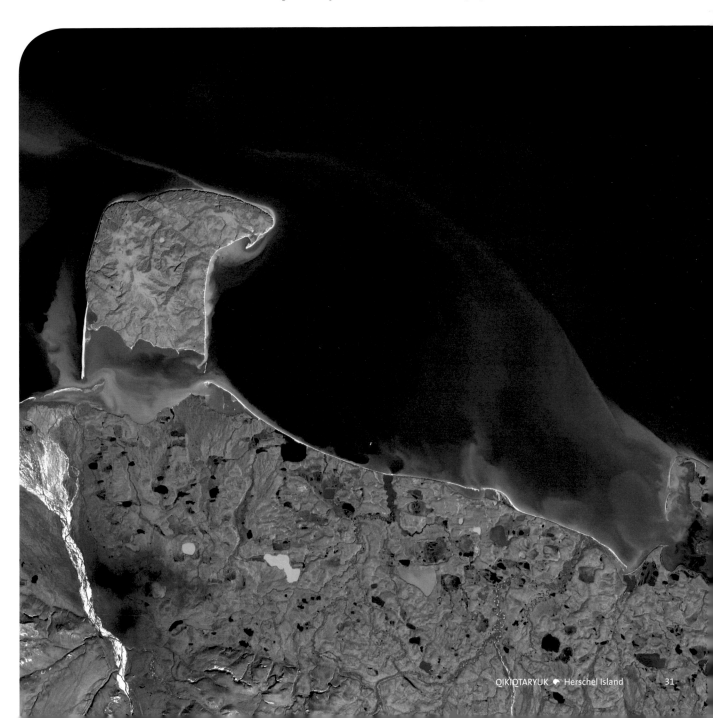

Fig. 4   Landfast ice in Thetis Bay, where the SDC offshore drilling platform was berthed for winter 2008–09. *Photo by Mary Beattie.*

Fig. 5   Rough ice on the west coast of Herschel Island, April 2009. *Photo by Mary Beattie.*

The island is separated from the mainland by Workboat Passage, a shallow strait less than three metres deep. The strait's deepest parts are near the island, with the bottom gradually rising from there to the mainland. Gravel spits that extend almost all the way across protect Workboat Passage at either end, greatly reducing the ocean swell. The shallow water in the strait suggests that the island has not been separated from the mainland for long. We know that sea level in the Beaufort Sea has been rising since the last ice age, turning the land of the coastal plain into the sea floor of the continental shelf. Given the depth of water and recent estimates for the rate of sea level rise, Herschel Island was probably separated from the mainland between 600 and 1,600 years ago. A similar separation of an island from the mainland happened during the last 25 years at Nicholson Peninsula (now Island) in Liverpool Bay, about 300 kilometres (190 miles) northeast of Inuvik.

The eastern edge of the Yukon–Alaskan continental shelf is 15 kilometres from Herschel Island, where it meets a wide submarine valley, the Mackenzie Trough (Fig. 1). The trough is critical to the ecology of the nearshore Beaufort Sea because it enables cold, nutrient-rich, deep ocean water to well up onto the shelf, especially when the ocean flow is from east to west. The streaming of sediment off the northern coast of the island, as shown in Figure 3, demonstrates this westerly flow. The coastal waters east of Herschel Island are a mixture of ocean water and fresh water flowing out of the Mackenzie River. In summer the outflow from the river mixes with the surface water to create a large body of ice-free ocean north of the Mackenzie Delta and westward past Herschel Island. In winter the Mackenzie's discharge, while reduced from the summer flow, is held beneath the sea ice by the pressure ridge at the seaward limit of landfast ice. The result is a massive, seasonal, freshwater "lake" between Herschel Island and the Delta.

The marine environment to the north and west of the island is quite different from the conditions to the south and east. In winter the landfast sea ice in Thetis Bay and Workboat Passage is relatively smooth, presenting few obstacles for travelling (Fig. 4). In contrast, the ice to the north and west is piled up in ridges and blocks (Fig. 5), making it impossible to cross by snow machine. These broken ice fields are preferred by bearded seals or **urgȓuk**, whereas ringed seals or **natchiq** inhabit the landfast ice of Thetis Bay. The difference in ice conditions is caused by ocean water welling up from Mackenzie Trough north of the island. This upwelling delays freeze-up and allows ice drifting in from the Beaufort Sea to break and pile up against the island.

Ground Materials

Bedrock, made up of sandstone and shale, lies about a kilometre below the surface of the coastal plain and continental shelf. These rocks, which have been folded and faulted, were formed from sediments brought down from the mountains during the last 10 million years. The sediments above the bedrock were also brought down from the mountains and at various times settled out as beach or marine deposits. Figure 6 shows the pattern of drainage from the British Mountains toward the coast.

As the great ice sheets waxed and waned during the last two and a half million years, sea level has fallen and risen. As a result, the deposits in the continental shelf that were pushed up to form Herschel Island are remarkably saline. Most of the sediments revealed in the northern and western cliffs of the island are such beach and marine deposits. They are often fine sands and silts, usually in well-defined layers (Fig. 7).

At the surface, Qikiqtaryuk is covered by a thin layer of sediment left behind by the glacial ice that once blanketed the island, reaching its maximum extent 12 kilometres farther west (Fig. 6). This glacial advance took place between 40,000 and 16,000 years ago. The glacial sediments are a mixture of sand, silt, and clay, but also contain erratic rocks that are unrelated to any of the bedrock nearby and were brought a great distance by the ice sheet.

Below the uppermost 40 to 60 centimetres of the ground, which is the seasonally thawed active layer, Herschel Island is perennially frozen. The top of permafrost has a high ice content to a depth of about 15 metres. Some of the ice shows signs of deformation, as might be expected in ground pushed up from the continental shelf, but other bodies of ice show little evidence of external force. The ice itself is from several sources, including bodies found at depths of 20 to 60 metres that were in the ground before the sediments were pushed up out of the coastal plain. Other sources include glacier ice that has remained since the last ice age (Fig. 8), ice that formed from the freezing of glacial meltwater, and other ice, near the surface, that has formed more recently.

Fig. 6 Drainage from the British Mountains across the coastal plain. The interior drainage to the south joins the Porcupine River at Old Crow and flows to the Bering Strait. The shaded area represents the portion of the Yukon Coastal Plain that was glaciated in the last ice age. *Cartography by Christine Earl.*

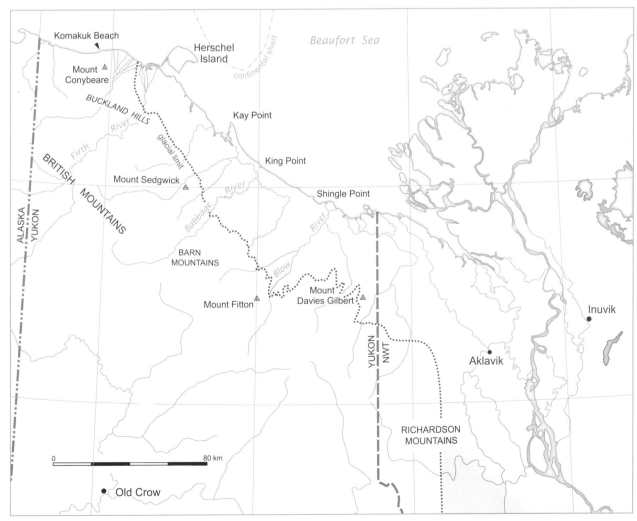

Fig. 7 Sediments exposed in the northern bluffs of Herschel Island, showing well-defined layering of the deposits. *Photo by Mary Beattie.*

Fig. 8 Exposed ground ice in a thaw slump on the eastern coast of the island. The massive ice directly below the V-shaped ice wedge is a glacial ice remnant from the last ice age. *Photo by Louis Schilder.*

At the surface, organic material usually accumulates in the ground just below the active layer. This organic material is made up of decomposed black peat and pieces of wood (Fig. 8). Soil development occurs in the active layer, but it is difficult to distinguish different soil layers because annual freezing and thawing mixes up the sediments through a process called cryoturbation. The cryoturbation occurs in units of the active layer one to two metres in diameter, gradually burying surface vegetation at the top of permafrost. Many parts of the island have extensive fields of small, circular hummocks, a surface feature caused by this soil movement (Fig. 9).

Climate

Herschel Island has an arctic climate. Mean monthly temperatures are above 5°C only in July and August, while average temperatures in January and February are below -25°C. The mean annual air temperature is about -9°C. The winter snow cover normally arrives in September and lasts until June, but snow drifts in gullies, built up by winter storms, may last through the summer, especially if insulated from melting by plant detritus (Fig. 10). The storms, however, blow much of the upland surfaces clear of snow because

there is little vegetation to trap it, and big drifts also develop around obstacles such as the buildings at Pauline Cove (Fig. 11). The strong winds come from the north, usually the northwest or northeast, making Thetis Bay a sheltered anchorage. The ocean freezes in Thetis Bay in November and breaks up in late June, so that by early July it is possible to reach the island from the Mackenzie Delta by boat.

The winter at Herschel Island is a relatively dry season. Most snow arrives in the fall before the ice cover has formed, when ocean water may still evaporate. The summer months may be wetter, often bringing fog (Fig. 12). The low temperatures, short growing season, and frequent fogs combine to limit the plants that grow on the island to tundra species. Evaporation is restricted in summer because the air is moist due to the ocean surrounding the island. As a result the ground remains damp even though the annual precipitation is only about 160 millimetres.

Permafrost

All of Herschel Island is underlain by permafrost. The mean annual ground temperature over the windswept uplands, where large areas have only

a thin snow cover, is -8°C. Beneath snow drifts in gullies, valleys, and depressions, where the snow is an effective insulator preventing loss of heat, annual temperatures up to 4°C higher have been measured. The minimum recorded temperature in such areas is only -8°C, compared with a minimum ground temperature of -21°C at a one-metre depth at exposed sites. Thawing at the ground surface, and development of the

Fig. 9 Soil hummocks on Collinson Head. Each circular feature has a diameter of about one metre. The hummocks are exposed in winter because the snow is blown off the raised tops by the wind. *Photo by Christopher Burn.*

Fig. 10 A snow bank near Pauline Cove that fills the lower part of a valley and is insulated from melting by plant detritus that is blown with the snow during winter storms. *Photo by Christopher Burn.*

Fig. 11 Northeasterly blizzard conditions in Pauline Cove. *Photo by Lee John Meyook.*

seasonal active layer, begins when the snow cover melts in late May or early June. Freeze-back of the active layer is completed by mid-November over most of the island, but may take a month longer beneath snow banks.

Over most of the island the top metre of permafrost consists of ice and soil in thin layers, each one or two centimetres thick (Fig. 13). Much of this near-surface ground

was in a deeper active layer that developed about 9,000 years ago when the summer climate was warmer. Since then the climate has cooled and the active layer has become thinner. Beneath these layers lies almost pure massive ice, visible at many places along the coast in large thaw slumps. These slumps, the most dynamic landforms on the island, often form at the coast, where they trigger erosion at a rate of up to 10 metres per year.

Numerous V-shaped masses of similarly pure ice called "ice wedges" are visible in these slumps (Fig. 8). These ice wedges can be distinguished by their vertical structure in the horizontal layering of the massive ice. They are formed from snowmelt that infiltrates the cracks that open up in winter when the ground is extremely cold. Many of the ice wedges have formed in the millennia since the end of the last ice age.

Fig. 12 A fog bank off the northwest coast of Herschel Island. *Photo by Catherine Kennedy.*

Fig. 13 Ice-rich permafrost near the ground surface. The trowel is 22 centimetres long. *Photo by Christopher Burn.*

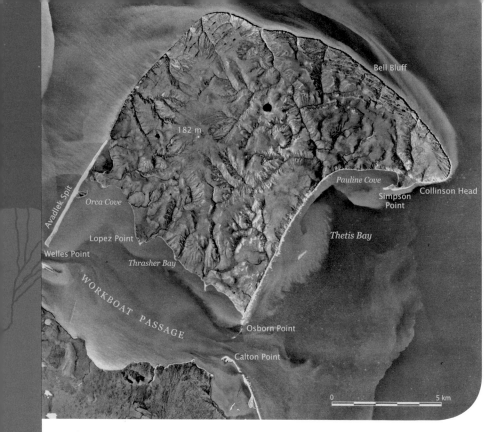

Fig. 14 Aerial photograph mosaic of Herschel Island from photographs A22974 212-214 and A22975 23-25. *Image courtesy of Her Majesty the Queen in Right of Canada and reproduced by permission of Natural Resources Canada. The mosaic was assembled by Jon Tunnicliffe.*

Landforms

Herschel Island itself is a landform pushed out of the continental shelf by advancing glacier ice. Figure 14 is an aerial photograph mosaic of the island showing a series of straight parallel faults that appear as lines along the northwest coast. These linear features curve around to follow the northeast coast. They are surface evidence of the deformation that took place when the island was pushed up in a northwesterly direction. In some places the sedimentary layers were overturned as the overriding ice pushed the sediments out of Herschel Basin (Fig. 15).

The coastal cliffs of Qikiqtaryuk are continually eroded during the open-water season. Although the annual erosion rate of less than one metre per year may seem small, the 60-metre-high cliffs and 10-kilometre-long coasts on the north and west of the island produce about a million tonnes of sediment each year. The cliffs themselves collapse in blocks of frozen ground (Fig. 7). In contrast, on the east coast of the island, coastal erosion happens largely through the

development of retrogressive thaw slumps (Fig. 16).

The thaw slumps are the most active landforms on the island, but the most constructive landforming activity occurs on the island's alluvial fans and sandspits (Fig. 14). The largest spits, at each end of Workboat Passage, are gravel beach remnants of the coast before the island was separated from the mainland. The gravel was winnowed from the debris of coastal erosion and the spits are the former beach. At the east end of Workboat Passage, Osborn Point is a few hundred metres from Calton Point, the tip of the spit protruding toward the island from the mainland. At the west end, Welles Point at the end of Avadlek Spit is close to Nunaluk Spit, which marks the end of the Firth River. The third spit forms one side of Pauline Cove, ending at Simpson Point. Because all the spits are gravel, they are relatively stable compared to the muddy sediments that make up the island. They are usually lined with driftwood brought down to the ocean by the Mackenzie River.

Alluvial fans occur where creeks leave their confining valleys, slow down, and deposit the sediment they carried. The island has two main alluvial fans at the coast—one in Workboat Passage at Lopez Point, the other at Pauline Cove. The fan at Pauline Cove forms the third side of the harbour between the island's bluffs and the sandspit where the buildings stand. This fan was built out onto the exposed coastal plain before sea level rose toward the present coastline. Like the rest of the coast of Thetis Bay, it is now being eroded.

Streams and Water Supply

The drainage network on Herschel Island is rectangular in shape, probably following fault lines inherited from the glacial thrusting (Fig. 14). Many of the small creeks run in steeply incised V-shaped valleys, though for most of the year they are either frozen or hold little water. Some internal drainages form wetlands in summer and a few contain lakes, but most creeks flow to the coast. Ice from the lakes is one of the few reliable sources of drinkable water on the island. In summer the poor water supply limits the number of park visitors, and was a reason for discounting the island as a tanker terminal location during planning for oil development in the 1970s.

Ecoregion

Herschel Island is part of the Yukon Coastal Plain ecoregion in the Southern Arctic ecozone. The climate, permafrost, and soil conditions together support low arctic vegetation, where willow bushes less than a metre high are the tallest plants. However, most of the island has a tussock tundra vegetation cover dominated by cotton-grass and low shrubs, apart from the coastal bluffs, retrogressive thaw slumps, and alluvial fans. Figure 3 shows the relatively uniform vegetation cover on the island. The dominant vegetation in each location varies with soil wetness. This relative uniformity means that the animals are unrestricted in range and can be found throughout the island, though

on warm summer days both caribou and muskoxen look for windy places to avoid biting insects.

Herschel Island is remarkable for an animal population that includes almost all those found on the Yukon North Slope (Table 1), except moose or **tuttuvak** and black bear or **iggarlik**. Ground squirrels or **siksik** are rarely seen. All the main marine mammals of the southeastern Beaufort Sea visit the island seasonally, as well as some stray visitors such as walrus or **aiviq**. The bird population includes land, coastal, and sea birds that use the island for nesting and rearing their young. The abundant and varied wildlife, the result of the island's relatively remote location and lack of major human activity, is a prime attraction of Herschel Island as a territorial park.

The history of human activities on the island is the result of Qikiqtaryuk's

Fig. 15 Glacially deformed beds at Bell Bluff on the north coast of Herschel Island, 1913–16.
Photo courtesy of Canadian Museum of Civilization, George Hubert Wilkins, 1916, 51384.

physical setting. The marine environment, with the Mackenzie Trough's upwelling waters diluted by the Mackenzie River, provided the concentration of resources that allowed aboriginal people to live on the island. The glacial history, and the development of an alluvial fan in the last 10,000 years, created the sheltered waters of Thetis Bay and Pauline Cove. These sheltered bays allowed the whalemen to develop their industry in the southeastern Beaufort Sea and still provide protection for ships and small boats. Sea level rise formed

Workboat Passage, which in turn partly shielded caribou and muskoxen from marauding predators on the mainland. Coastal erosion led to the growth of the spit at Pauline Cove, now used as a landing strip. All of these factors have contributed to Herschel Island's place in Inuvialuit and national history. In the future, Qikiqtaryuk's physical setting will bring the challenges of climate change, especially the effects of sea level rise on park infrastructure, and the potential development of oil and gas resources beneath the Beaufort Sea.

Fig. 16 Retrogressive thaw slumps across Thetis Bay from Simpson Point, behind CCGS *Nahidik*, and concrete caissons left in the Bay by the oil industry. *Photo by Bill Williams.*

COMMON NAME	LATIN NAME	INUVIALUKTUN NAME
Collared lemming	*Dicrostonyx groenlandicus*	Avingaq
Brown lemming	*Lemmus trimucronatus*	Avingaq
Tundra vole	*Microtus oeconomus*	Avingaq
Arctic ground squirrel	*Spermophilus parryii*	Siksik (S), Sikhirik (U)
Tundra shrew	*Sorex tundrensis*	Ugyungnaq (S), Uguřungnuraq (U)
Barren-ground shrew	*Sorex ugyunak*	Ugyungnaq (S), Uguřungnuraq (U)
Barren-ground caribou	*Rangifer tarandus*	Tuktu (S), Tuttu (U)
Muskox	*Ovibos moschatus*	Umingmak
Red fox	*Vulpes vulpes*	Aukpilaqtaq
Arctic fox	*Vulpes lagopus*	Tiriganniaq
Wolverine	*Gulo gulo*	Qavvik
Least weasel	*Mustela nivalis*	Itiriaq
Tundra wolf	*Canis lupus*	Amaruq
Lynx	*Lynx canadensis*	Niutuiyiq
Marten	*Martes americana*	Qavviatchiaq
Ermine or mink	*Mustela erminea*	Itiriaqpuk
Grizzly bear	*Ursus arctos*	Akłaq
Polar bear	*Ursus maritimus*	Nanuq
Beluga whale	*Delphinapterus leucas*	Qilalugaq
Bowhead whale	*Balaena mysticetus*	Arviq (S), Arvaq (U)
Ringed seal	*Phoca hispida*	Natchiq
Bearded seal	*Erignathus barbatus*	Ugyuk (S), Urgřuk (U)
Harbour seal	*Phoca vitulina*	Kusigiuk
Walrus	*Odobenus rosmarus*	Aiviq

Table 1 Mammals of Herschel Island. Note: Kayuqtuq is also a common collective Inuvialuktun word for fox. It refers to all foxes other than the arctic fox, such as cross, red and silver foxes. *Assistance with Inuvialuktun names was kindly provided by Esther McLeod.*

GEOLOGY

Larry Lane, Charlie Roots,
and Tiffani Fraser

The SDC (Steel Drilling Caisson) and concrete caissons stored in Thetis Bay by the petroleum industry, 2004. *Photo courtesy of Herschel Island Territorial Park.*

Looking south over Pauline Cove toward the Buckland Hills and British Mountains, 2011. *Photo by Graham Gilbert.*

Herschel Island now sits at the remote northern edge of the North American continent. However, until about 112 million years ago, when the Beaufort-Mackenzie sedimentary basin opened up, the area alternated between being a terrestrial lowland, lying beneath shallow water, or forming the foothills of a mountain range. The basin is of great interest today because it may contain significant reserves of oil and gas. Qikiqtaryuk itself, which lies on the edge of the basin, is made of unconsolidated glacial, marine, and alluvial sediments. These sediments form a veneer over a kilometre thick above the bedrock of the basin, which extends horizontally southward to the mainland. There, 30 kilometres from the island, bedrock is exposed in the British Mountains and the Buckland Hills that are often visible from Pauline Cove.

The convoluted sedimentary bedrock beneath Herschel Island has been deformed by repeated movements of the Earth's crust. The high number of these movements makes it difficult to determine the age of folds and faults in the rocks. Some rock units have been completely eroded, so the record is no longer continuous. The deformation and the limited bedrock exposure, except in the core of the British Mountains, have challenged geologists trying to interpret the area's history and development. Our knowledge comes from field observations in the mountains, geophysical surveys of the layers beneath the Beaufort Sea, and samples recovered during drilling for oil and gas.

The overall geology of the British Mountains and Herschel Island area is shown in Figure 1. The rock units are arranged by age on this map. Progressively younger rocks, labelled with higher numbers, appear at the surface to the northeast. Older rocks generally underlie the younger ones. Figure 2 is a schematic rock column showing the sequence of the region's geologic strata, or layers, as they have evolved over time.

Traces of a Supercontinent

During the late sixties, J. Tuzo Wilson, a Canadian geophysicist, proposed a new theory about the slow drift of continents over the surface of the Earth. According to Wilson, this movement resulted alternately in the joining up of continents into "supercontinents" and their spreading apart. When continents collide, he suggested, mountain belts form. When they drift apart, the trailing edges gradually sink, resulting in relatively shallow water above the continental shelf next to the land mass.

The theory of plate tectonics revolutionized our understanding of geological forces and processes that operate in the Earth's crust. Subsequently, several tectonic plates, including the continents, were identified as units that collide to form supercontinents and then separate.

The most recent supercontinent, Pangea, broke apart in stages. North America separated from Europe about 200 million years ago. The extension and thinning of the continental crust, known as rifting, continues today in the middle of the Atlantic Ocean at about 2.5 centimetres per year.

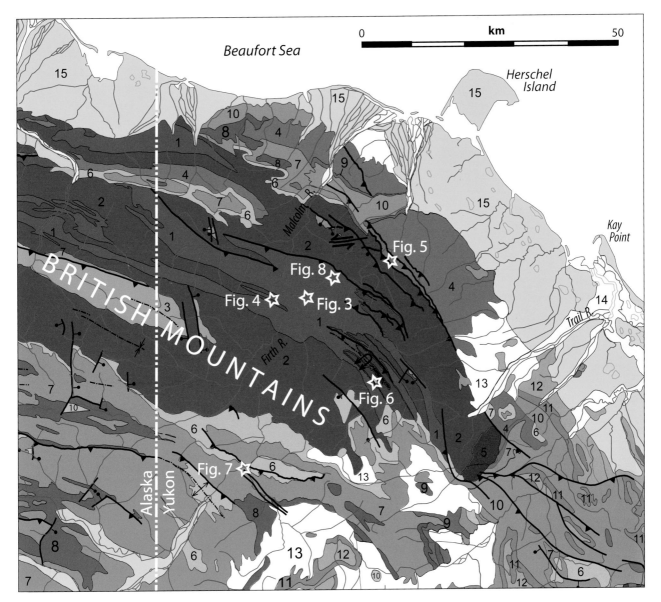

Fig. 1 General geologic units of the northern Yukon. The locations of photographs taken in the mountains are marked by stars. *Modified from Issler et al., 2011, sheet 4 of Geological Survey of Canada Open File 5689.*

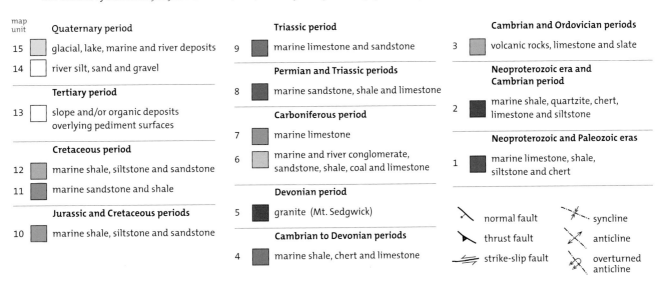

map unit	Quaternary period	
15		glacial, lake, marine and river deposits
14		river silt, sand and gravel

Tertiary period

13		slope and/or organic deposits overlying pediment surfaces

Cretaceous period

12		marine shale, siltstone and sandstone
11		marine sandstone and shale

Jurassic and Cretaceous periods

10		marine shale, siltstone and sandstone

Triassic period

9		marine limestone and sandstone

Permian and Triassic periods

8		marine sandstone, shale and limestone

Carboniferous period

7		marine limestone
6		marine and river conglomerate, sandstone, shale, coal and limestone

Devonian period

5		granite (Mt. Sedgwick)

Cambrian to Devonian periods

4		marine shale, chert and limestone

Cambrian and Ordovician periods

3		volcanic rocks, limestone and slate

Neoproterozoic era and Cambrian period

2		marine shale, quartzite, chert, limestone and siltstone

Neoproterozoic and Paleozoic eras

1		marine limestone, shale, siltstone and chert

normal fault   syncline
thrust fault   anticline
strike-slip fault   overturned anticline

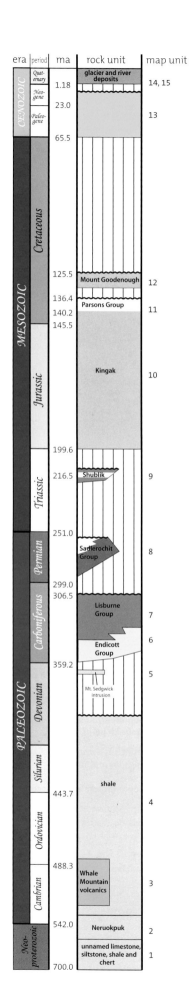

era	period	ma	rock unit	map unit
CENOZOIC	Quaternary	1.18	glacier and river deposits	14, 15
CENOZOIC	Neogene	23.0		13
CENOZOIC	Paleogene	65.5		13
MESOZOIC	Cretaceous	125.5		
MESOZOIC	Cretaceous	136.4	Mount Goodenough	12
MESOZOIC	Cretaceous	140.2	Parsons Group	11
MESOZOIC	Jurassic	145.5	Kingak	10
MESOZOIC	Jurassic	199.6	Kingak	10
MESOZOIC	Triassic	216.5	Shublik	9
MESOZOIC	Triassic	251.0		
PALEOZOIC	Permian	299.0	Sadlerochit Group	8
PALEOZOIC	Carboniferous	306.5	Lisburne Group	7
PALEOZOIC	Carboniferous	359.2	Endicott Group	6
PALEOZOIC	Devonian		Mt. Sedgwick intrusion	5
PALEOZOIC	Silurian	443.7	shale	4
PALEOZOIC	Ordovician	488.3		
PALEOZOIC	Cambrian	542.0	Whale Mountain volcanics	3
Neoproterozoic			Neruokpuk	2
Neoproterozoic		700.0	unnamed limestone, siltstone, shale and chert	1

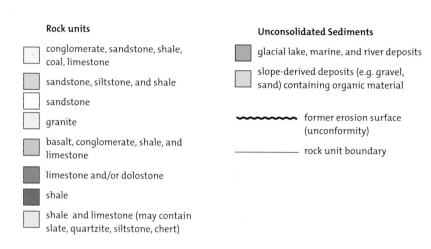

Fig. 2 Schematic column of major rock units of the Yukon north coast. *Extensively modified from D.W. Morrow, A.L. Jones, and J. Dixon, 2006. Infrastructure and Resources of the Northern Canadian Mainland Sedimentary Basin. Geological Survey of Canada Open File 5152, Figure 18.*

Rock units

- conglomerate, sandstone, shale, coal, limestone
- sandstone, siltstone, and shale
- sandstone
- granite
- basalt, conglomerate, shale, and limestone
- limestone and/or dolostone
- shale
- shale and limestone (may contain slate, quartzite, siltstone, chert)

Unconsolidated Sediments

- glacial lake, marine, and river deposits
- slope-derived deposits (e.g. gravel, sand) containing organic material

~~~~~~ former erosion surface (unconformity)

———— rock unit boundary

Rodinia, an earlier supercontinent, began to break apart about 700 million years ago. The separation of ancient North America, possibly from what is now Siberia, left an edge that extended from northwestern Yukon to northern Greenland. This edge, known today as the Franklinian margin, formed a slope from the newly created continental shelf of ancient North America to the ocean floor. The sedimentary rocks that accumulated on the continental shelf are now exposed in the western Arctic islands. Layers of limestone, siltstone, slate (hardened shale), and chert (rock formed from silica-dominated mud on the ocean floor) were deposited in deep water beyond the Franklinian margin (Fig. 3, and map unit 1 in Fig. 1). Some of the layers were formed from catastrophic underwater mudslides that flowed from the continental shelf to the ocean floor. These layers are the oldest rocks exposed in the British Mountains.

Up to about 540 million years ago, a thick succession of mud, sand, and silt, now called the Neruokpuk Formation, was deposited on the continental shelf (map unit 2, Fig. 1).

Fig. 3 The Firth River cuts through limestone and siltstone (map unit 1, Fig. 1), the oldest rocks exposed on the North Slope. *Photo by Michelle Sicotte.*

These rocks were subsequently pushed on top of the older deep-water sediments. Today, the weathered surfaces of the sandstone and siltstone of the Neruokpuk Formation, with limestone bands resistant to erosion, form a rugged landscape in the British Mountains (Fig. 4).

The next oldest rocks belong to the Whale Mountain volcanic unit and are exposed near the Alaska–Yukon border (map unit 3, Fig. 1). Pebbles of this dark reddish stone can be found along the Firth River from the confluence of Sheep Creek to the coast, including Nunaluk Spit. From about 530 to 415 million years ago, fine-grained, deep-water sediments (map unit 4, Fig. 1) covered the Neruokpuk Formation. These sediments included red and green mudstone (Fig. 5), limestone, and dark grey chert.

Mountain-building, Erosion, and a Warm Ocean

The collisions of tectonic plates formed mountain ranges on Pangea during the Devonian period (Fig. 2), folding sedimentary rocks so they were tilted almost vertically. In the British Mountains, however, these effects are difficult to separate from those that occurred during the Cretaceous and Tertiary periods when the great western mountains formed. Pulses of molten rock (magma) injected into the upper levels of the Earth's crust cooled about 365 million years ago. Since then, five to eight kilometres of rock have been eroded, revealing the magma as granite at Mount Sedgwick (map unit 5, Fig. 1).

By about 355 million years ago (the Carboniferous period; Fig. 2), the mountains of the region had been eroded. Rifting far to the southwest produced a new ocean. Fine-grained sediments from highlands to the north spread across the eroded and subsiding older rocks (the contact between them is known as an

Fig. 4 Ridges of multicoloured shale, siltstone (smooth slopes) and limestone (cliffs of the Neruokpuk Formation in the British Mountains above Sheep Creek) (map unit 2, Fig. 1). *Photo by Michelle Sicotte.*

Fig. 5 Bands of multicoloured mudstone interbedded with chert and limestone in the Buckland Hills (map units 2 and 4, Fig. 1). *Photo by Larry Lane.*

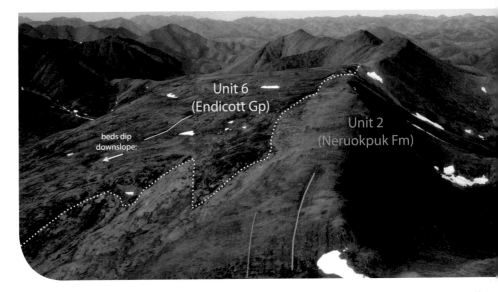

Fig. 6 Gently tilted dark-coloured conglomerate of the Endicott Group (map unit 6, Fig. 1) deposited on top of steeply dipping light brown beds of the older Neruokpuk Formation (map unit 2, Fig. 1), parallel to the orange lines. The sedimentary contact between the units (dotted line) represents about 200 million years during which the Neruokpuk layers were deformed, uplifted, and partly eroded. *Photo by Larry Lane.*

angular unconformity) (Fig. 6). The sediments (map unit 6, Fig. 1) contained swamp vegetation that eventually became coal, while clay and silt deposited offshore became shale. With the tropical climate of the time, the warm and shallow sea was home to a varied population of marine animals, including corals. Limestone (map unit 7, Fig. 1), which forms rugged, light-grey to yellowish ridges (Fig. 7) with bluffs and abundant fossils, reflects this marine environment.

Formation of the Arctic Continental Margin

The rocks that remain from the next hundred million years (Permian, Triassic, and Early Jurassic periods; Fig. 2) are thin deposits of shale, limestone, and sandstone (map unit 8, Fig. 1). The geologic history recorded by these scattered exposures is fragmentary. The alternating rock types suggest repeated submergence, uplift, and erosion, but evidence of the continental interactions which produced them has disappeared.

From about 200 to 100 million years ago (Early Jurassic to Early Cretaceous periods; Fig. 2), consecutive periods of faulting opened the basin of the western Arctic Ocean. The Jurassic rock sequences of sandstone, siltstone, and shale (map unit 9, Fig. 1) show that each rock type was deposited progressively farther from shore (sand accumulates near the coast while finer-grained silt, mud, and clay settle farther out). By mapping both the Jurassic and Early Cretaceous rocks (map unit 10, Fig. 1), geologists conclude that a shoreline lay some 200 kilometres to the south and east of the present western Arctic coast. A major episode of faulting took place in northern Yukon at the end of the Early Cretaceous period from 112 to 100 million years ago (Fig. 2). It was followed by a long period of slow subsidence, resulting in the ocean we now call the Beaufort Sea.

Fig. 7 A peak of limestone (map unit 7, Fig. 1) and low hills of sandstone and shale (map unit 6, Fig. 1). *Photo by Christopher Hunter, Parks Canada.*

Fig. 8 Rock arch (anticline) formed by folding of thick limestone beds (map unit 1, Fig. 1) exposed by erosion of the Firth River. *Photo by Christopher Hunter, Parks Canada.*

Rise of the Buckland Hills

During the Cretaceous period, the land mass south of Herschel Island was lifted up by the folding and faulting of sedimentary layers, as a result of tectonic forces acting on what is now the Pacific side of the Cordillera. The uplifted land was eroded into mountain ranges from which rivers carried sand and silt (map units 11 and 12, Fig. 1) into the rift basins on the Herschel Island side of the mountains. During this period the Mackenzie and Rocky mountains were separated from the rest of North America by a seaway that connected Arctic waters to the tropics. The shores of this sea were used by dinosaurs whose fossil bones and footprints are found from Montana to the northern shores of Alaska. The region had a much more temperate climate than it does today.

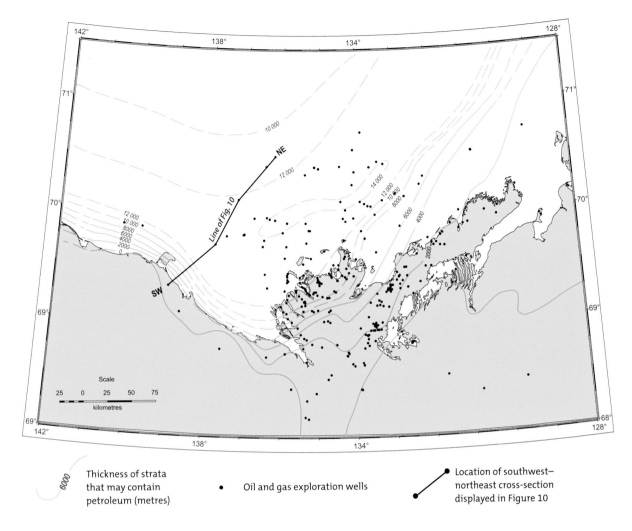

Thickness of strata that may contain petroleum (metres)

• Oil and gas exploration wells

Location of southwest–northeast cross-section displayed in Figure 10

Fig. 9 Thickness of the offshore sand and silt deposits that may contain petroleum, and location of exploration wells in the western Canadian Arctic. *Data from Geological Survey of Canada.*

Building the British Mountains

From about 70 to 45 million years ago (during the Late Cretaceous and early Tertiary periods; Fig. 2), North America drifted northwestward and collided with the landmass that now forms the Brooks Range of northern Alaska. Across northern Yukon the result was folding, faulting, and uplift (Fig. 8), with rocks pushed northeastward by about 120 kilometres and formations in the British Mountains lifted up by five to seven kilometres. Erosion by ancient rivers such as the Babbage, Firth, and Malcolm created valleys that were roughly perpendicular to the mountain ridges.

River Delta Sediments

As the Beaufort Sea opened up, a series of sedimentary basins were created between areas of local high relief. From the Late Cretaceous on, northward-flowing rivers transported fine-grained sediments to the ocean, forming deltas which slowly advanced into deeper water. Over time the weight of the sediments caused the bottom of the basins to sink, resulting in a gently sloping seafloor. Sandstone, mudstone, and siltstone, along with smaller amounts of conglomerate and lignite, formed the lowlands of the Yukon Coastal Plain, which has the same origin and age range as the

continental shelf. The warm ocean had considerable biological activity and some of the rocks formed from organic-rich mud. The continental shelf extends northward beneath Herschel Island, where the thickness of these sediments increases (Fig. 9).

During the last 10 million years or so, northern Yukon has moved northward at about 4 millimetres per year. In the process the rocks beneath the Beaufort Sea have folded and faulted, creating traps in the sedimentary rocks for oil and gas squeezed from the organic-rich layers. Herschel Island lies on top of a wedge-shaped package of gently crumpled, relatively soft, sedimentary rock, formed from these river deposits over the last 70 million years. The wedge is about two to eight kilometres thick close to the coast and increases in thickness northward to more than 12 kilometres (Fig. 10). The offshore search for oil and gas reservoirs focuses upon these sediments and the organic material trapped within them.

Landward, the gentle slopes leading from the coastal plain up into the Buckland Hills are known as pediments (map unit 13, Fig. 1). These are extensive sheets of eroded rock detritus, propelled slowly downslope by gravity, especially during snowmelt or heavy rainstorms.

These surfaces were relatively unaffected by glaciation in the last two million years because northern Yukon was at the margin of the ice sheets. At the foot of the pediments, glacial, marine, and river sediments lie at the surface of the Yukon Coastal Plain (map units 14 and 15, Fig. 1). It is these sediments, pushed up near the glacial limit, that form Herschel Island. The gravel bars and fans that form today at the mouths of the rivers on the coastal plain are relatively resistant to erosion. Most of the sediment that comes down from the mountains, however, is easily washed away by the Beaufort Sea and settles on the continental shelf, or is swept into the deep water of the Arctic Ocean.

Geological Setting for Hydrocarbon Reservoirs

The Herschel Island area may once again become economically important, as it was in the whaling era, if natural gas and oil are discovered below the sea floor nearby. The total hydrocarbon potential of the western Canadian Beaufort region is unclear because the area is underexplored. Offshore from the Mackenzie Delta, however, there are considerable oil and gas reserves. The best estimates of the resources discovered so far in the Mackenzie-Beaufort Sea region are 161 million cubic metres (one billion barrels) of recoverable oil and 255 billion cubic metres (9 trillion cubic feet) of marketable natural gas.

Fig. 10 Schematic cross-section of petroleum-bearing sediments near Herschel Island (location on Fig. 9). Note that wells were located to test for petroleum in folds and near faults (structural traps). Vertical exaggeration is approximately 3:1. *Modified from Dixon et al., 2008. Sedimentary Basins of the World, Vol. 5, p. 556.*

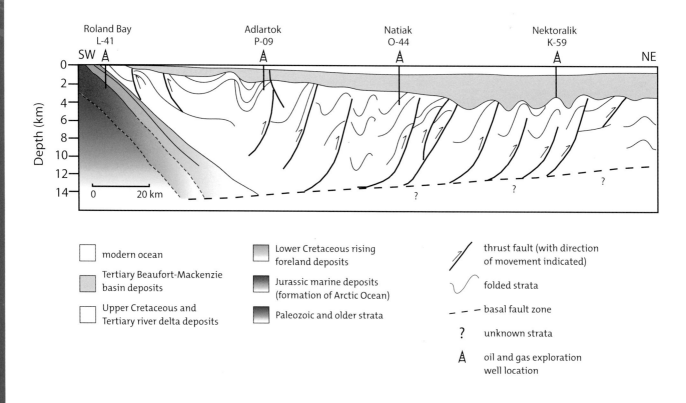

Along the coast of the Beaufort Sea, the hydrocarbons came from organic-rich shale, a rock formed from mineral sediments brought by rivers into warm coastal ocean waters filled with microscopic sea life. The organic material and mineral matter combined to form thick deposits of biological "sludge" that, over time, became petroleum-rich shale (Fig. 11). As northern Yukon moved northward, compression of the shale forced the petroleum fluid to migrate into porous sandstone. This sandstone is the reservoir rock (Fig. 12) necessary for a petroleum reserve, along with the shale source rock.

The shale and sandstone beneath Herschel Island contain all the elements of a petroleum system, including trapping and sealing mechanisms. Hydrocarbon traps and seals are important in keeping oil or natural gas isolated and preventing it from escaping to the surface. Traps are rock configurations, such as folds (Fig. 8) or faulted blocks, that hold the petroleum in one area. Seals include rocks such as shale that form a barrier to the flow of oil or natural gas.

Beneath these sediments housing the petroleum system, all less than 100 million years old, the underlying rocks are not considered suitable for hydrocarbons.

History of Oil and Gas Exploration

Petroleum exploration along the edge of the Canadian Beaufort Sea has concentrated on the east and northeast of Herschel Island, the Mackenzie Delta, the Tuktoyaktuk Peninsula, and the eastern Beaufort Sea (Fig. 9). Onshore exploration drilling in the Mackenzie Delta began in 1962 and peaked in the mid-1970s after the first discovery of oil in 1969. The offshore Mackenzie Delta area and the Beaufort Sea were explored in the late 1970s and 1980s, but the activity has been concentrated in the Delta area and to the east. Altogether, 274 wells have been drilled in the Mackenzie Delta and Beaufort Sea.

Fig. 11 Thinly-bedded shale, typical of petroleum source rock, at Rock River, northern Yukon.
Photo by Tiffani Fraser.

Fig. 12 Oil-stained sandstone, typical of petroleum reservoir rock in the Tuttle Formation, southern Richardson Mountains.
Photo by Tiffani Fraser.

Little petroleum exploration has taken place in the western Canadian Beaufort Sea and along the northern Yukon coast. Three wells were drilled onshore in the early 1970s, but no resources were discovered. The closest to Herschel Island was Roland Bay L-41, 21 kilometres southeast of the island (Fig. 9 and 10). This well was drilled in late 1972 and early 1973 to a depth of 2,752 metres. Natsek E-56 was drilled northwest of the island during the summers of 1978 and 1979 to a depth of 3,520 metres below the platform in a water depth of 34 metres, while Edlok N-56 was drilled offshore during the summer of 1985 to a depth of 2,530 metres below the platform. These wells were abandoned as no hydrocarbons were found. The closest oil discovery to Herschel Island is the Adlartok P-09 well, 43 kilometres northeast of the island.

Seven kilometres beyond this well is Kingark J-54, the closest gas discovery.

Large tracts of the Beaufort Sea to the west, north, and east of Herschel Island are being studied by the petroleum industry. These investigations are mostly seismic exploration, but further drilling offshore is expected in the next decade.

Seismic Hazard

The seismic network for northwestern Canada was installed in the early 1960s. Since then earthquakes have been recorded most frequently in the Mackenzie Mountains, along the southern half of the border between the Yukon and Northwest Territories. Earthquakes are less common in the Richardson Mountains west of the Mackenzie Delta. A third zone of infrequent, moderate earthquakes lies about 250 kilometres offshore, where the northern limit of Mackenzie Delta sediments overlaps the edge of the continental shelf. There, beyond the continental margin, the sedimentary wedge of the Mackenzie Delta, 15 kilometres thick, stretches onto weak oceanic crust. This mass of rapidly deposited sediment causes bending of the crust, with earthquakes being triggered deep within the basement rocks. The earthquake zone coincides with the area of thin oceanic crust. However, without records of large earthquakes in the area, the seismic hazard remains unclear. In contrast, the old rocks in the British Mountains seem to be, seismically, quite stable (Fig. 13).

Fig. 13 The oldest rocks in the region are in the British Mountains at the edge of the North American continent (units 1 and 2, Fig. 1). *Photo by Michelle Sicotte.*

THE OIL AND GAS BOOM

From 1978 to 1985, the federal government's National Energy Program provided substantial financial support to industry to stimulate oil and gas exploration in the Canadian Beaufort Sea. Over $5 billion of public and private funds were spent in offshore exploration, which required drilling in both open water and ice-covered conditions. Some of the offshore drilling was from ships and other floating platforms, but a number of wells were attempted from artificial islands.

Beaudril (Gulf Canada) used Thetis Bay as a marine base in the early 1980s. A dry dock was used for repairs to ships. *Photo courtesy of Bharat Dixit.*

The SDC (Steel Drilling Caisson), formerly the SSDC (Semi-submersible Drilling Caisson), in Thetis Bay, 2005. *Photo by Doug Larsen.*

In the early 1980s, Gulf Canada used Thetis Bay as its marine base, freezing in an oil tanker, two ice breakers, two supply boats, two mobile drilling platforms (*Molikpaq* and *Kulluk*), and a converted ferry (*Munaksee*) that served as a base camp. The vessels were serviced by a 210-kilometre ice road built out to Herschel Island from Inuvik. A 6,000-foot (1,800-metre) runway on the ice allowed Boeing 737 jet aircraft to fly directly to the island from Calgary in March and April, when the ice was at least 84 inches (214 centimetres) thick. Barges, dredges, and tugs also spent the winter in Thetis Bay. In summer various other ships, including Canadian Coast Guard research vessels, oil company ice breakers, oil-spill clean-up auxiliaries, and even a dry dock, arrived. Around the clock the air buzzed with the sounds of helicopters and tenders travelling between ships. All the activity was reminiscent of the busy days when fifteen ships overwintered in Pauline Cove at the peak of the whaling era.

Standing on the quiet beach today, in summer or winter, it is difficult to imagine the level of activity in Thetis Bay during the early 1980s, or to believe that industrial activity will return once market conditions are favourable. Since 2004–05 the SDC (Steel Drilling Caisson) has been berthed in Thetis Bay or near Roland Bay for most of the time, along with steel and concrete caissons used as the foundations for artificial islands. Any renewed development activity will have environmental oversight as specified by the 1984 Inuvialuit Final Agreement.

Hercules transport aircraft on the runway in Thetis Bay. The runway was built throughout winter to reach the thickness required to land large aircraft, including Boeing 737 jets and Hercules transports, in March and April. *Photo courtesy of Bharat Dixit.*

CLIMATE

Christopher Burn

Herschel Island has a truly arctic climate, with a long, cold winter and a short summer bathed in continuous daylight. The weather at Qikiqtaryuk is a result of its far northern latitude, the presence of mountains throughout the Yukon and Alaska, and the cold waters and ice of the Beaufort Sea. The latitude means that the amount of light varies from twenty-four hours a day in summer to merely a short, faint twilight in midwinter around the winter solstice on December 22. The mountain ranges to the south prevent the relatively warm, moist air that travels from the Pacific through the Yukon from reaching the Arctic Ocean. The Beaufort Sea moderates the annual range in temperature by cooling the area in summer and warming the region slightly in winter with heat from the unfrozen ocean water beneath the ice cover. However, the same seasonal ice cover leads to a dry winter and reflects much of the incoming solar radiation, delaying the arrival of spring and summer.

Herschel Island is one of the few places in the Arctic with climate records from over a hundred years ago. These records show that freeze-up now occurs about four weeks later than it did in 1890–1900. Today, when there is great interest in changes to the extent of arctic sea ice brought about by climate change, such records are an invaluable resource.

Climate data were recorded at Herschel Island in 1899–1905 and occasionally thereafter until an automatic weather station was erected at Pauline Cove in 1995 (Fig. 1). The closest weather stations to Herschel Island are at Shingle Point and Komakuk Beach on the mainland, where records began in 1958 (Fig. 2). Data for many months from Herschel Island since 1995 are missing, due to malfunction of the equipment when no one is on the island. The automatic measurements do not include precipitation. However, the records from nearby stations provide a summary of both the present climate and the changes that have occurred over the last hundred years.

Fig. 1 The automatic weather station at Pauline Cove. Data are transmitted from here to the Canadian weather service by satellite. *Photo by Graham Gilbert.*

The midnight sun seen over the Beaufort Sea on July 15, 2010, near Herschel Island (69° 37' N, 138° 50' W) at 3:15 am local time. *Photo by Christopher Burn.*

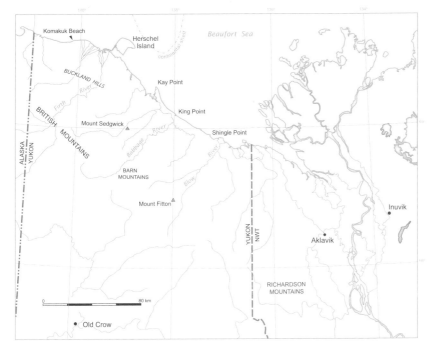

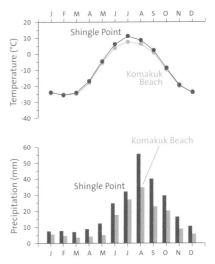

Fig. 2 Herschel Island and northern Yukon Territory, with the location of weather stations at Komakuk Beach and Shingle Point. The rivers south of Herschel Island, such as the Firth and Babbage, flow out of the British Mountains. *Cartography by Christine Earl.*

Fig. 3 Mean monthly temperature and precipitation for Komakuk Beach and Shingle Point, Yukon Territory. The mean annual temperatures at Komakuk Beach and Shingle Point are -11.0°C and -9.9°C, respectively, and the mean annual precipitation totals are 161 millimetres and 254 millimetres. *Data courtesy of Environment Canada.*

Temperature

The data from the automatic weather station at Herschel Island may be unreliable in winter if the equipment is buried by a snowdrift. The most representative long-term measurements of the climate at Qikiqtaryuk are from Komakuk Beach, 40 kilometres west of the island (Fig. 2). Table 1 (overleaf) presents the average air temperature and precipitation at Komakuk Beach. Weather records for over 100 months have been collected at both Komakuk Beach and the automatic station at Herschel Island. The data from the two stations are closely correlated—that is, they vary together closely—with conditions at Herschel about 1°C warmer, on average, than at Komakuk. The temperature difference is a little less in summer and slightly more in winter. In the last decade, the average annual temperature recorded at Herschel Island has been about -9°C.

Air temperatures along the Yukon coast are similar throughout the year, as shown by the records from Shingle Point and Komakuk Beach, with the greatest difference in summer (Fig. 3).

During this season, discharge from the Mackenzie River warms the ocean near Shingle Point, and the sea ice breaks up about a month earlier than at Herschel Island.

The seasonal sea-ice cover near Qikiqtaryuk delays the arrival of daily mean, or average, air temperatures above 0°C until June, even though twenty-four-hour daylight is established in May. The daily average is above 5°C only in July and August. Conditions in winter are cold, but generally do not fall to the temperatures measured inland. Figure 4 presents the mean monthly temperatures for Komakuk Beach and Old Crow, 200 kilometres south of Herschel Island. It shows the noticeable increase in annual range of temperature inland, and demonstrates the importance of the British Mountains in separating the arctic maritime climate of Herschel Island from the continental climate to the south. Figure 4 also illustrates the cooling influence of the ocean in summer and its warming influence in winter, even when there is ice cover.

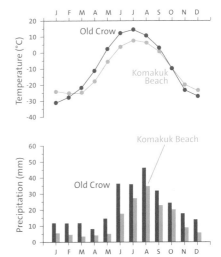

Fig. 4 Mean monthly temperature and precipitation for Komakuk Beach and Old Crow, Yukon Territory. The mean annual temperatures at Komakuk Beach and Old Crow are -11.0°C and -9.0°C, respectively, and the mean annual precipitation totals are 161 millimetres and 266 millimetres. *Data courtesy of Environment Canada.*

Precipitation

Like most of the western Arctic coast, the area near Komakuk Beach has a dry climate, with total annual precipitation (166 millimetres) similar to Tuktoyaktuk's (142 millimetres). Just over half of the precipitation arrives as rain between June and September (Table 1). Although there is little precipitation, the cool conditions and the moist air from the nearby ocean lead to low evaporation rates. As a result, the landscape remains damp throughout the summer. From November onward there is little precipitation in winter once the sea-ice cover is established and evaporation from the ocean more or less ends. Shingle Point receives more precipitation (254 millimetres) than the Herschel Island area throughout the year (Fig. 3), especially in late summer and autumn, partly because the Mackenzie's discharge keeps the ocean open longer.

Figure 4 shows the difference in precipitation between Old Crow and the Herschel Island area, with wetter conditions south of the British Mountains. Most of the precipitation at Old Crow in winter is from weather systems that are generated in the Pacific Ocean. In summer the precipitation comes from similar air masses and from evaporation and transpiration of the forests and lakes of Yukon and Alaska. The biggest difference illustrated in Figure 4 happens in June, when

summer has arrived inland but the persistent ice cover keeps conditions cool and dry at the coast.

The low precipitation does not mean the ground on Qikiqtaryuk is dry. Many mornings, and even parts of days, may be foggy throughout the year (Fig. 5), creating fog drip that collects on the ground. As the nights lengthen in late summer, we usually find dew on the ground in the morning. Dew and fog drip combine to increase the effective precipitation above the rather low amount recorded in the region.

Snow Depth

Relative to the mainland, little snow accumulates on much of Herschel Island because the vegetation is too low to hold it in place during the strong winds of winter (Fig. 6). Measurements of late-winter snow depth on Collinson Head between 1999 and 2009 showed an overall average of only 17 centimetres. In contrast, the average snow depths on the mainland at Komakuk Beach and Shingle Point were 34 and 40 centimetres respectively. However, snow banks several metres deep build up on the island in valleys and at the bottom of sheltered slopes because the snow that is blown off the uplands is deposited there (Fig. 7). Deep snow drifts also accumulate around the buildings at Pauline Cove. The thin snow cover over much of Qikiqtaryuk was noticed by the nineteenth-century whalemen, who had difficulty hauling sleds across the snow-free tundra.

Fig. 5 The settlement at Pauline Cove in fog. *Photo by Doug Larsen.*

Wind

Qikiqtaryuk's coastal location means that a breeze blows most of the time, mercifully reducing the presence of mosquitoes in summer. The strongest winds in summer at Komakuk Beach have been easterlies, which are associated with good weather and high water. In 2008 several days of strong easterly winds raised water levels at Simpson Point and flooded it. Strong, steady easterlies are responsible for significant changes in sea level from time to time because the normal tidal range in this portion of the Beaufort Sea is less than 30 centimetres. In contrast, northwesterlies coming off the open Beaufort Sea bring rain, snow, and cold weather in summer. The strong winds of winter responsible for drifting snow also blow predominantly from the northwest or northeast. Police reports from the early twentieth century refer to Herschel Island as a "blow hole," suggesting that local conditions could bring severe blizzards.

MONTH	JAN	FEB	MAR	APR	MAY	JUN	JUL	AUG	SEP	OCT	NOV	DEC	YEAR
Daily maximum temperature (°C)	-19.7	-20.9	-21.2	-13.6	-2.6	7.5	12.2	10.3	3.8	-6.4	-16.1	-19.6	-7.2
Daily minimum temperature (°C)	-28.7	-29.8	-29.2	-21.9	-8.6	0.5	3.4	2.2	-2.4	-13.0	-23.8	-27.9	-14.9
Daily average temperature (°C)	-24.0	-25.3	-25.1	-17.8	-5.6	4.0	7.8	6.3	0.7	-9.7	-19.9	-23.1	-11.0
Extreme maximum temperature (°C)	8.3	18.2	10.1	13.3	17.2	30.2	30.0	29.6	24.1	13.1	10.0	8.9	30.2
Extreme minimum temperature (°C)	-51.8	-50.0	-47.8	-38.5	-26.7	-9.4	-5.6	-7.8	-17.8	-31.8	-39.5	-44.4	-51.8
Monthly rainfall (mm)	0.0	0.0	0.0	0.1	0.7	14.5	26.2	31.1	10.0	0.8	0.1	0.0	83.5
Monthly snowfall (centimetres)	5.7	6.0	3.6	4.3	4.4	3.2	1.2	3.7	12.7	19.5	9.0	5.8	77.0
Monthly precipitation (mm)	5.7	4.7	3.6	4.3	5.2	17.7	27.3	34.8	22.9	20.3	9.0	5.8	161.3

Table 1. Climatic Normal temperatures and precipitation (1971–2000) at Komakuk Beach, 40 kilometres from Herschel Island. Monthly mean air temperatures at Komakuk Beach and Pauline Cove are closely related, with Pauline Cove warmer by less than 1°C in summer and by about 1.5°C in winter. *Data courtesy of Environment Canada.*

Fig. 7 Snowbank in a valley near Pauline Cove that accumulated in winter 2004–05 and was insulated in summer 2005 by organic debris scoured from the tundra that winter. *Photo by Christopher Burn.*

Fig. 6 View from Collinson Head looking down toward Pauline Cove, April 22, 2005. The thin and patchy late-winter snow cover is due to the lack of vegetation that would hold snow and prevent it from blowing away during winter storms. *Photo by Christopher Burn.*

Day Length

Herschel Island lies at 69° 35′ N, and experiences a long period of daylight in summer but little in December and January. In summer, "midnight" at Herschel Island occurs at about 3:15 am local time. The territorial park operates on Mountain Daylight Time, which is coordinated with 90°W, but the island's longitude is 139°W. The mountains to the south create an irregular horizon, so the precise time of daily sunrise in winter differs from sunrise over a flat horizon (as at sea, for example). In the 1890s, the whalemen recorded the disappearance of the sun on November 29 and celebrated its return on January 12, but in some years, when clouds obscured the horizon, they waited longer. However, even at the winter solstice, it is not completely dark for twenty-four hours because of twilight that illuminates the southern sky around midday. Figure 8 gives both the day length from the beginning to the end of civil twilight, when the sun is 6° below the horizon, and the daily period when the sun is visible with a clear sky.

In summer the visibility at Herschel Island is sometimes obscured by smoke from wildfires burning in Alaska, but fog-like conditions due to smoke are unusual.

Climate Change

Since the Ice Age, climate change on the western Arctic coast has been influenced by three sets of forces. First, there have been periods when changes in solar radiation have created a warmer climate, especially about 10,000 years ago, several thousand years after the ice melted from the coastal plain. Over most of Qikiqtaryuk there is a top layer in permafrost up to about a metre thick, which formerly thawed in summer but is now frozen year-round. The thawing of this layer is primary evidence for the existence of an earlier warmer climate.

Second, sea level has been rising in the Beaufort Sea, reaching the northern coastline of the island about 4,000 years ago and creating Workboat Passage (and thus Qiqiktaryuk itself) in the last 1,600 years. The increasing proximity of the area to the sea ice has progressively delayed the arrival of summer, shortening the growing season. As a result, Herschel Island has a tundra environment, although trees grow on the mainland only a few tens of kilometres to the south. In many places where the top layer of permafrost has thawed, pieces of preserved wood have been exposed. Such former vegetation is no longer able to grow on Herschel Island because of the deterioration in summer conditions.

TWILIGHT

There are three periods of twilight: civil, nautical, and astronomical. Their limits occur when the sun is 6°, 12°, and 18° below the horizon. During civil twilight most objects are still visible and a person can read without a lamp. At the end of civil twilight, drivers must use their headlights and visual aviation is not allowed. The horizon can still be identified during nautical twilight, but not in astronomical twilight.

Fig. 8 Hours of daylight in each day, and the hours in each day that the sun is above the horizon throughout the year, at Qikiqtaryuk. The hours of daylight include civil twilight when the sun is less than 6° below the horizon. In this diagram the effect of the mountains in raising the horizon is not shown.

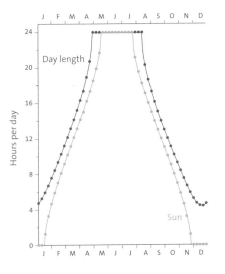

Third, recent climate change has been part of the worldwide trend to higher temperatures associated with increasing concentrations of greenhouse gases in the atmosphere. The data collected by Rev. Isaac Stringer beginning in 1897 (Fig. 9) show annual mean air temperatures for 1899–1903 that are about 3°C lower than similar data collected on the island since 1995, indicating the climate warming that has occurred during the twentieth century (Fig. 10). The observations at Herschel Island are amongst the oldest in northern Canada, but only records from Dawson City provide a continuous series for the Canadian North from 1899 to the present. The longest series in the western Arctic are for the Mackenzie Delta, represented by data from Inuvik (Fig. 10). These series indicate that the bulk of the climate warming in the western Arctic has occurred since 1970. This trend has also been observed at Komakuk Beach and Shingle Point. The variation in the monthly temperature records from these stations are remarkably similar to each other and to data collected at Inuvik.

No reliable records of precipitation have been kept at Herschel Island, but since 1957 records have been maintained at Komakuk Beach and Shingle Point. Unlike the temperature records, these data show no trend over time, and are not closely related to each other or to the Inuvik data. However, there is little snow accumulation in winter on the island today, and as this was also noted by the whalemen, snow depths have probably been similar throughout the last hundred years or so.

Freeze-up and Break-up

The whalemen noted the date of freeze-up in Pauline Cove because it represented the end of their commercial season and the start of preparing their vessels for the winter. The steam whalers could travel through light ice, so the dates of final anchorage for the winter are

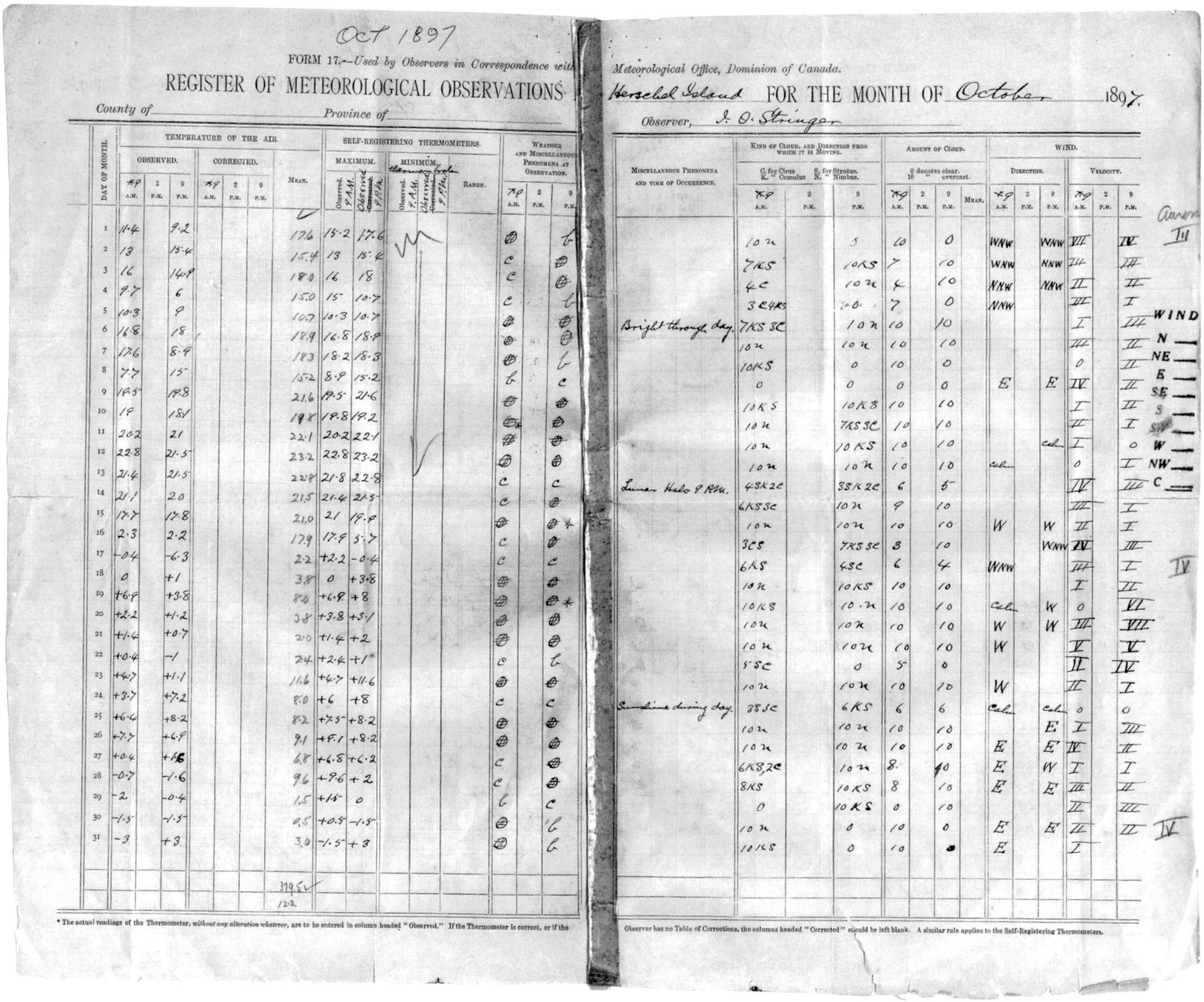
Oct 1897
FORM 17.—Used by Observers in Correspondence with Meteorological Office, Dominion of Canada.
REGISTER OF METEOROLOGICAL OBSERVATIONS
Herschel Island FOR THE MONTH OF October 1897.
Observer, I. O. Stringer

Fig. 9 Weather observations for October 1897 made by Rev. Isaac Stringer. *Image courtesy of Environment Canada.*

YEAR	DATE	DAYS AFTER 31 AUG	YEAR	DATE	DAYS AFTER 31 AUG
1890	18 Sep.	18	2000	30 Oct.	60
1891	13 Oct.	43	2001	22 Oct.	52
1892	13 Oct.	43	2002	4 Nov.	65
1893	9 Oct.	39	2003	17 Nov.	78
1894	12 Oct.	42	2004	1 Nov.	62
1895	12 Oct.	42	2005	7 Nov.	68
1896	30 Sep.	30	2006	6 Nov.	67
1897	4 Oct.	34	2007	29 Oct.	59
1898	14 Oct.	44	2008	3 Nov.	64
1899	16 Oct.	46	2009	9 Nov.	70
1900	5 Oct.	35	2010	1 Nov.	62
Middle (Median)	12 Oct.	42	Middle (Median)	3 Nov.	64
Average (Mean)	8 Oct.	38	Average (Mean)	3 Nov.	64

Table 2. Dates of freeze-up in Pauline Cove for 1890–1900 during the whaling era, and 2000–2010 as detected by satellite. The dates from 1890 to 1900 were recorded in ship's logs and represent conditions that are comparable to grey ice in close pack. *The satellite data were interpreted by Thai Nguyen, Canadian Ice Service.*

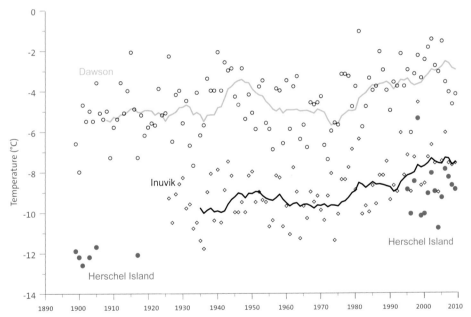

Fig. 10 Annual mean air temperatures, 1899–2009, at Herschel Island, Inuvik, and Dawson City. Data for Herschel Island were either recorded on the island or are interpreted from measurements at Komakuk Beach. Data for Inuvik are from Inuvik Airport for 1958–2009 and are interpreted from the Aklavik record for 1926–1957. For Dawson City and Inuvik, the lines present the average of the previous 10 years' data.

a little later than those of the first ice in Pauline Cove. Records of freeze-up were also kept by Rev. Isaac Stringer. The freeze-up dates recorded between 1890 and 1900 vary between mid-September and mid-October (Table 2).

The first transit of the Northwest Passage, made by Roald Amundsen's *Gjøa*, was prolonged by a year because of an early freeze-up. The ship was frozen into her winter berth at King Point by September 7, 1905. Amundsen recorded that he could walk around his ship on September 9. At present, satellite observations record comparable freeze-up in late October to early November.

At the other end of the season, the American whaling crews celebrated July 4 at Herschel Island and left as soon as possible thereafter, usually by July 10. Navigation begins at a similar time today, or perhaps a week earlier.

Herschel Island's tundra is due to its arctic climate. From mid-September through early June, the island is blanketed by snow, but during the short summer the ground is almost entirely covered by growing plants. Sea ice leaves Thetis Bay between late June and early July, assisted by the outflow from the Mackenzie River. Then, for six to eight weeks, the area is biologically productive, sustaining grazing animals on land and abundant fish and sea mammals in the ocean. Climate change is most apparent in the autumn, extending the period of open water. We must anticipate ecological changes driven by climate change on land, such as the continuing development of the vegetation cover and growth of more willow shrubs, while in the ocean the ecosystem may be most affected by the declining sea ice extent and duration. Effects observed in the Hudson's Bay area that have been driven by changes in sea-ice conditions, such as the declining polar bear population, are also underway in the southern Beaufort Sea.

OCEAN WATER AND SEA ICE

Bill Williams and Eddy Carmack

Herschel Island is surrounded by four bodies of water: Workboat Passage to the southwest, Herschel Basin to the southeast, Mackenzie Trough to the northeast, and the Yukon–Alaskan Beaufort Shelf to the northwest (Fig. 1). Each of these parts of the ocean has its own particular character, thanks to the island's special location on the continental shelf, both close to shore and close to the slope that descends from the shelf to the depths of the Beaufort Sea.

Continental Shelves

The continental shelf is the offshore extension of the continent. Commonly, this shelf has a gentle slope and extends tens of kilometres into the ocean to a depth of about 100 to 200 metres. Here the edge of the continent appears as a steep slope that plunges thousands of metres to the ocean floor. The place where the slope changes at the continent's edge is called the shelf break. In the Beaufort Sea, the shelf break is at a water depth of about 80 metres, which is quite shallow, and the ocean floor is at a depth of about 3,800 metres.

In the southern Beaufort Sea, the continental shelf is divided near Herschel Island into the Yukon–Alaskan Beaufort Shelf to the west and the Canadian Beaufort Shelf to the east (Fig. 1). These two shelves have significantly different widths and alignments. The Yukon–Alaskan shelf is about 50 kilometres wide and runs east-southeast (on a bearing of 105°), whereas the Canadian shelf is approximately 110 kilometres wide and runs northeast (on a bearing of 052°). When moving along the continental shelf from west to east, shelf width doubles, while the along-shelf direction changes by 53°.

Just east of Herschel Island, the Yukon shelf and the Canadian shelf are separated by Mackenzie Trough, a broad, deep, submarine canyon that rises southeastwards (Fig. 1). Together, Herschel Island and Mackenzie Trough form a complex constriction at the corner where the two continental shelves meet. Mackenzie Trough cuts through the shelf so that at Herschel Island it is only 25 kilometres from the mainland to the shelf break, and the island itself covers much of the shelf. Surface water can only pass between the Yukon and Canadian shelves through Workboat Passage, which is extremely shallow, or around the northeastern edge of Herschel Island, where the steep undersea slope forms the southwestern wall of Mackenzie Trough. Water that does not pass via one of these two routes must leave the shelf and head out to the deep ocean across Mackenzie Trough.

Blocks of sea ice north of Collinson Head forming a pressure ridge at the edge of landfast ice on the west side of Mackenzie Trough in April 2009. *Photo by Mary Beattie.*

Fig. 1 Bathymetry of the southeastern Beaufort Sea, with Herschel Island and Herschel Basin lying near the head of Mackenzie Trough between the Yukon–Alaskan Beaufort Shelf and the Canadian Beaufort Shelf. The isobaths, indicating water depths, are in metres. *Cartography by Christine Earl.*

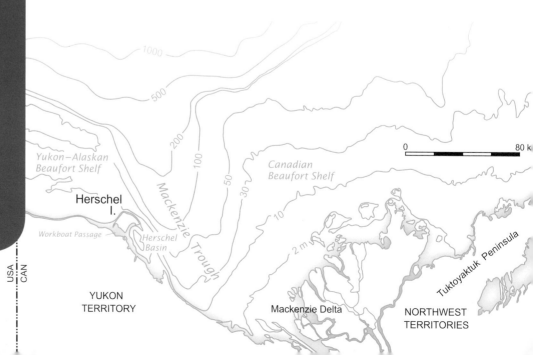

The Mackenzie River Plume

Each year about 300 cubic kilometres of fresh water and 85 million tonnes of sediment flow through the Mackenzie Delta to the Canadian Beaufort Shelf. The Mackenzie has the fourth greatest annual discharge of all rivers to the Arctic Ocean (after the Ob, Yenisey, and Lena rivers in Russia), delivers about 10 percent of all the river water input to the Arctic Ocean, and is the largest single source of sediment. Because the Mackenzie River draws water from Great Slave and Great Bear lakes, it maintains moderate flows throughout winter and then is the largest river entering the Arctic Ocean.

Mackenzie River water spills out from the delta onto the Canadian Beaufort Shelf, where it plays a dominant role in the nearshore waters of the southeastern Beaufort Sea. In winter, the reduced flow spreads out under the sea ice to form an under-ice plume that is eventually hemmed in by the large ice ridge (known as a stamukhi) at the seaward edge of landfast ice. By the end of winter each year, this effectively creates one of the 20 largest "lakes" in the world. The freshwater extends toward Herschel Basin and as far as Workboat Passage, but not north or west of Herschel Island. Throughout the winter of 1905–06, when Amundsen's *Gjøa* was at King Point, the crew obtained fresh water for their domestic use from beneath the sea ice. This brackish (salty or briny) feature, the so-called Lake Herlinveaux, provides a relatively predictable habitat for the Arctic Cisco that migrate between the Mackenzie River and the Colville River on the north coast of Alaska.

During spring and summer, the huge discharge of the Mackenzie forms a brackish plume six to eight metres thick on the ocean surface. The plume is large and irregular and contains many fronts and swirls. Figures 2 and 3 are satellite images taken in summer showing the sediment-laden plume and the corresponding surface temperatures of the ocean. These images show that river outflow is warm, with temperatures that may rise above 16°C.

The plume responds to surface winds in summer, when the ice cover of the ocean is reduced (Fig. 2). During easterly winds, such as in Figure 2, the wind blowing along the continental shelf moves the sediment-laden plume offshore toward the ice. As the surface water moves offshore, cold water welling up from the bottom replaces it near the shore. Figure 3 shows the low sea-surface temperatures that are the result of this upwelling, and the change in temperature between the

Fig. 2 A visible satellite image taken on July 26, 2006, showing the turbidity, or cloudiness, of the ocean surface due to the sediment-laden Mackenzie River water plume. Sediment appears to be streaming off Herschel Island toward the northwest, suggesting rapid upwelling and flow along the western side of Mackenzie Trough and erosion of the coast. *Image available from MODIS, NASA Goddard Space Flight Center.*

Mackenzie River plume and the area covered by ice. Northeast of Herschel Island there is significant upwelling that is amplified by Mackenzie Trough, and the temperature at the ocean surface is only 1°C. During westerly winds, the wind stress favours downwelling, which pushes surface waters toward the shore. The river plume is then compressed against the coast and tends to form a boundary current that flows eastward along the Tuktoyakuk Peninsula.

We do not know how much the summer plume influences the ocean environment near Herschel Island. However, its influence is probably strong on the eastern side of the island and in Workboat Passage, but weaker on the western side because the island largely blocks the plume. Anadromous (sea-run) fish, such as Arctic Cisco, Least Cisco, and Dolly Varden Char, use the brackish plume of water close to the coast as a migration route. In particular, cisco that begin their life in the Mackenzie River migrate west along this brackish coastal corridor to the Colville River and so pass near Herschel Island. The corridor may not be continuous around the northern side of Herschel Island, where the flow is fast and there is little fresh water, so Workboat Passage is principally used by these fish.

Tides

The Arctic Ocean has small tides in comparison to the other oceans because at northerly latitudes tidal forcing by the moon and sun is less direct than at lower latitudes. At Herschel Island the daily tidal range is less than 30 centimetres. In other oceans, vertical mixing from the movement of the tides can keep sediment suspended in the sea water, and can also mix dissolved nutrients from the depths into the surface water. However, near Mackenzie Trough and the Mackenzie Delta, the tidal water movement is very slow (less than five centimetres per second), which increases the relative importance of vertical mixing driven by wind and ice. The small tidal effects also help the deposition of river sediment to form the Mackenzie Delta.

Sea Ice

Sea ice surrounds Herschel Island from roughly October to June, with landfast ice generally reaching as far as the north coast of the island. Herschel Basin is usually covered with a relatively smooth surface of landfast ice from early winter on. Beyond the edge of the landfast ice, the pack ice generally moves westward as part of the overall clockwise flow of sea ice in the Beaufort Sea (known as the Beaufort Gyre). The westward movement is forced by prevailing easterly winds caused by high pressure over the Beaufort Sea to the north. In contrast, eastward ice movement during less common westerly winds tends to be blocked by the islands of the Canadian Arctic Archipelago. As a result, the preferential movement of the ice pack in the southern Beaufort Sea is westward.

An example of rapid westward ice motion during easterly winds in February–March 2003 is shown in Figure 4. The flaw lead (the gap between the landfast ice and the pack ice) opened up to

Fig. 3 Sea-surface temperatures on the same day Figure 2 was taken (July 26, 2006). Near the Mackenzie Delta, the Mackenzie River water flowing into the Beaufort Sea is very warm, but to the north the ice cover is just above 0°C, probably due to pools of meltwater on the surface. *Satellite image courtesy of T.J. Weingartner and G.M. Schmidt, data from NASA Goddard Space Flight Center.*

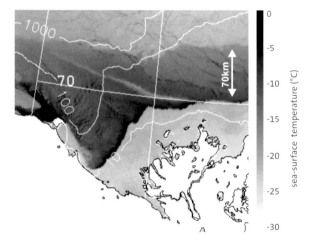

Fig. 4 A late-winter satellite image of sea-surface temperatures from March 4, 2003, when wind and ice forcing opened the flaw lead between landfast and pack ice to 70 kilometres wide. New, warmer ice mostly fills the flaw lead. There is open water (shown in black) at the edge of the landfast ice and west of Herschel Island, the latter due to upwelling from Mackenzie Trough. *Satellite image courtesy of T.J. Weingartner and G.M. Schmidt, data from NASA Goddard Space Flight Center.*

70 kilometres wide and became filled with new ice, which has an intermediate grey tone on the satellite image. The image shows landfast ice in Herschel Basin but a large area of open water, known as a polynya, on the western side of Herschel Island. This unusually large area of open water is due to the Mackenzie Trough upwelling that, in winter, is relatively "warm."

Mackenzie Trough

Mackenzie Trough is a deep submarine canyon approximately 50 kilometres wide and 300 metres deep. The trough is a major channel for the upwelling of deep ocean waters onto the continental shelf (Fig. 2). When the surface stress on the ocean from wind or ice motion is from the east, it favours upwelling, and Mackenzie Trough, like other undersea canyons, amplifies the effect. Thus the water in Mackenzie Trough may be lifted over 600 metres from its original depth. The measurements in Figure 5 show upwelling in late September 2002. At the time of measurement, water was flowing along the shelf from east to west, and there was movement into the mouth of the trough on its eastern side and out on the western side. However, nearly all the flow that crossed the head of the trough moved up and out onto the continental shelf north of Herschel Island.

Satellite images, and water temp- erature and salinity measurements, suggest that upwelling happens along the northeastern edge of Herschel Island and then spills onto the Yukon–Alaskan shelf immediately to the west. Figure 3 gives a good example of such upwelling, with cold water (below 1°C) streaming off northwestern Herschel Island onto the Yukon–Alaskan shelf. The upwelling creates concentrations of nutrients on the shelf that are brought from the deeper ocean, which produce phytoplankton (or microscopic plant organisms) that in

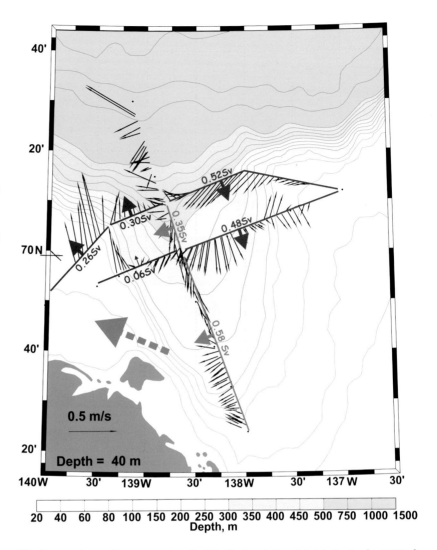

Fig. 5 Overall water flow at 40 metres depth in Mackenzie Trough in late September 2002 after a week of strong easterly winds favouring upwelling. The units of water transport are Sverdrups (1 Sv = 1 million cubic metres per second). *Measurements from Dr. Koji Shimada, Tokyo University of Marine Science and Technology.*

turn feed zooplankton (microscopic animal organisms). The upwelling also likely sweeps copepods (large zooplankton) up onto the shelf. The possible presence of these zooplankton may explain why the sea near Herschel Island is a preferred feeding place for bowhead whales.

Workboat Passage

Workboat Passage is a very shallow waterway between Herschel Island and the mainland. Much of the passage is less than two metres deep and varies in width from about three kilometres at the southeastern end to about six kilometres at the northwestern

end. Long discontinuous spits constrict the entrances at either end of the passage (Fig. 6). The water is about ten metres deep in the northwestern entrance and eight metres deep at the southeastern entrance. This depth is much greater than inside or immediately outside the passage, and suggests that the faster water flow within these narrow entrances has eroded the seafloor. The relatively calm water between the barrier spits at each end of Workboat Passage helps make the area important habitat for coastal fishes and waterfowl.

Fig. 6 Aerial photograph looking west along Workboat Passage, with the sandspits leading to Calton Point on the left and Osborn Point on the right, and the projection of Lopez Point in the background on the right. *Photo by Cameron Eckert.*

Herschel Basin

Herschel Island was thrust upward by the advancing Laurentide ice sheet from the depression we now call Herschel Basin. The basin lies between Herschel Island and Kay Point, southeast of the island. This depression in the sea floor is roughly 40 kilometres long, 15 kilometres wide, and 73 metres below sea level in its deepest part. Below a depth of 30 metres, it has a number of deep holes, and soft sediment covers the sea floor. The sediment has probably been deposited since the ice sheet retreated from the coastal plain.

Figure 7 shows temperatures and salinities across Herschel Basin and out into Mackenzie Trough as measured in July 2008. Unusually, the basin was brim-full of salty water at the freezing-point, formed the previous winter from both upwelling of deep-ocean water in Mackenzie Trough and ice growth in Herschel Basin. Exceptionally strong westward wind and ice motion in the winter of 2007–08 provided favourable conditions for both the upwelling and ice formation.

Herschel Sill and Northeastern Herschel Island

Herschel Sill is a 13-metre-deep narrow ledge that forms the offshore boundary of Herschel Basin. Unlike the basin, the sill has hard sediment and rocks that were probably deposited by glacial ice. Water that flows from either the Canadian Beaufort Shelf or the Yukon–Alaskan Beaufort Shelf must speed up as it passes from the wide shelf to the narrow sill. This creates rapid flows on the sill that limit both sedimentation and the development of a soft surface layer.

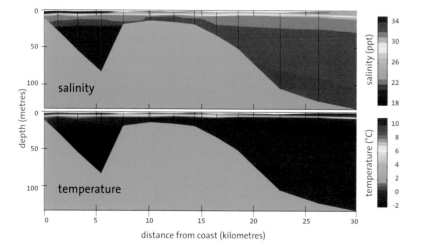

Fig. 7 Water temperature and salinity in Herschel Basin and Mackenzie Trough, measured in late July 2008.

The diversity of physical characteristics in the waters surrounding Herschel Island, from the extremely shallow sea in Workboat Passage to the deep Mackenzie Trough, creates a remarkable environment unlike any other part of the Canadian Arctic Ocean. The key factors responsible for such conditions are the influence of the Mackenzie River, the growth of sea ice, and the force of the wind acting at the island's unique location across a constriction in the sea-floor topography between the Yukon–Alaskan and Canadian Beaufort shelves. Upwelling of nutrient-rich water onto the shelf from Mackenzie Trough is the foundation of an ecosystem in which the bowhead whale or **arviq** (*Balaena mysticetus*), the largest arctic mammal, thrives. Polar bears or **nanuq** (*Ursus maritimus*) are at the top of the food chain in late winter and spring, living off seals that for hundreds of years also sustained the Qiqiktaryungmiut. Today, Inuvialuit harvesters are less interested in seals than in the anadromous (sea-run) fish, particularly Dolly Varden Char or Qalukpik (*Salvelinus malma*), that migrate along the coastal corridor of brackish water between the mouths of the Mackenzie and Colville rivers. The upwelling and the presence of the brackish corridor are both significant, so the specific rates of upwelling and the continued presence of the corridor under varying wind and sea ice conditions remain important areas of research.

CCGS *NAHIDIK*

CCGS (Canadian Coast Guard Ship) *Nahidik* was a shallow-draft vessel built in 1974 by Allied Shipbuilders of North Vancouver. It was 53 metres (175 feet) long and drew less than two metres (6.5 feet) of water. For 35 years *Nahidik* was used to deploy and retrieve buoys and other navigation aids along the Mackenzie River from Great Slave Lake to the Beaufort Sea. The Dempster Highway had not been completed when *Nahidik* entered service, so the river was the primary route for the shipment of goods to the western Arctic. The vessel descended the river in June, spent the summer near the western Arctic coast, and returned to its home port of Hay River in early October.

From 1976 on, *Nahidik* was also used as a research platform for investigating the continental shelves of the southeastern Beaufort Sea. The main programs included mapping ice scours for the assessment of potential risk to pipelines laid on the seabed, and the examination of seafloor materials necessary for foundation design. Extensive seismic investigations to determine the extent of subsea permafrost and temperature studies to determine its character were also conducted. In the 2000s, *Nahidik* was used to study gas vents and associated mounds on the Canadian Beaufort Shelf. Ecological research focused on the invertebrate fauna, or benthos, at the sea bed, fish populations, and the physical and chemical structure of the water.

Nahidik's great advantage was its shallow draft, enabling surveys close to shore and resupply in Tuktoyaktuk or Inuvik. Surveillance of weather and ice conditions in the Beaufort Sea during the 1970s and 80s was poor, so the success of the research depended heavily on the seamanship of the officers and crew. Pauline Cove was often used as a temporary anchorage during storms.

CCGS *Nahidik* in Thetis Bay, 2007. This vessel, now retired from service, was the platform for much scientific research in the southeastern Beaufort Sea for about 40 years beginning in the mid-1970s. *Photo by Bill Williams.*

ICE AGE

Grant Zazula

The Quaternary

Climatic changes during the last two-and-a-half million years have had dramatic effects on environments and landscapes around the world. This geological time period is known as the Quaternary and is subdivided into two main parts: the Pleistocene, or Ice Age, and the Holocene, the present climate interval, which spans the last 10,000 years. Large fluctuations in climate between glacial and interglacial periods occurred during the Pleistocene. The glacial periods, or ice ages, were times of prolonged cold in which ice sheets accumulated and advanced across Europe, North America, and Antarctica. These glaciations, which altogether lasted for over 80 percent of the Quaternary, were interrupted by relatively short interglacials, with climates similar to ours. This chapter takes a look at Herschel Island's unique glacial history.

Much of our world was formed during the Quaternary—from the landforms we live on and the shape of coast lines to the distribution of plants and animals, especially in the circumpolar North. The ground that forms Herschel Island was excavated from the coastal plain by a glacial advance during the Pleistocene, and the island was created by the ongoing rise in sea level that has accompanied the melting of the ice sheets. Our own species— *Homo sapiens*—is also a product of Quaternary climate changes, which provided the backdrop for human evolution, cultural innovation, and global colonization.

Glacials and Interglacials

The major Pleistocene glaciations began in periods of reduced solar energy, lasted about 100,000 years each, and were separated by interglacials about 10,000 years long. Fluctuations in the Earth's orbit around the sun, and in the tilt of the Earth toward or away from the sun, caused these changes in solar energy reaching the Earth. The tilt of the Earth also controls the location of the Arctic Circle. At the moment, the tilt is gradually decreasing, and the Arctic Circle is moving slowly northward.

Between 140,000 and 125,000 years ago, the Earth's climate was similar to the present climate interval—the Holocene. Then the last glaciation began. It culminated in the extreme cold climate of the Last Glacial Maximum around 20,000 years ago, when glaciers all around the world advanced to their maximum positions.

Fig. 1 The St. Elias Icefields, southwestern Yukon, are the most extensive remains of the Cordilleran ice sheet in Canada. *Photo by Luke Copland.*

Fig. 2 Reconstruction of the steppe-tundra and Ice Age mammal community in Beringia. *Painting by George Teichmann.*

The climate began to warm again around 14,000 years ago, with the transition to the interglacial conditions our world now experiences. However, even during our present Holocene period, the climate has not remained constant. Instead, periods of relative warmth and cold have occurred throughout the last 10,000 years. The most recent of these Holocene cold periods is known as the Little Ice Age. Beginning in the Middle Ages, glaciers throughout the Northern Hemisphere expanded, reaching their maximum around 1850 AD. Since the Little Ice Age, most glaciers have been receding.

Events such as the Little Ice Age show that the climate is naturally unstable over periods of centuries. However, since about 1850, the climate system has been measurably disturbed by human activity. Changes in land use have altered the Earth's surface, while the burning of fossil fuels has significantly altered the chemical composition of the atmosphere, contributing to the forcing of climate change today.

Glaciers

Glaciers are a signature feature of the Ice Age, and have advanced and retreated with the cycles of Quaternary climate change (Fig. 1). Almost all of Canada was covered by three major continental ice sheets during the Last Glacial Maximum. The ice sheets were several kilometres thick, advanced from distinct centres, and eventually joined to form a nearly continuous ice mass.

The first of these ice sheets, the Innuitian, covered Ellesmere Island and the adjacent High Arctic islands of northernmost Canada. The Laurentide ice sheet was centered over the Canadian Shield and the interior plains of Alberta and Saskatchewan, extending west to the Mackenzie and Rocky mountains and south to the northern United States. The third sheet, the Cordilleran, was formed

Fig. 3 The extinct Ice Age Beringian lions (*Panthera spelaea vereshchagini*) looked much like their present-day African cousins, but were 25 per cent larger. *Painting by George Teichmann.*

by accumulating and merging valley glaciers in the mountainous terrain of British Columbia, Yukon, and Alaska. Dramatic drops in global sea level accompanied these major periods of glaciation because large portions of the Earth's water resources were locked up on land in glacial ice. At the Last Glacial Maximum, sea level was as much as 120 metres lower than now. With vast areas of the continental shelves exposed, land masses previously separated by water became connected.

Because glaciers have immense power to erode land and deposit debris, they leave behind a legacy of sediments and landforms. The three main types of glacial deposits include those sediments left behind directly by glaciers; those that accumulate in lakes fed by glaciers and meltwater; and those that are washed out from beneath glaciers in meltwater torrents. The most common material left by glaciers is till, a mixture of silt, sand, gravel, and boulders that remains when the ice melts. Glaciers also have the erosive power to pick up sediment from the land they flow over, which they deposit in ridges at the edge of the ice sheet, where the ice melts. These ridges are called

terminal moraines, and mark the point of maximum glacier advance. Herschel Island itself began life as a terminal moraine pushed up by the northwestern extent of the Laurentide ice sheet.

The Yukon has a unique Quaternary glacial history because parts of it—including the Herschel Island area—were ice-free during the latter part of the Ice Age. When the Laurentide ice sheet advanced over the Yukon north coast from the Mackenzie Delta region to near the Alaska border, vast tracts of land on the continental shelf in the southern Beaufort Sea were exposed as sea level fell. The unglaciated regions in northern Yukon bordering this ice sheet formed the easternmost area of Beringia, the landmass that was connected through Alaska to Siberia by the exposed Bering land bridge. When the Laurentide ice receded from the Yukon north coast, the Herschel ridge was left in its wake and became part of the larger region of Beringia.

Fig. 4 Woolly mammoth (*Mammuthus primigenius*) and Yukon horse (*Equus lambei*) grazing. *Painting by George Teichmann.*

Fig. 5 The highly specialized nose of saiga antelope (*Saiga tatarica*) enabled them to breathe the dry, dusty air on the steppe-tundra of Beringia. *Painting by George Teichmann.*

Beringia

Beringia has played an integral role in the Ice Age history of the circumpolar regions. The landmass was exposed numerous times over the Quaternary whenever global sea levels dropped significantly. The landscape was nearly treeless, with little vegetation at higher elevations. The deposits of wind-blown silt, or loess, that are found throughout the former Beringia testify to the harsh, cold, and dry climate. However, these glacial conditions with loess soils enabled a type of grassland called steppe-tundra to spread across Beringia. The steppe-tundra featured grasses and dryland sedges, sage, and small alpine and tundra flowers. Today we can see similar vegetation to Beringian conditions on some south-facing slopes in southern and central Yukon that are too dry to support trees. However, where there was plenty of glacial meltwater, the environment may have been particularly fertile, and would have supported the large mammals for which Beringia is famous. In fact, the Ice Age steppe was much better drained and more hospitable to large mammals than today's northern tundra communities.

Mammal communities during cold Beringian times were much more diverse than they are in the Yukon today. The steppe-tundra supported a huge variety of animals, some of which still exist in Yukon, while others went extinct near the end of the Ice Age (Fig. 2). The best known of the extinct mammals include the Beringian lion (Fig. 3), woolly mammoth and Yukon horse (Fig. 4), saiga antelope (Fig. 5), scimitar cat (*Homotherium serium*), camel (*Camelops hesternus*), and steppe bison (*Bison priscus*). Those species still present today include moose, caribou, muskoxen, and arctic ground squirrels.

The Bering land bridge not only enabled the exchange of plants and animals back and forth between North America and Eurasia, but was also the route used by the first people to colonize North America, probably around 15,000 years ago. These first inhabitants relied on the mammals for food, clothing, and shelter. In fact, the Beringian ecosystem is sometimes called the mammoth-steppe. However, this ecosystem came to a crashing halt about 10,000 years ago, at the end of the Pleistocene. Climates in the northern hemisphere warmed, the glaciers melted, sea levels rose to flood the land bridge, and the rich steppe-tundra vegetation was replaced by boreal forest and boggy tundra. These changes were too much for many of Beringia's mammals. Human hunters may also have helped to push Beringia's mammal populations past the point of no return, though scientists are still investigating the precise cause of the extinctions.

Herschel Island

Herschel Island is a landform of Pleistocene glacial origin. Pioneering work by geographer J. Ross Mackay in the late 1950s suggested that Herschel Island is composed of sediments pushed up from the now-

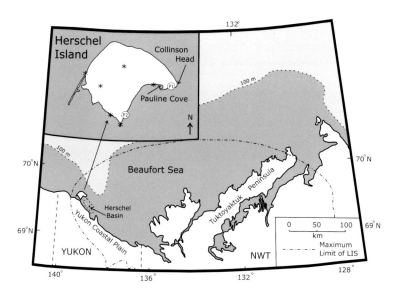

Fig. 6 Map of the Beaufort Sea coastlands of Yukon and Northwest Territories and maximum limit of the Laurentide ice sheet (LIS). The shaded area, extending from the coast to 100 metres below sea level, demonstrates the approximate extent of the exposed Beaufort Shelf during the Late Pleistocene. Inset map shows fossil-collecting localities on Herschel Island (marked with *). *Map courtesy of Government of Yukon.*

submerged Beaufort Sea shelf and thrust westward into a moraine ridge by advancing glacier ice (Fig. 6). Mackay charted the submerged Herschel Basin, a depression in the sea floor of the same volume as Herschel Island, providing further evidence of the proposed ice-thrust origin of the island. Geological mapping of the land surface by Vernon Rampton in the late 1970s confirmed that the Yukon north coast and adjacent areas, including Herschel Island, were covered during the late Pleistocene by a lobe of the Laurentide ice sheet he called the "Buckland Glaciation." A mixture of terrestrial and marine sediments found along eroding sea cliffs around the island reveals this dynamic glacial history. The skull of a Yukon horse, found near the top of a high bluff by geologist Stephen Wolfe, was determined to be 16,000 years old, suggesting that the Buckland glacial ice had receded eastward by this time.

The moraine ridge that eventually became Herschel Island was connected to the mainland until recent times. Post-glacial sea-level rise flooded the Beaufort Sea shelf, leaving the moraine as the northernmost landform in the Yukon. Given the known rate of recent sea-level rise in the Beaufort Sea, Herschel Island was probably only severed from the mainland within the last 1,600 years. Today the island is separated from the Yukon mainland by a narrow stretch of water only two metres deep called Workboat Passage.

Fossil pollen grains found in the sediments of a drained pond dating to about 9,400 years ago provide evidence of climate change on Herschel Island after the Ice Age. During the early Holocene, the vegetation was dominated by shrub birch, which contrasts with the present sedge- and herb-dominated tussock tundra on the island. The shrubby vegetation suggests that summer temperatures on the Herschel ridge were probably warmer during the early Holocene than they are today. This time of increased summer warmth between 10,000 and 8,000 years ago is called the Early Holocene Thermal Maximum, a warm climatic period recognized throughout the western Arctic and in the Yukon.

Herschel Island Fossils

Fossil bones, teeth, and antlers along the beaches provide evidence for ancient life on Herschel Island (Fig. 7). Palaeontologist Dick Harington from the Canadian Museum of Nature made the first systematic collection of Ice Age mammal bones on the island in 1973. Since 1985, researchers from the Yukon government, with assistance from the park rangers, have collected fossil bones as part of their heritage resource management activities. The vast majority of Ice Age fossil bones recovered on the island is from beach debris at Pauline Cove, near the historic whaling settlement. Most fossils display evidence of abrasion and typically have rounded edges as a result of wave action.

Herschel Island is Yukon's third most productive locality for collecting Ice Age fossils, after the internationally renowned fossil sites of the Old Crow basin and the Klondike goldfields. Ice Age fossil bones from the island represent a wide range of mammal species still living there, such as caribou and muskoxen (Fig. 8). Other fossil bones are from typical members of the now-extinct mammoth-fauna, including woolly mammoth (Fig. 9), steppe bison, Yukon horse (Fig. 10), and American mastodon. Radiocarbon ages obtained from these land mammal bones span a range from greater than 50,000 years to 16,000 years old.

Fossil evidence also indicates that muskoxen have inhabited areas surrounding Herschel Island for at least the last 50,000 years (Fig. 11). Not surprisingly, given the prominence of muskoxen in the Arctic today, Herschel Island has provided more fossil bones from Ice Age muskoxen than any other site in the Yukon.

Fig. 7 Yukon horse bone washed up on the gravelly beach at Herschel Island. *Photo courtesy of Government of Yukon.*

Fig. 8 Muskox metacarpal (leg) bone from Herschel Island. The bars on the scale in this figure and the two below are centimetres. *Photo courtesy of Government of Yukon.*

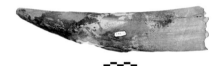

Fig. 9 Woolly mammoth tusk from Herschel Island. *Photo courtesy of Government of Yukon.*

Fig. 10 Yukon horse mandible (jaw bone) from Herschel Island. *Photo courtesy of Government of Yukon.*

However, the most abundant Ice Age fossil bones discovered on Herschel Island are from Yukon horses. In fact, 40 percent of the fossil bones identified from the island represent these small, Ice Age ponies that went extinct in Yukon around 12,500 years ago. The recovery of American mastodon remains, an animal known to browse on shrubs and small trees, suggests that forests extended as far as the Yukon north coast during the Last Interglacial period, around 125,000 years ago (Fig. 12).

The dominance of horses over steppe bison on Herschel Island contrasts with areas in the interior of Beringia. In the gold mining districts near Dawson City and Fairbanks, Alaska, palaeontologists estimate that steppe bison account for 80 percent of the Ice Age fossil bones. The dominance of horses over steppe bison also found in fossil assemblages from the north coast of Alaska suggests that northernmost areas of Beringia were extremely arid during the Pleistocene. Because horses can survive long periods without free water and on large amounts of low-quality dry grass, they were able to out-compete other Ice Age mammals such as bison and caribou. The presence of saiga antelope along the southern Beaufort coastal plain also indicates a very cold, dry environment. Saiga antelope are currently found only on the windswept steppes of Asia, where there is sporadic, thin snow cover.

As well as land mammals, evidence for ancient marine mammals has been recovered from the beaches of Herschel Island. A fossil polar bear bone recovered near Simpson Point confirms this species' presence on Herschel Island 1,500 years ago. A wide range of bones from seals and whales have also been recovered on the beach at Pauline Cove, and likely represent animals living throughout the Holocene. Bones of Pleistocene walrus, dating to more than 45,000 years ago, indicate this species has a long history in the southern Beaufort Sea region. However, the origin of the Pleistocene marine mammal bones is not clear. Since the coastline was north of the Herschel ridge during the Pleistocene, marine mammal bones must either have been deposited on the ridge by glacier ice, or may have washed in as sea level rose and the coast moved southward.

Fig. 11 Muskoxen (*Ovibus moschatus*) were widespread throughout Beringia, but are now restricted to the Arctic, including Herschel Island. *Painting by George Teichmann.*

The radiocarbon dates obtained from Ice Age bones found on Herschel Island help to determine the timing of Herschel Island's formation. It seems likely that the Laurentide ice sheet's Buckland advance reached its maximum position near the Last Glacial Maximum, around 20,000 years ago. However, some radiocarbon-dated fossil bones from land mammals on the ridge are greater than 50,000 years old, suggesting that the island was already formed and animals were living there during a previous glaciation. An alternative explanation for these very old bones is that they represent animals that lived and died on the exposed Beaufort Sea shelf, and were picked up by the advancing glacier during the Last Glacial Maximum.

There are many questions still to be answered about the Ice Age history of Herschel Island. Most fossils are found washed up on the beach rather than in the cliff sediments, so it is difficult to determine where they originate or how they relate to Pleistocene glacial events. What does seem certain is that the Herschel ridge was part of Beringia for thousands of years toward the end of the last glaciation. Through the regular monitoring and collection of fossils from the beach, and by examining exposed sediments along sea cliffs, we will continue to learn about the dynamic history of Yukon's only Arctic island.

Fig. 12 Mastodon (*Mammut americanum*) fossils recovered on Herschel Island likely date to the Last Interglacial period, around 125,000 years ago, when trees grew at the Beaufort Sea coast. The two smaller images illustrate the differences in appearance between the mastodon *left* and its cousin, the woolly mammoth. *Painting by George Teichmann.*

PERMAFROST

Christopher Burn

Herschel Island is almost entirely composed of permafrost—ground that remains at or below 0°C for two or more years. Most of the ground in the western Arctic, however, has probably been frozen for hundreds of thousands of years. The island originated as a body of frozen ground pushed up from the continental shelf by glacier ice toward the end of the last ice age. Ice from that glacier is preserved in Qikiqtaryuk and exposed from time to time at the coast. The permafrost at Herschel Island predates the last ice age because deformed sediments that were thrust upward by the glacial advance contain bodies of ice (ice wedges, discussed later) several tens of metres below the surface (Fig. 1). These ice bodies formed near the surface when the ground was exposed and were subsequently buried by marine sediments.

Fig. 2 Thaw slump on the east coast of Herschel Island. *Photo by Louis Schilder.*

The thawing of frozen ground is key to many of the active landscape processes on the island, such as coastal erosion and the development of thaw slumps (Fig. 2). During summer, thawing of the ground forms an "active layer" (the top layer of soil that thaws in summer and freezes again in the fall) above the permafrost (Fig. 3). At Qikiqtaryuk, the active layer is less than a metre thick over most of the island, but is greater in the gravel beaches and spits.

Permafrost has been used at Herschel Island as a freezer to store food since the whaling era. The first "ice house" was blasted out of a hillslope in March 1891 and covered over with a wood and sod roof. Five such ice cellars were excavated on the island, but four have collapsed and only one is still functional (Fig. 4).

Fig. 1 An ice wedge preserved in deformed sediments on the northeast side of Herschel Island. The ice wedge is about 30 metres below the top of the cliff. *Photo by Mary Beattie.*

Massive ice in permafrost exposed in the head wall of a retrogressive thaw slump on the coast of Thetis Bay, summer 2008. *Photo by Louis Schilder.*

Ground Temperatures

The temperature in permafrost is largely controlled by climate, but any variation in surface conditions causes the exact value to change from one site to another. The most important of these surface conditions is the snow cover. Snow acts as an insulator, trapping summer heat in the ground so that, as a rule, the average temperature of the ground is higher than that of the air. At Qikiqtaryuk, however, the snow cover over most of the island is thin because the tundra vegetation is insufficient to hold more than about 20 centimetres of snow. Even the whalemen noticed that the lack of snow meant it was hard to drag sleds across the island. As a result, the ground is relatively cold. The low average annual air temperature and thin snow cover ensure that permafrost is found everywhere at Herschel Island.

Fig. 3 The active layer of ground that thaws each summer above permafrost. The active layer is shown here above the ice wedge. *Photo by Louis Schilder.*

Over the year, temperatures vary in the upper 15 metres of the ground. Figure 5 shows the maximum and minimum temperatures between depths of 1 metre and 14 metres recorded on Collinson Head from April to August since 2001.

(Temperatures are recorded when park staff are on the island.) The two curves converge at depth on the mean annual ground temperature, which is -8°C. This value is close to the mean annual air temperature (-9.6°C) because of the thin snow cover at the top of Collinson Head.

In valleys and gullies, where the snow does accumulate in deep drifts, the ground may be much warmer. On a hillslope leading up to Collinson Head, the ground temperature at a depth of 1 metre has been collected daily at a series of 10 stations since 2003. The annual mean temperature at this depth varies by about 5°C between these sites, with the warmest ground in a depression where relatively deep snow builds up during winter. The range in annual average temperature is from -9.0°C to -4.0°C, with -4.0°C beneath the snow drift and the other sites mostly 4°C lower (or -8.0°C). Ground temperatures measured at another location beneath a snow drift were similarly "warm" (-4.5°C for the annual average).

The thickness of permafrost at Herschel Island is not known directly, but must be at least the height of the cliffs at Bell Bluff (60 metres) because they are made up of frozen sediments. The thickness can be estimated from the mean ground temperature if we know the ground materials and the heat flow from the Earth's interior.

Fig. 4 Four of the five "ice houses" (cellars) on Herschel Island that were dug out of the permafrost and built during the whaling era. *Photo courtesy of Library and Archives Canada, PA 211733.*

On this basis it seems that permafrost beneath the hills of the island may reach a depth of about 450 metres. In newer landforms, such as the alluvial fan at Pauline Cove, where sediments brought down from the interior of the island spread out at the coast, the thickness is likely to be similar, as the landform was built on top of pre-existing permafrost in the coastal plain.

Surprisingly, permafrost is also found in the seabed surrounding the island. Even though the continental shelf near the island has been submerged for about 4,000 years, the water is cold and salty and has a temperature below 0°C for much of the year. The water temperature rises in summer because of the influence of the warmer Mackenzie River. Workboat Passage has probably only been an ocean passage for less than 1,600 years, and is so shallow that sea ice freezes to the bottom over much of the strait. The deepest water and highest seabed temperatures are on the north side of Workboat Passage near Lopez Point, where there is water beneath the ice throughout the winter. The annual average temperature at the seabed is -0.1°C, indicating that permafrost is being maintained.

Massive Ice

A spectacular element of the terrain at Herschel Island is the almost pure ice that forms the uppermost 15 metres of permafrost in many areas. This massive ground ice is typically exposed in the broad headwalls of thaw slumps that develop along the shore of Thetis Bay and on the northwest coast of the island. Figure 6 is a photograph of exposed massive ice, with the effects of deformation clearly visible. The deformation may have been created when the island was pushed up from the continental shelf by the overriding glacier, or the deformed ice may actually be a remnant body of glacier ice. Both types of massive ice occur on Herschel Island. The depth of the massive ice is evident in the repeated thaw slumps at the coast, begun and continued by coastal erosion (Fig. 7).

Massive ice will be important in the future if the active layer thickens because of climate change. Melting of this ice will lead to ground subsidence and, most likely, development of new ponds and wetlands.

Deformed ground ice at Collinson Head, either distorted when the island was pushed up, or left from the bottom of the overriding glacier. *Photo by Christopher Burn.*

DEFORMATION OF GROUND ICE

Ice that is close to 0°C and near its melting point is not strong because its molecular bonds are close to their breaking point. If pressure is applied constantly to the ice, in the movement of a glacier, the ice may creep or deform rather than breaking. Ice at the base of a glacier is usually highly deformed. When this occurs, structures in the ice are bent, folded, or faulted. Some of the ground ice near the surface of Herschel Island shows such deformation, suggesting it may be glacier ice that was subsequently buried.

Other ground ice, deeper in the sediments, was in the ground that was pushed up to form Herschel Island. These deposits were deformed at a larger scale than in the bottom few metres of a glacier, and whole beds of sediment were folded and faulted. The ice in these units was deformed with, rather than within, each unit.

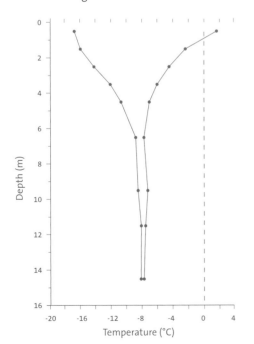

Fig. 5 Maximum and minimum temperatures recorded in the uppermost 15 metres of the ground at Collinson Head, 2003–09. The data were collected between April and August each year.

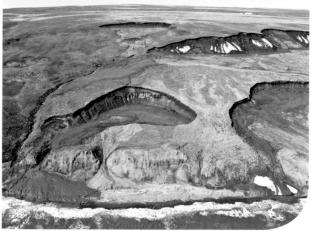

Fig. 6 Deformed massive ice exposed near the coast of Thetis Bay. *Photo by Louis Schilder.*

Fig. 7 Repeated development of thaw slumps in massive ice at Thetis Bay. *Photo by Fritz Mueller.*

The presence of ground ice close to the surface presents a challenge for new structures on the island. The park buildings currently stand on the gravel spit at Pauline Cove, where there is little excess ice. If rising sea level forces their relocation, careful site selection and new foundation design will be needed. The alluvial fan at Pauline Cove, which makes up the rest of the low, flat ground in the area, is covered in peat and contains large amounts of ground ice, making it unsuitable for building.

Ice Wedges

Ice wedges, V-shaped structures of almost pure ice, are often seen in exposed near-surface permafrost at Herschel Island (Fig. 3). These wedges form when snowmelt in the spring infiltrates cracks in the ground created during winter when the terrain becomes so cold that it contracts, or shrinks, and splits. Over many winters, these V-shaped wedges grow and deform the surrounding ground. The tops of the ice wedges are in permafrost and are normally near the base of the active layer. The wedges are thickest at the top and become narrower with depth, partly because the cracks are widest near the surface, but also because deep cracks that penetrate the full wedge depth are rarer than near-surface cracks, and because the snowmelt often freezes near the top of the crack rather than filling it.

The ice wedges may develop into irregular networks of tundra polygons, 10 to 15 metres wide (Fig. 8). The polygons have between four and seven sides, and are outlined by troughs that may be filled with water. The ice wedges are located below the troughs. The shrinking of the ground during winter cooling occurs all over the landscape, but the polygons develop best in flat ground and are not easy to see over much of the island because of the rolling terrain. Slow downslope movement may obscure these hillslope troughs, as above the ice wedge in Figure 3.

The ice wedges exposed in the thaw slumps on Herschel Island are relatively large for such features in Canada's western Arctic (Fig. 9), partly because they have grown for thousands of years since the overriding glacier ice melted, and partly because the thin snow cover helps the ground to cool, increasing the frequency of cracking. Some of the wedges may be exposed obliquely, not in true cross-section, and their widths are exaggerated.

Ice wedges can be used as evidence of landform development, as in the alluvial fan at Pauline Cove. Figure 10 shows an ice wedge that was buried during the growth of the alluvial fan. A thin column of ice above the wedge extends up toward the bottom of the active layer. The top of the wedge is 107 centimetres below the ground surface, or 62 centimetres below the

active layer, and represents the level in the ground that was the top of permafrost, or "permafrost table," when the surface was lower. Its width suggests that the growth of deposits on the alluvial fan's surface stalled for some time, allowing the wedge to develop. As sediment accumulation resumed on the surface, the permafrost table—while remaining a consistent distance below the surface—also rose. The thin column of ice is from renewed ice-wedge cracking reaching down from the active layer into permafrost.

Active Layer

The active layer is a biologically critical part of the landscape because plants can grow in the thawed ground. It is also important for the water cycle because almost all seepage of snowmelt or summer rain is stored in this zone. The thickness of the active layer varies with soil type, slope direction, and soil wetness. Relatively thin active layers develop in organic soils, on north-facing slopes, and at wet sites. Thick active layers develop in gravels, on beaches, and at other dry sites. At Herschel Island, the active layer in the wet, organic-rich soil of the alluvial fan at Pauline Cove is up to about 40 centimetres thick, while on the dry slopes leading up to Collinson Head it is 40 to 60 centimetres. The fox dens on the island are at very dry sites at the top of slopes where the active layer is deepest. Measurements of

Fig. 8 Ice-wedge polygons near Thetis Bay. *Photo by Nicole Couture.*

Fig. 9 Ice wedge exposed in the headwall of a thaw slump. The deformation of the ground to the side of the wedge is partly caused by the extra volume that the permafrost must accommodate as the ice wedge grows. *Photo by Graham Gilbert.*

active-layer thicknesses on the uplands of Herschel Island in the late 1980s were 15–30 centimetres less than the thicknesses measured since 2005. The thickening of the active layer is one indicator that the climate has warmed since the 1980s.

The ground just below the top of permafrost is usually ice-rich, so as the active layer thickens, melting this icy ground, the surface may sink. On Herschel Island we find evidence in the ground ice of a former active layer, much thicker than at present (Fig. 11). In places where the current active layer is 45 centimetres thick, the former thickness may have been about 95 centimetres. This deeper active layer probably developed about 9,000 years ago when the climate was considerably warmer.

The present active layer supports a vegetation cover similar to many other places in the western Arctic. However, when the ground is disturbed at Herschel Island, as in the thaw slumps, revegetation is by salt-tolerant species. The lower sediments that are thawed in the slumps are the original coastal permafrost that was pushed up by glacial ice. The salt in these marine sediments is diluted when they are in the active layer for a long time. The freshly exposed coastal sediments are too saline to support the dominant tundra vegetation, which can only grow in soil that has been flushed with rain and snowmelt for many years.

Permafrost and Climate Change

Some of the most convincing Canadian evidence that twentieth-century climate change has affected permafrost was collected at Herschel Island. In 2006 ground temperatures were collected in a borehole drilled to a depth of 42 metres at Collinson Head. Normally, ground temperatures are expected to increase with depth because of the heat flowing through the Earth's crust. When this trend occurs throughout the ground, the permafrost may be considered as being in equilibrium with the climate. However, in the upper 50 metres of the ground at Collinson Head the temperature is higher than at depth, echoing a pattern found at many sites in Alaska. This data suggests that permafrost temperatures are rising, driven by warming at the ground surface (Fig. 12).

At Herschel Island, the weather observations by Rev. Isaac Stringer at the end of the nineteenth century provide a snapshot of the climate over a hundred years ago. As described in the chapter on Climate, conditions were considerably colder then than now. We can calculate the increase in ground temperature that should have taken place as a result of the climate warming during the twentieth century to the present. In fact, we find a remarkable agreement between observed and calculated ground temperatures when the calculations

Fig. 10 An ice wedge exposed at the coast in the alluvial fan near Pauline Cove. It has been buried by sediment deposits and vegetation growth on the alluvial fan. The active layer, just below the vegetation mat, is 45 centimetres thick. *Photo by Christopher Burn.*

assume that the ground at the end of the nineteenth century was in equilibrium with the climate back then (Fig. 12). The calculations show that temperatures at the top of permafrost have risen by about 4°C, from -10.6°C to -7.0°C, through the last century. At a depth of 20 metres, the ground has warmed by about 2°C, from -10.2°C to -8.3°C. The effects of warming have likely reached a depth of about 120 metres so far.

Changes to active-layer thickness can only be considered over a shorter period, because the first systematic measurements of the active layer were made in the 1980s when the park was being established. However, even since then the active layer has become thicker by 10–15 centimetres and vegetation has increased, perhaps because of the slow release of nutrients and moisture during thawing of near-surface permafrost in summer.

Continued deepening of the active layer is almost certain to be a consequence of further climate change. It is also only a matter of time until permafrost with massive ice begins to thaw. This thawing has happened in the past, particularly about 9,000 years ago, during the period with the warmest climate since the Ice Age. The present rate of active-layer deepening suggests that it may overtake the previous maximum thickness in the next 50 to 75 years.

Fig. 11 The top of permafrost exposed in the headwall of a thaw slump. The current layer is brown and lies at the ground surface. The black ground between the active layer and the grey massive ice is now permafrost, but was seasonally thawed in the past.
Photo by Graham Gilbert.

Fig. 12 Ground temperatures at Collinson Head in July 2006, showing warming during the twentieth century. Measurements to 42 metres depth were made in July 2006. Other values were calculated using the observed climate warming since 1899. The temperatures for 1899 were calculated assuming that ground conditions then were in equilibrium with the climate.

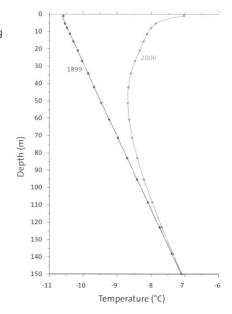

THE ICE HOUSE

The functioning ice cellar or "ice house" at Pauline Cove was excavated in the footslope of a stabilized and revegetated thaw slump. It is the structure near the right margin of Figure 4. An insulated double door provides entry to the cellar, which is about 2.5 metres deep, 3 metres wide, and 4 metres long. The cellar hole was blasted out of the permafrost. The cellar walls show the ground ice at the site, with about one-half of the wall area composed of ice. A log roof, supported by wooden posts, was erected and topped with sod. The ceiling is covered with hexagonal ice crystals that have grown from the vapour in the cellar's atmosphere. These crystals can be up to 6 centimetres across but are normally less than 3 millimetres thick.

The temperature in the cellar has been recorded with data loggers over several years. For 2007–09, the average temperature in the cellar was -6.2°C, falling as low as -12.3°C. Most summers the temperature has risen to -3.9°C in the lower part of the cellar, demonstrating that it works well for storing frozen food or hanging caribou harvested on the island.

The operational ice house at Herschel Island, with a collapsed cellar in the background. *Photo by Christopher Burn.*

Ground ice in the wall of the ice house at Pauline Cove. The dark layers are ice, while the light layers are sediment. The shovel is 75 centimetres from the handle to the blade. *Photo by Christopher Burn.*

Ice crystals from the ceiling of the ice house that have grown from the vapour in the cellar's atmosphere. *Photo by Christopher Burn.*

Temperatures measured by data logger at the top and bottom of the ice house at Pauline Cove between January 2007 and December 2009.

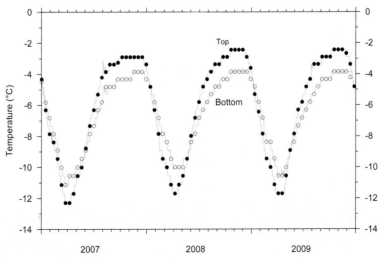

COASTAL ENVIRONMENT

Wayne H. Pollard, Nicole Couture, and Hugues Lantuit

Three facets of Herschel Island's geologic history meet in its coastal environment. That history includes, first, the long unglaciated period during which cold climatic conditions created permafrost; second, the island's evolution during the Ice Age as the permafrost was pushed up out of the continental shelf; and, third, the recent encounter with the ocean as the Beaufort Sea has risen to create the island. Coastal processes have been shaping the island relatively recently in geological terms, probably during the last four or five thousand years.

The erosion of arctic coasts involves both mechanical processes directly related to waves and ice (Fig. 1), and thermal processes driven by the ocean water temperature and the heat in breaking waves. In ice-rich permafrost environments like Herschel Island, considerable coastal erosion is also related to the thawing of permafrost, which meets the ocean at the Arctic coast. Melting ground ice and shoreline erosion due to wave action are the main processes currently reshaping the island. Permafrost, sea ice, and ocean waves all depend on the climate of the area, interacting so that a change in one often affects the others. Throughout the summer and fall, the coastline responds to the action of the open ocean, but in winter and spring the land is locked up by sea ice, restricting the amount of change that can occur. The ice cover limits the open-water season to only a few months at Herschel Island, from late June to early November.

Fig. 2 Massive ice body exposed in the headwall of a retrogressive thaw slump. Several ice wedges can be seen in the headwall.
Photo by Wayne Pollard.

Topography and Geology

The topography of Herschel Island and its coastal landscape is closely linked to the region's Quaternary glacial and periglacial (cold climate) history. Although we do not know the precise timing of some key events, we can be certain about the glacial ice-thrust origin of the island and its role in determining the island's relief and sedimentary structure.

The north and northwest sides of the island have high bluffs that overlook the Beaufort Sea. These parts of the island have a series of tightly packed layers of sediment that form pronounced ridges and valleys, and a parallel drainage pattern. In contrast, on the east and southeast sides of the island, the rolling hills are dissected by shallow valleys. The terrain is lower in this area, with horizontal or near-horizontal layers of sediment containing massive ground ice at the coast. The shore of Thetis Bay has the highest concentration on the island of retrogressive thaw slumps, the large features that form from melting permafrost.

Fig. 1 Ocean water and drifting ice near the shore at Simpson Point, July 2006. *Photo by Nicole Couture.*

The coast at Simpson Point with Collinson Head in the background. *Photo by Nicole Couture.*

Zones of deformed and sheared ground ice in Pauline Cove, and stones and boulders from remote sources, show that glaciers overrode the eastern portion of the island and pushed it out of the continental shelf. The folding and faulting due to glacial thrusting piled up slabs of sediment, producing the high bluffs on the north and west sides of the island. Some of the massive ice may well be glacier ice that was buried either during the folding and faulting or as the ice sheet melted, and has been preserved as permafrost. The widespread massive ice along the coast of Thetis Bay has led to extensive thermokarst (ground collapse due to melting ice) that is closely linked to coastal erosion.

The fine-grained and ice-rich sediments that make up Herschel Island are extremely vulnerable to coastal erosion, mass wasting, and thermokarst development. The ground ice on the island occurs in a variety of forms, including discrete ice lenses (separate layers of ice, often with convex upper and lower surfaces), V-shaped ice wedges, and massive icy bodies (Fig. 2). Our information on ground ice is based on examining exposures along the coast, including numerous retrogressive thaw slumps. The thaw slumps on Qikiqtaryuk are among the largest and most spatially concentrated in the Canadian Arctic. They typically occur as back-wasting headwalls fronted by pools of liquefied mud that slowly flow down to the ocean. As these headwalls retreat, they form C-shaped depressions that commonly coalesce into large and irregularly shaped features (Fig. 3). Along the coast, the retreating headwalls are broadly parallel to the shoreline. Average headwall retreat rates are about 15 metres per year.

Fig. 3 C-shaped retrogressive thaw slumps in bluffs of intermediate height along Thetis Bay.
Photo by Wayne Pollard.

Fig. 4 High bluffs with steep faces occur along the north and west sides of the island.
Photo by Wayne Pollard.

Fig. 5 High bluffs along the island's west side extend to the base of Avadlek Spit.
Photo by Wayne Pollard.

Coastal Morphology

Herschel Island covers an area of 116 square kilometres, with approximately 60 kilometres of coastline. Of that coastline, 38 percent consists of bluffs more than 25 metres high, while 17 percent consists of bluffs five to 25 metres high and 22 percent of bluffs less than five metres high. The highest bluffs occur along the north and west sides of the island, from Collinson Head and Bell Bluff (Fig. 4) around to the base of Avadlek Spit (Fig. 5). The intermediate bluffs are in Thetis Bay (Fig. 3), while the low bluffs are along the south side of the island between Osborn Point and Avadlek Spit, especially at Thrasher Bay.

Fig. 6 In addition to bluffs, spits are another prominent coastal feature. Avadlek Spit is shown here. *Photo by Wayne Pollard.*

Fig. 7 Low bluffs and delta at Orca Cove. *Photo by Wayne Pollard.*

The remaining coastline is characterized by three well-developed sand and gravel spits (Fig. 6)—Avadlek, Osborn, and Simpson spits—and a series of small deltas, most notably at Lopez Point, near Orca Cove (Fig. 7), and at Pauline Cove.

Along much of the coast, the high and intermediate bluffs are fronted by sandy beaches one to two metres wide at low tide, with many intermittent mudflows in areas of thermokarst. Low bluffs tend to have wider and more stable beaches.

These beaches are usually covered by driftwood from the Mackenzie River (Fig. 8). Most of the driftwood is on the south and east sides of the island. The higher bluffs consist of steep (50-70°) straight slopes of frozen sediment cut by closely spaced gullies, channels, and small valleys (Fig. 9). Large, regularly spaced, V-shaped valleys incise the bluffs almost to sea level every one to two kilometres along the coast. As bluff and channel slopes gradually thaw during the summer and become over-steepened

because of wave and channel erosion at their base, they are prone to slope movements. Block failures, active-layer detachments (Fig. 10), mud slides, debris flows, and retrogressive thaw slumps are common. Low bluffs, however, either slope gently toward the beach with tundra vegetation extending close to the beach line, or end in low near-vertical cliffs of frozen sediment one to five metres high. These low bluffs have only sporadic thermokarst activity and localized slope movement.

Most retrogressive thaw slumps are on the coast, where they contribute to its erosion. Since 2000, annual aerial surveys of the coast in late July or early August have identified between 70 and 90 active coastal thaw slumps. The bluffs in Thetis Bay and on the west side of the island near Avadlek Spit are so heavily modified by retrogressive thaw slumps that they might be more accurately described as thermokarst coasts. These areas have many large, active retrogressive thaw slumps ranging from 100 to 700 metres long, with headwalls five to 20 metres high that have eroded the upper part of the bluff up to 200–300 metres back from the present coast. These slumps go through multiple cycles and are triggered by shoreline erosion. They dramatically modify coastal structures and contribute large amounts of sediment to the nearshore zone. During the summer, coastal retreat may be temporarily slowed by the growing mudflows along the coast.

Medium and high bluff coasts are areas of highest coastal retreat, while low bluff areas tend to be fairly stable. The areas with low bluffs have less thermokarst both because ice contents are lower and because they are situated along the protected shores of Workboat Passage. In this strait, small deltas are currently forming near Avadlek Spit and Lopez Point, and the shoreline is growing out from the coast.

Spits are areas where sediment is transported by wave action along the shore face. Longshore currents, breaking waves, back wash, and beach drift keep particles moving, and the coarse sand, gravel, and cobbles of these sediments indicate a fairly high-energy wave environment. The three well-developed spits are constantly changing. They occur where the Herschel shoreline changes direction, with longshore drift and wave refraction compensating for the abrupt change.

Avadlek Spit, an impressive structure 5.8 kilometres long and in places more than 100 metres wide, has played a pivotal role in both the human and natural history of the island (Fig. 6). It contains sites of major archeological significance and remains the main route for wildlife crossing back and forth between the island and the mainland.

Wave Climate

Waves generated by high winds are responsible for most of the coastal erosion and nearshore sediment transport on Herschel Island. Strong winds lasting for several days also produce storm surges that raise water levels and cause flooding and erosion. Inuvialuit who travel by boat and camp along the coast during the open-water period provide most of our information about wave and storm patterns. A second source of data, based on wave height, length, and speed in a particular direction, comes from wave climate analysis. Wave climates may reflect wave conditions during a single storm event, varying with location and distance from the centre of the storm, or the overall conditions for a fixed period of time.

Most wave climate analyses for the southeastern Beaufort Sea come from a combination of wind observations at Tuktoyaktuk, Sachs Harbour, Shingle Point, and Pelly Island, and from computer models.

Fig. 8 Driftwood on Simpson Point. The wood comes from the Mackenzie River. *Photo by Nicole Couture.*

Fig. 9 Incised cliffs at Collinson Head, the northeast point of Herschel Island, with Pauline Cove behind. *Photo by Fritz Mueller.*

Fig. 10 Mass wasting due to active-layer detachment slides along the island's northeast coast. *Photo by Wayne Pollard.*

Fig. 11 Flooding on Simpson Point due to a storm surge in August 2010.
Photo by Wayne Pollard.

These models calculate wave conditions based on wind duration, velocity, open-water area (fetch), and direction. The major storms come mainly from the northwest and tend to generate more extreme waves. Storm surges can cause water levels along the coast to rise up to 1.2 metres, flooding low-lying areas and washing over spits and barrier islands. Sustained winds lasting three to four days, especially easterly winds, have caused extensive flooding in the main camp area on Simpson Point (Fig. 11). In recent years Inuvialuit hunters have seen an increase in the area of open water in summer and less ice drifting near the shore. However, most of them comment that storm patterns are variable from year to year.

Wave climate simulations take into consideration Herschel Island's location in the southern Beaufort Sea and its position only a few kilometres offshore. The placement of the island means that significant waves may come from a 180° arc running between the southeast and the northwest. The average number of storms per year varies between two and 14, depending on the criteria used to define a storm, with frequency and intensity increasing between August and October. Most years have at least 4 major storms during which maximum wave heights in deep water are between 1.5 and 2.0 metres, with an extreme wave height of 3.0 metres.

As storm waves approach the coast, releasing a tremendous amount of kinetic and thermal energy as they break, their pattern of breaking depends on the nearshore profile of the seafloor.

Coastal Erosion

Almost the entire coastline of Herschel Island is eroding, with sediment buildup taking place at only a few sites. Recent studies that calculated rates of coastal retreat based on aerial photo and satellite image analysis have measured horizontal shoreline loss of up to 59 metres in 50 years. However, the intensity of shoreline erosion during the second half of the twentieth century seems to have declined. The average erosion rates for Herschel Island per year were 0.61 metres for 1952–70 and 0.45 metres for 1970–2000 (Fig. 12). The highest rates of shoreline retreat occur at high bluff sections that face the northwest, the main direction of wave attack during storms.

At some sites near the northern tip of the island and Bell Bluff, retreat rates have decreased, but they are still relatively high. However, the rates have increased for south- and southeast-facing shorelines along Thetis Bay. These areas are marked by high ice contents and the highest density of retrogressive thaw slumps. The coastal erosion here may be linked to thaw slump activity as a result of the lowering of the cliff profile (from cliff base to cliff top) and the removal of fine-grained sediments by mudflows. The difference between coastal retreat rate and slump headwall retreat rate leads to the repeated development of slumps along this shoreline.

Between 1952 and 2000 the number of retrogressive thaw slumps on Herschel Island increased by 125 percent, while the total area of these slumps increased by 160 percent. The increase in air temperatures in the western Arctic over the past several decades seems to be one of the most important factors speeding up their development.

Along with the direct physical effects of coastal retreat, erosion has other major consequences. Eroded sediments can bury or change the habitats of plants and animals that live in nearshore areas. The sediments also add organic carbon to the Arctic Ocean, thereby affecting how much carbon dioxide the ocean can absorb from the atmosphere.

Climate Change

Herschel Island's coastal environment has been shaped by its geologic history and Quaternary evolution. The southern Beaufort Sea region is one of the most ice-rich areas in the Canadian Arctic, with widespread massive ground ice and numerous retrogressive thaw slumps. Ice-rich coasts such as the ones found on Herschel Island are vulnerable not only to mechanical and thermal erosion by waves, but also to more regional patterns of global warming and sea level rise. Climate change is expected to further reduce the extent and duration of sea ice, leading to increased exposure of coasts to storm-related wave activity. The warming of permafrost will lead to increases in the depth of the active layer. The combined effect of these processes on ice-rich permafrost coasts will be an increase in the rates of thermokarst and shoreline loss.

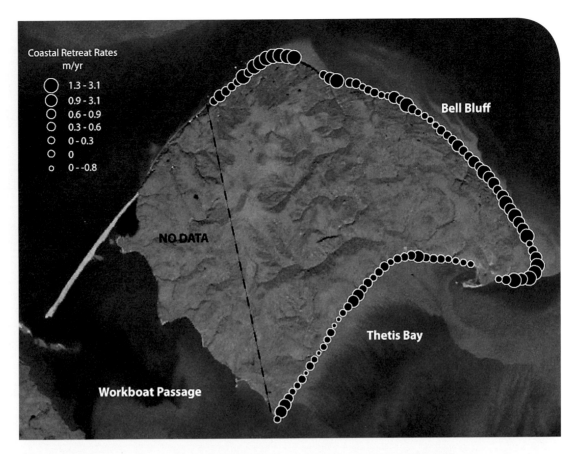

Fig. 12 *Above* Coastal retreat rates for 1952–70. The northwest section of the island's coast is the most affected by erosion as a result of prevailing storm winds. *Below* Coastal retreat rates for 1970–2000.

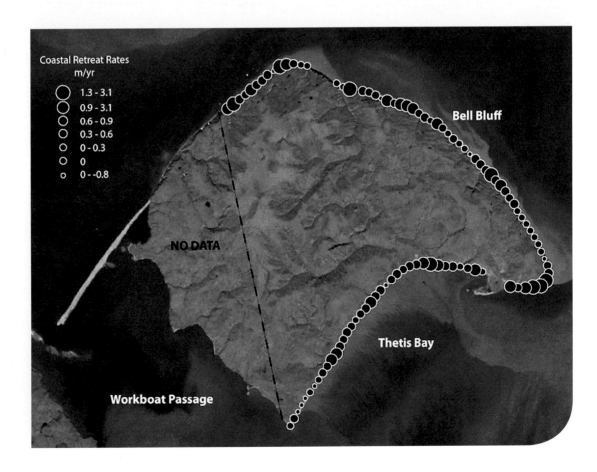

FLORA AND FAUNA

flora and fauna

VEGETATION

Catherine Kennedy

From a bird's eye view, Herschel Island looks like a pancake of frozen tundra, melting around the edges. On the ground, however, a lush arctic oasis awaits the summer visitor. From late June until the middle of August, Qikiqtaryuk is saturated with the brilliant colours of flowers in bloom (Fig. 1). About 200 species of plants thrive in the maritime climate, the fine-textured, moist soils, and the continuous daylight of the short growing season.

The plant ecology is influenced by the arctic climate, the thin active layer of soil above permafrost, and the island's unusual geological origin. Its landscape, with features developed in a range of cold-climate terrain types, provides micro-environments for diverse and abundant vegetation. The most active landforms on the island are the numerous retrogressive thaw slumps, resulting from the thawing of permafrost (see page 73). These slumps are noticeable in summer because of their headwalls of melting ground ice and the progression of plant communities in the stabilizing ground.

Fig. 2 Cotton-grass (*Eriophorum* spp.) tussock tundra is a stable plant community that dominates level uplands on the island. *Photo by Catherine Kennedy.*

The diverse flora of Qikiqtaryuk includes species that occur throughout the Yukon, as well as species that occur only in the Arctic. Of particular interest are plants of limited range in Canada that only grow on the seashore in the western Arctic, and species which evolved during the Ice Age in Beringia, the ice-free parts of Alaska, Yukon, and Siberia. The main vegetation communities and where they occur on the island are described in this chapter.

Fig. 1 Northern sweet-vetch (*Hedysarum boreale*). *Photo by Michael Kawerninski.*

A hillslope covered by arctic lupines (*Lupinus arcticus*) in full colour. In July and early August, abundant wildflowers bloom on Herschel Island. *Photo by Fritz Mueller.*

Fig. 7 Alpine milk-vetch (*Astralagus alpinus*). Photo by Michael Kawerninski.

Uplands: Cotton-grass Tussock Tundra

Cotton-grass sedge tussocks (Fig. 2) cover the smooth, level uplands of the island. These tussocks present a formidable challenge for hikers, although caribou navigate effortlessly across them. Interspersed with a continuous moss cover, the tussocks provide a thick blanket of insulation, so only a thin active layer develops above permafrost.

There is little plant variety in this stable vegetation community. The sparse dwarf shrubs include net-veined willow, arctic willow, mountain cranberry, and diamond-leaf willow. Colourful forbs (herbaceous flowering plants that are not grasses) such as alpine bistort, capitate lousewort (Fig. 3), arctic and Lapland poppies (Fig. 4), heart-leaved saxifrage, capitate valerian, and narrow-leafed sawwort (Fig. 5) dot the landscape. Few lichens grow in this terrain.

Uplands: Dry Low Shrub Tundra

On steeper upland slopes, the vegetation changes from cotton-grass tussocks to a dry tundra, dominated by dwarf willows (arctic willow, net-veined willow), mountain avens, and arctic lupine (Fig. 6). A variety of flowering plants grow on these slopes, with numerous vetches such as alpine milk-vetch (Fig. 7), hairy arctic milk-vetch, arctic oxytrope, and blackish oxytrope. Lapland poppy, alpine forget-me-not, capitate lousewort, and naked-stemmed parrya are the other main flowering plants.

Without an insulating blanket of moss, the soil thaws in summer to depths of up to 80 centimetres and freezes again in winter. In moist soils, the freezing and thawing churns the ground, a process known as cryoturbation, and prevents plants from rooting. As a result, bare mud hummocks, circular mounds about a metre in diameter, are common in this terrain. Between the hummocks, plants establish themselves in nets of vegetation (Fig. 8). On steep slopes, where the hummocks are elongated downslope, the vegetation nets become stripes.

Fig. 3 Capitate lousewort (*Pedicularis capitata*). Photo by Catherine Kennedy.

Fig. 4 Lapland poppy (*Papaver lapponicum*). Photo by Catherine Kennedy.

Fig. 5 Narrow-leafed sawwort (*Saussurea angustifolia*). Photo by Catherine Kennedy.

Fig. 6 Arctic lupine (*Lupinus arcticus*). Photo by Catherine Kennedy.

Fig. 10 Turner's buttercups (*Ranunculus turneri*). *Photo by Catherine Kennedy.*

Fig. 11 Slopes on Herschel Island may have rough surfaces that provide a range of micro-environments for various plants. Hard-packed winter snow persists in gulley bottoms late into the summer, delaying plant development. *Photo by Fritz Mueller.*

Interior Wetlands

Well-developed ice-wedge polygons are commonly visible in wet depressions on Qikiqtaryuk (Fig. 9), but these polygonal areas make up less than five percent of the island's total area. The depressions are recognizable by their bright green colour (Fig. 8). Irregular ice-wedge polygons, up to 30 metres in diameter, are separated by troughs containing wetland vegetation. Ridges on each side of the troughs separate the wetland species from the vegetation in the centre of the polygons. Cotton-grass tussocks usually grow in polygons with moist, low centres, but if the centres of the polygons are raised, their surface may be covered by mosses, dwarf willows, and other small shrubs. In the troughs between the polygons, willows and water sedge are the main species. Where there is standing water underlain by ice, which is common in the troughs, horsetails, yellow marsh saxifrage, sweet coltsfoot, and yellow water buttercups are often present.

Small thaw ponds, formed through the melting of ice-rich permafrost, also occur in the interior upland tundra. The shorelines of these small ponds are bordered with mare's-tails, water sedges, tawny arctophila, Fisher's dupontia, marsh marigold, buttercups (Fig. 10), and mosses.

Erosional Slopes and Gullies

Both inland and at the coast, the hillslopes on Herschel Island show the effects of varying amounts of erosion, often demonstrated by the vegetation cover. Active erosion usually prevents plants from becoming established, while plant diversity increases as roughness of the slope surface creates a greater variety of micro-habitats (Fig. 11).

On slopes with active cryoturbation, the well-developed hummocks provide a range of plant micro-environments. Dense mats of mountain avens grow here (Fig. 12) along with a wide variety of flowering plants including

Fig. 8 Mud hummocks, common in upland dry low-shrub tundra, lead to development of vegetation nets, particularly on exposed knobs and ridges, as in the foreground. A green wetland complex stands out in the background. *Photo by Catherine Kennedy.*

Fig. 9 Ice-wedge polygons in wet depressions are dominated by sedges in the troughs above the ice wedges and the low-lying polygon centres, but support willows, grasses, and colourful flowers on the dry ridges adjacent to the troughs. *Photo by Nicole Couture.*

Fig. 12 Mountain avens (*Dryas integrifolia*). *Photo by Bruce Bennett.*

Fig. 13 Pink elegant paintbrush (*Castilleja elegans*) and blue arctic lupine (*Lupinus arcticus*). *Photo by Dorothy Cooley.*

Fig. 14 The diverse vegetation growing on the alluvial fan at Pauline Cove. *Photo by Michael Kawerninski.*

arctic lupines and elegant paintbrush (Fig. 13), capitate lousewort (Fig. 3), arctic willow, alpine and meadow bistort, alpine forget-me-not, and capitate valerian, as well as numerous colourful vetches.

Gentle concave slopes, where eroded sediments are deposited, are carpeted by moisture-loving dwarf willows, such as net-veined willow and arctic willow, as well as horsetails, sweet coltsfoot, and mosses. Sparse flowering plants include hairy arctic milk-vetch, alpine bistort, Sudeten lousewort, and yellow marsh saxifrage.

Fig. 15 Arctic dock (*Rumex arcticus*). *Photo by Catherine Kennedy.*

Little muddy streams flowing out of active gullies deposit fine sediments where early establishing plants grow, such as mountain sorrel, sweet coltsfoot, and numerous species of the mustard family. The diverse and colourful plants in these settings include alpine forget-me-not, buttercups, saxifrages, grass-of-Parnassus, northern Jacob's ladder, arctic wormwood, low fleabane, alpine sandwort, and common yarrow.

Alluvial Fans

Herschel Island has several alluvial fans, usually where streams come down to the coast, such as the fan at Pauline Cove which contains the graveyards. Lopez Point is on a similar fan. These fans support several different plant communities, depending on the underlying moisture and soil (Fig. 14). Water sedges and willows grow on moister sites that receive water from the stream or are flooded seasonally. Understory species include horsetails, sweet coltsfoot, buttercups (Fig. 10), nodding saxifrage, and yellow marsh saxifrage. Canopy species include Richardson's willow, which forms a dense cover on the alluvial fan at Pauline Cove. Photographs taken on this fan show that the willow patches have expanded over the last 40 years.

In Qikiqtaryuk's interior, where several streams come together, alluvial fans form level or slightly sloping grassy meadows. These meadows have a vigorous variety of flowering plants, including tall Jacob's ladder, tall delphinium, arctic dock (Fig. 15), grass-of-Parnassus, and groundsels.

The alluvial fan at Pauline Cove with extensive patches of willow-dominated vegetation near the stream. These Richardson's willows (*Salix richardsonii*) are some of the tallest (60 centimetres) vegetation on the island. *Photo by Catherine Kennedy.*

ALLUVIAL FANS

Where a stream flows out of a valley onto flat ground, the water slows down and drops much of the sediment it may have been carrying. As the sediment builds up, the stream characteristically flows around the deposit and makes a new channel. Over time, the deposits accumulate in a fan shape. The apex (the highest point of the fan) is at the end of the valley, and the greatest thickness of deposits is commonly down the middle of the fan. The ground slopes down from the apex to the arc-shaped edge. The alluvial fans of Herschel Island have gentle slopes and wet ground in summer.

Fig. 16 Ice-rich permafrost in the headwall of a retrogressive thaw slump and the gentle footslope, which is colonized by plants. *Photo by Michael Kawerninski.*

Fig. 17 Marsh ragwort (*Tephroseris palustris*)—formerly known as marsh fleabane or mastodon flower (*Senecio congestus*)—is a primary colonizer of retrogressive thaw slumps. *Photo by Michael Kawerninski.*

Fig. 18 View from the southwest coast of Herschel Island along the beach toward Avadlek Spit and the British Mountains. *Photo by Catherine Kennedy.*

Retrogressive Thaw Slumps

Slope failures resulting from the thawing of permafrost are spectacular features on the island's coast, but also occur on some inland hillslopes (Fig. 16). Broken pieces of mature vegetation may slide down the steep headwall of ice-rich permafrost and establish themselves on the mud when the slope stabilizes. Alternatively, plant propagules from species that colonize bare ground may land on the mud and start growing. These species often include grasses—spiked trisetum, alpine foxtail, polar grass—as well as marsh ragwort, sea-shore chamomile, and Tilesius' wormwood. There are few mosses, except on the fallen pieces of mature vegetation, and no lichens. Many of these early colonizers do not grow anywhere else on the island except in recently disturbed soils, and some (e.g., marsh ragwort) grow exclusively on fresh thaw slumps, forming dense stands (Fig. 17). The grasses that grow on stabilized surfaces are salt tolerant, because the soil comes from marine sediments that were originally pushed up from the coastal plain. While the salts have been leached from the surface soils over time, they have not been diluted within the permafrost. When thaw slumping occurs, the soil that comes to the surface is usually saline.

Beaches and Spits

The coastline has plant communities that do not occur anywhere else on Herschel Island, due to the proximity of the ocean, which inundates the ground from time to time. The spits and beaches provide a range of habitats with moist depressions, shifting sand and gravel deposits, and varying exposure to salt water (Fig. 18). The spits have the thickest active layers on the island, as a result of the relatively warm ground in these coarse materials in summer. Some plants that are not normally associated with beaches have varieties that are adapted to these habitats, such as Sabine's buttercup (Fig. 19).

The low tidal range in this part of the Beaufort Sea prevents the development of a tidal vegetation zone. On the active beaches, hardy plants are adapted to growing in barren sand and gravel, and must withstand salt spray and abrasion from waves, wind, ice, and woody debris. Tufts of lyme grass grow here, and two conspicuous mat-forming species, seabeach sandwort and sea lungwort (Fig. 20).

In the slightly raised bench above the active beachline, there is a sparse community of coarse grasses, mainly lyme grass and fescue, and flowering plants, including sea-shore chamomile (Fig. 21). Northern primrose, restricted to Beringia (Fig. 22), grows on the landward side of the beach. Shorebirds are often seen feeding in the moist depressions and on the margins of brackish lagoons, where Hoppner's sedge, salt-tolerant arctic goose grass, and low chickweed form a reddish vegetation mat over a muddy layer, together with algae and moss.

Alteration by Animals

Warm, loamy soils on well-drained sites throughout Herschel Island are ideal for denning animals, particularly foxes. Their digging and burrowing activities aerate the soil and accelerate the composting of scat, food, and plant material. This compost enriches the available nutrients near the dens, allowing plants to flourish. Over time, these sites significantly increase in biological diversity and mass, conditions that last long after the animals have left the den.

Fox dens can be recognized from a distance by their green colour, due to a combination of dense grass and flowering plants (Fig. 23). The diversity of plants is unsurpassed at these sites, and up to 50 species may be found at a single den, including arctic lupine, thoroughwort, northern hemlock parsley, tall Jacob's ladder, capitate valerian, alpine arnica, Porsild's fleabane (Fig. 24), alpine forget-me-not, and elegant paintbrush (Fig. 13). Grasses, including foxtail, alpine fescue, holy grass, blue grass, and polar grass, occur in much higher proportions than in other communities of flowering plants on the island.

Vegetation change also occurs to a lesser degree on small elevated points on the landscape where birds may perch and leave droppings. Small promontories associated with polygonal ground tend to host a similar high proportion of grass species and colourful flowering plants such as tall Jacob's ladder, capitate valerian, and alpine bistort.

Fig. 19 Sabine's buttercup (*Ranunculus sabinei*). *Photo by Catherine Kennedy.*

Fig. 20 Sea lungwort (*Mertensia maritima*). *Photo by Catherine Kennedy.*

Fig. 21 Sea-shore chamomile (*Tripleurospermum maritimum*) is rare in the Yukon, but common on the coast and in disturbed ground at Herschel Island. *Photo by Dorothy Cooley.*

Fig. 22 Northern primrose (*Primula borealis*). *Photo by Catherine Kennedy.*

Fig. 24 Porsild's fleabane (*Erigeron porsildii*). *Photo by Catherine Kennedy.*

Fig. 23 A fox den near Pauline Cove with a long history of use. Such dens are clearly visible because foxes often choose sites on the drier ridges or exposed slopes. Nutrients from urine, scat, and the remains of prey create unusually fertile soil in which vegetation is relatively abundant. *Photo by Daniel Gallant.*

COMMON NAME	LATIN NAME	INUVIALUKTUN NAME
Horsetails	**Equisetaceae**	
Field horsetail	*Equisetum arvense*	Ivik (U)
Dwarf scouring-rush	*Equisetum scirpoides*	
Variegated horsetail	*Equisetum variegatum*	
Grasses	**Poaceae**	
Alpine foxtail	*Alopecurus alpinus*	
Alpine sweet grass	*Anthoxanthum monticolum*	
Polar grass	*Arctagrostis latifolia*	
Tawny arctophila	*Arctophila fulva*	
Fisher's dupontia	*Dupontia fisheri*	
Baffin fescue	*Festuca baffinensis*	
Alpine fescue	*Festuca brachyphylla*	
Richardson's fescue	*Festuca richardsonii*	
Lyme grass	*Leymus mollis*	Ivik (U)
Arctic blue grass	*Poa arctica*	
Blue grass	*Poa glauca*	
Arctic alkali grass	*Puccinellia arctica*	
Spiked trisetum	*Trisetum spicatum*	
Sedges	**Cyperaceae**	
Water sedge	*Carex aquatilis*	
Loose-flowered alpine sedge	*Carex rariflora*	
Hoppner's sedge	*Carex subspathacea*	
Common cotton-grass	*Eriophorum angustifolium*	Qivyuřuaq (U)
Sheathed cotton-grass	*Eriophorum vaginatum*	Palliksaq (U)
Willows	**Salicaceae**	
Arctic willow	*Salix arctica*	Uqpipiat (U)
Blue-green willow	*Salix glauca*	
Diamond-leafed willow	*Salix pulchra*	
Net-veined willow	*Salix reticulata*	
Richardson's willow	*Salix richardsonii*	Uqpik (U, S)
Buckwheats	**Polygonaceae**	
Meadow bistort	*Bistorta plumosa*	Ippit (S)
Alpine bistort	*Bistorta vivipara*	Quaraq (S)
Mountain sorrel	*Oxyria digyna*	Qunulliq (U), Qungiliq (S)
Arctic dock	*Rumex arcticus*	Quaguq (U), Quaqqat (S)
Pinks	**Caryophyllaceae**	
Seabeach sandwort	*Honckenya peploides* var. *diffusa*	Iviuyat (S)
Arctic stitchwort	*Minuartia arctica*	
Arctic catchfly	*Silene involucrata*	
Low chickweed	*Stellaria humifosa*	
Crowfoots	**Ranunculaceae**	
Marsh marigold	*Caltha palustris* ssp. *arctica*	Nauřiaq (U)
Tall delphinium	*Delphinium glaucum*	
Yellow water buttercup	*Ranunculus gmelinii*	
Sabine's buttercup	*Ranunculus sabinei*	
Turner's buttercup	*Ranunculus turneri*	
Poppies	**Papaveraceae**	
Lapland poppy	*Papaver lapponicum*	
Arctic poppy	*Papaver radicatum* ssp. *radicatum*	
Mustards	**Brassicaceae**	
Alpine bittercress	*Cardamine bellidifolia*	
Richardson's bittercress	*Cardamine digitata*	
Cuckoo flower	*Cardamine pratensis*	
Scurvy grass	*Cochlearia officinalis* ssp. *arctica*	
Naked-stemmed parrya	*Parrya nudicaulis*	

COMMON NAME	LATIN NAME	INUVIALUKTUN NAME
Saxifrages	**Saxifragaceae**	
Grass-of-Parnassus	*Parnassia kotzebuei*	
Nodding saxifrage	*Saxifraga cernua*	
Yellow marsh saxifrage	*Saxifraga hirculus*	
Heart-leafed saxifrage	*Saxifraga nelsoniana* ssp. *nelsoniana*	
Roses	**Rosaceae**	
Mountain avens	*Dryas integrifolia*	
Cloudberry	*Rubus chamaemorus*	Aqpik (U, S)
Legumes	**Fabaceae**	
Alpine milk-vetch	*Astragalus alpinus*	
Hairy arctic milk-vetch	*Astragalus umbellatus*	
Northern sweet-vetch	*Hedysarum boreale*	
Arctic lupine	*Lupinus arcticus*	Nauřiaq (U), Nautchiaq (S)
Arctic oxytrope	*Oxytropis arctica*	
Blackish oxytrope	*Oxytropis nigrescens*	
Crowberries	**Empetraceae**	
Black crowberry	*Empetrum nigrum*	Kablaq (S)
Mare's-tails	**Hippuridaceae**	
Four-leaved mare's-tail	*Hippuris tetraphylla*	
Common mare's-tail	*Hippuris vulgaris*	
Parsleys	**Apiaceae**	
Thoroughwort	*Bupleurum americanum*	
Hemlock parsley	*Conioselinum cnidiifolium*	
Heaths	**Ericaceae**	
Mountain cranberry	*Vaccinium vitis-idaea*	Kimmingnaq (U, S)
Primrose Family	**Primulaceae**	
Northern primrose	*Primula borealis*	
Gentians	**Gentianaceae**	
Marsh felwort	*Lomatogonium rotatum* ssp. *rotatum*	
Phloxes	**Polemoniaceae**	
Tall Jacob's ladder	*Polemonium acutiflorum*	
Northern Jacob's ladder	*Polemonium boreale*	
Borages	**Boraginaceae**	
Sea lungwort	*Mertensia maritima*	Iviuyat (S)
Alpine forget-me-not	*Myosotis alpestris* ssp. *asiatica*	
Figworts	**Scrophulariaceae**	
Elegant paintbrush	*Castilleja elegans*	
Capitate lousewort	*Pedicularis capitata*	
Woolly lousewort	*Pedicularis lanata*	
Langsdorff's lousewort	*Pedicularis langsdorfii* ssp. *arctica*	
Sudeten lousewort	*Pedicularis sudetica*	
Valerians	**Valerianaceae**	
Capitate valerian	*Valeriana capitata*	
Composites	**Asteraceae**	
Common yarrow	*Achillea millefolium* ssp. *borealis*	Nauřiaq (U)
Alpine arnica	*Arnica angustifolia* ssp. *angustifolia*	
Tilesius' wormwood	*Artemisia tilesii*	Nauřiaq (U)
Low fleabane	*Erigeron humilis*	
Large-headed fleabane	*Erigeron muirii*	
Porsild's fleabane	*Erigeron porsildii*	
Sweet coltsfoot	*Petasites frigidus* ssp. *frigidus*	
Sea-shore chamomile	*Tripleurospermum maritimum*	
Narrow-leafed sawwort	*Saussurea angustifolia* ssp. *angustifolia*	
Black-tipped ragwort	*Senecio lugens*	
Marsh ragwort	*Tephroseris palustris*	

Table 1 Principal plant species found on Herschel Island. Names are from *Flora of the Yukon Territory* by W.J. Cody, and *Inuvialuit Nautchiangit* by Inuvialuit elders with R.W. Bandringa—(U) indicates Uummarmiutun name; (S) indicates Siglitun name.

INSECTS AND SPIDERS

Donald Reid and Maria Leung

Although we perceive the tundra as a harsh environment, it is home to a remarkable diversity of insects, spiders, and other small creatures. We call these creatures invertebrates because they don't have the vertebrae to make up a backbone. In 2007 and 2008 on Herschel Island, we systematically trapped invertebrates that are key foods for young birds so we could discover their timing and numbers. We used a combination of containers dug into the ground (pitfall traps) to catch those that travel along the surface or through the leaf litter, and vertical netting and suspended bottles (malaise traps) to catch flying species (Fig. 1). In 2007, when 70 percent of the upland tundra was snow-free by June 8 and the spring and summer weather was mixed, we caught 4,867 individual invertebrates in the traps. In 2008, when snowmelt was earlier by a week and it was unusually warm through early summer and midsummer, we caught 7,713 individuals.

Most of the invertebrate types on Herschel Island are well-known: slugs, spiders or **akłauȓaq**, mites, flies or **nuviuvak**, mosquitoes or **kikturiaq**, crane flies, beetles or **miñ'nguq**, bees or **igutchaq**, and moths. When the specimens from our traps were sorted into taxonomic order (classification by type of organism), the flies far outnumbered any other group. Fungus gnats, midges, and winter crane flies dominated this sample. Three other invertebrate orders—spiders, bees and wasps or **tuggayuuq**, and beetles—were almost equally numerous in the collections. By far the most numerous beetle family was the ground beetles. Among the bees and wasps, the most numerous were the ichneumons, a diverse group of parasitic insects with a long appendage on the abdomen that the adult females use to lay eggs in the larvae of butterflies, beetles, and moths. The ichneumon larvae grow in their hosts, killing them, and eventually emerge as adults.

A bee collecting nectar from sea lungwort (*Mertensia maritima*) on the beach at Pauline Cove. This is a rare northern plant, found in the Yukon only along the Beaufort Sea coast. *Photo by Maria Leung.*

Fig. 1 A combination pitfall and malaise trap used for catching invertebrates on Herschel Island. Invertebrates at ground level fall into the white trough (pitfall), or, when flying, hit the 40 x 50 centimetre vertical netting. Here they go up into the bottle or fall into the pitfall and are immobilized in water. *Photo by Maria Leung.*

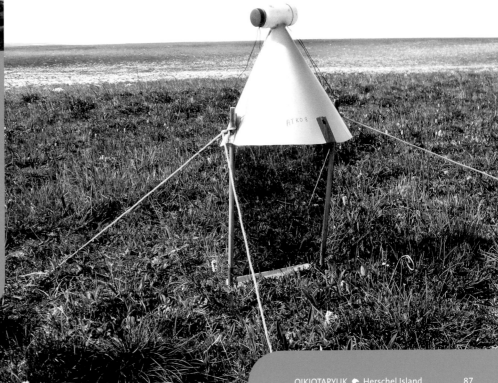

Fig. 3 The silken cocoon of a tiger moth allows warm air to be trapped around the developing body of the pupa. These cocoons are quite numerous in early summer on Herschel Island.
Photo by Maria Leung.

Fig. 2 Woolly-bear caterpillar, showing the dark body colour and multiple rows of hairs.
Photo by Donald Reid.

The particular species of invertebrates we find on Herschel Island today arrived either from the nearby unglaciated steppe and tundra of Beringia, where they were probably well-adapted to northern life, or from regions south of the continental glaciers as those receded. Early arriving species may have evolved into new ones on or near the island. Scientists infer the origin of a species from its current distribution, from fossil records across western North America and Siberia, and from the genetic makeup of the species in the different areas where it lives. A significant number of black fly, noctuid moth, and ground beetle species in northern Yukon originated in Beringia.

In successfully adapting to life at northern latitudes, invertebrates have had to deal with the daily and seasonal patterns of sunlight as well as patterns of precipitation. Long summer daylight can provide excellent growing conditions and plentiful food, especially in micro-environments with lots of exposure to the sun. But little or no sunlight through many winter months means intense cold, penetrating right through the soil to permafrost, and resident life cannot escape the freezing conditions. An uncommon summer rain may be catastrophic if winged forms cannot find cover, whereas the early arrival of winter snow can be a great benefit by insulating the ground from heavy frost. An additional complication is that invertebrates don't reproduce simply by making copies of themselves, which then grow to be adults. They generally go through multiple life stages, with each stage often dependent on a different habitat. For example, adult moths and butterflies lay eggs that become larvae (caterpillars or **auřvik**), which turn into pupae (cocoons or chrysalises) that then form new adults. Control over the timing of all these changes, especially with winter cold, becomes crucial.

Many species of invertebrates that live above ground are herbivores, feeding on stems, leaves, flowers, or nectar. Some beetles, however, are predators of other invertebrates, and the ichneumons in particular are parasitic. Some invertebrates do not feed at all in their adult stage above ground. However, all these species synchronize their life cycle with the pulse of summer plant growth, because it brings food for them, their prey, or their subsequent life stages. This pattern contrasts with that of the numerous species that live largely underground, including the tiny springtails, mites, and nematode worms. Their life stages are not necessarily timed to coincide with the seasons, so individuals of the same species may be at different life stages at the same time. Many of these below-ground dwellers are important detritivores, eating rotting vegetation and speeding up the rate of decomposition so that nutrients can be reabsorbed by roots.

Many herbivores can fit their life cycle into a year, but different species choose to overwinter in different stages. Aphids generally overwinter as eggs, then go through a series of asexual and sexual reproduction stages during the summer. Other herbivores cannot fit their life cycle into a year because they cannot grow fast enough, and they overwinter as larvae. An extreme example is the tussock moth (*Gynaephora groenlandicum*), whose life cycle can take many years. The moth actually spends most of this time as a caterpillar, feeding only on young willow buds and leaves during a short period in early summer. The caterpillars run a high risk of parasitism by flies or ichneumons, so they find refuge in vegetation and leaf litter for the remainder of the growing season and winter. The short pupal and adult stages are compressed into the last summer of the moth's life cycle.

Fig. 4 Two individuals of the rare arctic tiger moth (*Acerbia alpina*). They are mating. Herschel Island is one of two sites in western Canada where this species has been found. *Photo by Colin Gordon.*

The "woolly-bear" caterpillars of arctiid (tiger) moths benefit from their dark colour and hairy coats, which together absorb and retain heat from the sun. This heat retention gives them the energy to be active at temperatures that otherwise would be too cold (Fig. 2). Even the silken, fluffy cocoons they weave act as mini-greenhouses to speed up their development to the adult stage (Fig. 3). Herschel Island is one of only two places in Canada (the other site is in the Mackenzie Mountains, far to the south) where biologists have found the arctic tiger moth (*Acerbia alpina*) (Fig. 4).

A number of other easy-to-see species on Herschel Island are also remarkably hairy, including adult butterflies and bees (Fig. 5). One can find bumblebees actively exploring flowers on cool, foggy days when virtually no other insects are moving. These large bees search out sheltered cavities, such as lemming burrows, in which to build their hives. These consist of just a few chambers with sweet liquid and pollen to sustain a small number of young.

It is the above-ground carnivorous invertebrates (black flies and mosquitoes) that are usually most interesting—or horrifying—to people. These invertebrates feed on blood and emerge in frenzied swarms on hot summer days. Some larger mosquitoes emerge very early in summer after overwintering as adults. Other species overwinter as eggs, then develop in standing water through the larval stages to emerge as adults later in summer. However, only adult female mosquitoes seek out a blood meal, in order to promote the rapid development of their eggs.

In fact a relatively high proportion of Beringian black fly species do not feed on blood at all. Their aquatic larvae feed on algae, and adults use these larval food reserves in their bodies to produce eggs.

Flight is common to the adult stage of many invertebrates, and is often necessary for finding mates, food, and suitable sites to start the next stage (most often eggs) in the life cycle. But flight requires the energy to develop wings and use them, and the weather is not always warm enough. For some species, including some Beringian black flies, the investment is not worth the cost, so flightless adults have evolved. Flightless forms of some species are quite common on small islands, since a flight in the almost incessant arctic wind might mean a quick trip out to sea for weak fliers. Biologist Benoit Godin has identified flightless species of rove beetles from our Herschel collections.

Fig. 5 A bumblebee gathers nectar from a willow flower in spring. Note the dark body colour for absorbing energy from the sunlight, and the hairy coat for trapping warm air close to the body. *Photo by Alice Kenney.*

Fig. 6 A sow bug (*Mesidotea entomon*), washed up on the beach at Simpson Point. *Photo by Fritz Mueller.*

Invertebrates in the Arctic deal with the inevitability of freezing temperatures through either freeze-avoidance or freeze-tolerance. With both strategies, they make antifreeze alcohols and proteins to lower the freezing point of their tissues. Freeze-avoiding invertebrates try to eliminate all chemicals or other structures from their bodies that might act as a nucleus for crystal formation in their tissues, and then allow their tissues to super-cool. This strategy may not work below -20°C and can result in high death rates, but organisms that live in the soil and have reasonable snow cover to insulate them usually survive. The other strategy, freeze-tolerance, is common in invertebrates that live on the surface and allows them to survive at lower temperatures. These invertebrates move the potential nuclei on which ice crystals form in their bodies to the spaces between cells, where any freezing that does occur will not burst the cells. They also avoid crystal development inside the cells with antifreeze chemicals.

More marine invertebrate species have been collected around Herschel Island than in other parts of the southern Beaufort Sea. The large carcasses of one such species—the sow bug (*Mesidotea entomon*) (Fig. 6)—readily catch the attention of many visitors strolling the Herschel shoreline. Sow bugs are isopod crustaceans that have heavily armoured bodies flattened top to bottom. Live specimens of this ravenous scavenger are visible swimming in the sea close to shore. In spring 2009, Herschel Island Park rangers used these scavenging abilities to clean the head of a muskox that they wanted as a specimen and that had died during the winter. They immersed the head offshore and employed these isopods, along with other marine crustaceans such as pink-coloured amphipods (small crustaceans with curved bodies flattened side-to-side), to remove the flesh from the skull. These isopods and amphipods, in turn, are food for char, cisco, and other fish that commonly feed in Pauline Cove.

Invertebrates are an easily overlooked but very influential component of the tundra food web. They enhance the rate of decomposition, which is particularly slow in tundra environments, and eat much of the annual plant growth. In doing so they convert the plants' energy and nutrients into their own bodies, which then become relatively nitrogen-rich, high-energy packets of food for numerous birds. If you watch a bird on the tundra in late June or early July, the chances are it will quickly find a spider, beetle, crane fly, or caterpillar, often taking its catch straight to the nest to feed its rapidly growing nestlings. The fast growth of young birds, ranging in size from Lapland Longspurs through Rock Ptarmigan to Sandhill Cranes, is fuelled by the huge numbers of tundra invertebrates that emerge when temperatures are right in early summer. As the young birds leave their nests, the tundra flowers reach full bloom, inviting the nectar-feeding bees, flies, mosquitoes, butterflies, and moths to pollinate them. These adult invertebrates will eventually lay eggs in their turn, starting the cycle that is such an essential part of the Arctic web of life all over again.

COMMON NAME	LATIN NAME
Nematode worms	**Nematoda**
Isopod crustaceans	**Isopoda**
Amphipod crustaceans	**Amphipoda**
Springtails	**Colembola**
Mayflies	**Ephemeroptera**
Stoneflies	**Plecoptera**
Thrips	**Thysanoptera**
Bugs	**Hemiptera**
Leaf or plant bugs	Miridae
Shore bugs	Saldidae
Aphids and hoppers	**Homoptera**
Pine and spruce aphids	Adelgidae
Aphids	Aphididae
Leafhoppers	Cicadellidae
Delphacid planthoppers	Delphacidae
Woolly and gall-making aphids	Eriosomatidae
Mealybugs	Pseudococcidae
Psyllids	Psyllidae
Lacewings	**Neuroptera**
Green lacewings	Chrysopidae
Beetles	**Coleoptera**
Pill beetles	Byrrhidae
Ground beetles	Carabidae
Leaf beetles	Chrysomelidae
Checkered beetles	Cleridae
Lady bird beetles	Coccinelidae
Snout beetles	Curculionidae
Predaceous diving beetles	Dytiscidae
Handsome fungus beetles	Endomychidae
Minute brown scavenger beetles	Lathridiidae
Round fungus beetles	Leiodidae
Rove beetles	Staphylinidae
Twisted-winged parasites	**Strepsiptera**
Halictophagids	Halictophagidae

COMMON NAME	LATIN NAME
Scorpionflies	**Mecoptera**
Caddisflies	**Trichoptera**
Butterflies and moths	**Lepidoptera**
Tiger moths	Arctiidae
Gossamer-winged butterflies	Lycaenidae
Tussock moths	Lymantriidae
Noctuid moths	Noctuidae
Flies	**Diptera**
Leaf miner flies	Agromyzidae
Anthomyiid flies	Anthomyiidae
March flies	Bibionidae
Blow flies	Calliphoridae
Gall gnats	Cecidomyiidae
Biting midges	Ceratopogonidae
Midges	Chironomidae
Fruit flies	Chloropidae
Mosquitoes	Culicidae
Long-legged flies	Dolichopodidae
Dance flies	Empididae
Shore flies	Ephydridae
Heleomyzid flies	Heleomyzidae
Milichiid flies	Milichiidae
Muscid flies	Muscidae
Fungus gnats	Mycetophilidae
Bot and warble flies	Oestridae
Humpbacked flies	Phoridae
Skipper flies	Piophilidae
Moth and sand flies	Psychodidae
Snipe flies	Rhagionidae
Dung flies	Scatophagidae
Minute black scavenger flies	Scatopsidae
Dark-winged fungus gnats	Sciaridae
Marsh flies	Sciomyzidae
Black scavenger flies	Sepsidae
Black flies	Simuliidae
Small dung flies	Sphaeroceridae
Syrphid flies	Syrphidae
Tachinid flies	Tachinidae
Crane flies	Tipulidae
Winter crane flies	Trichoceridae

COMMON NAME	LATIN NAME
Bees and wasps	**Hymenoptera**
Bees	Apidae
Braconids	Braconidae
Ceraphronids	Ceraphronidae
Chalcids	Chalcidoidea
Diapriids	Diapriidae
Encrytids	Encrytidae
Gall wasps	Eucoilidae
Eulophids	Eulophidae
Ichneumons	Ichneumonidae
Megaspilids	Megaspilidae
Fairyflies	Mymaridae
Platygasterids	Platygasteridae
Proctotrupids	Proctotrupidae
Pteromalids	Pteromalidae
Common sawflies	Tenthredinidae
Vespoid wasps	Vespoidea
Spiders	**Araneae**
Mites	**Acarina**
Terrestrial slugs	**Stylommatophora**
Limacid slugs	Limacidae

Table 1 Invertebrate Families trapped on Herschel Island in summers 2007 and 2008, or referred to in the text. These are arranged by taxonomic Order (bold) and Family, except the Phylum Nematoda. *The invertebrates were identified by Élise Bolduc, Hirondelle Varady-Szabo, and Samuel Pinna.*

BUTTERFLIES

Maria Leung

Herschel Island is in the part of the North American tundra that has the largest number of butterfly species. Before 2006, fifteen species of butterflies (**saqalikitaaq** or **haqalukihaq**) had been documented from Qikiqtaryuk, with records dating back to 1916. Several of these species, including the Arctic Fritillary (*Boloria chariclea*) (Fig. 1), Polaris Fritillary (*Boloria polaris*), Hecla Sulphur (*Colias hecla*) (Fig. 2), Labrador Sulphur (*Colias nastes*), and Polixenes Arctic (*Oeneis polixenes*), are typical tundra butterflies.

Butterflies have complex life cycles that involve several transformations. They begin as eggs, from which tiny larvae hatch. The larvae, also known as caterpillars, grow and moult up to six times before hardening into chrysalises from which adult butterflies emerge. The life stage that overwinters depends on the species, but may be the egg, larva, chrysalis, or adult. In the Arctic, it is the larvae that most commonly overwinter. They survive by releasing antifreeze compounds such as sorbitol and propylene glycol into their bodies as freezing begins. Some northern butterflies cope with limiting temperatures and short growing seasons by taking two years to develop from egg to adult, instead of one.

Adults of some species tolerate sub-zero temperatures for several days in spring and summer while waiting for more favourable conditions in which to feed and find mates.

The timing of egg-laying depends on the life history of the species, spanning early to late summer. On Herschel Island, the Northern Blue (*Plebejus idas*) is among the last of the species to emerge each year. Eggs of this species are laid relatively late and are left over winter. In general, adult butterflies lay eggs close to or on the plants that the larvae will feed upon. Such plants are known as "host plants" and are specific to each species, but may differ slightly depending on the region. For example, the larvae of the Dingy Fritillary (*Boloria improba*) (Fig. 3) feed on dwarf willows in Europe, so it is probable that they feed on willows at Herschel Island. In contrast, adult butterflies do not exhibit strong preferences for particular plant species and will feed on the nectar of many different flowering plants. Adults can also be found drinking from nutrient-rich mud puddles.

Fritillary butterflies at Herschel Island. *Photo by Clara Reid.*

Fritillary butterfly, probably an Arctic Fritillary, at Herschel Island in July 2008. *Photo by Fritz Mueller.*

Fig. 2 Hecla Sulphur (*Colias hecla*) at Herschel Island in July 2008.
Photo by Fritz Mueller.

Fig. 1 Arctic Fritillary (*Boloria chariclea*) at Herschel Island in July 2009.
Photo by Maria Leung.

Butterfly surveys in the early summers of 2007 to 2009 detected six species not previously recorded on Herschel Island. Three of the new species found during the recent surveys are the Mourning Cloak (*Nymphalis antiopa*), Compton Tortoiseshell (*Nymphalis l-album*), and Western White (*Pontia occidentalis*) (Fig. 4). The Mourning Cloak and Compton Tortoiseshell belong to a group of butterflies that hibernate as adults and are not common north of the Yukon coast. Sightings of Mourning Cloaks in late summer 2007 and early summer 2008 suggest that they overwinter on Herschel Island. However, the Compton Tortoiseshell may have been a vagrant as it was only seen once. Among the species known to Herschel Island and recorded again during 2007 to 2009 is Booth's Sulphur (*Colias tyche*), a species thought by some to be a hybrid of the Hecla Sulphur (Fig. 2) with the Labrador Sulphur. Hecla Sulphur males reflect ultraviolet light, whereas Labrador Sulphur males absorb ultraviolet light. Females of these species may use this difference to distinguish mates, and it is possible that foggy conditions may impair the females' vision and lead to hybrid offspring. Such chance hybridization may explain why Booth's Sulphurs are far less common than either Hecla or Labrador Sulphurs on Herschel Island.

Fig. 3 Dingy Fritillary (*Boloria improba*) at Herschel Island in July 2009.
Photo by Maria Leung.

Fig. 4 Western White (*Pontia occidentalis*) at Herschel Island in July 2009.
Photo by Maria Leung.

Fig. 5 Four-dotted Alpine (*Erebia youngi*) at Herschel Island in July 2009. The subspecies *herscheli* is only found on Herschel Island and the adjacent mainland.
Photo by Maria Leung.

The number of butterflies visible is strongly associated with air temperature, as few adult butterflies actively feed and fly when it is below 8°C. Conditions were much warmer in early summer 2008 than at the same time in 2009. This difference explains why there were five times as many butterflies counted at Collinson Head in July 2008 as in July 2009. The maturity of individual butterflies was also noticeably more advanced in 2008 compared to 2007 and 2009. The early emerging species such as the Alpines (*Erebia* spp.) (Figs 5 and 6) were waning, and more of the later emerging species, such as the Hecla Sulphur and Alaskan Fritillary (*Boloria alaskensis*), were seen.

The greatest butterfly activity on the island in early summer occurs in areas vegetated by willows, especially in dry tundra areas where vetch, lupine, and other flowers also grow. The abundance of butterflies in these areas is due both to the presence of plant species upon which larvae feed, and the many opportunities to sip nectar from the rich diversity of flowers found in these vegetation types. Most butterfly species were found in this type of habitat, although the Banded Alpine (*Erebia fasciata*) (Fig. 6) had a preference for moist areas with sedges, grasses, and mosses. The specific larval plant food for this species is unknown, but it is likely to be grasses or sedges, as for many other Alpines.

Butterflies are good indicators of climate change because they are short-lived, highly visible, and can respond relatively rapidly to changes in habitat conditions. There are well-documented range shifts of butterflies associated with regional warming elsewhere, such as in Britain. The butterfly database established for Herschel Island, and the observed differences in butterfly numbers and types in warm and cold spring weather from 2007 to 2009, provide a good starting point to monitor such patterns of change.

Fig. 6 Banded Alpine (*Erebia fasciata*) at Herschel Island in July 2009.
Photo by Maria Leung.

COMMON NAME	LATIN NAME
Swallowtails	**Papilionidae**
Old World Swallowtail	*Papilio machaon*
Whites and Sulphurs	**Pieridae**
Canada Sulphur	*Colias canadensis*
Hecla Sulphur	*Colias hecla*
Labrador Sulphur	*Colias nastes*
Palaeno Sulphur	*Colias palaeno*
Booth's Sulphur	*Colias tyche*
Western White	*Pontia occidentalis*
Gossamerwings	**Lycaenidae**
Little Copper	*Lycaena phlaeas*
Northern Blue	*Plebejus idas*
Brushfoots	**Nymphalidae**
Alaskan Fritillary	*Boloria alaskensis*
Arctic Fritillary	*Boloria chariclea*
Frigga Fritillary	*Boloria frigga*
Dingy Fritillary	*Boloria improba*
Polaris Fritillary	*Boloria polaris*
Mourning Cloak	*Nymphalis antiopa*
Compton Tortoiseshell	*Nymphalis l-album*
Banded Alpine	*Erebia fasciata*
Ross's Alpine	*Erebia rossii*
Four-dotted Alpine	*Erebia youngi*
Melissa Arctic	*Oeneis melissa*
Polixenes Arctic	*Oeneis polixenes*

Table 1 Butterflies found on Herschel Island. Family names are given in bold. *Latin names follow NatureServe (www.natureserve.org/explorer).*

BIRDS

Cameron D. Eckert

On Herschel Island, the winter sun disappears below the horizon on November 29 and isn't seen again for another 48 days. The island itself is barely discernible in the snow- and ice-bound expanse of the Beaufort Sea. During this long harsh season, there are few birds to be found on the island. Small coveys of Rock Ptarmigan or **Nikhaaktungiq** (Fig. 1) survive by roosting in the snow and feeding on wind-swept exposures. An occasional passing Gyrfalcon or **Kidjgavik** finds little in the way of prey and keeps moving in search of better hunting on the mainland.

The light returns rapidly in January, though winter will not loosen its grip on the island for another three months. Mid-April marks the beginning of spring migration with the arrival of the first Snow Buntings or **Amauligaruk** (Fig. 2) and Common Ravens or **Tulugaq**. Snowy Owls or **Ukpik** are also seen at this time, likely returning from nearby wintering locations. By late April, the first Rough-legged Hawks or **Qilriq** and Peregrine Falcons or **Kir̂gavik** return to their nesting cliffs around the island, though actual nesting won't begin for weeks.

Spring Migration

In May temperatures rise considerably, expansive leads open up in the sea ice, and meltwater pools form. Spring migration is now in full swing, with birds on the move and new arrivals every day.

Fig. 2 Snow Bunting or Amauligaruk (*Plectrophenax nivalis*). *Photo by Cameron Eckert.*

Fig. 3 Common Eider or Amaolik (*Somateria mollissima*). *Photo by Cameron Eckert.*

Common Eiders or **Amaolik** (Fig. 3) and, less commonly, King Eiders or **Qingalik** following open leads on their eastward migration, appear in the first week of May, with numbers peaking by mid-May. Flock sizes are generally small, usually not more than 80 to 90 birds. The King Eiders will continue northeast to their more northerly nesting grounds, while at least some of the Common Eiders will remain at Qikiqtaryuk to nest. During spring migration, eiders are vulnerable to sea-ice conditions, and in some years

Fig. 1 Rock Ptarmigan or Nikhaaktungiq (*Lagopus mutus*) in winter plumage. *Photo by Alice Kenney.*

Black Guillemots or Atpa (*Cepphus grylle*) in Thetis Bay. *Photo by Michael Kawerninski.*

Fig. 6 Glaucous Gull or Nauyaq (*Larus hyperboreus*). *Photo by Cameron Eckert.*

Fig. 4 Sandhill Crane or Tatiṛgaq (*Grus canadensis*). *Photo by Cameron Eckert.*

flocks may die when the leads in the sea ice close. In May 1990, Herschel Island rangers found 17 King Eiders that had died because of closed leads.

Despite the lack of ice-free shoreline at Pauline Cove in early May, the snow has disappeared from large areas of tundra. The first migrant geese arrive in early May—flocks of Brant or **Nirlivniq** as well as Greater White-fronted or **Nirliq** and Snow geese or **Kanguq**, sometimes numbering upward of 100–200 birds. They continue arriving through the month, along with small flocks of Canada geese. By the second week of May, Sandhill Cranes or **Tatiṛgaq** (Fig. 4) and Tundra Swans or **Qugȓuk** (Fig. 5) appear, as well as a variety of dabbling ducks such as American Wigeon or **Uhiuhuq**, Green-winged Teal or **Kurugaruq**, Mallard or **Kurukgakpuk**, Northern Pintail or **Kuȓugaq**, and

Northern Shoveler, though none in significant numbers. Small numbers of cranes, swans, Snow and Canada geese or **Uluagullik**, and Brant, along with the various dabbling ducks, will remain to nest on Herschel.

The first Glaucous Gulls or **Nauyaq** (Fig. 6), returning in early May, take advantage of the casualties of winter. A dead caribou, wolf, or even bear provides a welcome meal for these keen scavengers.

A few pairs of Glaucous Gulls nest on the island's beaches and spits. A small flock of non-breeding Glaucous Gulls, and in recent years a lone Glaucous-winged Gull, loaf at Pauline Cove through the summer, eating fish scraps or making the rounds to any dead seals or whales that may be in the area. Pure Herring Gulls are fairly rare at Herschel Island, though hybrid

Glaucous crossed with Herring gulls are relatively common throughout the Beaufort Sea region.

Shorebird migration peaks during mid- to late May when Pauline Cove is still ice-covered, though ponds and marshes have opened up, offering feeding habitat. While shorebird numbers are not high, the diversity is impressive, with a parade of Arctic breeders that includes American Golden-Plover (Fig. 7), Black-bellied and Semipalmated plovers (Fig. 8), Whimbrel, and Semipalmated, Baird's, Pectoral, and Stilt sandpipers, as well as Long-billed Dowitchers (Fig. 9) and Red-necked and Red phalaropes (Fig. 10). The distances these birds have travelled are astounding. For the Semipalmated Sandpiper, a small shorebird weighing just 25 grams, its spring flight from a location such as Ecuador represents

Fig. 5 Tundra Swan or Qugȓuk (*Cygnus columbianus*). *Photo by Cameron Eckert.*

Fig. 10 Red Phalarope or Aukruaq (*Phalaropus fulicarius*). *Photo by Cameron Eckert.*

a distance of over 9,000 kilometres. A Buff-breasted Sandpiper will have flown over 13,000 kilometres from its wintering grounds in Argentina to Qikiqtaryuk. The challenges these birds face are extraordinary, and the survival of shorebird populations requires the conservation of breeding, migration, and wintering habitats. However, the populations of many North American shorebird species are declining seriously. This includes breeders and migrants that come to Herschel Island, such as American Golden-Plover, Ruddy Turnstone or **Taliruq**, Semipalmated Sandpiper, and Red-necked and Red phalaropes. Protected areas like Herschel Island play an essential role in shorebird conservation.

The end of spring migration often brings unusual wanderers to the island. Visitors from the south in the past have included Yellow and Yellow-rumped warblers, White-throated and Harris's sparrows, and Rusty and Red-winged blackbirds. Vagrants from the Bering Sea region, venturing upward of 1,000 kilometres beyond their range, have included Red-necked Stint, McKay's Bunting, and Whooper Swan.

Summer Nesting Season

The breeding season is short at Qikiqtaryuk, and by early June most species have turned their energies to nesting (Fig. 11). American Golden-Plovers (Fig. 7), Horned Larks, Lapland Longspurs or **Putukeluk** (Fig. 12), and Snow Buntings animate the landscape with their spectacular songs and aerial displays. In the evenings a low, cooing "hoo hoo," reminiscent of a dove, drifts across the ice at Pauline Cove. This haunting sound is the courtship call of the male Common Eider, given as he throws his head back and points his bill to the sky. Later in the evening, as activity in the cove quietens down, the female Common Eider ventures onto land to mate and scout out suitable nest sites. In the coming days she will build her nest of eider down, hidden between deep tussocks or low shrubs, or positioned right up against one of the settlement buildings. Her only defense against predation is camouflage, and she will sit tight on the nest until the point at which a predator literally stands over her. By mid-June she will be sitting on eggs, and by early to mid-July the first chicks will hatch. The female and her brood will then move to the ocean to spend the remainder of the summer and early fall feeding in the nearshore waters.

Fig. 7 American Golden-Plover or Siuktavak (*Pluvialis dominica*). *Photo by Cameron Eckert.*

Fig. 8 Semipalmated Plover or Taliviak (*Charadrius semipalmatus*). *Photo by Cameron Eckert.*

Fig. 9 Long-billed Dowitcher or Kilatallik (*Limnodromus scolopaceus*). *Photo by Cameron Eckert.*

Fig. 11 Nest of Greater White-fronted Goose or Nirliq (*Anser albifrons*). *Photo by Fritz Mueller.*

Jaegers are true seabirds that spend their lives at sea, only coming to land to nest. Their migration is largely offshore, with Long-tailed Jaegers or **Isungaq** (Fig. 13) travelling from wintering areas in the South Atlantic off South America, and Pomarine or **Ihunngaq** and Parasitic jaegers coming from the South Atlantic off Africa. All three jaeger species migrate past Qikiqtaryuk from the third week of May through early June, with the Long-tailed regularly remaining to nest, and the Parasitic being a rare breeder on the island. During the nesting season, the Long-tailed Jaeger adopts a somewhat raptor-like lifestyle, preying on small mammals and birds. Its minimalist nest is much like that of a shorebird, being nothing more than a sparsely lined depression in the tundra. The first eggs are laid in early June and will hatch about 25 days later. These enthusiastic nest defenders will aggressively attack all unwanted intruders. In years when small mammal populations are low, they will downgrade their diet to insects and spiders and may forego nesting altogether.

The Lapland Longspur (Fig. 12), the island's most common nesting bird, returns in early May. By the end of the month, nests have been built and females are sitting on eggs. Their ground nests are a tight weave of grasses, invariably lined with ptarmigan feathers and positioned against the side of a tussock or driftwood log for predator and thermal cover. They usually have a southerly exposure to further ensure warmth. The young will begin to fledge by the end of June, even before they can fly, preferring to scuttle for cover at the approach of a predator rather than remain in the nest. Savannah Sparrows also nest in tundra habitats, in areas where low sparse shrub cover provides singing perches for the males and cover for the nests.

The island's rather limited dense shrubby habitats are inhabited by Common and Hoary redpolls. Like the longspurs, they build well-insulated nests of grasses and feathers with a southerly exposure, usually in shrubs or in the larger driftwood logs along the shoreline. The Snow Bunting (Fig. 2), by contrast, is a cavity nester, and what better place to find suitable nest holes than in the community buildings around Pauline Cove? Nest building begins in mid- to late May, and by mid-June adults are packing beak-loads of insects to the nest to feed hungry young. The first fledglings venture out of the nest in early July.

American Pipits and Horned Larks are somewhat less widespread than the longspurs, with the pipits preferring the sloping tundra around the margins of the island, and the larks nesting on the driest tundra habitat. Common Ravens would probably not nest on the island if it were not for the tall navigation towers along Workboat Passage. In recent years, ravens have used the large stick nests on the towers, likely first built by Rough-legged Hawks.

Shorebird species share some aspects of their life histories. For example, the nests of most are barely more than a depression in the sand or sedge, lightly lined with lichens, and usually just four eggs are laid. However, each species has its own specific habitat requirements for nesting. American Golden-Plovers seek out the drier patches of upland tundra, while Semipalmated Plovers nest on the gravel and sand flats of Simpson Point and Avadlek Spit.

Fig. 12 Lapland Longspur or Putukeluk (*Calcarius lapponicus*): *left* male in breeding plumage; *right* immature. *Photos by Cameron Eckert.*

Semipalmated Sandpipers nest in the moister lowland tundra, and Red-necked Phalaropes prefer even wetter sedge habitat at the edges of ponds.

One nesting shorebird, the Ruddy Turnstone, has apparently disappeared from Herschel Island. Twenty years ago this species was known as an uncommon nester and a fairly common migrant. In recent years no nesting birds have been found, and turnstones are only rarely seen on migration. While habitat change is underway on the island—for example, the recent proliferation of polargrass (*Arctagrostis latifolia*)—this would not likely account for the disappearance of the turnstones. The continent-wide declines experienced by this species seem to have reached Herschel Island.

Predation by arctic and red foxes is one of the major causes of nesting failure for the many ground-nesting birds at Qikiqtaryuk. Camouflage, distraction displays, and mobbing provide some defence if a fox wanders close to a nest. Even so, the foxes are persistent and, during their late evening forays, will plunder many nests. Summer is short, with only just enough time

Fig. 13 Long-tailed Jaeger or Isungaq (*Stercorarius longicaudus*). *Photo by Cameron Eckert.*

to nest and rear young before the weather starts to turn. There is no allowance for second chances, and a failed nesting attempt means the end of the breeding season for most birds. By late June, small flocks of failed or non-breeding shorebirds feed along the edges of ponds and will soon leave the island to begin their southward migration.

The Black Guillemot or **Atpa** (Fig. 14), a striking black and white seabird with brilliant red legs, does not return to the island in some years until mid-June.

For the guillemots, nesting can apparently wait until there is at least some open water around Pauline Cove. This species, a cavity nester, uses the historic Anglican mission house at Pauline Cove, which has an abundance of cavities along with an array of nest boxes put up in the mid-1980s. Twenty years ago the colony numbered over 100 adults; since then the population has declined to about 60 adults. While we don't know the cause, climate change is altering the ocean environment and is almost certainly affecting the productivity of many marine species.

The guillemots lay their eggs, usually just one or two, in late June, and after an incubation period of about 30 days the chicks hatch in August. In recent years these birds appear to be nesting later in the summer. For example, in 1994–2001, many chicks had hatched by 19 July to 1 August; yet in 2005, no chicks had hatched by 28 July. Once the chicks hatch, the adults are busy making trips to sea to feed their hungry young. They bring back Arctic Cod, their preferred prey (Fig. 14), and Sculpin, an abundant but less palatable fish, along with a variety of other species such as Arctic Lamprey, Slender Eelblenny, Eelpout, and Capelin, all of which are fed whole to their chicks.

Fig. 14 Black Guillemot carrying an Arctic Cod. *Photo by Cameron Eckert.*

The maniacal cackle of the Red-throated Loon or **Qaqȓauq** is one of the characteristic sounds of summer at Qikiqtaryuk. It nests on small fish-less ponds and marshes on the island and flies out to the ocean to feed. A pair of Red-throated Loons nested in the small marsh at Pauline Cove over a number of seasons, but has not been there recently. Pacific Loons (**Maliriq**) also regularly occur in summer, though their nesting status on the island is uncertain. Common and Yellow-billed loons (**Tulik**) both visit the waters around the island, but are not known to nest on Qikiqtaryuk.

Sandhill Cranes (Fig. 4) are not numerous on Herschel Island, but with their loud vibrant calls and spirited breeding displays, they do not go unnoticed. A few pairs nest each summer in open wetland meadows or wetter tundra habitats along creeks. Following their arrival in early May, the cranes are sitting on eggs by early June, with the first young hatching by the third week of June. Sandhill Cranes have borrowed a trick from the plovers, producing a very convincing broken wing display when intruders approach a nest too closely. Later in summer and fall, small flocks of cranes—local breeders as well as migrants—feed on the wetland flats in preparation for their long trip south.

The summer passes quickly, and by mid-July the chorus of bird song has long since faded. It's replaced by the begging cries of young and the flight calls of southbound migrant shorebirds. During this period of frenetic nesting activity, the ice disappears from the waters of Pauline Cove and Workboat Passage, and Surf and White-winged scoters or **Taakłagȓuaq** and Long-tailed Ducks or **Ahaanliq** (Fig. 15) arrive in the thousands. These sea ducks do not come to the island to nest, but rather to take advantage of a safe haven and rich feeding while they undergo their summer moult. They will spend the rest of the summer here, eventually departing on a new set of flight feathers in early to mid-September.

Fall Migration

By August the nesting season is all but finished for most species and fall migration is well underway.

Large flocks of migrant Lapland Longspurs and American Pipits, numbering in the many hundreds, feed in the meadows and among driftwood along the beaches. Juvenile shorebirds are also on the move, and each day the island's marshes and beaches host small flocks of American Golden-Plovers (Fig. 7), Semipalmated Plovers (Fig. 8), Pectoral, Baird's, and Semipalmated sandpipers, and Long-billed Dowitchers (Fig. 9). There is also the occasional Black-bellied Plover, Western Sandpiper, Sanderling, or Dunlin. Likewise, small flocks of Red-necked and a few Red phalaropes (Fig. 10) feed in the ponds and near the cobble shoreline. The Long-tailed Jaegers (Fig. 13) that nested on Qikiqtaryuk depart by mid-August, returning to their seafaring life for another nine months. The geese are on the move again, with large flocks of Greater White-fronted, Snow, and Brant geese passing by the island, occasionally touching down to feed and rest. This is also a time when unexpected species appear on the island. In late July 1991 a juvenile Ross's Gull arrived, while in August

Fig. 15 Long-tailed Ducks or Ahaanliq (*Clangula hyemalis*) taking off from the water in Workboat Passage. *Photo by Michael Kawerninski.*

Fig. 16 Arctic Tern or Mitqutailaq (*Sterna paradisaea*). *Photo by Michael Kawerninski.*

1996 a string of rarities appeared, with an Eastern Yellow Wagtail followed by a Wood Sandpiper from Eurasia, and then a Yellow-headed Blackbird from southern Canada.

The migrant songbirds and shorebirds do not go unnoticed by birds of prey. Peregrine Falcons make forays from their nesting cliffs to hunt shorebirds at Pauline Cove. Merlins, which do not nest on the island, often appear in mid-August, no doubt attracted by the abundance of prey. These small falcons display extraordinary speed and agility, powering through a flock of pipits and easily snatching one of the fleeing songbirds from the air. An occasional roving Gyrfalcon, looking massive in comparison to the Merlin, puts the waterbirds and ptarmigan in a state of high alert.

Bird numbers dwindle quickly through late August and September. A juvenile Northern Shrike, off-track from its southbound migration, might spend a few days on the island fuelling up on voles or songbirds. An occasional

Arctic Tern or **Mitqutailaq** (Fig. 16), Parasitic Jaeger, or Pomarine Jaeger cruises the shoreline, migrating west along the coast. The first dusting of snow and hard freeze in early September sends the last shorebirds, pipits, and longspurs on their way. The adult Snowy Owls that nest on the island remain until mid-September, when their own innate estimates of prey densities tell them it's time to move on. The adults may spend the winter nearby in the Firth River valley or the northern Ogilvie Mountains of central Yukon, while the juveniles will likely travel further south.

The last of the juvenile Snow Buntings, feeding on the grasses still poking above the snow, finally depart as winter conditions deepen. Activity at the Black Guillemot colony continues through mid-September as the latest of the nestlings, now grown to near-adult size, fledge and touch the waters of the Beaufort Sea for the first time. The guillemots linger in the waters around Pauline Cove until freeze-up forces them ever further

out into the Beaufort Sea. Eventually they will head northwest to winter in the polynyas (open-water areas) of the Arctic Ocean. Infrequent flocks of migrating eiders move northwest past the island during early October to their wintering areas in the Bering Sea. In early November, a Common Raven looking for a winter home circles Pauline Cove to check for signs of life; seeing nothing, it continues southeast to the Mackenzie Delta. Winter has returned.

COMMON NAME	LATIN NAME	INUVIALUKTUN NAME
Geese, Swans, and Ducks	**Anatidae**	
Greater White-fronted Goose	*Anser albifrons*	Niglik (S), Nirliq (U)
Snow Goose	*Chen caerulescens*	Kanguq (S, U)
Brant	*Branta bernicla*	Niglignak (S), Nirlirnaq (U)
Canada Goose	*Branta canadensis*	Uluagullik (S, U)
Tundra Swan	*Cygnus columbianus*	Qugyuq (S), Qugȓuk (U)
Whooper Swan	*Cygnus cygnus*	
American Wigeon	*Anas americana*	Ugguigik (S, U)
Mallard	*Anas platyrhynchos*	Kurugakpak (S, U)
Northern Shoveler	*Anas clypeata*	Kuluarpak (S, U)
Northern Pintail	*Anas acuta*	Kuȓugaq (S, U)
Green-winged Teal	*Anas crecca*	Saviligaaluk (S, U)
Greater Scaup	*Aythya marila*	Qaqtuatug (S, U)
Lesser Scaup	*Aythya affinis*	Nunagelak (S)
King Eider	*Somateria spectabilis*	Qingalik (S, U)
Common Eider	*Somateria mollissima*	Amaolik (S, U)
Harlequin Duck	*Histrionicus histrionicus*	
Surf Scoter	*Melanitta perspicillata*	
White-winged Scoter	*Melanitta fusca*	Taakȓagȓuaq (S, U)
Black Scoter	*Melanitta nigra*	Taakruaq (S, U)
Long-tailed Duck	*Clangula hyemalis*	Ahaanliq
Common Goldeneye	*Bucephala clangula*	Aviluqtuq
Red-breasted Merganser	*Mergus serrator*	Arparsayoayoq (S)
Common Merganser	*Mergus merganser*	

COMMON NAME	LATIN NAME	INUVIALUKTUN NAME
Grouse and Ptarmigan	**Phasianidae**	
Willow Ptarmigan	*Lagopus lagopus*	Aqidjigiq (S), Qaȓgiq (U)
Rock Ptarmigan	*Lagopus mutus*	Nikhaaktungiq (S, U)
Loons	**Gaviidae**	
Red-throated Loon	*Gavia stellata*	Maligik (S), Qaqȓauq (U)
Pacific Loon	*Gavia pacifica*	Maliri
Common Loon	*Gavia immer*	Tuuliik
Yellow-billed Loon	*Gavia adamsii*	Qaqsauq (S, U)
Grebes	**Podicipedidae**	
Horned Grebe	*Podiceps auritus*	Pairaaluk (S), Sorolatsiak (U)
Red-necked Grebe	*Podiceps grisegena*	Paiqłuk (S), Soroleq (U)

Table continues on following page.

Table 1 Birds of Herschel Island Territorial Park. Species are arranged taxonomically according to the American Ornithologists' Union, with Family names in bold. *Inuvialuktun (Siglitun and Uummarmiutun) names are from A.E. Porsild, Birds of the Mackenzie Delta, The Canadian Field-Naturalist (1943), and P.H. Sinclair et al. (ed.) The Birds of the Yukon Territory (2003).*

Birds of Herschel Island Territorial Park, continued

COMMON NAME	LATIN NAME	INUVIALUKTUN NAME
Hawks and Eagles	**Accipitridae**	
Bald Eagle	*Haliaeetus leucocephalus*	Kilerak
Northern Harrier	*Circus cyaneus*	
Sharp-shinned Hawk	*Accipiter striatus*	
Rough-legged Hawk	*Buteo lagopus*	Qilrig (S, U)
Golden Eagle	*Aquila chrysaetos*	Tingmiakpak (S, U)
Falcons	**Falconidae**	
American Kestrel	*Falco sparverius*	
Merlin	*Falco columbarius*	
Gyrfalcon	*Falco rusticolus*	Kidjgavik
Peregrine Falcon	*Falco peregrinus*	Kidjgaviraraq (S), Kirgavik (U)
Cranes	**Gruidae**	
Sandhill Crane	*Grus canadensis*	Tatidjgaq (S), Tatiȓgaq (U)
Plovers	**Charadriidae**	
Black-bellied Plover	*Pluvialis squatarola*	
American Golden-Plover	*Pluvialis dominica*	Siuktavak
Semipalmated Plover	*Charadrius semipalmatus*	Taliviak
Sandpipers	**Scolopacidae**	
Lesser Yellowlegs	*Tringa flavipes*	
Wood Sandpiper	*Tringa glareola*	
Spotted Sandpiper	*Actitis macularia*	Tusatusaq
Whimbrel	*Numenius phaeopus*	
Hudsonian Godwit	*Limosa haemastica*	
Ruddy Turnstone	*Arenaria interpres*	
Sanderling	*Calidris alba*	
Semipalmated Sandpiper	*Calidris pusilla*	Livilivilaaluk (S), Livalivauȓaq (U)
Western Sandpiper	*Calidris mauri*	
Red-necked Stint	*Calidris ruficollis*	
Least Sandpiper	*Calidris minutilla*	
White-rumped Sandpiper	*Calidris fuscicollis*	
Baird's Sandpiper	*Calidris bairdii*	
Pectoral Sandpiper	*Calidris melanotos*	
Dunlin	*Calidris alpina*	
Stilt Sandpiper	*Calidris himantopus*	
Buff-breasted Sandpiper	*Tryngites subruficollis*	
Long-billed Dowitcher	*Limnodromus scolopaceus*	Kilatallik
Wilson's Snipe	*Gallinago delicata*	Aivaktayaq
Red-necked Phalarope	*Phalaropus lobatus*	Livalivauraq
Red Phalarope	*Phalaropus fulicarius*	Aukruaq
Gulls and Terns	**Laridae**	Nauyaq (S, U)
Bonaparte's Gull	*Larus philadelphia*	
Mew Gull	*Larus canus*	
Herring Gull	*Larus argentatus*	
Thayer's Gull	*Larus thayeri*	
Glaucous-winged Gull	*Larus glaucescens*	
Glaucous Gull	*Larus hyperboreus*	
Sabine's Gull	*Xema sabini*	
Black-legged Kittiwake	*Rissa tridactyla*	
Ross's Gull	*Rhodostethia rosea*	
Ivory Gull	*Pagophila eburnea*	
Arctic Tern	*Sterna paradisaea*	Mitqutailaq/Tekatekȓiaq
Skuas and Jaegers	**Stercorariidae**	
Pomarine Jaeger	*Stercorarius pomarinus*	Ihunngaq

COMMON NAME	LATIN NAME	INUVIALUKTUN NAME
Parasitic Jaeger	*Stercorarius parasiticus*	Isugnaq
Long-tailed Jaeger	*Stercorarius longicaudus*	Isugnaq
Auks and Murres	**Alcidae**	
Thick-billed Murre	*Uria lomvia*	
Black Guillemot	*Cepphus grylle*	Atpa
Owls	**Strigidae**	
Snowy Owl	*Bubo scandiaca*	Ukpik/Okpik
Northern Hawk Owl	*Surnia ulula*	Naiquqtuarȓuk
Short-eared Owl	*Asio flammeus*	Nipaiłuktaq (U)
Woodpeckers	**Picidae**	
Northern Flicker	*Colaptes auratus*	
Tyrant Flycatchers	**Tyrannidae**	
Say's Phoebe	*Sayornis saya*	
Shrikes	**Laniidae**	
Northern Shrike	*Lanius excubitor*	
Crows and Jays	**Corvidae**	
Common Raven	*Corvus corax*	Tulugaq
Larks	**Alaudidae**	
Horned Lark	*Eremophila alpestris*	
Swallows	**Hirundinidae**	
Tree Swallow	*Tachycineta bicolor*	
Bank Swallow	*Riparia riparia*	
Cliff Swallow	*Petrochelidon pyrrhonota*	
Barn Swallow	*Hirundo rustica*	
Thrushes	**Turdidae**	
Northern Wheatear	*Oenanthe oenanthe*	
American Robin	*Turdus migratorius*	Kuyapigaqturutin (S, U)
Varied Thrush	*Ixoreus naevius*	
Pipits and Wagtails	**Motacillidae**	
Eastern Yellow Wagtail	*Motacilla tschutschensis*	
American Pipit	*Anthus rubescens*	
Longspurs and Buntings	**Calcariidae**	
Lapland Longspur	*Calcarius lapponicus*	Putukeluk
Smith's Longspur	*Calcarius pictus*	
Snow Bunting	*Plectrophenax nivalis*	Amauligaruk (U)
McKay's Bunting	*Plectrophenax hyperboreus*	
Wood-Warblers	**Parulidae**	
Yellow Warbler	*Dendroica petechia*	
Yellow-rumped Warbler	*Dendroica coronata*	
Sparrows	**Emberizidae**	
American Tree Sparrow	*Spizella arborea*	Saksagaq
Savannah Sparrow	*Passerculus sandwichensis*	
White-throated Sparrow	*Zonotrichia albicollis*	
Harris's Sparrow	*Zonotrichia querula*	
White-crowned Sparrow	*Zonotrichia leucophrys*	
Dark-eyed Junco	*Junco hyemalis*	
Blackbirds	**Icteridae**	
Red-winged Blackbird	*Agelaius phoeniceus*	
Meadowlark sp.	*Sturnella* sp.	
Yellow-headed Blackbird	*Xanthocephalus xanthocephalus*	
Rusty Blackbird	*Euphagus carolinus*	
Finches	**Fringillidae**	
Common Redpoll	*Carduelis flammea*	
Hoary Redpoll	*Carduelis hornemanni*	

Fig. 2 Peregrine Falcon or Kirgavik (*Falco peregrinus*). *Photo by Cameron Eckert.*

BIRDS OF PREY
David Mossop

Hawks and owls are at the top of the food chain on Herschel Island, and these raptors, or birds of prey, are powerful indicators of the health and productivity of natural communities. Four species nest annually at Qikiqtaryuk, while another eight have been seen there from time to time. Herschel Island's raptors provide some of the best, most reliable wildlife viewing for visitors because the open tundra puts their lives on such clear display. Their nests are on the ground at the edges and on the ledges of creek-side and ocean bluffs and on other prominent landmarks. Some of the nests are perched precariously on eroding ocean cliffs (Fig. 1). Their courting displays, hunting strategies, predator-defence behaviour, and regal presence are almost impossible to miss. The breeding status and success of these birds is recorded annually by park rangers and visiting biologists as part of the island's ecological monitoring program.

Breeding Pairs
Peregrine Falcon or Kirgavik
(*Falco peregrinus*). The Peregrine Falcon, one of the most exciting of all birds, is the flagship species of the modern conservation movement (Fig. 2). It was listed as endangered after populations declined sharply in the 1960s due to pesticide-induced thinning of egg shells. The subsequent North American ban on DDT use, and captive-rearing programs, led to the recovery of populations throughout its range. The numbers are largely recovered, but the species is still listed as of special concern, and it remains high on the most-wanted list of many birdwatchers. Figure 3 illustrates the decline and recovery of this species along the Yukon coast as detected by periodic surveys.

Fig. 1 Peregrine Falcon nest on the cliff-top at Bell Bluff. *Photo by Cameron Eckert.*

Juvenile Snowy Owls or Ukpik (*Bubo scandiaca*). *Photo by Cameron Eckert.*

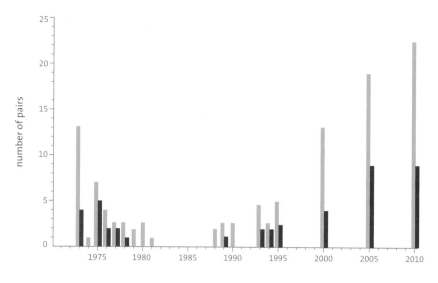

Herschel Island is an excellent place to view Peregrine Falcons. The "tundra" form of the species bred on the island until about 1980 when it disappeared. A pair suddenly reappeared in the early 1990s, and, more recently, six or seven pairs have occupied well-spaced nesting sites along cliff and gully tops. Two to four of these pairs use the cliffs northeast of the settlement, where they are monitored by Park staff. From the records collected between 2002 and 2009, it seems that chicks fledge from over half of the nests, and in some years all the nests are successful. The adults return from their South American winter range in mid-May when Herschel Island is mostly snow-covered. They choose an exposed pinnacle that can be easily defended, lay three or four reddish-brown eggs without the benefit of nest material (Fig. 1), and settle down to a 32-day incubation. Both adults share nest and young duties and are well known for their fierce defence in the face of all intruders. The young are flying by mid-August and are ready to migrate south around the first of September.

With a little perseverance, a visitor hiking along the ocean bluff tops will be rewarded with the "cacking" of its alarm call and defensive aerial displays from this superlative bird. Its long, often back-swept, pointed wings and longish tail, along with its light breast, dark back, and head accentuated by its identifying dark "whisker" marks make it one of the most readily recognized of the birds of prey. Probably the fastest bird on Earth, its high speed stoops, or dives, and chases during hunting are some of the most thrilling events the field naturalist can see. On Herschel Island, these falcons hunt a variety of other birds, often small shorebirds but also water birds such as the Black Guillemot.

Rough-legged Hawk or Qilrig

(*Buteo lagopus*). Without question, this largish, broad-winged, soaring hawk or "buteo" is the signature raptor of Herschel Island (Fig. 4). Its haunting, mewing scream is characteristic of tundra wilderness as few other sounds are. The breeding density of these hawks on the island varies from year to year, apparently in step with the density of the lemmings and voles that are its prime prey. Its talons and hunting style seem superbly adapted for catching small mammals. The population of these hawks on Qikiqtaryuk may be the densest anywhere when prey is abundant, as 37 nests have been located across the entire island (Fig. 5).

In 1986, 24 of these sites were known to be occupied, leading to a breeding density of at least one pair per four square kilometres. The number and success rates of Rough-legged Hawk nests near to Pauline Cove are similar to those of the Peregrine Falcon.

Fig. 5 Rough-legged Hawk young almost ready to fledge from their nest on the north coast of Herschel Island. *Photo by Louis Schilder.*

Fig. 6 Rough-legged Hawk nest.
Photo by Cameron Eckert.

Fig. 7 Snowy Owl. *Photo by Cameron Eckert.*

Fig. 8 Snowy Owl chick. *Photo by Fritz Mueller.*

Rough-legged Hawks build nests of sticks lined with finer grasses at the tops or on ledges of the clay bluffs and cliffs of the island's coasts and interior streams. In early June, the female usually lays four or five beautiful creamy eggs blotched with reddish brown, which are incubated for about a month (Fig. 6). The young are ready to migrate south by early September. Two of the enduring mysteries regarding the behaviour of Rough-legged Hawks are how these birds judge the abundance of prey, and where they disappear to when they decide not to breed.

Snowy Owl or Ukpik (*Bubo scandiaca*). Two species of owl breed on the island. The Snowy Owl is a well-known resident of the Arctic, and more closely associated with tundra regions than any other bird (Fig. 7). In some years, apparently when the lemming population is near its peak, up to 11 pairs have been found on Herschel Island, but in other years virtually none. These owls lay their clutches of up to six pure white eggs in ground scrapes, usually on top of a hummock, without the addition of nesting material. Snowy Owls nest early on Herschel Island, with the eggs hatching in mid- to late June (Fig. 8). In some years these owls have been found on the island throughout the winter, but individual birds commonly range far and wide. The annual movements of these birds were studied using radio tags during the International Polar Year, 2007–09. In 2008–09, a radio-tagged owl from Herschel Island travelled across the eastern Beaufort Sea to Banks Island.

Most hikers on Qikiqtaryuk, even in years when the bird isn't breeding, may suddenly find they are being watched by this tundra ghost. The clear white form standing out against the hills from which it hunts is one of the tundra's most memorable sights. The owls' strategies for dealing with poor prey years, especially during winter, remain an intriguing mystery.

Short-eared Owl or Nipaiłuktaq (*Asio flammeus*). This bird is another of the island's species listed as of special concern because it is at risk further south in its range. However, the population on Herschel Island, likely just a small number of pairs, seems relatively secure, although years have gone by without any known breeding effort. Ground nests in sedge or other meadow vegetation have only rarely been found, but the wonderful aerial displays of the male and the strange calls of courtship can be enjoyed most summers (Fig. 9).

The four species described above are known to breed on Herschel Island. Eight other species of raptor have been sighted hunting on the island, although most of them are not regular visitors.

Fig. 9 Short-eared Owl or Nipaiłuktaq (*Asio flammeus*). *Photo by Jukka Jantunen.*

Fig. 10 Merlin (*Falco columbarius*).
Photo by Cameron Eckert.

Visitors

Bald Eagle or Kilerak (*Haliaeetus leucocephalus*). The closest nesting pairs are in the Mackenzie Delta, about 100 kilometres away. Immature individuals are occasional visitors to the island.

Golden Eagle or Tingmiakpak (*Aquila chrysaetos*). A very large population of this magnificent predator breeds throughout the British Mountains, south of Herschel Island. It's known to hunt mostly arctic ground squirrels but also commonly preys on animals up to the size of young caribou. The closest breeding pair are normally only about 15 kilometres away from Qikiqtaryuk, yet the species has rarely been seen on the island.

Gyrfalcon or Kidjgavik (*Falco rusticolus*). A large population of about 200 pairs of Gyrfalcon breed on the Yukon North Slope, immediately south of

the island. The closest known nesting pair is about 20 kilometres away. The Gyrfalcon is the largest of the falcons and is a must-see species for most visiting birders. Hunting forays by Gyrfalcons onto Qikiqtaryuk seem to occur irregularly, so a sharp-eyed visitor may spot one on the island.

Merlin (*Falco columbarius*). This little falcon also nests on the mainland within about 60 kilometres of the island. It is a regular visitor to Herschel Island in the autumn (Fig. 10).

Northern Hawk Owl or Niaquqtuarr̂uk (*Surnia ulula*). This northern owl has only been seen on the island a few times. It breeds at the tree line further south, so regular excursions onto the open tundra are likely.

Northern Harrier (*Circus cyaneus*). A relatively sparse population of this species, which is also called the Marsh Hawk, breeds on the coastal plain and in Old Crow Flats

to the south. However, these birds with the characteristic white band on their rump have been seen hunting in the meadows of Herschel Island fairly regularly.

Accidentals

American Kestrel (*Falco sparverius*). The only record of this diminutive falcon on Herschel Island was of a female that appeared at Pauline Cove on August 9–10, 2010, and was later found dead. This species nests as far north as Old Crow Flats and has been seen at various locations across the North Slope.

Sharp-shinned Hawk (*Accipiter striatus*). This small forest-dwelling hawk likely nests as far north as the southern Richardson Mountains and is a rare vagrant to the North Slope. It has been seen on Herschel Island just once: a female at Pauline Cove on August 24, 2010 (Fig. 11).

Fig. 11 Sharp-shinned Hawk (*Accipiter striatus*). This visit on August 24, 2010, established the first island record for this species. *Photo by Cameron Eckert.*

GETTING ALONG WITH RAPTORS

All the birds of prey and most other bird species nest on the tundra in exposed locations where they are open to disturbance. Nest timing is absolutely critical this far north as these birds need total, concentrated use of time and energy for raising their young. Raptors have developed strategies for dealing with disturbance from natural predators, but human disturbance is often quite different.

Lingering for that perfect photo near a nest, or just ignoring their desperate calls asking you to "move on," can seriously interfere with critical feeding and incubating. Eggs and young may freeze to death if adults are forced to leave their duties. In short, the right approach is to keep moving. That way the naturalist's behaviour is more like a natural event that these birds can deal with.

SMALL MAMMALS

Charles J. Krebs, Donald Reid,
Scott Gilbert, and Alice J. Kenney

The food chains of the Arctic would collapse without the small creatures that convert plants and insects into meat, and provide food for predators. Herschel Island has three small rodents (two lemmings and one vole), one medium-sized rodent (the arctic ground squirrel), and at least one shrew. These species are remarkably adapted to Arctic life and are vitally important to the Arctic terrestrial food web.

The Pauline Cove area offers a mix of vegetation that favours small mammals, making it a unique part of the island. Wild ryegrass, sedges, and other grasses, along with knee-high willows, grow on the relatively flat land around the cove, a cover not typically found in the upland of Qikiqtaryuk. In some years brown lemmings are particularly plentiful in this habitat, reaching numbers four to five times that of the upland areas. Tundra voles are especially common around the settled area of Pauline Cove and in the grassy vegetation near the beach. This wealth of lemmings and voles attracts many predators, both mammals and birds of prey. The latter arrive in the spring and autumn during bird migration, particularly just before the snow falls in September. Even minor vegetation complexes such as the Pauline Cove area can be important feeding areas for migratory birds of prey.

Fig. 2 A lemming winter nest after snowmelt.
Photo by Alice Kenney.

Lemmings

Like most of the Arctic, Herschel Island has two species of lemming or **avingaq**: the collared lemming (*Dicrostonyx groenlandicus*) (Fig. 1) and the brown lemming (*Lemmus trimucronatus*). Lemmings do not hibernate but instead are active all year round. In summer they burrow, but in winter they live on the ground surface directly below the snow pack. Here they build circular nests, 15 to 20 centimetres in diameter, out of dry grass and sedge leaves (Fig. 2). After the snow melts, these winter nests litter the landscape, giving some clue as to the lemming population of the previous winter. In summer they build the same kind of nest underground. Lemmings are good swimmers, with fur coats that allow them to float high in the water, a skill they use in crossing flooded areas or drainage creeks after snowmelt (Fig. 3). Popular myths about lemmings jumping into the sea are baseless.

Fig. 1 The collared lemming or avingaq (*Dicrostonyx groenlandicus*). The summer coat has numerous colours, excellent for camouflage. In winter, the coat changes to white to protect the lemmings from predators.
Photo by Alice Kenney.

A collared lemming surrounded by mountain avens, its staple food.
Photo by Fritz Mueller.

Fig. 3 A tundra vole or avingaq (*Microtus oeconomus*) swimming in a flooded marsh area. Voles and lemmings are excellent swimmers over short distances. *Photo by Alice Kenney.*

Fig. 4 *Right* The brown lemming (*Lemmus trimucronatus*). The summer coat is a rich brown colour. In winter the coats become thicker, but retain the overall brown colour. *Photo by Alice Kenney.*

The collared lemming ranges throughout the tundra areas of arctic North America and as far north as the tips of the Queen Elizabeth Islands and Greenland at 83°N. Adult collared lemmings weigh from about 45 to 100 grams and can sit comfortably in your hand. Their bodies are 13 to 15 centimetres long, they have short tails (20 millimetres), and their tiny ears are nearly invisible (Fig. 1). The small size of these body parts is an adaptation for life in the cold, ensuring that these animals lose little heat. The coats of collared lemmings, uniquely among rodents, turn white in winter.

The brown lemming (Fig. 4), the other lemming of the western Arctic, is not found as far north as the collared lemming but ranges further south, to the mountains of British Columbia. Brown lemmings also have short ears

Fig. 5 The tundra vole, commonly seen around the settlement at Pauline Cove. *Photo by Alice Kenney.*

and tails but keep their brown coats in both winter and summer. They are the same size as the collared lemmings but prefer wetter habitats. On Herschel Island, brown lemmings typically live in areas with many sedges, grasses, and mosses, while collared lemmings prefer areas with mountain avens (*Dryas* spp.) and willows.

Tundra Voles

The third small rodent of Herschel Island is the tundra vole, also called **avingaq** (*Microtus oeconomus*) (Fig. 5). A circumpolar species found all across Siberia and Nordic Europe, the tundra vole is limited to the northwestern part of North America. It is also called the root vole because it digs up roots for food. Runways in grass and sedge areas (Fig. 6) show the presence of this vole, along with piles of dirt left after winter by its root-digging activities. Figure 7 shows a winter cache of plant roots stored by tundra voles near the whalemen's graves at Pauline Cove.

Tundra voles are often found around the cove's buildings and in the grassy areas along the nearby beach, but are uncommon elsewhere on the island. Their bodies are 12 centimetres long, with an additional four to five centimetres of tail. With relatively large ears and a longer body shape than the two lemming species, they are not as well adapted to the cold.

Life Cycle of Lemmings

Populations of lemmings go up and down in number, and the Herschel Island lemmings are no exception (Fig. 8). Brown lemmings on Qikiqtaryuk were at peak numbers in 2008, while collared lemmings appeared to reach a peak in 2007. Biologists Darielle Talarico and Brian Slough trapped lemmings on Herschel in the mid-1980s and also recorded significant differences in numbers between years. In many parts of Arctic Canada, lemming numbers vary greatly, reaching their highest level quite regularly at the peak of a "cycle" every three or four years, though we do not have enough data to know whether this is also true on Herschel Island.

The numbers of lemmings on the island vary through changes in their birth and death rates. Like all small rodents, lemmings reproduce prolifically. Pregnancy lasts 21 days and litter size is typically five to eight babies. Females can become pregnant when they are 21 days old, and they mate again after giving birth. During the breeding season, female lemmings are nearly continuously pregnant, with numbers of offspring limited only by the season's length.

Fig. 6 Tundra vole runways and diggings exposed after snowmelt in spring. *Photo by Alice Kenney.*

Fig. 7 The tundra vole is sometimes called the root vole because it digs and caches roots for winter food. *Photo by Alice Kenney.*

Lemmings are able to breed under the snow during winter, but do not seem to do so every year. Unfortunately no direct observations of winter breeding exist because it is difficult to study lemmings in this season. They typically breed every spring, producing two-month-old juveniles by the time the snow melts on the island in late May or early June. Since they are active all winter long and need plenty of energy for reproduction, lemmings are unlikely to be short of food in most winters, although local food patches may be well-grazed.

Given that lemmings have tremendous breeding potential, why isn't the Arctic overrun with these animals? The answer lies in the death rate among the population. Nearly every carnivore on the tundra eats lemmings, from grizzly bears to wolves, foxes, weasels, Snowy Owls, Short-eared Owls, Common Ravens, gulls, and jaegers. Even the lowly arctic ground squirrel or **siksik** (*Spermophilus parryii*) (Fig. 9, overleaf), commonly thought of as a herbivore, digs out lemming burrows in summer and kills and eats the inhabitants. Summer is the best of times and the worst of times for lemmings, for good green plant growth is balanced by the arrival of many migratory predators. Lemmings do better in winter, when the snow protects them from some of these enemies.

The lemmings' most serious predators are probably weasels and foxes because they can hunt lemmings year-round. However, some deaths, paradoxically, come from the lemmings themselves, as females may practice infanticide. In the laboratory, female lemmings will kill the babies of other females if given the chance, though males rarely do so. The reason, we think, is that the promiscuous males have no way of knowing which offspring is theirs, but if breeding space or other resources are limited, females can give their own offspring more opportunities by reducing their neighbours' litters. We know this game of spite occurs in the field, but we don't know how common it is or how it affects lemming numbers, particularly at high population levels.

Although we are beginning to understand why lemming numbers go up and down, we don't know exactly what sets the upper limits for lemming numbers. The general answer is resources, which might mean food supplies, summer burrows, or winter snow conditions. We suspect that maximum lemming numbers are directly related to a rich supply of their main food plant. For the brown lemming, tundra grass (Fischer's dupontia—*Dupontia fischeri*) or vegetation such as mosses may be the key predictors of high numbers. For the collared lemming, mountain avens (*Dryas integrifolia*) may be the key predictor. Summer burrows are probably never in short supply, as there seem to be many unused ones even when lemming numbers are high.

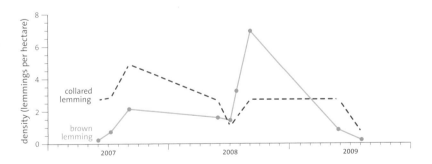

Fig. 8 Population density of lemmings on Herschel Island from 2007 to 2009.

Fig. 9 The arctic ground squirrel or siksik (*Spermophilus parryii*). *Photo by Alice Kenney.*

Fig. 10 The tundra shrew (*Sorex tundrensis*). *Drawing by Nancy Halliday, courtesy of the Smithsonian National Museum of Natural History, Washington, D.C.*

However, we have not studied burrow quality, so many of the burrows we see may be unsuitable for summer use.

Winter conditions could be important in limiting lemming numbers by preventing them from reaching food. Some habitats that look ideal in summer may be hopeless in winter if ice forms between the snow cover and the ground, making it impossible to burrow into the vegetation. Freezing rain or mid-winter melting in the North, which is increasing because of climate change, can contribute to this loss of habitat. Lemmings are also vulnerable if they get wet in winter, as they die quickly if their fur loses its insulation.

If winter conditions repeatedly cause many deaths or prevent reproduction, lemming numbers will go down, as they will have to depend on summer breeding during the short growing season for survival. The high numbers we see from time to time can only happen as a result of strong population growth, under the snow, during the winter months.

Ground Squirrels

The fourth rodent on Herschel Island is the arctic ground squirrel or **siksik** (Fig. 9), although it is a rare migrant. One was sighted in the 1980s, but elders confirm that ground squirrels are uncommon on Qikiqtaryuk. In fact arctic ground squirrels are not permanent residents of any of the Arctic islands, but are found along the Yukon North Slope in areas where they can dig burrow systems.

Because ground squirrels hibernate and cannot swim for long distances, they only travel to the Arctic islands in spring, over the ice. Females stay close to their burrow system when they wake up from hibernation; only the males go walkabout. If females reached Herschel Island, ground squirrels could become permanent residents there. However, this has not yet happened on any of the Arctic islands and is very unlikely to happen without human assistance.

Shrews

The tundra shrew or **ugyungnaq** (*Sorex tundrensis*) has been found on Herschel Island (Fig. 10), while another species, the barren-ground shrew (*Sorex ugyunak*), lives on the mainland nearby and may well inhabit the island, too. Few records of shrews exist anywhere further north in North America, although the tundra shrew also lives along the Alaska coastal plain. Shrews are not often seen, but have sometimes been caught in lemming traps, or their remains found in the regurgitated pellets from birds of prey. It is marvellous that an animal only eight centimetres long and weighing only five to 10 grams is active year-round on the arctic tundra, surviving on insects and spiders and scavenging meat. Perhaps the great variety and numbers of insects and spiders on the island is a key to the presence of shrews. They are hyper-active, foraging much of the time and burning energy constantly to keep warm. They can even change their body size and shape in winter, becoming lighter and shorter, a process called the Dehnel phenomenon. This includes losing weight in major organs, and reshaping the braincase and inter-vertebral discs to make a more compact body shape. The smaller size and more compact shape are believed to reduce energy requirements when food is scarce.

AN ARCTIC GROUND SQUIRREL SAGA

In the fall of 2008, park rangers from Herschel Island took pictures of a ground squirrel—the first sighting of this animal on the island in almost 25 years—near an abandoned fox den. In September 2008, biologists Alice Kenney and Liz Hofer found tracks of what appeared to be a ground squirrel along the beach at Pauline Cove. On May 24, 2009, Scott Gilbert and Alice Kenney came across a single ground squirrel track that left the snow-covered flats behind Pauline Cove and headed out on the sea ice. Scott and I followed on snowshoes and saw that the ground squirrel had climbed up a few of the pressure ridges close to shore (for a better view?). We followed the tracks out on the ice for two kilometres and then returned to camp for the night. The next morning one of us returned on skis and continued tracking. Snow conditions were perfect for our purpose, as there had been no wind and the ice was still covered with firm snow. (Within three days the ice was covered with pools of meltwater).

Our wandering ground squirrel took us on a surprising journey of 18 kilometres, travelling from the beach on Herschel Island to a beach east of Ptarmigan Bay on the mainland! The squirrel moved non-stop (based on the tracks), and remarkably directly toward the mainland for about six kilometres at the beginning of its trek (see map). There was then a hiatus in the tracks, where the squirrel seemed to have had trouble deciding whether to head inshore to the southern tip of the island or head to the mainland. It must be difficult for a small animal to see much of the horizon, and we wondered if it was

trying to get its direction based on soil or land scent. At one point the squirrel swerved sharply to check out a patch of yellowish snow, but kept going. Our tracker broke through a seal breathing hole that was hidden beneath this patch of snow.

About halfway through the journey, an arctic fox track crossed the trail and changed direction to follow the older squirrel track. After about 500 metres the fox had broken off the pursuit, perhaps realizing it was an old track, and resumed its original course across the sea ice.

The journey across this wide stretch of open ice seems amazing for such

a small rodent. We think this ground squirrel was an adult (a male?) that was returning to the mainland in search of females after spending a lonely year on the island. The ground squirrel chose to travel some way offshore when it could have run along the beach of Thetis Bay and crossed the relatively narrow ice of Workboat Passage. However, that route would have taken the squirrel past the territories or nests of at least two Peregrine Falcons, three or more Rough-legged Hawks, and one Common Raven. Heading out far from shore may have been a good strategy.

—Alice Kenney

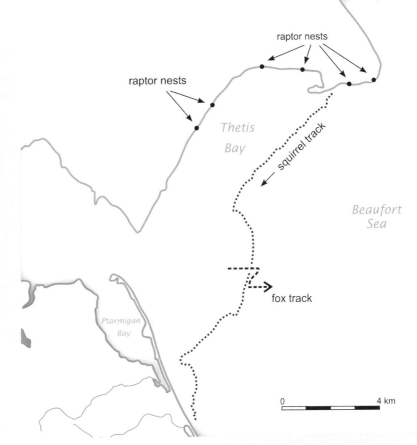

Ground squirrel track followed on May 24, 2009, from Herschel Island to mainland (a distance of 18 kilometres). The track was followed on skis and recorded by GPS.
Cartography by Christine Earl.

CARIBOU AND MUSKOXEN

Donald Reid, Dorothy Cooley,
Lee John Meyook, and
Richard Gordon

At Herschel Island, visitors have a good chance of seeing barren-ground caribou or **tuktu** (*Rangifer tarandus*) and a reasonable chance of seeing muskoxen or **umingmak** (*Ovibos moschatus*). During an aerial census of the 110-square-kilometre island in midsummer 2008, we counted 237 caribou and 46 muskoxen. These populations are high compared to other areas of similar size in the Canadian Arctic. Park rangers have observed muskoxen giving birth on Herschel Island, and caribou almost certainly do as well. Our 2008 census included 41 caribou and 11 muskox calves, relatively high proportions that indicate the herds are healthy.

Caribou

The Herschel Island caribou are part of the Porcupine Caribou Herd, which at last count in 2010 had about 169,000 individuals (Fig. 1). Like most barren-ground caribou, the Porcupine herd returns to the same calving grounds year after year. The cows calve mainly on the coastal tundra plain to the south of Herschel Island that runs west through the Arctic National Wildlife Refuge in Alaska. This area, including the island itself, has plenty of tussock cotton-grass meadows that produce the highly nutritious young flower heads needed by the cows in early June while nursing their newborn calves. Since they give birth after their arduous spring migration, they need a good food supply in order to recover their body reserves by autumn, when they may conceive again.

An ample supply of early summer foods is also vital to support the growth and health of calves. Although they weigh only five to nine kilograms at birth, calves must learn to walk and run with their mothers within hours of being born. They need to be able to avoid predators and grow big enough to survive the loss of blood from biting insects later in the summer.

Fig. 1 Three caribou or tuktu (*Rangifer tarandus*), two bulls and a cow, in July 2010. The animals are still shedding their winter hair. *Photo by Michael Kawerninski.*

A bull caribou emerges from the fog on Herschel Island. Note the shovel-shaped brow tine extending forward over the nose. *Photo by Alistair Blachford.*

Fig. 2 A bull caribou, with its brow tine facing the camera, near Pauline Cove. *Photo by Herschel Island park rangers.*

Fig. 3 A cow caribou in August 2006 near Pauline Cove. *Photo by Cameron Eckert.*

Uniquely among deer, caribou of both sexes grow antlers, but those of bulls are considerably larger. Caribou antlers have a distinctive shovel or brow tine over the face (Fig. 2). The animals grow new antlers each summer, with the bone growth sustained by a blood-rich velvet skin (Fig. 3). The bulls rub this skin off its bony core in autumn when they use the antlers as weapons while they push and jostle for breeding supremacy. Bulls drop their antlers during winter (Fig. 4), as do cows that are not pregnant. Pregnant cows, however, keep theirs through the winter and do not drop them until they give birth in the spring.

Caribou are the most nomadic of all deer species because feeding involves an ongoing search for the most nutritious plant morsels. They seem to move constantly across the tundra, appearing and disappearing with remarkable speed, in groups that often change in size and composition. Cows and calves tend to cluster together, as do the bulls, except during the rutting (mating) season in October. Adult cows (70–90 kilograms) are smaller than bulls (120–150 kilograms), but they all vary greatly in weight throughout the year, depending on the conditions they encounter.

Muskoxen

In contrast to caribou, muskoxen are relatively sedentary and close-knit. In the past few years, the Herschel Island muskoxen have almost always been in one large group of all sexes and ages. Adult bulls are often twice as large as cows, and weigh well over 300 kilograms (Fig. 5). The bulls' massive horns have central bases that merge to form a large boss or bulge, a crucial feature in the competitive head-butting of mating season (late August and September). Cows give birth to a single calf, usually in April or May, but calving is less synchronized than in caribou. Muskox cows may have to produce milk for up to two months before new vegetation emerges. Depending on how severe the previous summer or winter was, cows may fail either to conceive successfully or to bring a foetus to term each year.

The cohesive social behaviour of muskoxen serves them well in dealing with predators such as wolves and grizzly bears. When threatened, the larger adults move quickly to stand shoulder to shoulder, facing outward and forming a defensive circle around the calves and yearlings (Fig. 6). This strategy allows the adults to use their heavy horns to maximum advantage against an attack while limiting the vulnerability of any one individual. The best strategy for predators is to force the herd to run, perhaps through ambush or concerted harassment, and then single out a weak or small individual for attack. Although they can gallop at impressive speed, muskoxen rapidly overheat because of their remarkably heavy, dark coats.

On Qikiqtaryuk, the muskox group travels throughout the island (Fig. 7), but often stays in the same vicinity for many days in a row and may not return to a locale for months. Muskoxen are bulk feeders and fill up in winter on the most productive annual growth—last summer's grasses and sedges, which are found in many of the island's plant communities. Early in the growing season, however, they can be choosier, selecting the new leaves and flowers flourishing across the island. In summer their passage is easy to spot, as they leave their winter under-fur or **qiviuq** draped on willows or rubbed into the ground where they have wallowed. Their hooves, whether of adults walking together or—in the case of calves—running and playing, can disturb the vegetation and expose a lot of soil. In winter, digging through the snow with their hooves to reach food, they also leave a clear picture of their passage.

Population Dynamics

According to the reports of park rangers over the past 20 years, as well as those of local hunters, caribou and muskox numbers on the island vary considerably, with muskoxen being absent in some years. Both species readily cross the winter ice between mainland and island from mid-October through May, and may swim Workboat Passage in summer, so most of the changes in numbers probably reflect these movements. Some caribou and muskoxen appear to spend most or all of some winters on the island. Recently, hunters have readily harvested caribou on Herschel Island from December through May. The winter residency of muskoxen on the island is not surprising, as they are year-round residents on the north Yukon tundra, including the inland mountains, and do not seem to follow long-repeated seasonal movements. However, the winter residency of caribou is interesting because most of the Porcupine Caribou Herd spends only the summer months on the north Yukon tundra. The majority migrates far south through the British and Richardson mountains to winter in the taiga forests.

Caribou and muskoxen have not always been regular inhabitants of the island, even in recent history. Muskoxen had disappeared from north Yukon and northeastern Alaska by the 1860s, probably through overhunting, and were only reintroduced to Alaska's Arctic National Wildlife Refuge in 1969 and 1970. The core of the muskox range is now along the Yukon coast from the international border to the Babbage River. Herds are also found in the British Mountains, and there has been a breeding group in the northern Richardson Mountains since 2003.

As for the caribou, they were quickly eradicated on the island during the commercial whaling era. Hunting parties were sent as far east as the Mackenzie Delta and well south into the mountains in search of game. Although the huge Porcupine Caribou Herd was heavily hunted for quite a few years, the animals might well have learned to avoid the island and nearby coastal plain.

After the whalemen, missionaries, and RCMP had left Herschel, the Porcupine caribou slowly reinhabited the island and the nearby mainland. Families still resident on the island and along the coast relied on these caribou for subsistence. In summer 1972, Bob Mackenzie, a resident of Pauline Cove, reported that there were only about five caribou on Herschel Island, all of which had come across on the spring ice. Instead he relied on hunting moose or **tuttuvak** (*Alces alces*) on the mainland, along with the occasional muskox that had already moved east from the Alaska reintroduction, because caribou were scarce.

The eventual return of caribou to Herschel Island is not surprising, since for the most part it is a good place for them to spend the summer. From the tussock cotton-grass meadows that cover about 40 percent of the island and sustain the nursing cows, to the

Fig. 4 An antler shed by a bull caribou during winter lies among arctic lupines and mountain avens on the Herschel Island upland, providing evidence that caribou spend at least part of the winter on the island. *Photo by Donald Reid.*

Fig. 5 Bull muskox or umingmak (*Ovibos moschatus*) have horns with a massive boss and widely stretching curls.
Photo by Michael Kawerninski.

many flowering plants and willow shrubs of the rolling upland tundra, there is plenty of food for both adults and calves. Although the heat and the biting insects that follow make a caribou's life close to intolerable in late summer, the relatively deep valleys on Herschel Island trap deep snow drifts that last far later in summer than on the flatter coastal plain. These valleys, as well as shaded wet gullies with exposed permafrost, provide cool and relatively insect-free places for the caribou to rest. The fog that is commonplace along the Arctic coast also helps to make life much more pleasant for the caribou because it dramatically cools the island. On the windswept rolling uplands that rise well above the ocean, the caribou find relief from insects by moving into a headwind, reducing attacks to their vulnerable heads. Depending on the prevailing wind over a few days, the animals concentrate on one side of the island or the other.

Even the risk of encountering predators is lessened on the island. Golden eagles are the dominant predator on newborn calves on the coastal plain, but do not nest on Qikiqtaryuk and are rarely seen there. The island is too small to support a pack of wolves or a wolverine for the summer, and visits from these predators are unlikely when there is open water in Workboat Passage. All things considered, caribou traversing the coastal plain on their spring migration may well learn that crossing the ice to Herschel Island to spend the summer is worthwhile.

Why, however, would these animals choose to stay through the long winter? Most Porcupine caribou leave the coastal plain in August and September, well before the ice forms, so caribou on the island would have to swim at least one kilometre across Workboat Passage to join this migration. Such a task is quite feasible, but some caribou still choose to stay. In terms of sheer effort, migrating hundreds of kilometres through rough terrain takes a lot of energy, as does

finding food, and may increase the risk of predation. In addition, winter temperatures in the southern wintering grounds are no higher than on Herschel, especially early in the season when the open sea keeps the coastal air relatively warm.

The key issue for the caribou is probably the availability of winter food. Lichens, a vital but slow-growing winter food source, have proliferated on the island because of the lack of ungulate (hoofed-mammal) grazing through much of the twentieth century. With lots of wind-swept upland country on Herschel, caribou have probably found plenty of accessible lichen. This theory suggests that most of the Porcupine herd migrates because winter foods are not plentiful near their summer range on the mainland. In fact, botanists Donald McLennan and Bruce Bennett have found remarkably little lichen growth in the British Mountains, especially those subarctic forest species eaten by caribou on their winter ranges.

Botanist Catherine Kennedy has documented a decline in lichen abundance in upland habitats on Herschel Island from the 1980s until earlier this century, a trend also found at some other Arctic sites. The decrease in lichens is associated with rising temperatures and a proliferation of faster-growing plants, and may be a result of shading or drying. However, winter grazing by the growing ungulate population may also be a factor, raising the question of how well the island's vegetation can support caribou and muskoxen in the future. Island populations of these species elsewhere have been known to increase rapidly in numbers and then crash, apparently through lack of food. The risk of such a crash on Herschel is low because the animals can move off the island when food is harder to find, and because hunting by humans and bears reduces the growth rate of the population. In general, muskox grazing is more sustainable, since these animals feed on grasses and sedges that grow back each summer rather than on slow-growing lichen.

Compared with overgrazing of their winter foods, muskoxen and caribou face a higher risk to their winter survival from freezing rain, or from winter melting and refreezing of the snow pack. Such weather coats the ground with ice or hard snow, limiting the animals' ability to reach their food. In an era of climate warming, this risk has increased dramatically. Icing events in the past few decades have caused major die-offs of caribou and muskoxen on Canadian Arctic islands where these animals had nowhere else to go. In January 2009, air temperatures on Herschel Island rose well above freezing for almost a day, then dropped below 0°C again, turning the surface of the snow rock-hard. Rangers and researchers returning in April counted only about 19 caribou, compared to well over a hundred earlier in the winter. There were some caribou carcasses, but not the dozens expected if the animals had starved on the island. In fact, they probably moved to the mainland. In February 2009 hunters from Aklavik discovered a herd of caribou on a part of the mainland where Porcupine caribou rarely winter, well to the east of the island.

The numbers of caribou and muskoxen on Herschel Island are clearly far from stable, and a warming climate may produce yet another change in the island's ungulate population. Moose wintering in the British Mountains are now common summer residents of the coastal mainland, and one ventured far out into Workboat Passage in summer 2009. With a plentiful and growing supply of willows and flowering plants on Herschel, it may be only a matter of time before moose choose to spend the summer on the island.

Fig. 6 A group of muskoxen on the north coast of Herschel Island, May 2005. *Photo by Dorothy Cooley.*

Fig. 7 Muskoxen at Osborn Point, July 2010. *Photo by Michael Kawerninski.*

Two cabins at Lopez Point that are associated with the reindeer drive. They may have been occupied by the reindeer herders for about a month in December 1932. *Photo by Sara Nielsen.*

The more southerly cabin at Lopez Point, with the remains of its sod roof and wooden chimney. *Photo by Cameron Eckert.*

THE 1929–35 REINDEER DRIVE

In 1919 the Canadian government appointed a Royal Commission on Muskox and Reindeer to investigate the potential of these animals to be raised in domesticated herds, thereby providing a livelihood and secure food supply for northerners. The decision showed the government's desire to establish a western economy in the Arctic, but it was also a response to many reports of starvation when game periodically became scarce. Vilhjalmur Stefansson, who had recently returned to the south from Herschel Island after leading the Canadian Arctic Expedition, was one of the original Commissioners. The final report, issued in 1925, urged the government to introduce reindeer herds to the Canadian Arctic.

In response, the government hired Bob and Erling Porsild, who had been brought up in Greenland, to survey the vegetation from Alaska to the Mackenzie Delta and determine if it would support reindeer. They were also asked to study the commercially managed reindeer in Alaska and decide if the animals could be herded to Canada. Erling Porsild was a trained botanist who later produced the standard plant catalogue for the Northwest Territories. The Porsilds travelled along the north coast of

Alaska, crossing into Canada in March 1927. Erling injured himself near Herschel Island and was escorted to Aklavik by a police constable. The Porsilds then surveyed the land east of the Delta, and in September 1927 advised the government that the area was suitable as reindeer range.

The government proceeded to arrange for the movement of a herd from near Buckland in western Alaska to the east side of the Mackenzie Delta. A herd of 3,442 animals left Naboktoolik on December 26, 1929 under the management of Andrew Bahr, an experienced Saami herder working for Lomen Brothers of Seattle, the company supplying the deer. The drive took much longer than expected, mainly because of the recalcitrant nature of semi-wild animals and their tendency to bolt in the face of adversity. The Porsilds were in charge of preparations for receiving the animals in the new range, and at one point Erling urged that the herd spend the summer of 1932 on Herschel Island. Even though the reindeer were only 320 kilometres away in March, they were unable to reach the island that summer.

Instead, the herd crossed into Canada in December 1932, and reached Herschel Island later that month.

At that point, Bahr hoped to pick up supplies that the trader C.T. Pedersen had left for him the previous summer. Pedersen had left the supplies with the RCMP, but the officer stationed at Herschel for the winter had not received instructions to release the goods, and the herders could only pick up a few items from the Hudson's Bay Company store. The herders then pressed on to Kay Point, which they reached at the end of January 1933. Over the next two summers, Kay Point was a favoured pasture for the reindeer because of its exposure to sea breezes. After a failed attempt to cross the outer Mackenzie Delta in January 1934, the herd, by then down to 2,370 animals, was finally delivered in March 1935.

The descendants of these reindeer are still herded on Richards Island in summer, and in the Caribou Hills, north of Inuvik, in winter. The herd is an Inuvialuit-owned private concern of about 2,000 animals. The drive also brought Edwin Allen, an aboriginal herder from Kobuk, Alaska, to the Delta. He had joined the drive in summer 1930. Today the Allens are a prominent Inuvialuit family.

—*Christopher Burn*

SMALL CARNIVORES

Donald Reid, Daniel Gallant,
Dorothy Cooley, and
Lee John Meyook

For parts of the year, Herschel Island is home to red foxes or **kayuqtuq** (*Vulpes vulpes*), arctic foxes or **tiriganniaq** (*Vulpes lagopus*), wolverines or **qavvik** (*Gulo gulo*), and least weasels or **itiriaq** (*Mustela nivalis*). Other carnivores, such as the wolf or **amaruq** (*Canis lupus*), lynx or **niutuiyiq** (*Lynx canadensis*), pine marten or **qavviatchiaq** (*Martes americana*), and the ermine, also called the short-tailed weasel or stoat or **itiriaqpuk** (*Mustela erminea*), visit the island as well, but much less frequently.

Least Weasel

Least weasels or **itiriaq** live on the island year-round, raising their young and surviving on a diet of mostly small mammals such as lemmings and voles. These fierce little predators weigh only 40 to 90 grams as adults, with males about one and a half times the weight of females, and are no bigger than much of their prey (Fig. 1). They occupy most habitats on the island and are solitary hunters, largely with exclusive territories, although males do overlap with a number of females.

Fig. 1 A least weasel or itiriaq (*Mustela nivalis*) emerges from shelter in the shoreline driftwood near Pauline Cove, where it was probably hunting tundra voles. *Photo by Alice Kenney.*

Least weasels are unique among North American weasels because they can breed and raise young in winter as well as in summer if food is plentiful. Young least weasels, likely born in both winter and summer, have been live-trapped on Herschel Island. Females produce on average four or five young in a litter, and can produce two or three litters a year if prey is plentiful. Young females become sexually mature when only four months old. Least weasels increase when lemmings and voles are common, and probably slow down the population growth of lemmings since they respond so rapidly to plentiful prey. However, they can run into difficulty finding food, especially in winter, and starvation is a real risk.

An ermine or itiriakpuk (*Mustela erminea*) on a doorframe at Pauline Cove. *Photo by Cameron Eckert.*

An arctic fox or tiriganniaq amid purple fleabane (*Erigeron grandiflorus*), tall, yellow groundsel (*Senecio lugens*), whitish and tall hemlock-parsley (*Conioselinum cnidiifolium*), white wormwood (*Artemisia norvegica*) and yellow thoroughwort (*Bupleurum americanum*). *Photo by Michael Kawerninski.*

Fig. 2 An ermine at Pauline Cove carrying a brown lemming it has just killed.
Photo by Cameron Eckert.

Weasels make themselves inconspicuous because they themselves are preyed on by foxes and raptors. Few live longer than a year. They spend lots of time underground in summer, both for shelter and to hunt. They moult twice a year, turning completely white in winter, when they live mostly in the network of lemming passages at the bottom of the snow pack. Weasels are long and thin (about 2.5 centimetres in diameter on average) because they hunt lemmings in narrow tunnels and underground passages. However, this adaptation comes at a cost because their body shape is a poor one for conserving heat. In winter, least weasels take over the grass nests made by lemmings, lining the nests with their prey's fur to create a cosy home, and often leaving a cache of inedible body parts such as jaw bones, feet, and tails. In the spring we can obtain an index of both the weasel population and the number of lemmings killed during the winter from a thorough search for lemming winter nests.

Ermine

In many Arctic regions, the ermine, short-tailed weasel, or **itiriaqpuk** is more common than the least weasel, but on Herschel Island ermine are rare. Like least weasels, ermine rely on lemmings and voles in their diet (Fig. 2), and are aggressive toward least weasels. As a result, weasels tend to avoid areas occupied by ermine.

Ermine have thicker, longer bodies than the least weasel, are better adapted for energy conservation, and are capable of killing larger prey. However, male ermine cannot easily enter all lemming burrows because of their large size, so they have to use other structures as dens. On the tundra they often use ground squirrel burrows and crevices in bedrock and talus. Herschel Island, however, lacks bedrock and talus and has no ground squirrel colonies, so the only potential dens for ermine are either driftwood piles along the coast or fox dens. The lack of den sites may prevent ermine from living on the island in larger numbers. In contrast, least weasels of both sexes use lemming burrows fairly easily, so they can make most of the island their home.

Foxes

The arctic tundra of Yukon's coastal plain and Herschel Island is one of the few areas in the world where red and arctic foxes live close to each other, successfully raising young in dens just a few kilometres apart. In summer, the arctic fox or **tiriganniaq**, often called the white fox, loses its white winter coat to reveal a grey or tan coat with creamy belly (Fig. 3). In contrast, the red fox or **kayuqtuq** (despite its name) comes in numerous hues, from almost black with silver shading to rich red-brown, and remains coloured throughout the year (Fig. 4). A distinctive mark of the red fox is its white-tipped tail, regardless of the colour of its coat. In summer, the palest red foxes appear similar in colour to arctic foxes.

Fig. 3 The arctic fox or tiriganniaq (*Vulpes lagopus*) moults its white winter fur in June to reveal a dark grey muzzle and lower legs, while its body is tan coloured.
Photo by Michael Kawerninski.

The two species have very similar annual reproductive cycles, although we don't have as much information about red foxes at high latitudes. Both red and arctic foxes form pairs and mate in March. By early May the pairs have chosen den sites, with the pups arriving in May or early June. The number of pups varies between years and individual mothers, depending on how much food the female has been able to find during winter and especially during pregnancy. Arctic foxes can have more pups in a litter (usually six to 12) than red foxes (usually three to six). Pups are small (60 to 90 grams), helpless, and blind at birth, and are suckled for their first six or seven weeks. Their mother stays with them most of this time, while the adult male brings food to the den. Pups grow fast but don't come out of the den until they are three to four weeks old (Fig. 5). When food is scarce

many pups will die before ever coming above ground, so the number of young seen at a den may well be fewer than the number born. By autumn the pups are essentially adult-sized and independent, and they can breed in their first year.

Dens are crucial for foxes because of the shelter they provide from predators and the weather. When it is time to give birth in spring, the ground is still frozen, so foxes have to choose a den that is already well excavated. A good den for raising young (a natal den) has many entrances and a number of chambers, giving the foxes lots of options for quick escape underground and comfortable living. However, good den sites are rare. They need relatively dry soil that is easy enough to dig but not so coarse and soft that it will collapse, combined with a good vantage from which to search for danger, and a southerly

exposure to keep warm. Such sites are used repeatedly, and the foxes clean and fix them with extra digging most summers. Dens can last for decades, but will eventually collapse if not maintained.

In the 1970s, systematic surveys revealed both red and arctic foxes denning on Herschel Island and on the mainland coastal plain in what is now Ivvavik National Park. Extensive surveys in the 1980s, and again in 2008 and 2009, confirmed the pattern. Biologists conducting these den surveys have visited 50 dens at least four times each over a 20-year period. Only a small proportion of dens changed occupancy between species, and arctic foxes took over red fox dens as frequently as red foxes took over arctic fox dens. Interestingly, the natal den close to Pauline Cove has switched from one species to the other quite often (at least three times in the past five years).

Fig. 4 A red fox or aukpilaqtaq (*Vulpes vulpes*) delicately carrying a common eider egg in its mouth. (Kayuktuq is a general Inuvialuktun word for the species *Vulpes vulpes*. Strictly, red foxes are called aukpilaqtaq, silver foxes are marraq, and cross foxes are called kiasirutilik.) This male fox was caching eggs, and likely took some of them back to feed his mate while she was nursing her pups in the den. Note how the light-coloured fur on this individual is quite similar to the summer coat of an arctic fox. *Photo by Fritz Mueller.*

There are presently about 17 natal dens on Herschel Island, though there are rarely more than four active dens in any one year (1988 was an exception, with eight active breeding pairs). In summer, the den and associated foraging area is used exclusively by the breeding pair and young, but this territoriality breaks down in winter, when foxes become nomadic. The number of breeding pairs and their success at raising young depends mostly on the numbers of lemmings. Both species seem to use all the tundra habitats on the island for hunting. However, predation is a real risk. In 2008 one of the arctic fox dens was dug out by a grizzly bear, and an adult female arctic fox and her pups were found dead on the den.

In the past four decades, arctic foxes have declined, and even disappeared, in some tundra regions of northern Scandinavia and northwest Russia. Heavy fur trapping produced some of the decline, which coincided with a northward range expansion of red foxes. However, in the same period in northern Yukon, the range of the arctic fox has not contracted, and the red fox range has not expanded at the expense of the arctic fox. This relative stability is interesting because adult red foxes (four to seven kilograms) are larger than adult arctic foxes (three to five kilograms), and, as a result, are the dominant species. They are also, generally, the aggressor, even to the extent of killing arctic foxes. Yukon's red foxes are probably just as aggressive toward arctic foxes as the red foxes in other regions, including the Alaskan coastal plain. However, Yukon red foxes clearly do not reproduce and survive well enough to increase their numbers and force the arctic foxes out.

Part of the reason for such stability may be how these species survive the Yukon winter. Both species rely on a diet of small rodents, augmented by birds and berries in summer, and are avid scavengers at any time. In winter, snow makes rodent hunting much more difficult, but we know relatively little about how foxes—and especially the red fox—make a living on the tundra in this season. Both species may rely to some extent on food cached in summer. However, Herschel Island does not support colonies of geese or arctic ground squirrels, which would provide eggs or killed adult ground squirrels to cache—better choices than lemmings because they are larger. Both red and arctic foxes sometimes leave the island to search for food. Both fox species are known to head out onto the Beaufort Sea ice, probably to search out seals killed by polar bears.

Red foxes face two handicaps in winter: they are larger than arctic foxes, so they have to find considerably more food every day, and their dark coats make them conspicuous to competitors and potential predators such as wolverines, wolves, or polar bears. The arctic fox's size and white coat are no doubt adaptations to these circumstances, although they do not always guarantee survival in the hard tundra winters. Where red foxes have overcome these handicaps in other arctic regions, they may have benefited from extra food left by people, such as garbage or untended reindeer that die on the land. On Qikiqtaryuk, the return of wintering muskoxen and caribou in the last 25 years has probably provided similar help, because partial carcasses are sometimes available for foxes when these animals die or are killed by people or by grizzly bears in the spring. The way we manage garbage or other potential additions to the red fox winter diet in northern Yukon may affect the future of the arctic fox.

Between about 1895 and 1935, Herschel was a key trading post for arctic fox pelts. However, the huge numbers registered (up to 1,080 pelts in 1923–24) were trapped throughout the western Arctic and not just along the Yukon coast. Arctic fox trapping continued throughout the twentieth century, but the relatively large numbers trapped on the island and the North Slope (up to 108 in 1972–73) were well above the birth rate of these foxes in the area, according to biologists and resident trappers. The arctic fox population on Qikiqtaryuk is probably regularly supplemented by foxes from as far away as the Point Barrow region of northern Alaska or Banks Island, following the regular fluctuations in lemming populations.

Fig. 5 Four red fox pups at a den on Herschel Island. These pups are between two and three months old. *Photo by Daniel Gallant.*

Fig. 7 A pine marten or qavviatchiaq (*Martes americana*) on Herschel Island in May 2005. *Photo by Lee John Meyook.*

Fig. 6 Lynx or niutuiyiq (*Lynx canadensis*) are occasional visitors to Herschel Island, crossing Workboat Passage when it is still frozen. *Photo by Lee John Meyook.*

Foxes often travel widely to find food when the local lemming population crashes. Arctic foxes marked in northern Alaska have been known to travel many hundreds of kilometres away from their birth place, with some of them passing by Herschel Island on their way east to Banks Island or Victoria Island.

Wolverines and Wolves

If foxes find it difficult to eke out a living at Qikiqtaryuk year-round, then the larger wolverines or **qavvik** and wolves or **amaruq** have even less chance. Herschel Island represents about one-quarter of the annual range occupied by a male wolverine, and much less than that of a northern wolf pack. Wolves are rarely seen on the island, which is somewhat surprising given the fairly high numbers of caribou. They are probably careful not to get stuck on the island in summer after the ice has melted, when they risk having to swim to the mainland. In winter they probably follow the main caribou herd south.

Wolverines are seen less often on the island when the sea is open, even though they are strong swimmers. They are fairly frequent visitors in winter and spring, taking advantage of muskox and caribou remains, and venturing out on the ice to kill

or scavenge seals. Two wolverine dens found in deep snow banks in recent springs had a large number of wolverine scats, indicating that the animals had stayed there for quite some time.

The island is relatively poor summer habitat for these large carnivores, as there are very few arctic ground squirrels. Wolverines on the north slope of Alaska rely heavily on ground squirrels, caching many in late summer to be eaten in winter. The same wolverines that sometimes visit Herschel Island no doubt hunt ground squirrels in the mainland deltas of the Firth and Malcolm rivers.

Lynx and Marten

The lynx or **niutuiyiq** (Fig. 6) and pine marten or **qavviatchiaq** (Fig. 7) that have reached Qikiqtaryuk in recent years have been well north of the tree line, which is the normal limit for well-established populations of these species. These adventuresome travellers have only visited the island for short periods, and are likely dispersing individuals looking for country with sufficient food after prey has become scarce or hard to compete for in the northern forest. Lynx are known to roam far and wide when their principal prey, the snowshoe hare, declines from the

high point of its eight-to-eleven year cycle. Hares were quite abundant in the taiga forests of eastern Alaska and northern Yukon in 2007–2010, probably supporting cohorts of dispersing lynx and pine marten, a few of which reached Qikiqtaryuk. The tundra of northern Yukon cannot support lynx or pine marten at present, and visiting pine marten often try to make a living by raiding cabins. As shrubs become more prolific on the coastal tundra, they may provide sufficient food for snowshoe hares to colonize portions of the region, and they will trap more snow, perhaps to the advantage of wintering rodents. However, these changes will be gradual and patchy if they continue, and lynx and pine marten are unlikely to be resident on Herschel Island for a long time yet.

The Food Chain

Finding enough food is the common thread that binds the life stories of all these carnivores. Lemmings and voles are central characters in these stories, being prime prey for some and eaten by all. Some of the carnivores themselves can become prey in the competition for food. Weasels can fall prey to foxes, and foxes to other foxes, wolverines, wolves, and bears.

GRIZZLY BEARS

Ravmona Maraj

As you stand on the shore of Pauline Cove and look up to the tundra hills above, if you're lucky you might catch a glimpse of a female grizzly bear or **akłaq** (*Ursus arctos*) leading her two cubs in a feast of bog blueberries. The scene of a grizzly and her family lumbering along in an area without trees makes us think about what it might once have been like to see a grizzly on the prairies. The ecology and the bears' behaviour, as well as the aesthetics, may all be similar— but hopefully not their fate. Grizzlies became extinct on the prairies about 130 years ago. In fact, they have been extirpated from large parts of their historic range in North America, and are in decline in much of their current range. However, thanks to a great deal of isolation from humans, the grizzlies of Herschel Island and the surrounding area are doing well.

Every year one or two grizzlies spend at least a few weeks of their summer on Herschel Island, making Qikiqtaryuk the most northerly grizzly bear range in Yukon (Fig. 1). Grizzlies that visit the island are part of a larger bear population that uses the Alaska and Yukon North Slope, and they mingle with those of the Firth and Malcolm river corridors, where the Porcupine Caribou Herd sometimes calves. The isolation from people, the relationship of bears with caribou, the continuous daylight during the summer, and other aspects of Arctic ecology make the bears in this area slightly different from grizzly bears in the rest of North America.

Fig. 1 Grizzly bear or akłaq (*Ursus arctos*) on Herschel Island in August 2009. *Photo by Cameron Eckert.*

Grizzly bear on Herschel Island in May 2010. *Photo by Lee John Meyook.*

Fig. 2 Grizzly bear cubs-of-year. On average, grizzlies have two cubs per litter. *Photo by Ramona Maraj.*

When Did Grizzlies Arrive on Qikiqtaryuk?

Bears (ursids) are a relatively new evolutionary group, evolving from early dogs (canids) about 20–25 million years ago. Because this divergence is so recent, some taxonomists believe canids and ursids should really be considered one family, instead of dividing them according to a classification system established 100 years ago. Grizzly bears are thought to have descended from an ursid (*Ursus erectus*) that lived in Asia approximately half a million years ago. About 100,000 years ago, grizzlies crossed the Bering land bridge from eastern Russia to Alaska and northern Yukon. They were confined to Beringia by glacial ice until approximately 13,000 years ago, when they began to expand their range southward throughout what is now Canada, the lower contiguous United States, and northern Mexico. Grizzlies probably walked on the Herschel ridge as the climate warmed at the end of the Ice Age.

Grizzly Bear Characteristics

Despite being coastal animals, the grizzlies that use Qikiqtaryuk are similar in appearance to northern interior grizzlies. Grizzly bears are the second largest terrestrial carnivore in North America, smaller only than polar bears or **nanuq** (*Ursus maritimus*). The size and weight of grizzly bears varies widely across their range. Inland, a full-grown male grizzly bear, particularly from the Yukon, may weigh as little as 135 kilograms (300 pounds) in the fall. In contrast, bears on the Alaskan Peninsula may approach or just exceed 680 kilograms (1,500 pounds). The grizzlies of Qikiqtaryuk are larger than the average Yukon grizzly, with males weighing about 195 kilograms (430 pounds) in the fall. Females are 20 to 40 percent smaller than males.

A Grizzly Bear's Social Life

Grizzly bears generally do not interact with each other very much. They are not considered territorial, but they don't tolerate other bears except during mating season or while raising young. Occasionally, bears will also tolerate each other where food resources are concentrated, such as in a meadow lush with bear forage or on the calving grounds of the Porcupine Caribou Herd.

During mating season, males may travel long distances to find a female, and will shadow her until she is receptive. Grizzlies mate repeatedly over several days before they suddenly lose interest in each other. Both individuals may have multiple partners over the course of the mating season. In fact, siblings from the same litter may have different fathers.

Males wander much more widely than females, but both mark their home range by defecating, urinating, creating stomps (deep trails of bear footprints), or rubbing rocks (or trees when available) with their back to deposit fur. The markings are a type of communication to alert one bear to the presence of another. Occasionally, the buildings at Herschel have been used as makeshift rub trees.

Grizzly Bear Life Cycle

Grizzly bears have one of the lowest reproductive rates of all terrestrial mammals in North America. Although a few bears may start to reproduce at four or five years of age, grizzly bears on the North Slope do not reach sexual maturity until they are at least seven, and some females will not successfully raise a litter until they are ten. Once a female has mated with a male in the summer, she delays embryo implantation until hibernation. During this period, the female can abort her pregnancy if she hasn't had the proper nutrients and has not stored enough energy.

Fig. 3 Grizzly bear in spring on the ice of Workboat Passage. *Photo by Guillaume Szor.*

Fig. 4 Bearflower (*Boykinia richardsonii*) is a main food source for bears on the North Slope. *Photo by Ramona Maraj.*

Females produce one to four cubs, with an average of two cubs per litter (Fig. 2). After the cubs are born the mother will not mate again for up to two years while she cares for her young. Once the cubs leave or die, the mother may not produce another litter for three or more years, depending on environmental conditions.

Cub mortality and unsuccessful breeding result in an average of at least four years between litters. Probably fewer than 50 percent of grizzly bear cubs on the Yukon North Slope survive their first year. Such low survival rates are typical for most bear populations, particularly those near the maximum number that the landscape can support.

Interactions with Other Bear Species

The range of North Slope grizzlies, unlike that of many other grizzly bear populations, does not overlap with black bears or **iggarlik** (*Ursus americanus*). Although they are thought to be competitors with grizzly bears, black bears can exist at higher densities because they are smaller and able to forage more efficiently. Black bears are also more capable climbers, so when confronted by a grizzly they may escape up trees. In areas without trees, grizzly bears are able to chase black bears out of prime habitat. Black bears avoid Herschel Island and the adjacent North Slope, where there are no trees. The absence of black bears probably lets grizzlies exist at higher densities than in other places across the North. However, black bears are expanding their range into grizzly country, and Inuvialuit travellers are reporting more black bears on the North Slope.

The range of Qikiqtaryuk's grizzlies overlaps with polar bears just before and after the grizzlies emerge from dens (Fig. 3). Polar bears follow sea ice into shore in mid-September and then back out in late April. Only a few stragglers may be left behind when the sea ice retreats, giving grizzlies dominion of the land for most of their active season. During the periods when both species are using the area, grizzlies may follow polar bears onto the sea ice and capitalize on or scavenge polar bear kills. While polar bears and grizzlies have interbred in other parts of the western Canadian Arctic, there has been no evidence of species hybridization near Herschel Island.

Feeding Habits

Grizzly bears are omnivorous, but plants form the bulk of their diet. In spring they mainly feed on alpine liquorice-root (*Hedysarum alpinum*) and overwintered berries such as crowberry. In the summer they feed on common horsetail and bearflower (Fig. 4), and on bog blueberries, crowberries, horsetail, and bearflower in fall. When blueberries are not available, grizzly bears will dig for liquorice-roots. They will also kill or scavenge caribou and will sometimes eat microtines, such as lemmings and voles or **avingaq**.

Most primary forage plants in the North have nutritional quality similar to those in the grizzly bears' southern range. However, the northern growing season is short, with fewer suitable growing sites and less varied foods than in the south. Grizzly bears living in the Arctic must cope with a short season of forage availability, which places constraints on growth, maturation, and the reproductive rates of Arctic bears. They must also cope with a lack of protective cover and weather extremes. However, even with the summer daylight, northern bears do not forage longer each day than southern bears. Grizzly bears on Herschel Island seem to meet their energy requirements by having diets high in protein and fat from caribou as well as other small mammals.

Fig. 5 Partially excavated grizzly bear den on Herschel Island located by Lee John Meyook, July 2007. *Photo by Cameron Eckert.*

Dens and Denning

There are many grizzly bear dens on the North Slope, ranging from the coast to the mountains. People have seen dens on Herschel Island, but they are not common. Bears typically choose a denning location on a steep slope, stabilized by large rocks or shrub roots (Fig. 5). Most dens face southeast, where they receive a deep snow cover from prevailing north and northwest winds. Females with cubs start denning as early as mid-September and can leave their dens as late as mid-June. Lone adult females den between late September and May. Males stay out the longest, denning in late October or November and exiting as early as March.

Grizzly Bears and the Inuvialuit

Though Inuvialuit who use Qikiqtaryuk have a longstanding relationship with grizzly bears, the bears have never been associated with daily life in the same way as other species such as caribou. Grizzlies have always been harvested opportunistically for their meat, fat, hides, and claws. People ate the meat, especially in years when other food sources were scarce, with grizzly paws considered an especially good part of the bear. People used the fat in baking bread or mixed it with certain roots, treated skins with rendered grizzly fat so they could be used as tarpaulins, and also used the rendered fat as oil for lamps and for cooking because it was odourless. Grizzly hides were used to make shoes or as sleeping mattresses.

At the start of the fur trade, grizzly hides were not highly valued because they cost too much to ship to southern markets. However, transportation became easier in the 1970s and people realized the hides were a prized commodity. By the 1980s the sale of the hides could generate a significant supplemental income for a household, and people began harvesting more bears. Today, grizzly bear hides are still highly valued in southern markets, where a single good-quality hide can fetch several thousand dollars. Some Inuvialuit hunters still take meat home—such as a hindquarter—along with the skin, but the majority of the meat is left on the land.

Inuvialuit who were raised on the land say they have important memories of grizzly bears, and they hope that their grandchildren will have the opportunity to grow up with grizzlies as well. They talk about the silvertip bears around Qikiqtaryuk, as this is one of the places they see the old males regularly.

Grizzly Bear Research

In the fall of 2002, members of the Aklavik Hunters and Trappers Committee, the Wildlife Management Advisory Council (North Slope), Government of Yukon, and Parks Canada met to discuss needs for managing grizzly bear populations on the Yukon North Slope. Previous grizzly bear population estimates were around 316 bears, but these estimates were over 30 years old (1974) and were best guesses based on population studies in neighbouring jurisdictions. Since the 1970s, techniques to estimate bear populations have considerably advanced and the Arctic coast has undergone many ecological changes.

At the 2002 meeting, all management agencies agreed that there was a need to update population estimates and assess grizzly population health. Fieldwork for the Yukon North Slope Grizzly Bear Study began in 2004,

Fig. 6 Hair samples are trapped on barbed wire. The DNA is then extracted and used for mark-recapture analysis to count the number of bears in the population. *Photo by Ramona Maraj.*

Fig. 7 Sixty bears have been collared and tracked for the Yukon North Slope Grizzly Bear Study. *Photo by Ramona Maraj.*

with a completion date of 2012. The information will be used to establish harvest quotas for grizzly bears and assess ecological threats to the population. To date, 60 grizzly bears have been collared for the study and tracked to monitor survival rates and movements (Fig. 7).

A DNA mark-recapture study to estimate the population size and examine its genetic diversity is also underway. This study involves placing 107 barbed wire stations over the landscape. Lures are used to draw bears to the stations, where they rub up against the barbed wire when they investigate the smell. DNA is then extracted from the grizzly hair caught in the wire (Fig. 6). Population size can be estimated by counting the number of different bears that leave their hair behind. Based on this count, the population size seems to be similar to the earlier estimates.

Management Outlook

The Inuvialuit have been good stewards of the grizzly bear. They have managed the harvest of grizzlies with conservative quotas, careful to ensure that bears remain for future generations. Under the Inuvialuit Final Agreement, they have protected the habitat of bears and many other species by permanently limiting development at Qikiqtaryuk and on the rest of the Yukon North Slope.

The Herschel Island park rangers have been at the forefront of human-bear conflict management. Bears regularly used to break into cabins at Pauline Cove, but the rangers frequently incinerate garbage and other waste, and conflicts have been virtually eliminated.

Currently, the main threats to the Yukon North Slope grizzly bear population come from climate change and its effects on their food supply. Bears that live on the North Slope rely on caribou, fish, and plants for food. How climate change will affect the habitat of grizzly bears on the North Slope is uncertain, but we must hope that grizzly families still have a while yet to lumber along the uplands of Qikiqtaryuk.

INUVIALUKTUN WORDS FOR GRIZZLY BEARS (Uummarmiutun dialect)

Akłaq
Grizzly bear

Akłaaluq
Old male grizzly bear

Angnuhalluq
Male grizzly bear, young or old

Akłaiyaaq
Young bear, male or female

Piatyaliq
Mother with cub(s)

Akarvik
A place where someone harvested a grizzly bear.

Aklavik
Grizzly bear place or place of the grizzly bear. Aklavik, which has 350 people, is one of the primary communities from which people hunt grizzly bears (and other animals) on and around Qikiqtaryuk.

POLAR BEARS

Andrew E. Derocher

Culturally, socially, and economically, the polar bear or **nanuq** (*Ursus maritimus*) (Fig. 1) has a long history in the Herschel Island area. The sea ice near the island is prime habitat for the species, which is the top predator in the Arctic marine ecosystem (Fig. 2). The polar bear is an icon of the North and has become the "poster species" for climate change because of its need for sea ice. With the summer extent of Arctic sea ice rapidly changing, the potential consequences for polar bears are severe.

Of the approximately 25,000 polar bears in the Arctic, about 1,500 live in the southern Beaufort Sea, making up one of nineteen polar bear populations that are recognized worldwide. The coastal range of this population extends from west of Point Barrow in Alaska to east of Paulatuk in Darnley Bay (Fig. 3). Since 2000, the population is thought to have declined from about 1,800 bears because of poor ecological conditions brought about the rapidly changing sea ice and low numbers of cubs joining the population. Herschel Island is toward the centre of the range for the southern Beaufort population, but the bears mainly use the island when the ice retreats or when pregnant females are looking for a suitable site to build a den. As the sea ice changes in the Beaufort Sea, the population boundaries may be shifting, and some bears are wandering further, presumably searching for suitable habitat.

Range

Individual polar bears in the southern Beaufort Sea region range over an area of 300,000 to 400,000 square kilometres each year. Satellite tracking of bears tagged near Herschel Island shows that they mostly stay north of the western Arctic coast, but they have been tracked around Banks Island in the east and as far west as the Chukchi Sea and Wrangel Island in Russia (Fig. 3).

A young polar bear or nanuq (*Ursus maritimus*) on newly formed ice. *Photo by Andrew Derocher.*

A female polar bear swims across a narrow lead in the Beaufort Sea near Herschel Island. *Photo by Andrew Derocher.*

Fig. 1 Cub-of-the-year or nanuaraaluk (approximately four months old) caught near Herschel Island in May during a population ecology study. *Photo by Andrew Derocher.*

Fig. 2 Adult male polar bear on the sea ice east of Herschel Island. *Photo by Andrew Derocher.*

Until recently, all the bears in this population, with the exception of pregnant females, travelled northward in spring and summer as the ice front moved out of southern parts of the region. A flaw lead, or channel of open water, appears in late winter and spring, running east-west just north of Herschel Island toward the Cape Bathurst polynya, an area of open water in the sea ice maintained by ocean currents and winds, and north from there toward Banks Island. The flaw lead, which follows the boundary between the landfast ice and the more active pack ice, deflects the bears, because they prefer to avoid swimming in cold temperatures. As a result, the lead creates a "divided polar bear highway," with bears streaming east or west looking for food or, in the spring, for mates. When the flaw lead is closed by winds or cold weather, the bears are able to "change lanes" and move freely north and south.

The bears normally return southward in the autumn, as the ice reforms, to find better hunting over the shallow coastal waters of the continental shelf. Now, however, some bears spend the summer on land because of the seasonally reduced sea ice coverage, with the ice edge several hundred kilometres offshore. The coast on the Canadian side of the border is not used extensively by polar bears in summer, but a growing portion of the population, perhaps over 100 bears, remains on land in Alaska between Demarcation Point and Point Barrow. Some bears are drawn by the remains of bowhead whales hunted by Iñupiat harvesters from North Slope villages. These carcasses provide a substantial amount of food, and bears that feed in these areas may become abnormally obese. In the coming years we may expect more bears on Herschel Island in summer.

0   200 km

Sachs Harbour

Prudhoe Bay

Kaktovik

Paulatuk

ALASKA

NWT

Inuvik

YUKON

Fig. 3 Movement of 11 polar bears caught in the Southern Beaufort Sea population in spring 2008 near Herschel Island and followed by satellite telemetry over one year.

Fig. 4 Adult male ringed seal or natchiq (*Phoca hispida*) killed near Herschel Island in spring. Note the polar bears' clear preference for the blubber layer. The saw is 45 centimetres long. *Photo by Andrew Derocher.*

Diet

Polar bears are drawn to the area around Herschel Island by the abundance of their major prey—ringed seals and bearded seals. Regardless of the species, the bears seek seals for their energy-rich fat (Fig. 4). Overall, ringed seals form the bulk of the bears' diet (up to 70 percent), with bearded seals contributing about 20 percent. The remainder of their diet is made up of beluga and bowhead whales.

Several species exploit the leftovers from polar bear kills. Arctic foxes and glaucous gulls are the two most common scavengers. Arctic foxes often skip along behind polar bears, waiting for their next meal. Researchers and hunters keep a sharp eye out for gulls, which may indicate a recent seal kill and a nearby polar bear.

THE POLAR BEARS' SEAL LARDER

Both ringed seals and bearded seals give birth to their young on the ice around Herschel Island. The stable, landfast ice to the east and west of the island is ideal for the construction of birthing lairs by ringed seals. Many of the females give birth in the area from mid-March to April.

Bearded seals are found further offshore in the more active ice. They are large animals that may weigh over 400 kilograms. Female bearded seals give birth to their young in the broken active ice over the continental shelf in April and early May. Bearded seal pups weigh about 50 kilograms at birth and quickly reach 100 kilograms. The pups are particularly naïve and vulnerable to polar bears.

Denning

Mating pairs are commonly found on the sea ice near Herschel Island from March to June. The sexes are easily identified, as males weigh up to three times more than females (Fig. 5). By November or December, pregnant females seek out appropriate habitat to dig a snow den, and a few may choose suitable sites at Herschel Island. Dens are usually on the north and west sides of the island where deep snow drifts develop. These drifts allow the females to dig several metres down to make their round dens, each measuring one or two metres in diameter and one metre in height. They modify their dens throughout the winter, as more snow collects, to ensure an adequate oxygen supply through the icy layer that forms on the ceiling.

Many pregnant females of the southern Beaufort Sea population—unlike in most other areas—used to build dens on the stable multi-year ice in the area. In the last two decades, as the multi-year ice has retreated northward and become less predictable, more females have made their dens at the coast or on land. Herschel Island may see an increase in denning activity in the near future if this trend in sea-ice conditions continues. Because polar bears show high fidelity to their birth areas, we can expect female cubs born on Herschel Island to return at five to six years of age to produce their own cubs.

Polar bear cubs are born in December and remain in the den until they are old enough to move to the sea ice in April or May. Normally there are one or two cubs in the litter, but occasionally three are born. Mothers with young cubs stay close to the stable landfast ice in Mackenzie Bay to avoid encountering potentially infanticidal adult males, and to limit competition for seals that the mothers kill. Ringed seals and pups are the preferred prey. As spring progresses, the normal pattern is for the females and cubs to travel northward as the ice melts (Fig. 3). Females with older cubs, which stay with their mother until they are about two-and-a-half years old, are common in the fall, winter, and spring around Herschel Island. Subadults, three to five years old, are the true wanderers in the population, showing up almost anywhere a meal might be found.

Assuming a polar bear survives past the period of high mortality in its first two years, females can live to about twenty-six years and males to about twenty-four years. The most common cause of death for young animals is starvation. Juveniles are inexperienced hunters and often suffer higher mortality rates until their skills pick up. Old bears seem to die of an accumulation of small injuries. Broken teeth, failing eyesight, wounds acquired when fighting for breeding rights, and stiffening joints all take their toll. The bears slowly lose body condition and, in their last months, are often skinny.

Harvesting

Harvesting of polar bears by whalemen between 1870 and 1920 greatly reduced the number of bears denning along the mainland of Canada and Alaska. However, the population recovered after protection for mothers with cubs was introduced in the 1970s.

The Inuvialuit–Iñupiat Polar Bear Management Agreement in the southern Beaufort Sea aims to maintain a healthy, viable population of polar bears in perpetuity (Fig. 6). The region has an annual harvest of about sixty bears by Inuvialuit and Iñupiat hunters (Fig. 7). Inuvialuit hunters from Aklavik commonly hunt their bears on the sea ice near Herschel Island. There is some sport hunting of the bear population, but it usually occurs further east, based from Tuktoyaktuk and Paulatuk.

The hunt in the southern Beaufort Sea is conservatively managed to ensure a sustainable harvest. There are quotas for each community, which are set within a co-management system and in accordance with the Management Agreement.

Environmental Challenges

Pollutants carried into the Arctic Ocean by ocean currents and rivers are a threat to polar bears throughout the circumpolar north. However, they are of less concern in the southern Beaufort Sea because the pollution levels in the area are generally not as high as in other parts of the Arctic. Polar bears are particularly susceptible to pollutants because the concentration of toxic substances is magnified up the food web, and the bears are at the top! Most toxins are concentrated in animal fat, so the bears may receive high doses as a result of their high-fat diet. Pollutants can affect their growth, development, sexual activity, learning, and immune system, but we do not know if such effects are currently causing problems for the southern Beaufort Sea population.

Oil and gas exploration and development in polar bear habitat is rapidly expanding, and is worrying because polar bears are vulnerable to harmful effects from crude oil spills. The effects of oil and gas activity on polar bears in Alaska have not been substantial, but the accidental release of oil into polar bear habitat may have serious effects on bears in the area. In this context, the bowhead whale carcasses on the Alaskan coast mentioned earlier are a concern because they attract and keep bears in an area of industrial activity. If petroleum development continues in the Beaufort Sea, ships that tend drilling platforms will alter sea ice conditions in early winter. Such industrial activity will also attract bears, because seals like the open water and the bears like the seals.

Overall, however, the major threat to polar bears in the southern Beaufort Sea comes from climate change. A population of polar bears has inhabited the Herschel Island area for millennia, but the current climate warming is putting them at risk. The multi-year sea ice used by the bears in summer is disappearing, and some analyses suggest that the population could disappear within fifty years. At that point, the bears may only find sufficient habitat further north, perhaps even north of Banks Island. Already, as sea-ice distribution and extent changes, the signs of stress are showing. Changing bear movements, drowning bears, cannibalism, infanticide, evidence of reduced food intake, lower survival rates, and lower body growth rates all suggest that the population is under stress, and is reacting to the deterioration in the condition of their habitat.

Fig. 5 Adult male *left* and adult female in a mating pair of polar bears just east of Herschel Island in May 2008. *Photo by Andrew Derocher.*

Fig. 6 Long-term monitoring of the southern Beaufort Sea population is essential for management of sustainable harvests under the Inuvialuit–Iñupiat Polar Bear Management Agreement. Here, Andrew Derocher examines a polar bear on the sea ice east of Herschel Island. *Photo courtesy of Andrew Derocher.*

Fig. 7 Bill Cockney at Herschel Island with a polar bear he had shot. *Photo courtesy of Parks Canada, William McFarland Herschel Island 1953–55 Collection, #42, and reproduced with kind permission of Bill and Lucy Cockney.*

MARINE MAMMALS

Lois Harwood

The marine waters near Herschel Island provide a summer home for two species of whale, the beluga whale or **qilalugaq** (*Delphinapterus leucas*) and the bowhead whale or **arviq** (also **arvak**) (*Balaena mysticetus*) (Fig. 1). These seasonal migrants spend the summer in the southeastern Beaufort Sea and Amundsen Gulf, the same region where two species of seal, the ringed seal or **natchiq** (*Phoca hispida*) and the bearded seal or **urgȓuk** (*Erignathus barbatus*), are year-round residents. A few harbour seals or **kusigiuk** (*Phoca vitulina*) and occasionally walrus or **aiviq** (*Odobenus rosmarus*) have been seen at Pauline Cove (Fig. 2). There are reports of other marine mammals in the Beaufort Sea, such as the gray whale, the narwhal, and the killer whale, but these are sightings of the animals outside their normal range. The abundance of seals in autumn, and the ease with which they can be caught in nets at Pauline Cove, prompted Nuligak (Bob Cockney) to exclaim that "Herschel Island is a land where it is good to live."

Bowhead Whales

Arviq, the bowhead whale, is a large, ice-associated mysticete or baleen whale. Instead of teeth, bowheads have up to 600 thin, fringed baleen plates suspended from the upper jaw, and these are used to filter small, krill-like prey from the seawater. Bowheads are mostly black in colour and commonly have white markings on their chin and flukes (Fig. 3). The white markings may indicate maturity but do not confirm it. Female bowhead whales mature when they reach 12.5 to 14 metres in length (at 17 to 20 years or older) and calve once every three to five years. In the past two decades, stone harpoon blades dating back to the nineteenth century have been found in bowhead whales harvested in Alaska, indicating that some bowheads may live as long as 200 years.

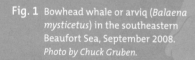

Fig. 1 Bowhead whale or arviq (*Balaena mysticetus*) in the southeastern Beaufort Sea, September 2008. *Photo by Chuck Gruben.*

Bearded seal or urgȓuk (*Erignathus barbatus*) swimming in Pauline Cove, July 2010. *Photo by Michael Kawerninski.*

The Bering Sea population of bowhead whales, also known as the Bering-Chukchi-Beaufort population, was estimated at 10,470 animals in 2001, although the numbers appear to have increased since then. This population was designated as of "Special Concern" by the Committee on the Status of Endangered Wildlife in Canada (COSEWIC) and under Canada's Species at Risk Act in 2007. An annual subsistence harvest by Iñupiat is regulated under a quota system by the Alaskan Eskimo Whaling Commission and the International Whaling Commission. In 2009, the quota allowed subsistence hunters to strike, or attempt to take, up to 79 bowhead whales. Only two bowheads from this population have been landed from Canadian waters in recent years by Inuvialuit harvesters (in 1991 and 1996). Previously, the last whale taken in Canadian waters was in 1921 near the Baillie Islands.

Bowheads arrive in the Canadian Beaufort Sea during late May and June through leads in the pack ice far from shore. During July, they are found throughout the offshore Beaufort Sea and Amundsen Gulf, singly or in small groups. By early to mid-August, ocean conditions favour the concentration of plankton—the bowhead's prey—and the whales begin to form large, loose feeding groups in four or five regular areas. They move among the different feeding areas, which are not all used in all years. One such feeding area is approximately 35 kilometres northeast of Herschel Island, where the water is 100 to 400 metres deep (Fig. 4). There is a particularly large and persistent feeding area to the east off the Tuktoyaktuk Peninsula. This area appears to support up to half of the bowhead whales in the Canadian Beaufort region at any one time, and more than all of the other feeding areas in the Beaufort Sea (including the Herschel feeding area) combined.

In some years Yukon coastal waters provide important feeding habitats

Fig. 2 Walrus or aiviq (*Odobenus rosmarus*) in Thetis Bay near Simpson Point.
Photo by Max Friesen.

Fig. 3 Bowhead whales near Herschel Island, north of the Babbage River, August 2007.
Photo by Cameron Eckert.

for subadult bowhead whales, usually when the prevailing winds are easterly. These winds induce an upwelling of nutrient-rich water from the deeper ocean, which in turn fosters the production of plankton. Harvesters from Aklavik travelling by boat to and from Herschel Island have seen large groups of bowhead whales feeding near the coast. At times the whales have been lying motionless at the surface, apparently sleeping. Bowheads favour the nearshore waters along the coast by Stokes Point, Shingle Point, and King Point.

The return fall migration of bowheads starts through Yukon coastal waters in late August, often within tens of kilometres of the coast. Bowhead whales can be spotted from the hills on Herschel Island or from other key vantage points along the Yukon coast.

During this migration the bowheads move relatively slowly, at between two and four kilometres per hour, stopping to feed in areas where plankton are concentrated. They may linger at such patches for days or even weeks before moving on to the next, on the way to their winter range in the Bering Sea.

Access to feeding areas, and the quality and quantity of prey available, are important to bowhead survival. Human activity such as shipping or seismic surveying may disturb feeding or migrating bowheads. Regulators work closely with Inuvialuit and Iñupiat communities and harvesters, with industry, and with scientists in Canada and Alaska to mitigate potential harmful effects.

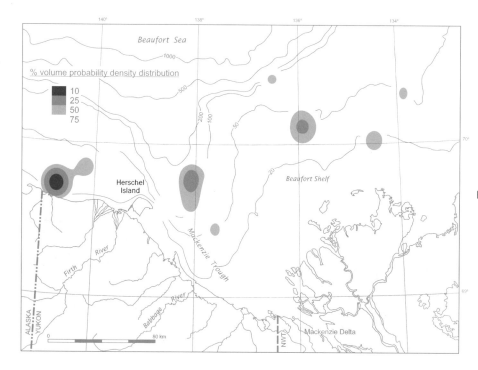

Fig. 4 Open-water habitats used by bowhead whales in southeastern Beaufort Sea, August 2007–09. *Surveys by Fisheries and Oceans Canada; cartography by Christine Earl.*

Beluga Whales

Qilalugaq, the beluga whale (Fig. 5), also known as the white whale (beluga means "the white one" in Russian), is an odontocete or toothed whale, and like the bowhead, lacks a dorsal fin. It is found throughout the Arctic and is the most common species of whale in the Beaufort Sea. Belugas are highly vocal and have a well-developed capacity for echolocation, a sonar-like system used to detect and locate objects. They are well-known for their habit of gathering together in nearshore estuaries during the summer (Fig. 6). We do not know exactly why belugas come into estuaries, but the reasons probably include calf rearing, socializing, and promoting the annual skin moult, when dead skin sloughs off and new skin cells grow. Belugas have a very thick skin, at least 10 times thicker than that of dolphins and 100 times thicker than that of land mammals, which provides insulation, stores high amounts of vitamin C, and possibly protects them from ice abrasion.

The population of belugas known as the Eastern Beaufort Sea stock arrives in the Canadian Beaufort Sea from wintering areas in the Bering Sea during late May and June. They are distinct from four other stocks of beluga found in Alaskan waters. They congregate in the Mackenzie River estuary in July. By late July they leave the estuary, some moving eastward into Amundsen Gulf and others northward into Viscount Melville Sound. The fall migration starts in late August, when the whales move westward along the Yukon and Alaskan North Slope, travelling mainly far offshore. At present the stock is thought to number at least 32,000 whales, and probably more.

The Inuvialuit have long depended on the beluga for their sustenance and survival, and these whales continue to be an important element of diet, tradition, and culture. Subsistence hunting for beluga has taken place in the Mackenzie estuary for at least 500 years. In the last decade, the annual average number of beluga harvested by subsistence hunters from Aklavik, Inuvik, and Tuktoyaktuk was 97, almost entirely from the Mackenzie River estuary. Herschel Island is 150 kilometres to the west of the main traditional beluga hunting areas. However, some families from Aklavik travel to Herschel Island to hunt and fish in July and August, and sometimes a beluga whale is taken and reported from this area.

During late July and August, the belugas move offshore. Feeding is an important activity at this time of year, with the preferred prey being Arctic Cod, squid, and other types of fish.

In late summer, pods of up to ten or more whales travel throughout the offshore, often where there is floating ice. The marine waters near Herschel Island are no exception. Belugas can be seen from suitable vantage points on the island when the westward fall migration is underway. Tagging studies have shown that most beluga prefer a route well north of Herschel Island and the continental shelf, although some of the beluga come relatively close to the island's shores. In 2003, hunters camped at Ptarmigan Bay saw three beluga—an adult female, a two-year-old, and a calf—swimming there. These whales were presumably on their return fall migration, stopping in areas of plentiful prey along the way.

Based on aerial counts, estimated harvest rates, and the ages and sexes of animals taken, the beluga population in the Canadian Beaufort Sea is healthy, and the present-day harvest is sustainable. The survival and well-being of these belugas depend on access to the warm waters of the Mackenzie estuary in July, offshore feeding areas during August, and migration corridors in late August and September. Human activity such as shipping or seismic surveying may disturb feeding or migrating belugas. Regulators work closely with Inuvialuit harvesters, industry, and scientists to mitigate potential harmful effects.

Fig. 5 Beluga whale or qilalugaq
(*Delphinapterus leucas*) in the
southeastern Beaufort Sea.
Photo by Frank Pokiak.

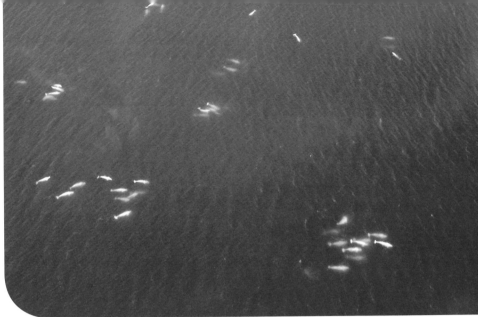

Fig. 6 Pods of beluga whales in the Husky Lakes area adjoining the southeastern
Beaufort Sea. *Photo by Lois Harwood.*

Ringed Seals

Natchiq, the ringed seal (*Phoca hispida*), is abundant throughout the circumpolar Arctic, is the most important prey of the polar bear, and is a keystone species of the Arctic marine ecosystem (Fig. 7). The smallest true (earless) seal, the ringed seal feeds at several levels in the Arctic food web, with seasonal and age-related differences in prey type and location. It continues to be important to the subsistence economies of the coastal Inuvialuit communities of Uluhaktok, Sachs Harbour, Tuktoyaktuk, and Paulatuk, although present-day harvests are approximately 20 percent of what they were in the 1960s, before the European anti-sealing campaigns. Today, about 1,000 ringed seals are taken annually in the Canadian Beaufort Sea region for food, dog food, and pelts to make handicrafts and clothing. We do not know the size of the ringed seal population in the southeastern Beaufort Sea, but it may be more than half a million.

Ringed seals occupy the fast ice as it forms in early winter, where they keep breathing holes open by scraping away the thickening ice with their strong fore-flipper claws. Stable landfast ice east and west of Herschel Island, where it occurs, provides habitat for ringed seals to have their pups. This area has one to two seals per square

kilometre of landfast ice during the pupping season, much like the rest of the fast ice areas in the southeastern Beaufort Sea. As the snow drifts over their breathing holes, ringed seals dig out lairs under the snow in which they haul out to rest. During mid-March to late April, pregnant females give birth to their single pups in these lairs and suckle them for approximately six weeks. The pups weigh about four kilograms at birth, and are vulnerable to polar bears while in the lairs.

By early June most of the lairs have melted open and ringed seals are basking on the sea ice. Pilots, hunters, and aerial observers have all reported large numbers of these seals basking along the Yukon coast during May and June, including the

Herschel Island area. The seals then undergo their annual moult, often staying close to the ice edge to be able to escape from polar bears. Once the sea ice melts, ringed seals begin travelling throughout the region. Like bowheads, they tend to form large, loose groups to take advantage of prey that concentrate in certain geographic areas. Harvesters have seen seals at the mouth of the Firth River, at Nunaluk Spit, at the entrance to Ptarmigan Bay, in Thetis Bay, and at Babbage Bight near Kay Point. Seals often go to the mouths of rivers at break-up, probably to prey on Dolly Varden Char and other ocean-bound fish. Large groups of ringed seals have also been seen between Shingle Point and Herschel Island.

Fig. 7 Ringed seal or natchiq (*Phoca hispida*) near Herschel Island, July 2010.
Photo by Michael Kawerninski.

Fig. 8 Bearded seal at Simpson Point, Herschel Island, August 2008. *Photo by Cameron Eckert.*

Ringed seals are opportunistic feeders, but they prefer Arctic Cod and the larger forms of crustaceous zooplankton (krill-like) such as marine amphipods and isopods. During the open-water period, they must find enough food to regain condition after their breeding and basking periods. Adult seals tend to make wide-ranging forays to distant areas to feed, returning to their breeding habitats just before freeze-up. Adolescents and pups of the year make extensive journeys in the fall, probably in response to food availability. For example, young seals tagged at Cape Parry migrated thousands of kilometres westward as far as Siberia and the Bering Sea, and we can see such waves of westward migrants at Herschel Island in the fall. During seal netting studies at Herschel Island in the 1970s, hundreds of seals were counted as they passed by on their way west. The seals tend to migrate closer to shore than belugas, following routes similar to those of bowhead whales along the continental shelf.

The ringed seal population appears to be stable, and the species is currently classified as not at risk in Canada. However, these seals are highly dependent on the sea ice for successful reproduction, and are proving to be a good indicator of environmental productivity and change in the Arctic. Climate change, coupled with a renewed interest by the oil and gas industry in northern offshore exploration, could have negative effects on seal populations.

Bearded Seals

Urgîuk, the bearded seal (*Erignathus barbatus*), also a true seal, is the largest seal species in the Canadian Beaufort Sea region (Fig. 8). Its name comes from its elaborate long whiskers (or vibrissae). It has not been as well studied as the ringed seal or the whales. Its body, weighing up to 340 kilograms during winter and spring, is much larger than that of the ringed seal. Bearded seals vary from light to dark brown without markings, and they have relatively long whiskers, paddle-shaped fore flippers (hence the name "square flipper"), relatively small eyes, and four mammary teats rather than two.

During April, at the start of the mating season, the adult males begin underwater "singing." The song is a unique, complex, and eerie whistle, parts of which are audible to humans. Their highly varied vocal repertoire suggests a complex social structure that may be related to claims of territory and breeding condition. Females give birth to a single pup on the moving ice, usually during late April or early May. The average weight of pups at birth is 34 kilograms, but by the end of 12 to 18 days of nursing, the pups have a thick blubber layer and their body weight is up to 100 kilograms.

Bearded seals prefer shallower waters than ringed seals so they can reach their favoured prey, which includes benthic (bottom-dwelling) invertebrates, fish, crustaceans, and molluscs. Because of their preference for shallow shelf waters less than 200 metres deep, they are not particularly common along the Yukon North Slope, including the Herschel Island area. Bearded seals are sighted from time to time during aerial surveys in spring when they are basking on the sea ice. Like the ringed seal, bearded seals haul out for basking and scratching to promote the annual moult of their skin. Harvesters report that both male and female bearded seals haul out regularly on Avadlek Spit during spring and summer.

Bearded seals are more common in other parts of the Beaufort Sea where the water is shallower, such as off the Tuktoyaktuk Peninsula and west Banks Island. However, we do not have enough sightings to describe other favoured areas or patterns or movements, and no bearded seals have been tagged or tracked in this region to date. Researchers in the 1970s estimated that the solitary bearded seal was approximately 1/16 as common as the ringed seal. The number of bearded seals taken by Inuvialuit harvesters in the Canadian Beaufort Sea region is small—less than 20 per year. Human disturbance, along with changing sea ice and potential changes in benthic food sources, are possible threats to the bearded seal population.

Harbour Seals

From time to time harbour seals or **kusigiuk** (*Phoca vitulina*) have been seen at Herschel Island. There are small numbers of harbour seals along the coast as far east as Husky Lakes. These seals generally avoid heavy winter ice environments, and they do not make or use breathing holes in fast ice. They need open water in which to spend the winter. Their occurrence in low numbers is well known to the Inuvialuit, and, as the climate continues to warm and there is more open water during winter, the numbers of harbour seals along the coast, including around Herschel Island, could increase.

FISHES

Lois Harwood,
Danny C. Gordon,
and Jim Johnson

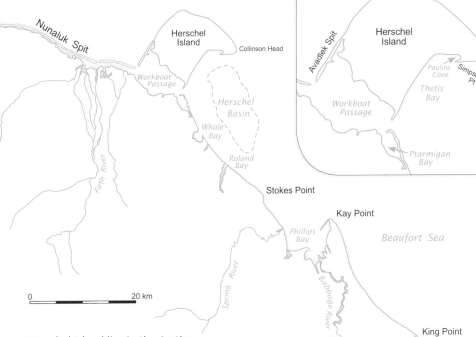

Bill Cockney checking his fish nets on the lee side of King Point. *Photo courtesy of Parks Canada, Jim Hickling Herschel Island 1953–56 Collection, #010, reproduced with kind permission of Bill and Lucy Cockney.*

Fig. 1 *Map* Yukon coast near Herschel Island. *Cartography by Christine Earl.*

Dolly Varden Char or Qalukpik (*Salvelinus malma*) drying at Pauline Cove, July 2010. *Photo by Christopher Burn.*

Herschel Island lies in the Arctic Ocean, but some of the waters near the island are diluted by freshwater from the Mackenzie and other rivers, creating brackish (salty) rather than pure marine (saline) environments. The mixture of waters surrounding Herschel Island provides habitat for at least 20, and probably over 30, different species of fish. Both marine and anadromous (sea-run) fish use the ocean near the island. Marine species remain in the ocean year-round, but anadromous species migrate to the ocean each spring from freshwater creeks, rivers, and lakes, where they spend the winter. There they feed near the shore, where plankton abound.

Many of the fish studies near Herschel Island were carried out in the 1980s, mostly in summer and in the more sheltered and productive areas. The five most common species of fish found near the shores of Herschel Island are Arctic Cisco or **Qaaktaq** (known locally as "herring") (Fig. 2), Dolly Varden Char or **Qalukpik** (Fig. 3), Least Cisco, also known as **Qaluhaq** (Fig. 2), Arctic Flounder or **Natarinaq** (Fig. 4), and the Fourhorn Sculpin or **Kanayuk** (known locally as "devil fish") (Fig. 5). The relative numbers vary from year to year, but there are consistent patterns from season to season.

Fig. 2 *Left* From top to bottom: Broad Whitefish or Anaqkiq (*Coregonus nasus*), Lake Whitefish or Pikuktuq (*Coregonus clupeaformis*), Inconnu or Higaq (*Stenodus leucichthys*), Arctic Cisco or Qaaktaq (*Coregonus autumnalis*), and Least Cisco or Qaluhaq (*Coregonus sardinella*). *Photo by Colin Gallagher.*

Fig. 3 *Above* Dolly Varden Char caught at Herschel Island, July 2010. *Photo by Cameron Eckert.*

During the open-water season, catches from nearshore waters are dominated by Dolly Varden Char, Least Cisco, and Arctic Cisco. Marine species, especially Arctic Flounder, predominate further from the coast. Common marine fishes that have been caught near Herschel Island include Arctic Flounder, Fourhorn Sculpin, Pacific Herring, Arctic Cod (Fig. 6), and Rainbow (Boreal) Smelt (Fig. 7). Arctic Cod or **Ikaluaq** is a keystone species of the Arctic marine ecosystem, as it is a major prey of seals, beluga whales, and seabirds, and is itself a major consumer of plankton. Inuvialuit have also occasionally caught freshwater species such as Burbot or **Tittaliq** (Fig. 8) near Herschel Island.

Although there are no spawning or overwintering areas for anadromous fish on Herschel Island, its coastal waters provide migration routes and feeding areas during the open-water season. Fish are concentrated mainly along the shore and in bays, lagoons, and neighbouring estuaries. The Babbage and Firth rivers provide overwintering and spawning areas for substantial runs of Dolly Varden Char, with more than 10,000 fish per run.

In 1985 a survey of the fishes at Herschel Island focused on the distribution of nearshore species. Ten species were captured, five of which were anadromous. The numbers of anadromous fish were four times higher than those of marine fish, and three-quarters of the anadromous catch was Arctic Cisco. The Arctic Cisco catch increased during July and reached a maximum by mid-August, with many juvenile and adult fish found in sheltered bays and coves. Nearshore protected areas, such as stream mouths and small sheltered bays, were particularly important for juvenile Arctic Cisco, Dolly Varden Char,

and Fourhorn Sculpin. The highest catch and the greatest variety of species occurred in Workboat Passage, followed by Pauline Cove, but few fish were caught in Thetis Bay. The plankton sampled near Herschel Island were dominated by Arctic Cod young-of-the-year. We do not know as much about the fish population on the north side of the island, because the coast is exposed to the open ocean and it is difficult to sample or catch fish there. However, in 1960 and 2006–07, biologists who were trawling in deeper waters off Herschel Island caught a variety of marine fish and a few anadromous species. These fish were caught up to 25 kilometres from shore. Thirty different species were found in the deep waters of Herschel Basin, with Arctic Cod (Fig. 6) dominating the catches, and making up 40 percent in one study.

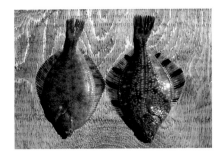

Fig. 4 Arctic Flounder or Natarinaq (*Liopsetta glacialis*) *left* and Starry Flounder (*Platichthys stellatas*) *right*. *Photo by Colin Gallagher.*

Fig. 5 Fourhorn Sculpin or Kanayuq (*Triglopis quadricornis*). *Photo by Colin Gallagher.*

Fig. 6 Arctic Cod or Ikaluaq (*Boreogadus saida*) caught by a Black Guillemot. *Photo by Cameron Eckert.*

Fig. 7 Rainbow Smelt (*Osmerus mordax*). *Photo by Colin Gallagher.*

Fig. 8 Burbot or Tittaaliq (*Lota lota*). *Photo courtesy of Fisheries and Oceans Canada.*

The ocean around Qikiqtaryuk has been a rich fishing area for many centuries, and today it is still important to the Inuvialuit for traditional harvesting. Four main sheltered sites are especially well-suited for fishing: Avadlek Spit and Pauline Cove on the island, and, on the mainland, Ptarmigan Bay to the southeast and Nunaluk Spit to the northwest (Fig. 1). Ptarmigan Bay has been fished for subsistence by one family from Aklavik since 1946 (Fig. 9), but others also go there in summer. The family travels to their cabin in summer by boat, and in winter and spring by snow machine. The most used fishing area on Herschel Island is Pauline Cove, where Inuvialuit, Iñupiat from Alaska, and others set nets or cast with rod and reel during the summer (Fig. 10).

Ocean and Wind Conditions Affecting Fish

Outflow from the Mackenzie River creates a narrow band of brackish water along the coast, extending westward from the Mackenzie Delta, in some years as far as Point Barrow, Alaska. More than any other factor, the presence of this brackish water affects the distribution and numbers of anadromous fish near the shore. The extent, chemical composition, and persistence of the brackish band depends on wind direction, precipitation, and distance from river mouths. Mountain streams such as the Babbage, Spring, and Firth rivers add large quantities of freshwater during spring runoff, but as summer progresses and stream flows lessen, the brackish band becomes narrower. Easterly winds tend to maintain the brackish water, while winds from the northwest drive marine waters toward the shore and disperse the brackish band. During late summer, easterly winds also promote the widespread upwelling of nutrient-rich waters along the Yukon coast.

The changing variety of fish species in the area is due to changing ocean conditions, the extent of the band of brackish water, prevailing winds, and upwelling. The arrival dates and numbers of Dolly Varden Char at Herschel Island are variable. In late July 1960, dense schools of spawning Capelin were caught in the shallow waters in Pauline Cove and at Simpson Point, but in other years no Capelin were found spawning there. Small silver fish that may be Capelin, Herring, or Arctic Cod provide food for the Black Guillemots on Herschel Island, which can often be seen feeding on them (Fig. 11).

The preferred prey of beluga whales is the Arctic Cod, which they feed on as they migrate through Yukon coastal waters during late summer and fall. They also eat huge quantities of Arctic Cisco, Least Cisco, and Pacific Herring. Bowhead whales likely eat young-of-the-year Arctic Cod when they graze on plankton patches in coastal waters near Herschel Island from mid-August to early October. Seals are common in the area and, like beluga, their preferred prey is the Arctic Cod, although they readily eat small crustaceans as well.

COMMERCIAL FISHING

In 1960, a two-season commercial fishery started at Shingle Point, targeting Dolly Varden Char and Arctic Cisco. The enterprise had two large barges, on-site freezers, and a cannery. The overall commercial catch was 18,000 pounds (8,165 kilograms) in 1960 and 12,000 pounds (5,443 kilograms) in 1961.

The fishery was organized by the Department of Northern Affairs and National Resources and included fishing near Ptarmigan Bay. No commercial fishing has been carried out near Herschel since then, and there are no plans to start a fishery.

Fig. 9 The Gordon family cabin at Ptarmigan Bay. Herschel Island is in the background to the right. The spit extends to Calton Point. *Photo by Danny C. Gordon.*

Fig. 10 Fishing at Pauline Cove. *Photo by Richard Gordon.*

Dolly Varden Char

The light spots on the sides of Dolly Varden Char or **Qalukpik** (*Salvelinus malma*) (Fig. 3) distinguish them from most trout and salmon, which are usually black-spotted or speckled. Young Dolly Varden Char have about eight to ten wide, dark parr marks (or oval blotches) that contrast with the mottled olive-brown colour of their bodies. The adult fish caught at Herschel Island are silvery with an olive-green to brown colour on their dorsal surface (back) and numerous faint red to orange spots on their sides. In coastal Yukon waters, including the Herschel Island area, Dolly Varden Char average one kilogram in weight and 42 centimetres in length, but may grow as large as 67 centimetres and weigh up to three kilograms (Fig. 3).

The char leave their freshwater overwintering areas in May and June, migrating downstream to the coast to feed over the summer in the nearshore zone. In July and August, they are often caught in nets set by Inuvialuit harvesters as the fish begin their return migration from the coast to their overwintering sites (Fig. 10). Although they can live 16 years or more, Dolly Varden over 10 years old are unusual near Herschel Island.

The Yukon North Slope has three river systems that are known to support genetically separate stocks of these fish. These rivers are Joe Creek and the Firth River to the west of Herschel Island, and the Babbage River to the east.

Arctic Cisco

Arctic Cisco or **Qaaktaq** (*Coregonus autumnalis*) (Fig. 2) are found along the Arctic coast from Point Barrow, Alaska, to Bathurst Inlet in Nunavut. They are known locally as "herring," but are different from "blue herring," which is a local term for Pacific Herring. Arctic Cisco are normally caught during their coastal migrations in July and August. They are an important part of the Arctic marine food chain, both as a predator of marine invertebrates and as prey for larger fish and marine mammals.

Arctic Cisco are distinguishable from Least Cisco by their smaller eyes and scales, a complete lack of dusky colouration, and transparent fins. Unlike the Least Cisco, their mouth is at the end of their head (Fig. 12), which indicates that they feed in the water column, rather than near the sea or river bed, and probably chase and capture their prey. Arctic Cisco are generally more tolerant of saline water than other whitefish species found in the nearshore Beaufort Sea. Their main summer feeding and rearing areas are in the bays and lagoons along the coast, including Workboat Passage and Pauline Cove. They spawn in the fall in the tributaries of the Mackenzie River, even travelling as far south as the Liard River near the border of the Northwest Territories and British Columbia. Arctic Ciscoes reach an average age of eight years, but they may live as long as 14 years. Along the Arctic coast they average 37 centimetres in length and 600 grams, but can reach 50 centimetres in length and weigh up to four kilograms.

Least Cisco

The Least Cisco or **Qaluhaq** (*Coregonus sardinella*) is found in Arctic coastal waters, and in certain inland lakes and drainages, from Russia eastward to the Northwest Territories. It is the smallest of the anadromous whitefish in this region, and was the third most abundant species found in surveys at Phillips Bay in 1985 and 1986. The Least Cisco is a slender herring-like fish whose lower jaw projects beyond the upper jaw (Fig. 12). Adults are brown to olive green and silvery on the belly. Least Cisco are less tolerant of saline waters than Arctic Cisco. They eat mainly crustaceous zooplankton, insects, fish, and plant material. Maximum age for this species is usually 12 years, although one specimen caught at Nunaluk Spit was estimated to be 16 years old. Least Cisco from the area average 24 centimetres in length and 165 grams, but they can reach 38 centimetres in length and weigh up to 450 grams.

Least Cisco are important in the food chain, as they are eaten by predacious fish such as Inconnu. They are taken as bycatch in the subsistence fishery for the more sought-after Arctic Cisco (Fig. 13).

Arctic Cod

Arctic Cod or **Ikaluaq** (*Boreogadus saida*) occur throughout the marine waters of northern North America. They are easily recognized by their slender body, deeply forked tail, and projecting mouth (Fig. 6). They are circumpolar and occur farther north than any other marine fish.

Fig. 11   An Arctic Lamprey (*Entosphenus japonicus*) caught by a Black Guillemot. *Photo by Cameron Eckert.*

Fig. 12   Arctic Cisco *above* and Least Cisco *below*, showing the different shape of their mouths. *Photo by Colin Gallagher.*

In the Beaufort Sea, Arctic Cod spawn each year in late fall and early winter. Females produce from 9,000 to 21,000 eggs that are 1.5 millimetres in diameter. Young of the year are planktonic, which means they are tiny and drift along with the other plants, animals, and bacteria that collectively make up the plankton "soup" in the ocean. Arctic Cod more than a year old disperse throughout the water column, including just below the ice where they can find places to hide from predators. They travel as individuals for part of the year, though they also occur in huge schools, particularly near the shore in the fall.

Arctic Cod are rarely fished in the Beaufort Sea. However, they are a key component of the Arctic marine food web. They are the main consumers of plankton in the water column, and in turn are a primary food source for beluga whales and ringed seals. They are small, short-lived fish, rarely over 30 centimetres long or more than seven years old. They thrive in temperatures below 0°C because of antifreeze proteins in their blood, so they are frequently found where ocean water is cold and the salinity high. The extent of the freshwater plume from the Mackenzie River influences the location and abundance of Arctic Cod along the Yukon coast.

Arctic Flounder

Arctic Flounder or **Natarinaq** (*Liopsetta glacialis*) are long-lived fish that survive almost anywhere in the marine waters of the Arctic. There have been reports of individuals reaching 26 years old.

They have an asymmetrical mouth and an almost straight lateral line with a distinct branch that points toward the dorsal fin (Fig. 4). These flat fish may reach a length of 44 centimetres and have eyes on their dorsal side, which is olive brown with dark spots that may form wide bands. Their blind side is white. Arctic Flounder prefer shallow, mud-bottomed coastal waters and may even enter rivers. By burying themselves in the mud, they can prey on other fish, but they prefer clams, crustaceans, sea squirts, and worms. They spawn under the ice during winter and spring, when females over eight years old may shed up to 200,000 eggs a season.

Fourhorn Sculpin

The Fourhorn Sculpin or **Kanayuq** (*Triglopis quadricornis*) has a dark, flecked body, large pelvic fins, a big head, and a large mouth. It has four rounded rough knobs and several straight spines on the head (Fig. 5). This fish is adapted to bottom living by means of eyes that are almost on top of the head, a slightly flattened body, and the absence of a swim bladder.

Fourhorn Sculpin spawn in winter. In coastal waters they reach sexual maturity at two to three years of age. Males dig a spawning pit on the seafloor in water depths of about 10–20 metres. The incubation period lasts slightly over three months. During that time, the male guards the eggs and fans them with his side fins to clean and aerate them. Eggs are usually greenish, but can be other shades from maroon to orange.

Male Dolly Varden Char in spawning colours. *Photo by Colin Gallagher.*

DOLLY VARDEN'S FASHIONABLE NAME

Dolly Varden, a young woman known for her colourful style of dress, is a character in Charles Dickens' 1839 novel *Barnaby Rudge*. In the 1870s, a brightly patterned, usually flowered, dress known as a Dolly Varden became popular in women's fashion in Britain and North America, and led in turn to the naming of the Dolly Varden Char. While in the sea these fish are silvery (Fig. 3), but when they return in autumn to their freshwater spawning grounds, their appearance, particularly the males, with their hooked lower jaw and bright spawning colours, is striking.

Fig. 13 Mrs. Elizabeth Mackenzie and Jonas Brower cleaning fish at Pauline Cove, July 2006. *Photo by Richard Gordon.*

Table 1 Fishes of Herschel Island and nearby waters. These are grouped by life history type and by Family in bold. *Names are based on Fish Base (www.fishbase.org/search.php), and the Catalog of Fishes (research.calacademy.org/ichthyology/catalog); Siglitun (S) and Uummarmiutun (U) names are from R. Lowe (2001), Siglit Inuvialuit Uqautchiita Nutaat Kipuktirutait Aglipkaqtat and the Wildlife Management Advisory Council (North Slope), with assistance from Esther McLeod, Danny C. Gordon, and Annie C. Gordon.*

COMMON NAME	LATIN NAME	INUVIALUKTUN NAME
FRESHWATER/ESTUARINE		
Pike	**Esocidae**	
Northern Pike	*Esox lucius*	Siulik (S), Hiulik (U)
Suckers	**Catostomidae**	
Longnose Sucker	*Catostomus catostomus*	Milugiaq
Salmon and Whitefish	**Salmonidae**	
Arctic Grayling	*Thymallus arcticus*	Sulukpaugaq (S), Hulukpaugaq (U)
Lake Herring	*Coregonus artedi*	
Round Whitefish	*Prosopium cylindraceum*	Anahluk
Burbots	**Lotidae**	
Burbot (Loche)	*Lota lota*	Tiktaalik (S), Tittaaliq (U)
Sticklebacks	**Gasterosteidae**	
Ninespine Stickleback	*Pungitius pungitius*	
ANADROMOUS		
Salmon and Whitefish	**Salmonidae**	
Dolly Varden Char	*Salvelinus malma*	Iqaluaqpak (S), Qalukpik (U)
Arctic Cisco (Blue Herring)	*Coregonus autumnalis*	Piqquaqtitaq (S), Qaaktaq (U)
Least Cisco (Big-eyed Herring)	*Coregonus sardinella*	Iqalusaaq (S), Qaluhaq (U)
Broad Whitefish	*Coregonus nasus*	Anaakliq (S), Anaqkiq (U)
Lake Whitefish	*Coregonus clupeaformis*	Pikuktuuq (S), Pikuktuq (U)
Inconnu (Coney)	*Stenodus leucichthys*	Siiraq (S), Higaq (U)
Pink Salmon	*Oncorhynchus gorbuscha*	
Chum Salmon	*Oncorhynchus keta*	
MARINE		
Lampreys	**Petromyzontidae**	
Arctic Lamprey	*Entosphenus japonicus*	
Herrings	**Clupeidae**	
Pacific Herring	*Clupea pallasii*	

COMMON NAME	LATIN NAME	INUVIALUKTUN NAME
Smelts	**Osmeridae**	
Rainbow (Boreal) Smelt	*Osmerus mordax*	
Pond Smelt	*Hypomesus olidus*	
Capelin	*Mallotus villosus*	
Cods	**Gadidae**	
Saffron Cod	*Eleginus gracilis*	
Arctic Cod	*Boreogadus saida*	Iqalugaq (S), Ikaluaq (U)
Alligatorfishes	**Agonidae**	
Arctic Alligatorfish	*Ulcina olrikii*	
Sculpins	**Cottidae**	**Kanayuq (S), Ganayuq (U)**
Hamecon	*Artediellus scaber*	
Arctic Staghorn Sculpin	*Gymnocanthus tricuspis*	
Twohorn Sculpin	*Icelus bicornis*	
Spatulate Sculpin	*Icelus spatula*	
Shorthorn Sculpin	*Myoxocephalus scorpius*	
Ribbed Sculpin	*Triglops pingelii*	
Fourhorn Sculpin	*Myoxocephalus quadricornis*	
Snailfishes	**Liparidae**	
Kelp Snailfish	*Liparis tunicatus*	
Eelblennies	**Stichaeidae**	
Slender Eelblenny	*Lumpenus fabricii*	
Pighead Prickleback	*Acantholumpemus mackayi*	
Eelpouts	**Zoarcidae**	
Pale Eelpout	*Lycodes pallidus*	
Arctic Eelpout	*Lycodes reticulatus*	
Threespot Eelpout	*Lycodes rossi*	
Shulupaoluk	*Lycodes jugoricus*	
Canadian Eelpout	*Lycodes polaris*	
Sand Lances	**Ammodytidae**	
Sand Lance	*Ammodytes hexapterus*	
Flounders	**Pleuronectidae**	**Nataarnaq (S), Natarinaq (U)**
Arctic Flounder	*Liopsetta glacialis*	
Starry Flounder	*Platichthys stellatus*	

FISHING IN PTARMIGAN BAY

Ptarmigan Bay lies southeast of Herschel Island on the mainland coast, just across Workboat Passage from Osborn Point. A spit leading to Calton Point shelters the bay from the Beaufort Sea (Fig. 9). The Gordon family members from Aklavik use their cabin on this spit for fishing in summer as well as hunting in spring. Between late July and mid-August they set fish nets, usually of 4.5-inch (11.5-centimetre) nylon, 75–100 feet (23–30 metres) in length, on either side of the spit. The nets are marked by a line of floats, and have weights on the bottom to extend the mesh to the sea bottom. Dolly Varden Char and Arctic Cisco are the main catch, and from time to time Least Cisco and Fourhorn Sculpin. The family caught four Broad Whitefish or **Anaqkiq** (*Coregonus nasus*) at Ptarmigan Bay in 2006, but this is the only record of such fish at this location.

Abandoned cabins from the 1940s stand at the inner reaches of Ptarmigan Bay, showing the richness of the fishing area.

Similar cabins stand along the coast 10 kilometres from Roland Bay toward Stokes Point. Traditionally, fishing was also successful at Pauline Cove and Nunaluk Spit. The cabins at Lopez Point (see page 117) and the archaeological evidence on Avadlek Spit both indicate that the north side of Workboat Passage, too, was a good place to fish.

The fish catch varies from year to year. When the sea ice drifts or is blown close to shore, as often happens near the Ptarmigan Bay camp, it seems that the char also come closer and are more readily caught in the nets. People fishing see small fish and invertebrates (amphipods) in the icy water with char feeding on them. Juvenile fish, however, seem to prefer stream mouths, bays, and coves along the coast of Herschel Island. The physical shelter provided in Workboat Passage attracts these small fish and invertebrates and, in turn, the water fowl that feed on them.

The Gordon family cabin at Ptarmigan Bay, with a fish net set in the water. *Photo by Danny C. Gordon.*

Floats mark the position of the nets and keep them upright. *Photo by Danny C. Gordon.*

Annie C. Gordon filleting fish in preparation for smoking. *Photo by Danny C. Gordon.*

Smoke tent at Ptarmigan Bay. *Photo by Danny C. Gordon.*

PEOPLE
AND CULTURE

people and culture

INUVIALUIT ARCHAEOLOGY

Max Friesen

While Inuvialuit elders and historians have a detailed understanding of regional history, archaeology—the study of the material objects, such as ancient houses, animal bones, and artifacts remaining from past activities (Fig. 1)—helps to fill in some of the gaps in our knowledge of the more distant past. This chapter considers the archaeological record of the period before Europeans arrived at Herschel Island.

Earliest Inuvialuit

The earliest Inuvialuit inhabitants of Qikiqtaryuk arrived around 800 years ago, not long after Workboat Passage became submerged and the island was separated from the mainland. We have not yet found earlier evidence of people on the island. This is surprising, since several nearby sites—including Engigtsciak, about 25 kilometres south on the mainland, Trout Lake near the Babbage River, and Richards Island in the outer Mackenzie Delta—have all been used by hunters at various times during the past 10,000 years. Some of these early peoples must have made forays to the coast and onto what was then Herschel Peninsula in search of game. However, their traces have not been found, probably due to coastal erosion.

Around 1200 AD, the ancestors of all modern Inuvialuit and Inuit in Canada and Greenland left Alaska in search of new lands to the east. After so much time, we can only speculate about the reasons for this migration, but it is probable that family groups left difficult lives in Alaska in search of a better home. They were likely looking for places that were rich in seals, whales, caribou, and other game, and where they could find valuable resources such as metal and wood.

These people reached Qikiqtaryuk very early in their migration along the Alaska and Yukon coast. Separated from a relatively flat coastal plain by only a few kilometres of sea water, Herschel Island looms in the path of any group travelling along the coast by boat or sled. The diverse nearshore environments of the continental shelf and Herschel Basin mean that the sea around the island is excellent habitat for seals and whales. As a result, Qikiqtaryuk contains the longest record of Inuvialuit occupation yet found in the western Canadian Arctic, with substantial settlements recorded throughout the last 800 years.

The First Inuvialuit Settlement

Traces of the first settlement of Qikiqtaryungmiut (or inhabitants of Qikiqtaryuk) were found at a site near Pauline Cove. This site is known as "Washout" because it was being washed away during excavation in 1954; today, no trace of the site remains (Fig. 2). When it was first described by archaeologist Richard

Fig. 1 A tiny ivory toggle in the shape of a seal head, recovered from Pauline Cove. *Photo courtesy of Government of Yukon.*

Fig. 2 The Washout site seen from the air during excavation, 1985. *Photo by Jeff Hunston.*

Fig. 5 Pauline Cove House 7. Entrance tunnel at front, main floor area at centre covered in driftwood logs, and sleeping alcoves at the rear and left side. *Photo by Max Friesen.*

Fig. 3 Washout House 3, fully excavated. On the right is a retaining barrel wall intended to keep the ocean from destroying the house. *Photo by Jeff Hunston.*

MacNeish, six eroding winter houses were seen, and an unknown number had already disappeared. Later, three additional houses were exposed and excavated by Brian Yorga and Jeff Hunston, so the site must have had a minimum of nine winter houses, although it was likely much larger. The original size of the Washout site will never be known. Some of the houses are known to be from different periods, but as there was little opportunity for archaeology before the site was destroyed, we do not know how many were occupied at any one time (Fig. 3).

Based on what we do know, however, the site was occupied for several centuries, beginning around 1200 AD and continuing until at least 1600 AD. We are sure about the beginning date because a type of harpoon head known as "Natchuk" was found on the site's surface. Natchuk harpoon heads were made in northern Alaska by people of the Birnirk culture, who were the ancestors of the earliest migrating Inuit. Whenever a Natchuk harpoon head is found in Canada, it indicates a very early occupation.

The earliest Inuvialuit house at Washout, excavated by Brian Yorga in 1978, reveals much about how these first Inuvialuit lived. The house was constructed entirely of driftwood, and had a rectangular main room about four metres long by three metres wide.

There was a raised sleeping platform at the rear and a separate kitchen outside the front wall. The house likely had an entrance tunnel, which served to trap cold air, but the tunnel was not preserved because of erosion.

Inside the house, the excavation team found an array of artifacts for hunting, fishing, tool-making, skin preparation, sewing, and cooking. The house contained a particularly large amount

of pottery, much of it decorated with circular patterns. Fragments of copper and iron, as well as ivory artifacts, provided evidence of trade. Almost 90 percent of the animal bones found at the house were from ringed seals, probably obtained by hunting in the open water in fall and from the ice edge in winter and spring. The house also contained large quantities of baleen or "whalebone"—the enormous flexible plates that hang from the

Fig. 4 Map of Pauline Cove, showing locations of major structures. *Cartography by Christine Earl.*

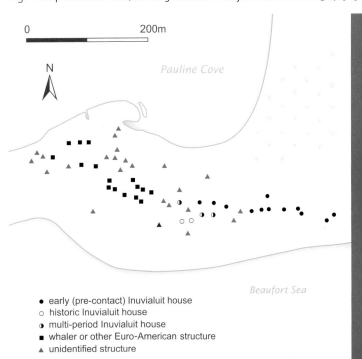

0   200m

N

Pauline Cove

Beaufort Sea

- ● early (pre-contact) Inuvialuit house
- ○ historic Inuvialuit house
- ◐ multi-period Inuvialuit house
- ■ whaler or other Euro-American structure
- ▲ unidentified structure

upper jaws of baleen whales, which they use when feeding to filter small animals from large mouthfuls of sea water. Baleen, which later became the object of commercial whaling, was used for many purposes, and large quantities at the Washout site almost certainly indicate that the earliest Inuvialuit actively hunted bowhead whales. In fact, the great numbers of bowhead whales in the Beaufort Sea may be why people migrated there from Alaska in the first place.

Seal Hunters at Pauline Cove

Following the earliest settlement at Washout, Herschel Island was continuously occupied until the twentieth century. During that time, the settlement gradually shifted westward along the beach toward Simpson Point, with later houses built at Pauline Cove (Fig. 4). Changes occurred in everything from the shape of the houses to the types of artifacts people made and used.

The best-preserved house from this more recent period is House 7 at Pauline Cove. Before it was excavated, the house was visible as a large mound just east of the historic whaling settlement. House 7 is larger than the earlier Washout houses, and contains two alcoves, one at the rear and one on the left side; each alcove contained a raised sleeping platform (Fig. 5). A short, deep entrance tunnel served as a cold trap, keeping the house's main room warm during the winter. The floor of large driftwood logs has a triangular burnt area in its centre, indicating the position of a hearth. The walls were made of upright driftwood logs angled inward toward what must have been a flat, square roof. The entire house would have been covered in skins and sod and must have been extremely comfortable in winter. It closely resembled the houses that were still built in the area in the 1890s.

Fig. 6 Artifacts from Pauline Cove House 7. Harpoon heads *(a–e)*; harpoon end blades *(f–h)*; harpoon foreshaft fragments *(i–j)*; toggle *(k)*; fish hooks *(l–m)*; fish hook barb *(n)*; decorated wrist guard used in archery *(o)*; blunt arrowheads for bird hunting *(p–q)*; arrowheads *(r–s)*. *Photo by Max Friesen.*

House 7 contained a broad array of artifacts, indicating a great variety of activities (Fig. 6). Harpoon heads, foreshafts, and a beautifully made toggle in the shape of a seal's head (Fig. 1) indicate sea mammal hunting, while arrowheads and a wrist guard, used to protect an archer's forearm, suggest the hunting of land mammals. Fishing is evident from an array of fish hook shanks and barbs, and two sled shoes indicate travelling. Other implements included ulus, men's knife handles and blades, engraving tools, drills, skin scrapers, needles, and lamps. Even items of personal adornment were found, including drilled teeth used as pendants and two labrets (lip plugs).

Animal bones also show that major changes had occurred between the occupation of the Washout site and the much later Pauline Cove House 7. In House 7, fish bones make up nearly 70 percent of all bones, indicating that they were crucial to the site's inhabitants. Most of the fish were probably caught in nets during the summer or fall and then dried or frozen to be used for winter food. However, the presence of numerous ringed seal bones suggests that this animal must have been a mainstay of the economy. The residents of House 7 also still hunted bowhead whales, at least occasionally, as seventeen bowhead bones were recovered from the house.

Based on radiocarbon dates and artifact types, House 7 is dated to around 1750 AD, just before European exploration began to have a major impact on the region.

Avadlek Spit

While the sites at or near Pauline Cove are clearly the largest and most important ancient Inuvialuit settlements on Qikiqtaryuk, there were also settlements at Osborn Point and Avadlek Spit. We know very little about Osborn Point, but the site at Avadlek Spit has yielded evidence of a small but very unusual occupation by early Inuvialuit (Fig. 7).

Two houses were excavated at Avadlek Spit; both probably date to around 1500 AD. Both houses were small and rectangular, with very well-preserved floors and walls of driftwood logs (Fig. 8). Each had a rear sleeping platform and a cooking hearth near the front wall. Outside one house a log-lined cache had been dug into the soil to store summer food for use during leaner winter times. A collapsed rack, possibly used for drying meat, was also found.

The Avadlek Spit occupation is particularly interesting because of the range of food sources used by the site's

Fig. 7 Avadlek Spit, seen from the air. The archaeological site is located at the dark patch near the centre of the photograph. *Photo by Max Friesen.*

inhabitants. Surprisingly, mammal bones were rare, and included only eight seal bones, making this probably the only coastal site in the entire western Canadian Arctic with such a low reliance on seals. However, this lack of mammals was made up for by huge numbers of fish and bird bones. In particular, the occupants ate Lake Whitefish, Inconnu, Arctic Char, Cisco, and Herring. There was also a large collection of sea duck bones, especially Long-tailed Ducks, White-winged Scoters, and Common Eiders.

Clearly, Avadlek Spit's inhabitants took advantage of its unusual location. The site is at the tip of a five-kilometre-long sandspit, which gave its inhabitants access to the very rich waters of Workboat Passage and the mouth of the Firth River. At this location, seals are not as common as at Pauline Cove, but in summer huge flocks of birds congregate on the water, and fish of several species are plentiful.

Regional Context

Throughout its archaeological history, Qikiqtaryuk has been home to communities consisting of Inuvialuit families interacting with each other and with people farther away. Avadlek Spit was a small community, with perhaps only one or two houses occupied in any one season, each

holding a single family. Washout and Pauline Cove must have been larger, but their exact size in any particular year is difficult to reconstruct. Much of the Washout site was destroyed by erosion, and many of the early Inuvialuit houses at Pauline Cove are buried under later historic buildings. Perhaps four to six winter houses were occupied at any one time, with thirty to fifty people living in them. Such a number would be large enough to provide a "social safety net" for sharing and mutual aid, but would not exhaust local seal and fish populations.

The houses described above were all partially dug into the earth by their builders and were almost certainly used during the winter. Some may have also been used during parts of the warm season, but a variety of summer activities probably took the early Inuvialuit of Qikiqtaryuk away from their winter settlements. Summer activities are often more difficult for archaeologists to recognize, since warm-season tents do not leave much evidence behind. However, one major summer activity would have been travelling to the mainland to hunt and fish. Caribou were plentiful on the Yukon North Slope and in the foothills of the British Mountains, and hunters would also have kept an eye out for moose, Dall's sheep, and smaller mammals. A site on the Trail River has provided evidence for late spring/early summer caribou hunting, and another site with dwelling structures is known from the Firth River, upstream from Engigtsciak. Mainland rivers such as the Firth were also excellent sources of fish. Trout Lake near the Babbage River has yielded evidence of its use for hunting and fishing as well.

During the summer, as well as during the mid-winter ceremonial season, people travelled to major social events. At these times, Inuvialuit from a broad region would congregate in larger settlements (probably including Pauline Cove) to meet, feast, tell stories, and dance (Fig. 9). There might also have been summer visits to important places such as the huge beluga-hunting villages of Kitigaaryuit and Kuukpak in the Mackenzie Delta, and the trade fairs at Kaktovik (Barter Island) and Nigalik in the Colville River delta, both on the Alaskan Beaufort coast.

Qikiqtaryuk was located on the important trade route between the major population centres of North Alaska, to the west, and the Mackenzie Delta, to the east. Early Qikiqtaryungmiut were thus in a vital position for the exchange of goods and information, and were likely central to inter-regional trade. Virtually all the houses excavated on Herschel Island contain trade goods in the form of copper, iron, soapstone, ivory, and other materials.

The Inuvialuit occupation of Herschel Island can be seen as a continuous and stable one from the time of their arrival, around 800 years ago, to Sir John Franklin's arrival in 1826. The first Inuvialuit quickly learned the best locations to hunt, fish, and build houses, with Pauline Cove preferred for its access to ringed seals and whales. Change on the island was gradual, with new ideas occasionally introduced by neighbours to the west, in Alaska, and to the east, in the Mackenzie Delta.

When Sir John Franklin landed on July 17, 1826, he met three Inuvialuit families living on Qikiqtaryuk. His arrival presaged the abrupt acceleration of the pace of social change for the Inuvialuit as the outside world became aware of their home.

Fig. 8 Avadlek Spit House 1. The excavated house, with well-preserved floor, is in the foreground; archaeologists are excavating cache areas in the background. *Photo by Max Friesen.*

Fig. 9 Archaeologists excavating part of a wooden drum rim at Pauline Cove. This artifact serves as a reminder of the social activities, including drum dances, that were part of Inuvialuit life on Herschel Island. *Photo by Max Friesen.*

QIKIQTARYUNGMIUT AND THE INTERCONTINENTAL FUR TRADE

By the first years of the nineteenth century, the Mackenzie Inuit had become part of an intercontinental fur trade that stretched from the shores of the eastern Beaufort Sea to the Kolyma River drainage in northeastern Siberia. The Mackenzie Inuit comprised several distinct societies whose territories covered the area from west of the 141st meridian to Cape Parry in the east. The westernmost of these societies, the Herschel Island

nation (Qikiqtaryungmiut, also known as Tuyurmiat), occupied the lands and waters from about King Point to near Barter Island. The interior lands to the south and west were occupied by Gwich'in. Inuit and Gwich'in had an uneasy co-existence, punctuated by periods of trade.

Captain John Franklin (later Sir John Franklin) was one of the first Europeans to learn about the complex relations between the Mackenzie Inuit and the Gwich'in

and among the Mackenzie Inuit nations themselves. In 1826 Franklin and a party of fifteen in two boats descended the Mackenzie River to the ocean and headed west to chart the coast. On July 7, at Tent Island in the western corner of the Mackenzie Delta, Franklin's men came upon a large encampment of Inuit, members of the Kuukpangmiut nation whose homelands occupied the delta. A crowd of 250 to 300 men surrounded Franklin's boats, clamouring to trade their labrets, bows and arrows, spears, and other items in return for Franklin's goods. Soon, however, the Inuit became hostile and aggressive and, with knives drawn, began to steal from the British.

Franklin and his men were lucky to escape with their lives. They were able to break away only by levelling their muskets at the Kuukpangmiut, who quickly retreated. They had encountered these weapons in the hands of the Gwich'in, and were afraid of them. Shortly afterward the explorers met a group of friendly Inuit from the Herschel Island nation farther along the coast. When Franklin's interpreter told them about the dangerous encounter at Tent Island, they said, "Those are bad men who never fail to quarrel with us, or steal from us, when we meet."

Near Herschel Island Franklin began to learn about the native trade of the region. The islanders received iron, knives, and beads from two sources—primarily from Inuit "who reside a great distance to the westward, and to meet whom they send their young men every spring with furs, seal-skins, and oil, to exchange for those articles," but also from the Gwich'in, whom Franklin called Indians, "who come every year from the interior to trade with them by a river" (today the Firth River).

A MIDDLE AGED MAN.

Engraved by Edwd Finden.

An Inuk from Qikiqtaryuk, 1826. This picture was sketched on July 9, 1826, by Lt. George Back during Franklin's visit to the Yukon coast, and published in his Narrative in 1828. The man had pierced his cheeks and the septum between his nostrils. The beads in his labrets came from China. They reached him via aboriginal trading networks that extended across Bering Strait, and had changed hands at Sheshalik, Nigliq, and Barter Island. *Part of Plate 13, facing p. 119, in Sir John Franklin,* Narrative of a Second Expedition to the Shores of the Polar Sea, in the Years 1825, 1826, and 1827, *published in 1828 by John Murray, London.*

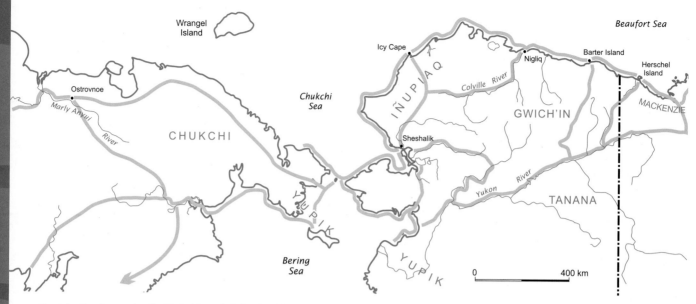

Aboriginal trading routes that linked Herschel Island and the western Canadian Arctic with Russian and Chinese traders in eastern Siberia. Metal goods, beads, and tobacco travelled east, while furs and skins travelled west. *Cartography by Christine Earl after the opening map in John R. Bockstoce,* Furs and Frontiers in the Far North, *published in 2009 by Yale University Press, New Haven, CT.*

Franklin also learned that the trade between Qikiqtaryungmiut and Inuit to the west had begun "so recent[ly] as to be within the memory of two of our present companions. ... As the articles we saw were not of British manufacture ... it cannot be doubted that they are furnished by the Russian Fur Traders who receive in return for them all the furs collected on this northern coast. Part of the Russian iron-work is conveyed to the Esquimaux dwelling on the coast east of the Mackenzie." A few days later Franklin's party crossed the 141st meridian and soon met the group of Qikiqtaryungmiut who were returning from their encounter with the "western Esquimaux." Because the exchange had taken place only a few days earlier, Franklin named his next campsite Barter Island.

Franklin discovered three important facts about the Herschel Islanders' trade. First, it was intercontinental and long-range, involving peoples as far apart as Russians in Siberia and Inuit east of the Mackenzie Delta. Second, Qikiqtaryungmiut were middlemen, receiving Russian goods

in return for Inuit furs. Finally, this trade had developed only recently, within the memory of his informants. In fact Franklin was among the first foreigners to begin to understand the nature of this native trade.

Although irregular trade exchanges had probably gone on between North Alaskan and Mackenzie Inuit earlier, it was not until the last decade of the eighteenth century that the trade intensified and became a regular occurrence. It developed because of events that had taken place in northeastern Siberia. In 1789 the Russians established an annual late-winter trade fair at Ostrovnoe on the Maly Anyui River, an eastern tributary of the Kolyma River. Chukchi traders brought furs to Ostrovnoe and bartered with the Russians for iron, kettles, tea, tobacco, beads, and many other ittems.

The Chukchi then carried the Russian goods 1,300 kilometres to the Bering Strait. In summer, with the help of Siberian Inuit (Yupik), they ferried the goods by **umiaq** across the strait to the great trade fair at Sheshalik on the shore of Kotzebue Sound.

Members of fifty aboriginal nations— as many as 1,750 people—met at the Sheshalik rendezvous and swapped their furs and other products for both foreign and domestic items. Other traders then carried the Russian goods onward via a number of over- land routes, but most often to the headwaters of the Kotzebue drainage.

The following summer these would be exchanged again at another annual trade fair, at Nigliq near the Beaufort Sea coast in the Colville River delta. From Nigliq other traders, primarily from Point Barrow, hauled the Russian products to the Barter Island rendezvous. Here the Qikiqtaryungmiut exchanged their own furs and took over as middlemen in the trade with other Mackenzie Inuit societies.

Thus furs from the Mackenzie Delta were carried a minimum of 3,500 kilometres by a series of aboriginal traders to northeasternmost Asia, where Russian traders took them onward to markets in China and western Europe.

—*John R. Bockstoce*

INUVIALUIT ANCESTORS

Murielle Nagy

Fig. 1 Inuvialuk in 1901 with kayak and two qaluurvik (dome-shaped tents) in the background. *Photo courtesy of Library and Archives Canada, Robert Bell fonds, PA 135821.*

Memeoane in his kayak at Herschel Island, 1909. *Photo courtesy of Library and Archives Canada, Royal Canadian Mounted Police fonds, PA 211730.*

Linguistic Groups

The contemporary Inuvialuit number about 5,000 people and belong to three distinct linguistic groups: the Siglit, who live in the coastal communities of Tuktoyaktuk, Paulatuk, and Sachs Harbour (on Banks Island); the Uummarmiut, who live in the Mackenzie Delta communities of Aklavik and Inuvik; and the Kangiryuarmiut, who live in Ulukhaktok on Victoria Island.

The meaning of the word Siglit (singular: Sigliq) is no longer known, but it refers to the indigenous Inuvialuit and was first recorded by Oblate missionary Émile Petitot as "Tchiglit" in the 1860s. The term Inuvialuit (singular: Inuvialuk), which means "real people," is used by speakers of the Siglit dialect to refer to themselves wherever they live. However, for over forty years the term has also been used to represent all western Canadian Inuit who signed the 1984 Inuvialuit Final Agreement.

The Uummarmiut ("people of the evergreens and willows") are the descendants of Iñupiaq speakers from Alaska who moved to the Mackenzie Delta and the Yukon coast. Linguistic evidence shows that the majority of these people came from the Anaktuvuk Pass area. The Uummarmiut are also called Nunatarmiut by Siglit speakers, a reference to the place they originally emigrated from. (Nunatarmiut is the Arctic Slope dialect form of Nuataarmiut, which means "people of the Noatak River.")

The first Nunatarmiut arrived in the 1870s, at the beginning of a drastic decline in the caribou population in Alaska, in order to find better hunting grounds. Later migrations took place in three distinct periods, beginning at the end of the nineteenth century when many moved to Canada to hunt caribou for the whalemen who had begun to winter at Herschel Island. Others arrived in the 1920s as muskrat trapping developed in the Delta, and a third wave of people arrived in the mid-1930s and 1940s as stores closed down near the Alaska–Yukon border. A few families who came from inland Alaska lived in the Old Crow Flats until the mid-1930s, and then moved to the Mackenzie Delta.

Indigenous Inuvialuit

The traditional territory of the indigenous Inuvialuit extended along the western Arctic coast from Barter Island in Alaska to Cape Lyon on the east side of Darnley Bay. Anthropologists divide the Inuvialuit population before contact with explorers, traders, whalemen, and missionaries in the nineteenth century into eight major groups, most of whose names end in the suffix "-*miut*," which means "the people of." From west to east, these were the Tuyurmiat of the Yukon coast; the Kuukpangmiut and the Kitigaaryungmiut of the Mackenzie Delta; the Imaryungmiut of Eskimo Lakes; the Nuvugarmiut of Point Atkinson; the Avvarmiut of Cape Bathurst; the Anderson River People; and the Igluyuaryungmiut of Franklin Bay. The pre-contact Inuvialuit population is estimated to have been between 2,000 and 2,500 people. The Inuvialuit were one of the largest Inuit populations in the Arctic before their drastic decline in the early twentieth century due to epidemics, particularly influenza. Contemporary police estimates, although possibly underestimates of the population at the time, indicate that the Inuvialuit were reduced to only 10 percent of their initial population in the early 1900s (Fig. 1).

Tuyurmiat and Qikiqtaryungmiut

Inuvialuit oral history tells us that the original people who lived along the Yukon North Slope were called Tuyurmiat by the people of the Tuktoyaktuk Peninsula and Mackenzie Delta, and probably spoke a language very similar to Siglitun. As the word Tuyurmiat can be translated as "guests" or "strangers," it may indicate that they visited their eastern neighbours, very likely at the village of Kitigaaryuit (now marked on maps as Kittigazuit) at the mouth of the East Channel of the Mackenzie River. Up to a thousand people are thought to have gathered there annually at the end of July or in August to hunt beluga whales. People lived year-round at Kitigaaryuit, but it was only during the summer that their numbers increased, because of the whale hunt. After the hunt, most people went back to their camps to fish during the winter. They only returned to Kitigaaryuit for major winter festivities.

Some cultural differences probably existed between the Tuyurmiat and the Kitigaaryungmiut. The people encountered by Capt. John Franklin near Shingle Point in July 1826 told him that they distinguished themselves by the fact that only women wore tattoos, while among the people living on the eastern side of the Mackenzie River, men also wore them.

Franklin gave the name Herschel Island to Qikiqtaryuk. At the time of his visit, he met people who had camps in three different parts of the island. He was told that people frequently visited Qikiqtaryuk in summer to hunt caribou and catch fish (Fig. 2). He also learned that the local population traded for iron, knives, and beads with the western Iñupiat at Barter Island, and with the Gwich'in, who travelled from the south along the Firth River. Although Inuvialuit and Gwich'in relations were not always good, the Inuvialuit who occupied the Yukon coast, and particularly the Nunatarmiut who migrated through the Old Crow Flats, developed a friendship with the Gwich'in.

According to Inuvialuit oral history, Qikiqtaryuk used to be linked to the mainland through Nunaaluk (Fig. 3). The people who lived there were then called Nuvurarmiut

Fig. 2 Avumnuk and his wife at Herschel Island in the 1890s. Avumnuk is wearing two labrets made of bone and blue glass beads. *Photo courtesy of Anglican Church of Canada, General Synod Archives, Stringer family collection, P7517-163.*

(people of the point of land) by the Siglit. After it became an island, they were referred to in Siglitun as the Qikiqtaryungmiut (also pronounced Qikiqtarr̂ungmiut in Uummarmiutun), meaning "people of the island." Tikiraq (Kay Point), Kiiñaq (King Point), and Tapqaq (Shingle Point) were the other major Tuyurmiat settlements along the Yukon coast before the arrival of the whalemen in the 1890s.

Fig. 3 Inuvialuktun names for places on and near Qikiqtaryuk mentioned in the text. *Cartography by Christine Earl.*

Fig. 4 Inuvialuktun names for places on the Yukon coast. In the early twentieth century, the largest settlement in the region was on Qikiqtaryuk. *Cartography by Christine Earl.*

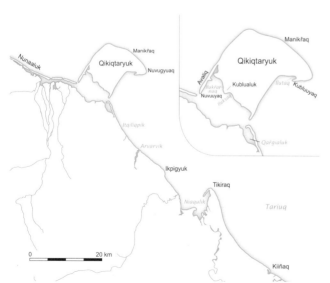

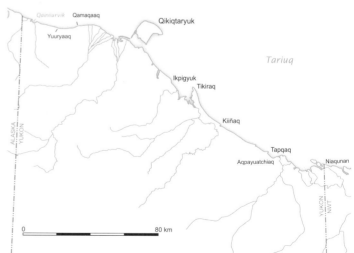

Fig. 5 Sod houses at Herschel Island. The dwellings were made of driftwood (and after contact with Euro-Americans sometimes of discarded lumber) covered by sod. The walls were lined with canvas. A hole in the roof served as a window. In 1903 there were 15 sod houses at Pauline Cove. *Photo courtesy of Library and Archives Canada, Royal Canadian Mounted Police fonds, PA 211737.*

Until the 1930s, small groups of three to six Inuvialuit families lived in the latter three locations, but also at Qainiiurvik (Clarence Lagoon), Yuuryaaq, Qamaqaaq (Komakuk), Nunaaluk, Qar̂gialuk (Ptarmigan Bay), Itqiliqpik (Whale Bay), Ikpigyuk (Stokes Point), Niaqulik, and Aqpayuatchiaq (Running River) (Fig. 4).

In summer, people would gather to fish and to hunt beluga whales at Tapqaq and Niaqunan (West Whitefish Station). Winter dwellings were made of sod and driftwood (Fig. 5), with interior hearths and oil lamps for light and heat. Inuvialuit elders reported that people also used some of these houses in the summer because they were cool. During the warmer months, people also lived in tents or round huts called **qaluurvik**, made of willow frames and traditionally covered with skins or moss (Fig. 1). These non-permanent structures were easily transported when people travelled along the coast. At Qikiqtaryuk, people used large houses made of sod and driftwood for communal activities such as drum dances.

Making a Living

Although food sources fluctuated over the years, people were able to occupy the Yukon North Slope on a relatively permanent basis, living on seals, bowhead and beluga whales, caribou, fish, and birds. They also

occasionally travelled inland to hunt caribou and sheep or to catch fish. Food surpluses stored in caches and ice houses during the warmer months eventually allowed people to occupy the coast permanently. Drying meat and storing food and oil in containers also ensured food supplies for the cold winter months.

The traditional life of the Tuyurmiat changed rapidly after the arrival of the whalemen who wintered at Herschel Island from 1890 to 1912 (Fig. 6).

The whalemen brought exotic goods to trade, mainly for meat, furs, and labour. Catastrophic change, however, occurred when diseases from the south, against which the local population had no immunity, arrived in the western Arctic between 1902 and 1930. These infections, particularly influenza, were carried to the Yukon coast first from the Klondike, and then by traffic on the Mackenzie River. Within thirty years, three epidemics tragically killed a major part of the Inuvialuit population (Fig. 7).

Fig. 6 Inuvialuit women visiting the *Jesse. H. Freeman* at Herschel Island in the 1890s. *Photo courtesy of Anglican Church of Canada, General Synod Archives, Stringer family collection, P7517-381.*

Whaling was overtaken by the fur trade, as trapping for furs became a major activity for all the Inuvialuit and eventually transformed their traditional economy. Trading posts were established at Qikiqtaryuk and Tapqaq, and the Inuvialuit went there in summer to trade their furs. In exchange they were given such goods as flour, tea, tobacco, and guns. Some people were also able to purchase schooners, allowing them to travel widely during the summer (Fig. 8).

Not all the Inuvialuit who exploited the resources of the Yukon coast in the first half of the twentieth century followed the same seasonal round. Although some people lived there on a permanent basis, most came only during the summer to fish and to hunt whales and caribou. Their seasonal travels depended on where they spent their winter: many in the Mackenzie Delta, some along the Yukon coast, including Qikiqtaryuk, others in the Old Crow area. Along the Yukon North Slope, people hunted caribou whenever they found them, mainly during the spring and fall migrations. In the early summer they used caribou to make summer clothes, and in the autumn to make winter clothes. Bull caribou were avoided during the rut because it affected the smell and taste of their meat.

People hunted polar bears along the coast and used their skins for the doors of sod houses and as mattresses. They also hunted seals, mainly in the spring and summer. They fished intensively in summer, and dried and stored the catch for later use. Bird hunting, particularly for ptarmigan, gulls, and geese, was an important activity in the springtime, when food was short and the season was not yet warm enough to hunt seals. During the spring ground squirrels were hunted for their meat and fur when they came out of their burrows. In the summer, people picked berries, roots, and the leaves of some plants, and stored the leaves in blubber for winter use.

Gender roles seem to have been more flexible than their usual portrayal among Inuit cultures, since many women were accomplished trappers and some hunted caribou and seal. Whale hunting, however, was done by the men. For bowhead whales, the activity was probably led by an **umialik**, the owner of an **umiaq** or large boat. Such men had a lot of prestige, as the whale they brought back was shared with everyone. Food preparation and storage, as well as making clothes, were mainly women's activities. When the trapping economy became dominant, both Inuvialuit men and women had their own traplines, although the fur trading was done almost exclusively by men. Children helped their parents and, when they were older, had their own traplines.

Fig. 7 The Inuvialuit graveyard at Pauline Cove. The whalemen's grave markers are in the background. *Photo courtesy of Canadian Museum of Civilization, George Hubert Wilkins, 1916, 51446.*

Fig. 8 Inuvialuit schooners at Herschel Island, 1930. *Photo courtesy of Yukon Archives, Finnie family fonds, 81/21, #156.*

Spiritual Life

Traditionally, the Inuvialuit had their own worldview, spiritual beliefs, rituals, and taboos, based on the belief that both humans and non-humans had souls and could be reincarnated. The shamans (**angatkuq**), who were able to contact the invisible world through their helping spirits, were the spiritual leaders. They were both feared and respected, as they could use their special powers not only to heal but also to kill. One of the last shamans remembered among the Inuvialuit was Kublualuk (Fig. 9), who could transform himself into a falcon and fly. Originally from Kitigaaryuit, he moved to Qikiqtaryuk around 1900. He was later baptized as a Christian.

Reports of the bad moral influence of the whalemen on the Inuvialuit prompted Anglican missionaries to visit Herschel Island from 1893 on. At first, few of the one hundred or so local residents of the island became Christians, but by the end of the 1910s most of the population was converted. These conversions were probably influenced by the deaths of many traditional spiritual leaders of the Inuvialuit communities during numerous epidemics. Church services soon became important and widely attended social gatherings (Fig. 10). Many traditional beliefs were still maintained alongside the new Christian faith.

Fig. 9 Kublualuk and his family at Herschel Island in 1925. *Photo courtesy of Yukon Archives, Finnie family fonds, 81/21, #206.*

Fig. 10 Wedding of James Atumiksana and Hanna Nasugaluak, August 14, 1909. *Photo courtesy of Anglican Church of Canada, General Synod Archives, Stringer family collection, P7517-148.*

Moving Out of the Yukon Coast

The last American whaling ship to spend the winter at Pauline Cove (the *Belvedere*) left Qikiqtaryuk in 1912. For the next twenty-five years, the island was an important trading centre in the summer. The Anglican mission at Pauline Cove moved to Tapqaq in 1920, where a school was established in 1929. However, activities at Tapqaq also declined as the economic focus shifted to the Mackenzie Delta, and the mission school was moved from Tapqaq to Aklavik in 1936. With the steady decline of fur markets, the Hudson's Bay Company posts at Qikiqtaryuk and Tapqaq closed down the next year. The absence of stores and the mission school led most of the few remaining Inuvialuit to move to the Mackenzie Delta. Another reason given by Inuvialuit elders for the move was that, along the Yukon coast, fewer animals could be hunted when the weather was bad, and without stores people might endure hard times. During the 1950s and 1960s, when seal skins could be sold for a good price, some Inuvialuit went back seasonally to Qikiqtaryuk to hunt seals with nets. However, Tapqaq was not abandoned by the Inuvialuit and is still a major fishing and whaling camp in summer. Although no Inuvialuit occupy the Yukon North Slope on a permanent basis anymore, the indigenous place names and the life stories associated with them demonstrate their profound attachment to the land that was occupied by their ancestors and will continue to be visited by their descendants.

WHALING

John R. Bockstoce

By the 1880s, American whaling ships were forced to travel farther and farther east along the Alaskan Beaufort Sea coast in search of new whale stocks. The whaling fleet, based in San Francisco, had been steadily reducing the bowhead whale or **arviq** (*Balaena mysticetus*) population in the western Arctic. In 1886 the fleet reached Barter Island, and two years later one of its ships approached the border between Canada and Alaska. It was a small whaleboat, however, and not a powerful steam whaler that first reached the Mackenzie whaling grounds.

In 1887 a group of Inuit traders returning to Point Barrow, Alaska, from a trip to the Mackenzie Delta reported to Charlie Brower, a trader and shore-based whaleman, that they had seen large numbers of bowheads in Mackenzie Bay. The following year Brower outfitted Joseph Tuckfield (Fig. 1), "a beachcomber of an adventurous turn of mind," with a whaleboat, gear, and a year's supplies, and sent him east with a local crew.

Tuckfield returned the following summer with news that "made about everybody crazy." He had wintered in the Mackenzie Delta and traded for furs, and had found a good harbour at Herschel Island (Fig. 2). Most importantly, he reported that the bowhead whales were "as thick as bees," and he had taken one—he had the baleen, or "whalebone," to prove it. He added that there was "plenty of open water up there in the forbidden sea." Seven steam whalers immediately headed east, anchoring on the east side of Herschel Island on August 12, 1889, but shortly afterwards five of them left when the *Jesse H. Freeman* encountered a shoal and they feared being wrecked. *Orca* and *Thrasher* stayed behind, each caught two bowheads, and on August 15 they met USS *Thetis*, a naval vessel that had sailed into Canadian waters to locate them. *Thetis* had encountered the other five whalers on August 14, before crossing the 141st meridian. Lt. Cdr. Charles Stockton of the *Thetis* ordered his men to chart Pauline Cove, which he named after his wife, while he named the adjacent sandspit after Ensign Edward Simpson.

Fig. 1 Joseph "Little Joe" Tuckfield, who in 1888 was sent to the Mackenzie Delta area from Point Barrow by trader Charlie Brower to look for whales and report on the conditions east of the international border. *US Government photo.*

The captain and officers of the whaling ship *Beluga* at Herschel Island in 1907. *Left to right:* Third Mate W.E. Cahill, First Officer Hugh Mackey, Captain George W. Porter, Boatheader Charles A. Sparks. *Photo courtesy of Library and Archives Canada, Royal Canadian Mounted Police fonds, e108693397.*

Before Stockton left on August 16, his men had surveyed the island sufficiently to produce the first chart of the area, which was published in March 1890 (see Fig. 2, page 21).

In San Francisco the Pacific Steam Whaling Company lost no time in capitalizing on Tuckfield's report. It outfitted the *Grampus*, one of its smallest vessels, and bought an even smaller one, a tug, the *Mary D. Hume*. The *Hume* was too small to carry tryworks for rendering blubber into oil, but with the price of baleen approaching four dollars per pound while whale oil fetched only 65 cents a gallon, it made economic sense to concentrate on the baleen from the bowheads, and not to bother much with the oil. This waste, in an already wasteful enterprise, was enormous, and regrettably it continued until the end of the industry.

The *Hume* reached Herschel Island on August 10, 1890. The crew off-loaded the supplies and the lumber to build a storehouse on Avadlek Spit, then cruised for whales near the island, but without success. They were unexpectedly frozen in for the winter at Pauline Cove on September 18 (Fig. 3). They had to man-haul all their supplies from Avadlek Spit and build a storehouse on Simpson Point, near the site of the present metal-clad warehouses. During the winter they built a cold storage cellar by blasting a hole in the permafrost and roofing it over with driftwood (Fig. 4).

Fig. 2 Aerial view of Pauline Cove, named in 1889 by Lt. Cdr. Charles Stockton of USS *Thetis* after his wife. Simpson Point is the spit on the left, where buildings from the whaling era are still standing. The line of white dots on the right mark the whalemen's graves. *Photo by Fritz Mueller.*

Fig. 3 The first season that whaling vessels overwintered at Herschel Island was 1890–91. The bowsprit of the *Grampus* is on the left and the *Mary D. Hume* is on the right. *Photo courtesy of Collections of Martha's Vineyard Museum, Edgartown, MA.*

Fig. 4 Five ice cellars for food storage were blasted in the permafrost at Pauline Cove, the first in March 1891 by the crew of the *Mary D. Hume*. One of the cellars is still in use. It is 4 metres long, 3 metres wide, and 2.5 metres deep, with a wooden ceiling covered by soil and turf. *Photo by Alice Kenney.*

The next summer, in 1891, both ships headed to Cape Bathurst and made phenomenal harvests, with the *Hume* taking 27 bowheads and the *Grampus* 21. The *Grampus* then headed for San Francisco, carrying the baleen and the news, while the *Hume* returned to Pauline Cove for another winter. The following summer the *Hume* took 10 more whales before heading out of the Arctic.

On the way, the *Hume* passed four other inbound Pacific Steam Whaling Company ships planning to winter at Herschel Island. The company had decided that Pauline Cove would now be used as an advance base from which the ships could exploit the whaling grounds at Cape Bathurst as early as July each summer (Fig. 5). At Qikiqtaryuk, the ships could winter in safety, make repairs, and await the company's tender that would provide them with food, supplies, and fresh crews each summer (Fig. 6). The tender would then return to San Francisco with the whalebone and furloughed men, thereby saving the whale ships the time wasted shuttling to and from California.

Pauline Cove quickly became the port of choice in the western Arctic. Four ships wintered there in 1892–93, seven in 1893–94, fifteen in 1894–95, and thirteen in 1895–96 (Fig. 7). By then the fleet had severely reduced the bowhead population. In 1893, the thirteen ships that hunted east of Herschel Island took 286 whales in what Capt. George Leavitt of the *Mary D. Hume* described in his logbook as "the greatest whaling season on record." As a result, the future of Herschel as a permanent whaling station was in doubt by winter 1896–97. Many ships were forced to winter farther east, at Baillie Island, Langton Bay, and Cape Parry, in order to make a catch. Nevertheless, during the two decades when the whaling fleet visited Herschel Island, a routine developed for the whalemen.

Fig. 5 The Pacific Steam Whaling Company's buildings at Pauline Cove, 1894. The far building was used as the mission station from 1897, the police barracks from 1906, and is now the community house (see Fig. 11). *Photo courtesy of Peabody Museum of Archaeology and Ethnology, Harvard University, 2004.29.3121.*

Fig. 6 Some of the fo'c'sle hands of the S.S. *Beluga* at Herschel Island in 1907. *Photo courtesy of Library and Archives Canada, Royal Canadian Mounted Police fonds, e10869398.*

Fig. 7 The whaling fleet at Herschel Island, 1895. *Photo courtesy of Mystic Seaport, Mystic, Conn.*

The whale ships and tenders usually reached the island from California around the middle of August (Fig. 8). They frantically discharged their stores and set off for Cape Bathurst, often meeting the "inside" fleet on its way to Herschel to exchange crews and ship out whalebone. The fleet then returned to whaling, following the bowheads as they gradually worked their way west.

By the middle of September, most of the wintering fleet was close to the island in case of an early freeze-up, and most of the bowheads were well to the west. As the whaling tapered off, the ships went to the mainland to collect firewood, since the island's supply had long since been exhausted. Depending on the particular ship's requirement, the crew took on board 100 to 300 cords of wood. By the beginning of October, all the ships were in Pauline Cove, where the last task was to secure sufficient dog food. Usually a few whale carcasses had washed ashore near the island, and a couple were towed to the outside of the sandspit, where great chunks of meat could be chopped out during the winter for the dogs.

When the ice was a couple of inches thick, the ships hove up their anchors and drove southeast into the young ice, minimizing their exposure to the northwest winds of winter. Each crew then housed over the decks with spars and sails. They put ashore the ship's boats and extra stores, and as snow accumulated they cut blocks from the wind-compacted drifts and banked the ship in to insulate it from the cold.

The men also cut ice for drinking water from ponds on the island and stored the blocks on racks near the ship. As the harbour ice thickened, they chopped the rudder free to protect it from damage and cut a fire hole in the ice to have quick access to water in an emergency. Both of these holes were housed over with snow blocks to retard ice from forming.

During the winter the crews obtained fresh meat and fish by trading with aboriginal people who were camped on the sandspit. They also sent parties made up of the ship's officers, Iñupiat, and Siberians to hunt for caribou and mountain sheep on the mainland. Provisioning the ships with fresh meat soon became a source of income for both the Gwich'in and Inuvialuit.

Fig. 8 The settlement at Pauline Cove.
Photo courtesy of Canadian Museum of Civilization, George Hubert Wilkins, 1916, 51368.

Fig. 9 A variety of accommodations at Herschel Island during the whaling era. *Photo courtesy of Library and Archives Canada, Royal Canadian Mounted Police fonds, PA211736.*

Hunting and trading parties travelled as far as 250 kilometres from Herschel Island and took a wide variety of game, although they preferred caribou meat. For the years 1894 to 1896, when the wintering fleet was largest, the ships' crews probably consumed as many as 2,000 caribou each year. Fortunately, the Porcupine Caribou Herd from which most animals were taken was undergoing a natural increase and may have numbered more than 100,000. At the end of the whaling era, the herd was probably larger than in 1890. The whalemen's kill, averaged from 1890 to 1908, likely amounted to little more than one percent annually of the herd's size.

The price of meat seems to have remained relatively steady between 1890 and 1910. The whalemen bought it for six or seven cents a pound, paying in trade goods valued at San Francisco wholesale prices. As a result, these goods cost only 20 or 30 percent of the prices charged by the Hudson's Bay Company at Fort McPherson. Ready access to these trade goods and to alcohol, among other things, drew local people to the island. With a mix of Inuvialuit, Iñupiat, Gwich'in, Siberian Yupik Inuit, whaling crews, and a few "beachcombers," the Herschel Island settlement approached one thousand people at its height in 1894–96. Its members lived amid "a mixture of wooden and canvas buildings, native huts, spare casks, boats, wood and all spare stuff put on shore to

make room ... on the ships" (Fig. 9). It was also a community of many languages. A trade jargon grew up that allowed residents to communicate basic ideas more or less effectively in an agglomeration of words drawn from various local dialects, Polynesian (some of the crewmen came from Hawaii and the South Pacific), Danish, French, English, and other languages.

With so many people living in close quarters, problems inevitably cropped up. Enforced idleness and rumours of gold on the tributaries of the Yukon River combined to cause desertions from the whaling crews every winter. Few deserters made good their escape; some froze to death, and many returned badly frostbitten. Occasionally groups of

Fig. 10 Several whaling captains brought their familes along to overwinter at Herschel Island, including Capt. W.P.S. Porter of the *Jesse H. Freeman. Left to right:* Miss Dorothy Porter, unidentified, Capt. Porter, unidentified, at Herschel Island, c. 1894–95. *Photo courtesy of the New Bedford Whaling Museum, New Bedford, MA.*

men left together. Seventeen deserted in January 1896 and twelve more in March. A party of officers and aboriginal people always went after the deserters because "as long as any number of deserters remained at large, it was a temptation to other men to desert and join them." When the pursuers caught up with the group that left in March 1896, more than 160 kilometres from the island, a gun battle broke out and two of the deserters were killed. Only one or two of all those who deserted reached the Yukon goldfields.

Alcohol also caused its familiar problems. The Pacific Steam Whaling Company forbade its men from trading whiskey, and most captains were opposed to the trade. Even so, an alcohol trade developed, and aboriginal and non-native people

on the sandspit also made hooch using gun-barrel stills. Rumours of debauchery at Herschel Island began to appear in southern newspapers. Few whaling masters, however, would have wintered there or brought their wives and children along if the rumours had been true (Fig. 10). In fact, when Rev. Isaac Stringer made his first visit to the island in 1893, he was surprised to be warmly welcomed by the whaling captains. He wrote to his fiancée, Sadie, that he "did not *see* much liquor or drinking, but I can't have my ears open without knowing that there is a good deal given to the Eskimos." According to Police Inspector D.M. Howard, the wild reports in the newspapers were greatly exaggerated: "The Esquimaux greeting at the ships' arrival belies stories of abuse and mistreatment; the women would certainly stay away." The whaling

captains also welcomed the arrival of the North-West Mounted Police in 1903, because the police reinforced the captains' authority over the crews. (The NWMP became the RNWMP in 1904.)

Winter life at Herschel Island included sports, games, and a social life of sorts. In summer 1893, when seven ships arrived in Pauline Cove, men from all the crews built a community house that contained a games and billiard room. The building, known today as the "RCMP House" or "community house," still stands, and is the oldest frame house in the Yukon (Fig. 11). The building served as a focal point for indoor activities throughout the winter, and the men performed minstrel and theatrical shows there. They also amused themselves by skiing and tobogganing in the hills to

Fig. 11 The community house at Herschel Island, built by the Pacific Steam Whaling Company in 1893. This sturdy and excellently finished building is the oldest standing frame building in the Yukon Territory. *Photo by Christopher Burn.*

Fig. 12 The row of whalemen's grave markers at Herschel Island. *Photo by Sara Nielsen.*

Fig. 13 Fancy dress party at Herschel Island, 1895–1896. Whaling captains and their families maintained a semblance of normal life through the winter. *Left to right, back row:* Sophie Porter, Capt. George Leavitt, Capt. James Wing, Capt. Hartson Bodfish, Capt. James McKenna; *front row:* Mrs. F.M. Green, Lucy McGuire, Viola Cook, Bertie Sherman, Mrs. Joseph Whiteside, Dorothy Porter. *Photo courtesy of the New Bedford Whaling Museum, New Bedford, MA.*

the north and east of the cove, and by playing baseball and soccer on the harbour ice. They organized a baseball league with four teams: the Herschels, the Northern Lights, the Arctics, and the Pick-ups. On February 19, 1894, the men played what one whaling captain considered to be the first baseball game north of the Arctic Circle.

But baseball could also be dangerous. On March 7, 1897, the men were just starting a game in unseasonably warm weather when suddenly a dark, billowing cloud loomed over the island. Within minutes the worst gale that some of the men could remember was blowing. As they ran for the ships, they could see only a few feet ahead and the temperature plunged

toward minus 30°C. Unable to find their way, they simply ran to the first ship or building, staying all night while the wind shrieked around them. At eight o'clock the next morning the wind stopped as suddenly as it had started. The ships' crews fanned out and found five frozen corpses: three whalemen and two aboriginal people.

Fig. 14 *Below* Fourth of July obstacle race at Herschel Island, 1896, with men atop the community house. *Photo courtesy of the New Bedford Whaling Museum, New Bedford, MA..*

Fig. 15 S.S. *Beluga*, Capt. George W. Porter, at Herschel Island in 1907. *Beluga* was fitted out as both a whaling and trading ship. *Photo courtesy of Library and Archives Canada, Royal Canadian Mounted Police fonds, e10869399.*

The bodies were buried in the graveyard on the east side of Pauline Cove (Fig. 12).

The winter of 1894–1895 was the first in which the wives of whaling masters stayed over at Herschel Island. Five of them, several with children, added a certain flair to the island's social life (Fig. 13). Masters with wives soon became known as "the Four Hundred," an allusion to New York City's high society; those without wives organized into "Hoodlums" and "Dry Throats." The wives put on elaborate parties among the three groups. With women in short supply, one captain wrote that he had had a fine time at one affair where "for a partner in the Virginia Reel I had Miss Dorothy Porter aged five years."

The season's last event, a celebration of the Fourth of July, took place just before the ships were able to break out of the harbour. The men dressed the ships with all their flags, and at eight A.M. they fired a salute to begin a day of games and contests: tugs-of-war, jumping, foot races, wheelbarrow races, sack races, tub races, three-legged races, obstacle races, a whaleboat race, shooting contests for whalemen and aboriginal people, and, of course, baseball (Fig. 14). The ships were usually able to buck their way out of Pauline Cove by the tenth of July. Then the fleet, having spent ten months in the ice, set out on its way to Cape Bathurst.

By 1895, the whaling ships had exploited almost the whole range of the bowhead whales, whose numbers were in steep decline due to overhunting. However, until the winter of 1907–08, Herschel Island continued to be the resupply point as well as a fall-back harbour in case of heavy ice. In 1908 the whalebone market collapsed and the whaling fleet soon left the Beaufort Sea. However, at the same time the price of fur was rising, and thereafter Herschel Island was only visited by whalers fitted for the fur trade (Fig. 15). Smaller trading vessels dominated the shipping, and Herschel Island gradually became a centre of the fur trade instead.

THE SHIPPING NEWS

Twenty-seven whaling ships wintered over at Herschel Island between 1890 and 1907. The *Grampus*, one of the first, spent seven winters in Pauline Cove between 1890 and 1899. The *Karluk* spent six winters and four other ships spent five winters each at Herschel, but most of them overwintered only once or twice. In 1894–95 fifteen ships overwintered and in 1895–96 thirteen ships stayed in the cove. Many of those that spent only one or two winters at Herschel Island did so in 1894–95 and 1895–96. Of the twenty-eight whaling captains who wintered over at the island, George B. Leavitt, the master of the *Mary D. Hume*, the *Newport*, the *Grampus*, and the *Narwhal*, did so seven times. John A. Cook and James A. Tilton each stayed through five winters.

Whalemen's Graves

Between 1890 and 1916, whalemen died at Herschel in all sorts of circumstances, natural and unnatural. The bodies of two officers were carefully preserved and shipped home on a southbound ship, but crewmen were buried on the island. Hartson Bodfish, a whaling captain whose career covered the whole of the period, wrote that between 1890 and 1905 only "thirty-seven graves [were] made on Herschel Island, and but two bodies shipped home," stressing the relatively low mortality. Even an individual limb was buried (though exactly where is unclear). Capt. John A. Cook related that a young officer called West had his arm amputated in June 1896, and as he came round from the operation to a glass of whiskey, said, " 'Kindly bury that here on the island,' which was done as he requested."

As of 2010, twenty-two whalemen's grave markers remain in a rough line at Pauline Cove. The original grave-markers are stored in Whitehorse;

the present markers are exact replicas of the originals, made in the 1980s. The splendid manufacture and variety of form reflects a concern for decency in burial and commemoration. The markers are all painted white with inscriptions in black, though the lettering varies from simple black painting to carved letters of varied quality (always painted black) to letters carefully cut from lead sheeting and nailed to the boards. Two markers in particular, those of Charles Morton and Frank Jones, are splendidly elaborate, suggesting perhaps that these men were held in high esteem. Morton died a shocking death, frozen in a sudden storm while playing baseball out on the ice of the cove; Jones, who was second mate on the *Balaena*, was murdered, shot through the head by the third mate of his own ship during a drunken argument. Jones's death was recorded by Bodfish. His murderer, H.P. Bowen, was a notorious thug and was shipped south for trial, but the jury failed to convict.

The first recorded death at Herschel, in November 1890, was that of J.A. Drayton, first mate of the *Grampus*, who died of dropsy (edema). As Bodfish wrote, "we had buried him ashore, cutting the grave in the solid ice that is encountered after little more than a foot of digging." The difficulties encountered may have taught the whalemen patience for future occasions, because Drayton is the only man we know to have been directly buried in the permafrost. In most cases of winter death, the bodies were preserved frozen and covered by logs until a grave was more easily dug out in early summer.

Two officers' bodies were preserved for shipping home on a southbound vessel: Captain C.E. Weeks of the *Thrasher*, who died after falling down a hatch on his ship in March 1895, and Peake (or Peakes), the chief engineer of the *Jesse H. Freeman*, who "died instantly of heart disease" the previous December. Cook noted that Weeks's body "was prepared for

Three of the whalemen's graves at Herschel Island. *Photo courtesy of Government of Yukon.*

sending the remains back next fall, and on the 31st there was a funeral service aboard the *Thrasher*, after which his body was placed in one of the ice-cellars to be kept there until ready for shipment home." The following June, "we took Captain Weeks's body from the ice house and put it in a tight box constructed for the purpose, the box being filled with salt and brine to preserve the body." Weeks was not much loved, but Chief Engineer Peake seems to have inspired greater affection and may actually have been temporarily buried in the ground: Cook records that "his body was put into a grave." Peake "was a member of the Masonic order, and on the following day twenty-four members of the fraternity held the Masonic burial service for him."

What we know of the whalemen's deaths from Bodfish and Cook illustrates the multiracial nature of the whaling crews. In March 1892 John Meyers, a 60-year-old "coloured

seaman," died of inflammatory rheum-atism and "was buried in a snow bank and covered with logs until the ground should thaw," being properly interred only when the ice softened in May (his grave was evidently in the Inuvialuit cemetery). Henry Cruiz, another "coloured man," died aboard the *Rosario* in April 1895. Meyers and Cruiz were two of many black men who served with the whaling fleet and whom the Inuvialuit called "maktokkabluna," or black-whites. George Kealoha, who died in February 1895, was a Kanaka from Hawaii sailing on the *Alexander*.

Many of the dead are now just names, but a few stand out, if only in tiny anecdotal glimpses. William Mosher, mate of the *John & Winthrop*, who died of dropsy in May 1896, was "an old whale man, having been engaged in the business from boyhood." August Arnike, blacksmith on the *Navarch*, died of tuberculosis in May 1895. Another victim of TB was

young Robert Hansen, who died in June 1904 after a long illness by the end of which he was "living entirely on condensed milk." He was clearly popular, because after the funeral conducted for him by Rev. Charles Whittaker on the ship, he was buried in the graveyard where a "wreath and cross and anchor ... made of flowers gathered by the crew from the island ... were laid upon his grave." His captain, John Cook, wrote that "he was a good shipmate."

Some funeral services were recorded shortly after death, like Peake's Masonic rite in 1894 and Hansen's in 1904. From 1893 Rev. Isaac Stringer visited each year, wintering over from 1897 when he established a mission. He was on hand to bury Jones in September 1896, laying him to rest in what must be one of the most northerly of Christian burial grounds.

Jones was shot in the head during a drunken argument. The inscription is made of lead lettering nailed onto the board. *Photo by Martin Rose.*

Morton froze to death in a sudden storm while playing baseball. *Photo by Martin Rose.*

Kealoha was a Kanaka from Hawaii. The inscription is carved and painted on a panel of two-inch wood. *Photo by Martin Rose.*

The whalemen's grave markers presently visible form a north-south line. Starting from the north end they commemorate:

1. **Louis Mahoney**, who died on June 25, 1916.

2. **Fred Morand**, who "froze to death on the ice between Herschel Island and the mainland while deserting" from the *Karluk* on November 24, 1907, aged 31.

3. **Michael Thurn**, ship's carpenter on the *Mary D. Hume*, who died March 22, 1899, aged 27.

4. **Georgie**, infant son of George Edson, born on February 22, 1897, and died on February 17, 1898.

5. **George Sorenson**, from Denmark, engaged as a seaman on the *Wanderer*, who died on December 17, 1897, aged 32.

6. **Charles Morton**, who sailed on the *Grampus*, but was frozen to death when a baseball game was overwhelmed by a sudden storm on March 7, 1897, aged 41.

7. **Henry Williams**, a cabin boy on the *Wanderer*, who died on September 2, 1896, aged 20.

8. **Edwin Isler**, of the *Jesse H. Freeman*, another casualty of the baseball game, who died aged 21.

9. **Frank Jones**, aged 30, the second mate of the *Balaena*, who was killed by the third mate, H. P. Bowen, on September 1, 1896.

10. **William Mosher**, mate of the *John & Winthrop*, who perished of dropsy (edema) on May 19, 1896, aged 65.

11. **G. Santos**, a seaman on the *Northern Light*, who was born in September 1872 and died on November 4, 1895, aged 23.

12. **Joe Peters**, probably a sailor on the *Triton*, who froze to death while on a hunting trip. He was born on November 15, 1867, and died on February 20, 1895, aged 27.

13. **August Arnike**, the blacksmith on the *Navarch*, who died of consumption (tuberculosis) on May 27, 1895, aged 36.

14. **Robert Hansen**, on the *Bowhead*, who was born on February 24, 1882, and died of consumption on June 22, 1904, aged 22.

15. **George Kealoha**, a Kanaka seaman from Hawaii on the *Alexander*, who died of frostbite on February 12, 1895, aged 18.

16. **Arthur**, who died on September 4, 1903 (age and position unknown).

17. **J.A. Drayton**, who died of dropsy on November 4, 1890, aged 32. He was first mate on the *Grampus*.

18. **John Regan**, a seaman on the *Narwhal*, who froze to death on February 21, 1894, aged 29.

19. **Joseph White**, who died on August 11, 1894, aged 19.

20. **John Wilke**, probably a seaman on the *Rosario*, who died on November 8, 1894, aged 20.

21. **Henry Cruiz**, a seaman on the *Rosario*, who died on April 9, 1895, aged 29.

22. **Frank Swartz**, of the *Bonanza*, who was born in October 1876 and died on February 11, 1904, aged 27.

23. There is a marker for the bark *Triton*, an old sailing whaler condemned by a captains' meeting in September 1895. *Triton* was damaged in the ice and leaked very badly.

The markers for the remainder of the 37 graves described by Bodfish are not visible. The marker for John Myers, "a Black from Baltimore," serving as a seaman on the *Mary D. Hume*, who died in March 1892, is among Inuvialuit graves close to the slope leading up to Collinson Head. Markers for aboriginal whalemen, photographed by Roald Amundsen in 1905–06, were also placed in the Inuvialuit graveyard. These markers are quite unlike those standing today. Amundsen's picture shows three markers in the form of crosses and one in the rough outline of a keyhole. The inscriptions are difficult to read, but three appear to be TSIUGAK, INKICZOOAK, and MUSKOW.

—*Martin Rose*

We know little about Arthur other than the date of his death. His grave is not included in the list published by the RNWMP in 1911.
Photo by Sara Nielsen.

Sorenson was a seaman on the *Wanderer*.
Photo by Louis Schilder.

MISSIONARIES

Glenn Iceton

In autumn 1890, the whaling vessels *Grampus*, *Mary D. Hume*, and *Nicoline* anchored in Pauline Cove, hoping for a head start on other whalers the following summer. As news travelled throughout Canada's western Arctic and subarctic about trading opportunities with these ships, the coastal aboriginal people and the Gwich'in responded, taking their business away from the established Hudson's Bay Company (HBC) trading posts at Peel River (Fort McPherson) and Rampart House.

At the same time, the Anglican Diocese of Mackenzie River, under Bishop W.D. Reeve, was trying to recruit a young man to serve in the western Arctic. He would work in the Mackenzie Delta and along the coast westward to Herschel Island and eastward to Baillie Island. The call was answered by Isaac O. Stringer, a student at Wycliffe College in Toronto. Stringer's curriculum suddenly changed to include training in areas such as medical and dental care that would prepare him for the realities of northern work. Stringer was physically strong and possessed "marked powers of endurance."

The First Mission: Isaac Stringer

On May 16, 1892, the day after he was ordained deacon, Stringer left his family and his fiancée Sarah Ann (Sadie) Alexander, and embarked at Toronto for the western Arctic. Two months later he arrived at Fort McPherson, where there had been missionary activity since 1861. He spent the fall and winter learning the ropes of missionary work in the

Fig. 2 Rev. Isaac Stringer and Sadie Stringer in traditional Inuvialuit clothing at Herschel Island in 1898. *Photo courtesy of Anglican Church of Canada, General Synod Archives, Stringer family collection, P7517-51.*

North, and began to study Siglitun, the language spoken by people in the Mackenzie Delta, helped by his interpreter George Greenland.

In April 1893, Stringer set out on his first journey to Herschel Island, travelling by dog team. Much to his surprise, the young missionary was welcomed by the whaling captains. They recognized his potential as a moderating influence on their crews and were glad of conversation with another educated man. However, Stringer discovered the aboriginal residents of the island were largely Nunatarmiut and spoke a different language from the people in the Delta. His stay at Herschel Island lasted about three weeks. Back in Fort McPherson, he was ordained priest by Bishop Reeve on July 15, 1893.

Fig. 1 View of the whaling settlement at Pauline Cove in late summer 1893, the first year that Isaac Stringer visited the island. *Photo courtesy of Yukon Archives, Anglican Church, General Synod Archives fonds, 78/67 #106.*

Missionaries (from left to right) Edward Hester, Bishop Isaac Stringer, and Herbert Girling with an Inuit congregation. *Photo courtesy of Yukon Archives, Anglican Church, Diocese of Yukon fonds, 89/41 #87*

Stringer returned to Herschel Island five times between November 1893 and spring 1895 (Fig. 1), and each time was warmly welcomed by the local population. He enjoyed the hospitality of the whalemen, with whom he developed a strong rapport, and held regular services for them and the aboriginal residents. When Mrs. Albert Sherman, wife of the captain of the *Beluga*, gave birth to a girl in May 1895, Stringer baptized her Helen Herschel four days later. He also collected over $650 from 31 of the whaling captains and officers toward the establishment of a permanent mission on the island.

During the same visit in May 1895, Stringer convinced the captains of 22 vessels to stop supplying liquor to the local residents. He was backed by a letter from the senior Anglican missionary at Fort McPherson, Archdeacon Robert McDonald, and also by two HBC fur traders, Julian Camsell and John Firth. While this decision reduced the availability of spirits on the island, it did not bring an end to the distillation of *tonga*, a home-brewed liquor.

In September 1895, Stringer left Herschel Island aboard the *Jeanie* for furlough in Ontario, where he married his fiancée Sadie. The following year,

in May 1896, he began the trip back to Herschel Island, together with Sadie and her uncle, William Dobbs Young, a skilled carpenter, who had sold his farm and volunteered to go north as a lay worker. Stringer's salary was $750 per year, with an additional $250 for expenses, but William Young was not paid. Sadie was carrying the Stringers' first child, Rowena, who was born at Fort McPherson in December.

Although the Stringers made a short visit to Herschel Island in late August and early September 1896, they spent the winter of 1896–97 at the Peel River mission. They bought a building at Herschel, probably a sod house, after Isaac was told that both white and aboriginal people wanted a permanent mission established at Pauline Cove. The following summer, in August 1897, they returned to Herschel to spend the next four years on the island (Fig. 2). The Pacific Steam Whaling Company offered them the community house as a residence and mission, in return for keeping an eye on the whalemen's materials and supplies (Fig. 3). It was also compensation from the company, who had used the lumber sent north in 1896 for the mission to construct a separate building.

The Stringers turned the community building into a home, schoolhouse, infirmary, and chapel. Sadie acted as a partner in her husband's mission work, holding a day school for aboriginal people and teaching a course in shorthand to those whalemen wanting to spend their winter productively. This training allowed a number of crewmen to find steady jobs when they returned to San Francisco. On May 25, 1900, Sadie gave birth to the Stringers' second child, a son, assisted only by the limited help Isaac could give. In honour of his birthplace, they named their newest family member Frederick Herschel.

The Stringers offered medical services to the whalemen, but mostly to aboriginal people (Fig. 4). Isaac had received rudimentary training as a physician, dentist, and druggist at Wycliffe College, and put these skills to use at Pauline Cove and while travelling throughout the region. From time to time the Stringers took particularly ill people into their home, giving them a better chance of recovery with regular meals in warm and dry conditions. A turning point in their work arrived in February 1899, when they took in a boy called Okpik. He was in terrible condition and

Fig. 3 The community house, which served as the Herschel Island Mission and residence of Rev. Isaac Stringer, his wife Sadie, and their daughter Rowena between 1897 and 1901, and where their son Frederick Herschel was born on 25 May 1900. *Photo courtesy of Anglican Church of Canada, General Synod Archives, Stringer family collection, P7517-185.*

Fig. 4 Sadie Stringer bandaging the frostbitten feet of Robert Ship, a Gwich'in man, 1900. *Photo courtesy of Anglican Church of Canada, General Synod Archives, Stringer family collection, P7517-66.*

Fig. 5 The Inuvialuit graveyard at Pauline Cove, showing crosses on some of the graves.
Photo courtesy of Canadian Museum of Civilization, George Hubert Wilkins, 1916, 51378.

Fig. 6 James Atumiksana and his wife Hanna Nasugaluak were two of the first Inuvialuit to be baptized by the Anglican Church in 1909.
Anglican Church of Canada, General Synod Archives, Stringer family collection, P7517-307.

had been diagnosed by shamans as fatally ill. Okpik stayed with them for six weeks as they nursed him back to health, fully aware that if Okpik died, their influence would end and no aboriginal person would enter their house again.

Shortly after the arrival of outsiders, and throughout the first decades of the twentieth century, a series of epidemics—primarily influenza—spread along the coast. The local people had little resistance to these diseases and many died. Those who had been at the Pauline Cove settlement were buried at the foot of the hills (Fig. 5), some distance from the graves of whalemen who fell victim to the Arctic's harsh climate, or died of other illnesses and accidents. Isaac conducted the funerals for some of these unfortunate men, who were buried on the island.

In 1896 Isaac had developed snow blindness, which gave him acute pain and led to recurring problems with his eyes throughout the next five years. In 1899 he commented on the challenges the affliction posed in carrying out his missionary duties:

"I do not think my eyes would stand a long trip. They are worse now than they have ever been perhaps. This week I cannot do anything at all with them. It seems to be nothing but a common inflammation, but it has become so chronic now that very little usage

makes them worse, and I will soon be useless if I keep on this way. It is very discouraging as there is so much to be done that has to be left undone."

Ultimately, this condition prevented the Stringers from returning to live in the Arctic after they took furlough in 1901.

Although they failed to convert any of the Herschel Islanders, they significantly reduced the potentially harmful influence of the whalemen, they made many friends, and several of the seeds they sowed took root over a longer period. The Stringers' legacy among the Inuvialuit was summed up by Peter Thrasher, who stated:

[Bishop Stringer] is the one my dad saw and talked about. Also my grandmother, they saw him at Herschel, for the first time. But then, they never let him baptize them. Bishop Stringer was a good man 'cause my grandmother used to really like that man and his wife.

The couple maintained a lifelong interest in Herschel Island, making numerous return journeys after Isaac was consecrated Bishop of Selkirk (later Yukon) Diocese in 1905.

"A Man Who Never Deviates from Duty:" Charles Edward Whittaker

Following the Stringers' departure, Charles Edward Whittaker took responsibility for the missionary

activities at Herschel Island. Whittaker, like Stringer, had been recruited from Wycliffe College in Toronto by Bishop Reeve for Arctic work. He arrived in 1895 and spent the winter of 1895–96 at Herschel Island on board the *Jesse H. Freeman*. He temporarily replaced Stringer, particularly in medical work, gaining experience in the region, and developing a reputation as a forthright, but rather unpopular and patronizing character. In 1897 he assumed responsibilities at Fort McPherson, but continued to travel to the coast from time to time, and when the Stringers left took up residence at Herschel Island. He later became involved in a celebrated row with the explorer and anthropologist Vilhjalmur Stefansson, taking offence at Stefansson's public criticisms of missionary activities in the Arctic. In response, Whittaker pointed out that no native people were forced to convert to Christianity, but had decided to do so after many years of experience with the missionaries; he also publicly attacked Stefansson for neglecting Fanny Pannigabluk, his Nunatarmiut wife, and Alex, their son.

Whittaker's problems at Herschel Island included tragedies within his own family. In a letter written to Isaac Stringer in spring 1905, Whittaker mentioned that his daughter, Winnie, was suffering from rickets and needed "iron legs" in order to walk. She died of brain lesions the following year, and Roald Amundsen on the *Gjøa* at King Point described the desperate sight of the Whittakers dragging their dead child behind them on a sled. They took her body to Fort McPherson to be buried next to her younger brother, Cecil, who had died in 1903. Subsequently, Whittaker was based at Fort McPherson, where he worked as a missionary until he left the Arctic in 1918. William Henry Fry, who served as missionary at Herschel Island from 1916 to 1919, diplomatically wrote of the embattled missionary: "To the white men, Indians and Eskimos, Mr. Whittaker stands out as a man who never deviates from duty no matter how stern or disagreeable it may be."

Re-establishing the Mission: William Fry

When Whittaker and his family left for Fort McPherson, Herschel Island was again served only periodically by missionaries. Bishop Stringer still visited, and on August 15th, 1909, baptized the first six Inuvialuit to become Christians: James Atumiksana and his wife Hanna Nasugaluak

(Fig. 6), Thomas Umaok and his wife Susie Atoogaok, Charlie Kelegak, and Elias Taotook. Atumiksana served as a lay worker from 1920 until his death in 1923. In 1917 Umaok became the first Inuvialuk to be licensed as a lay reader, and in 1927 the first to be ordained as a clergyman. Bishop Stringer also confirmed 47 Inuvialuit on the island in 1917, although some, such as Thomas Umaok and Susie Atoogaok, had been confirmed earlier at Fort McPherson.

By 1915, there were discussions about re-establishing a mission along the Yukon coast, and both Herschel Island and Shingle Point were considered as possible sites. In the end Herschel Island was chosen because of the HBC post located there. The Anglican Church sought to secure one of the whaling buildings for the mission, but they were all occupied by the Royal Northwest Mounted Police. In 1916, when William Fry took over responsibility with his wife Christina, plans were made for the construction of the long-delayed mission house (Fig. 7). In 1917, Edward Hester and

Herbert Girling joined the Frys at the new St. Patrick's Mission. Hester and Girling were primarily travelling ministers, whose parish extended from Herschel Island eastward along the coast to Cape Bathurst (Fig. 8).

In April 1918, the Frys enjoyed the company of the Anglican missionary and explorer Hudson Stuck, who is perhaps best known for his ascent of Denali (Mount McKinley). Stuck had crossed into the Yukon during his exploration of the Arctic coast of Alaska. Herschel Island was not the bustling Arctic metropolis that it had been in 1894–96. Stuck commented:

> It had a police post, a mission and a store, with their meagre staffs, and I think no more than two or three other white residents, while the Eskimos were much scattered at their trapping and hunting, so that only two score or so were at home.

Stuck seems to have enjoyed a good rapport with Fry, as the two shared an interest in Arctic geography and exploration. He wrote:

Fig. 7 Missionary Arthur Creighton McCullum on the front steps of the most northern mission in the Yukon, St. Patrick's at Herschel Island, built in 1916. *Photo courtesy of Yukon Archives, Anglican Church, Diocese of Yukon fonds, 86/61 #94.*

Fig. 8 Rev. Herbert Girling with Higluk, his travelling companion. In 1917, Girling and Edward Hester were stationed at Herschel Island, but travelled east along the coast to minister to people who did not have regular contact with missionaries. *Photo courtesy of Yukon Archives, Anglican Church, Diocese of Yukon fonds, 89/41 #75*

Fig. 9 Bishop Isaac Stringer, Rev. William Henry Fry, and Archdeacon Charles Edward Whittaker *behind* with the confirmation class at St. Patrick's Mission on Herschel Island, 1917. James Atumiksana and Hanna Nasugaluak are standing to the right of Bishop Stringer. Nuligak (Bob Cockney) is in front of Hannah in the first row. *Photo courtesy of Anglican Church of Canada, General Synod Archives, Vale collection, P7559-148.*

It was pleasant to me to find both the Hudson's Bay agent [Mr. Harding], and the missionary, the Rev. Mr. Fry, intelligently interested in the geography and exploration of the country, for it is surprising how little such interest is manifested all around this coast. The walls of the mission house were spread with the excellent Arctic charts of the British Admiralty, issued after the last of the Franklin search expeditions of the fifties, which there has been very little occasion to add to or alter, save for Amundsen's mapping of the east coast of Victoria Island, until this present time; and I found Mr. Stefánsson's three new islands of the Parry archipelago carefully inserted in their places.... I wish that every missionary would show as much interest in the country to which he is sent.

In contrast to his friendship with Stuck, William Fry became critical of Stefansson, like Whittaker before him, and like many of the traders in the region. Fry particularly objected to Stefansson's distance from the scientific personnel on the Canadian Arctic Expedition he was leading, and his exaggerated claims in *My Life with the Eskimo*. However, when Stefansson became seriously ill at the end of the expedition, Fry nursed him until it was safe to send him to the mission hospital at Fort Yukon.

The Frys enjoyed their work (Fig. 9), developed a great interest in Inuvialuit culture, and gained the cooperation of the police in assisting the destitute. Two of their sons were born at Herschel Island, the second on Christmas Day in 1918. Christina was a trained teacher and taught day school to the Inuvialuit. The missionaries' wives also had the potential to influence indigenous women more effectively than their husbands. Edward Hester wrote of Christina Fry: "We find that the moral influence of the missionary's wife is inestimable in its working for good particularly amongst the native women, and the softening and refining influence shed upon all." William Fry echoed a similar sentiment: "There are some things that only a woman can do. When our people need help she realizes their need long before I do and has been of great service where I should have failed utterly."

Decline of the Herschel Island Mission

In 1919 the Frys left Herschel Island due to William's failing health, and advised Bishop Stringer that the permanent mission should be moved to Shingle Point, as the Inuvialuit were moving along the coast to live closer to the Mackenzie Delta. Stringer accepted this advice and sent William Archibald Geddes, who served along the Yukon coast from 1920 to 1928, to construct a mission house and school at Shingle Point.

In 1922 Geddes oversaw the building of the first church on the Yukon coast, St. John's, at Shingle Point (Fig. 10). In 1929 a church residential school was opened under Harry Sherman Shepherd and a small staff. The residential school and mission operated until 1936, when they were moved to Aklavik. By the mid-1930s, the Herschel Island mission had been completely abandoned.

Fig. 10 St. John's Church and a mission house were built at Shingle Point in 1922, and were followed by a residential school in 1929, as the activities in the mission at Herschel Island declined. *Photo courtesy of Yukon Archives, Anglican Church, Diocese of Yukon fonds 89/41 #638*

Inuvialuit Ministers

From 1917 on, the first Inuvialuit—Gareth Notik (Garrett Nutik), James Atumiksana, and Thomas Umaok—were appointed and ordained as lay workers and clergy. Gareth Notik had attended the day school run by the Stringers on Herschel Island in the late 1890s, and by 1924 was a catechist who led services and preached to his people. James Atumiksana (Fig. 6) served formally as a lay worker from 1920 until his death in 1923, but had earlier been of great help to the mission. In 1912, Atumiksana took care of orphaned children whose parents died during an epidemic. Tragically, he lost his wife six years later in another outbreak of disease. In 1923, Atumiksana himself succumbed.

Thomas Umaok was ordained deacon at Herschel Island on July 30th, 1927 after serving as a lay worker for 10 years (Fig. 11). In 1960, Umaok recalled his decision to become a minister:

> Bishop Stringer, Mr. Whittaker and Mr. Webster come Herschel Island. Mr. Fry stay there. Every day I get wood in Tiliak (mission boat) for mission house. Bishop tell me he want me to be minister. I tell him I never go to school, I not be minister. Three nights he talk to me. He say never mind no go to school, only pray and ask God to help you in Church. I tell him I want to pray about go minister. He say all right, you pray, suppose He help you, then you know. That night I pray. Next morning I feel I want to help as minister.

Before his ordination, Umaok had held services regularly at Herschel Island, although the main mission had moved to Shingle Point. He also travelled east of Herschel Island and Shingle Point to minister to Inuit who did not have a permanent missionary amongst them. However, even Umaok moved to Shingle Point in 1929 to help run the new residential school, although he returned frequently to Herschel Island for supplies.

Missionaries' Legacy

Throughout Canada, the effect of missionary work on indigenous communities has been controversial, as they were part of the alternative to aboriginal culture. The missionaries on Herschel Island brought in elements of cultural change—specifically their spirituality—to the local people. William Fry noted that the people were afraid to speak of their traditional beliefs in case this angered the missionaries. Missionaries have also been criticized for encouraging indigenous people to rest on Sundays, a potentially damaging observance for people who live by hunting. However, the missionaries also made efforts to reduce other effects of contact with non-native people, such as the liquor trade and prostitution, and to help those afflicted by the epidemics that ripped through the Arctic.

Missionaries were agents of non-native culture, just like the whalemen, the police, and the traders, but they addressed spiritual and moral matters directly. Some people today may regard missionary activities as detrimental to the local inhabitants, but at the time a missionary presence was expected and welcomed. The Anglican boarding school at Shingle Point was established in response to a widely signed petition organized by Inuvialuit in 1926, demanding education for children living along the western Arctic coast. The Anglican Church in the Yukon rapidly ordained aboriginal people, such as Thomas Umaok, as catechists and priests, and it was the missionaries based at Herschel Island who brought education and medical care to the aboriginal people of the western Arctic coast.

Fig. 11 Thomas Umaok *left*, the first Inuvialuit member of the Anglican clergy, with an Inuvialuit couple and Sadie Stringer. Umaok was a cornerstone of the Herschel Island mission. *Photo courtesy of Yukon Archives, Anglican Church, Diocese of Yukon fonds, 89/41 #644.*

ISAAC STRINGER AND THE CANADIAN RED CROSS

When Isaac Stringer was Bishop of Yukon, he requested medical supplies from the Canadian Red Cross to help missionaries cope with the epidemics.

"The Eskimos for a distance of several hundred miles along the Arctic Coast depend on the missionaries for medical help. At times there is a doctor connected with the police force but even then the missionary must go far afield and meets many needy cases who are not able to get medical assistance in any other way. ... I should be glad if the Red Cross Society can lend their assistance ... for the benefit of humanity on the remote Canadian Frontier."

FUNERALS AND BURIALS

The missionaries in the western Arctic knew they had two congregations to serve. Services for aboriginal people were held in Siglitun or Uummarmiutun, with translation provided by a native speaker until the missionary spoke enough of the language. Rev. Isaac Stringer and his colleagues also had responsibilities for others who were in the region. Stringer baptized the newborn children of whalemen, and the clergy officiated at marriages. Inevitably, they were also called upon for funerals and interments. These events became frequent once epidemic diseases reached the region. In 1911, Rev. Charles Whittaker, then at Fort McPherson, presided at the funeral of the Lost Patrol.

January and February 1911 were grim months for the RNWMP in the western Arctic. Sgt. S.E.A. Selig died on January 29 at Herschel Island, leaving Cst. F.L.R. Wissenden in sole charge of the post for the rest of the winter (eight aboriginal families were then living on the island). That was also the winter that the Lost Patrol foundered in the mountains south of Fort McPherson on its way to Dawson City. Ex-Cst. Samuel Carter and Cst. George F. Kinney, both of whom had served at Herschel Island, perished first, along with the other member of the patrol, Cst. Richard O'H. Taylor. Insp. Francis J. Fitzgerald was the last of the four men to die, on or about February 14.

The interment of the Lost Patrol in the graveyard of St. Matthew's Church, Fort McPherson. The clergyman is the Rev. Charles E. Whittaker. *Photo courtesy of Anglican Church of Canada, General Synod Archives, C.E.Whittaker Album, P9901-B6-89.*

Fitzgerald had employed ex-Cst. Carter as the party's guide for the journey. Carter had been highly regarded by his superior officers, being described by Insp. A.M. Jarvis in 1908 as "one of the best all-round men in the force that I know of, a good four-in-hand teamster, dog driver, carpenter, and in canoe or whale boat is equally good. ... As a bread, pastry and meat cook he has no equal in the force. If sent on a trip, one has the feeling that he is going to get there and return." Tragically, this time he did not know the way well enough, and none of the patrol members survived.

Both men left widows behind. Fitzgerald was survived by Lena Unalina and their baby daughter Annie, while Carter was survived by Mabel Rauchenna. Bishop Stringer had married Carter and Mabel Rauchenna a mere 18 months earlier, in August 1909. The women in the photograph at the graveside of the Lost Patrol are in obvious mourning.

—Christopher Burn

The original grave markers of the Lost Patrol at Fort McPherson. *Photo courtesy of Anglican Church of Canada, General Synod Archives, C.E. Whittaker Album, P9901-B7-67.*

FUR TRADERS

John R. Bockstoce, Rob Ingram, and Helene Dobrowolsky

Fig. 1 The winter coat of the arctic fox or tiriganniaq (*Vulpes lagopus*) was the focus of the fur trade at Herschel Island in the twentieth century. *Photo by Christopher Burn.*

H. Liebes and Company's *Herman* at anchor in Pauline Cove. *Photo courtesy of Library and Archives Canada, Royal Canadian Mounted Police fonds, e010836741.*

When the whaling fleet reached Herschel Island, the whalemen encountered aboriginal peoples who were already familiar with European goods. Since the seventeenth century, these peoples had supplied furs to a vast inter-regional trade network that included both British and Russian products. The rising demand for furs in the late nineteenth and early twentieth centuries made Herschel Island the centre of the western Arctic fur trade for more than forty years (Fig. 1).

Whalemen as Traders

Arctic whalemen had always made a profitable sideline in trading furs with aboriginal peoples. In 1890, when the whaling fleet began wintering in Pauline Cove, the crews also began trading for fresh game and fish. Aboriginal traders, both Inuvialuit and Gwich'in, provided a substantial portion of the whalemen's winter diet, though the ships also sent out hunting parties. The whalemen acquired a wide variety of meat, but found caribou the most plentiful and palatable. Between 1890 and 1908, whaleships made more than seventy overwinterings at the island, and with crews of up to fifty persons, food consumption was prodigious. During the winter of 1894–95, when 15 ships wintered at Qikiqtaryuk, and 1895–96, when 13 ships overwintered, more than two thousand caribou were probably traded each year.

The Gwich'in, who lived in the forested regions south of the British Mountains, profited especially, because caribou were more plentiful in their homelands during the cold months. Groups of Gwich'in traders arrived at the island two or three times each winter, hauling as many as twenty-two toboggans carrying caribou, moose, and fish. Their arrival usually touched off a scramble among the captains for their trade (Fig. 2).

Aboriginal traders were drawn to the island because it was a convenient source of manufactured goods. They traded game and furs for gunpowder, primers (for igniting the powder), lead shot, rifles, cartridges, flour, sugar, tea, calico, tobacco, soap, knives, combs, files, whaleboats, small stoves, clothing, and other items, including alcohol. Although we have few records of the prices paid for furs, the whalemen offered a relatively steady six or seven cents per pound for meat, paid in trade goods that were valued at San Francisco wholesale prices.

Their prices were only 20 to 30 percent of those charged by the Hudson's Bay Company (HBC) at Fort McPherson, Lapierre House, and Rampart House because the whalemen did not add transportation costs or profit to their trade goods. The HBC, of course, had to make a profit, and the cost of shipping the goods to the northern posts was substantial.

Fig. 2   Chief Christian of the Neetsaii Gwich'in visiting Herschel Island to trade in May 1895. *Photo courtesy of Mystic Seaport, Mystic, Conn.*

Fig. 3   Christian (Charlie) Klengenberg, a trader of uneven reputation, who was charged with murder but acquitted. He opened up trade with the central Arctic, and brought word to Stefansson in 1906 of Inuit on Victoria Island who had not met white men. *Photo courtesy of Library and Archives Canada, Royal Canadian Mounted Police fonds, e010869396.*

This disparity in prices became dramatically apparent to John Firth, the HBC factor at Fort McPherson. In 1892 a group of Inuvialuit arrived from Herschel Island in a whaleboat loaded with trade goods obtained from the whalemen. At Fort McPherson the Inuvialuit became middlemen, bartering with others and then returning to the island with the furs. As a result, the number of fox and beaver skins offered to the HBC declined at the post.

Firth then played his only high card. In winter 1894–95, he apparently sent word to the whalemen that, unless they stopped trading in furs, the company would no longer forward mail to them. In their intense isolation at Herschel, the whalemen eagerly awaited the winter mail; news from home was more important than the profits from fur trading. When Firth visited the island in the autumn of 1896, he reported that the whalemen had largely stopped encouraging the aboriginal people to bring them furs. The whalemen continued to trade for meat, of course. Even after 1903, when they had begun paying customs duty to the police, they were able to sell 100-pound bags of flour for two dollars, while the HBC was asking thirty.

Independent Traders and the Hudson's Bay Company

The price of furs began to rise in 1900, especially the price of white fox pelts (Fig. 1), partly because they could be dyed to imitate more expensive skins. This rise in prices drew a number of small independent trapper-traders into the region. One of the first was Franz "Fritz" Wolki, a veteran whaleman. In 1900, with the backing of Capt. Hartson Bodfish, he became a successful trapper at Horton River. In 1908 he bought his own schooner, the *Rosie H.*, and later the *Gladiator*.

Following him was Christian "Charlie" Klengenberg (Fig. 3), who spent a series of winters in the western Arctic aboard a number of vessels (Fig. 4). At the same time several Inuvialuit began trapping on the Arctic coast, having traded goods for boats at Herschel Island. The merchants of Nome, Alaska, soon saw the opportunities, outfitting independent trapper-traders to overwinter in Northern Alaska and the western Arctic. Many of these men visited Pauline Cove to rendezvous and resupply.

Fig. 4   The gasoline schooner *Olga*, a whaling and trading ship, at Herschel Island. Charlie Klengenberg disappeared from Herschel Island with the *Olga* in 1905. When he returned the next year several of the crew were missing, and Klengenberg was suspected of murdering them. *Photo courtesy of Library and Archives Canada, Royal Canadian Mounted Police fonds, e010869400.*

Fig. 5 Mr. Breyton with white fox skins at Herschel Island, 1928. *Photo courtesy of Library and Archives Canada, J.F. Moran fonds, PA 167648.*

Fig. 6 Herschel Island harbour in 1930. *Photo courtesy of Library and Archives Canada, Post Office fonds, PA 61884.*

Fur prices declined so sharply when the First World War broke out that many aboriginal people stopped trapping for one or two seasons. In 1916, however, the prices recovered and then soared, a fact which invited excessive market speculation and resulted in another temporary slump in 1920. After that correction, the price of furs, especially white fox and muskrat, began a dazzling ascent that reached its zenith in 1929. In that year trappers in the Arctic received goods valued at more than fifty dollars for a large, first-class, white fox pelt—twenty-five times its 1900 value (Fig. 5). Many aboriginal trappers were able to buy gasoline-powered boats ("schooners") and set up trapping camps throughout the Mackenzie Delta and along the coast. Each summer most of them sailed with their winter's catch to Herschel to trade with ships arriving from Pacific Ocean ports (Fig. 6).

The HBC finally established a post on Herschel Island in 1915 (Fig. 7), but from the beginning it faced stiff competition from several rivals. These included Capt. Steven Cottle and his steam whaling bark *Belvedere*, Capt. Louis Lane with the auxiliary schooner *Polar Bear,* and—most importantly—H. Liebes and Company, furriers from San Francisco.

This company, which had been engaged in Alaskan whaling and trading for two decades, had been operating the *Herman* in the western Arctic since 1904, first as a whaler, with trading as a sideline, and later as a trading ship, with whaling as a sideline. In 1916 the company expanded its shore-based operations eastward and set up a post near Demarcation Point, Alaska, four miles (6.4 kilometres) west of the international boundary. The following year it went farther and established trading posts at Shingle Point and Kittigazuit, adding Aklavik in 1918. In 1921, the HBC's response was to buy H. Liebes and Company's Canadian posts.

Fig. 7 A fleet of Inuvialuit schooners and the settlement at Pauline Cove, from the foremast of the *Patterson*, 1930. The RCMP buildings (on the extreme right of the photograph) were white with red roofs, while the HBC buildings were painted white with green trim. *Photos courtesy Library and Archives Canada, R.S. Finnie fonds, C 66708 and PA 100660. Photos merged by David Neufeld.*

Inuvialuit schooner at Herschel Island, early 1950s. *Photo courtesy of Parks Canada, William McFarland Herschel Island 1953–55 Collection, #006.*

The *North Star*, later the *North Star of Herschel Island,* in 1958. This schooner arrived at Herschel Island in 1935 on board the *Patterson. Photo by Morley Riske, courtesy of Alan and Marilyn Fehr.*

INUVIALUIT SCHOONERS

Through the 1920s high fur prices, particularly for white fox, enabled the Inuvialuit to become some of the wealthiest people in Canada. They not only bought rifles, fish nets, and camp gear; they also commissioned the construction of motor schooners so that they could sail along the western Arctic coast and over to Banks Island to trap there as well. In early summer Pauline Cove became a busy harbour as the schooners arrived, loaded with furs, to wait for the arrival of the trading ships.

In the early 1950s Cst. W.L. (Bill) McFarland, stationed at Herschel Island, recalled: "The Inuit had schooners, left over from the heydays of the fur trade. These were boats built in the 1920s and had little one-lung engines in them. You could hear them coming for miles—'putt, putt, putt, putt, putt, putt.' Dogs and kids and everything loaded aboard. You wouldn't believe the stuff they had loaded on those schooners. Amazing they had the gas to run them around because furs weren't worth very

much and they'd come out and hunt white whale and seal and whatnot in the summertime. Bill Cockney's dad had a schooner. He came out there one summer. [You] see the dogs and the sled on the back there and just everything you can imagine [that] you needed for camping and travelling. I think it was probably their worldly possessions loaded on there on the boats."

–David Neufeld

H. Liebes and Company proved to be a particularly difficult competitor for the HBC because of the skill and reputation of the *Herman's* captain, Christian Theodore Pedersen (Fig. 8). Pedersen was a widely experienced Arctic whaleman and trader and a supremely competent ice pilot. He was held in high regard by virtually all residents of the western Arctic, aboriginal and non-aboriginal alike, and obtained large quantities of furs despite HBC competition. His honesty, reliability, and willingness to help others, along with both his prices and the quality and variety of his trade goods, are remembered to this day.

Fig. 8 Capt. C.T. Pedersen and Capt. W.H. Gillen, the first captain of the *St. Roch,* at Herschel Island in 1928. Capt. Gillen commanded the schooner from Vancouver to Herschel Island, where he handed over command to Cst. H.A. Larsen on August 26. *Photo courtesy of Vancouver Maritime Museum, HCRO–20-08.*

In early 1923, however, Pedersen left H. Liebes and Company in a bitter salary dispute. He promptly arranged financing from furriers in New York and formed the Northern Whaling and Trading Company, buying a three-masted motor schooner, the *Nanuk*. Pedersen not only traded on behalf of his own company but also supplied many independent traders as well. Almost single-handedly, he prevented the HBC from establishing a monopoly in western Arctic Canada. The Inuvialuit and independent trappers were the beneficiaries of this competition and were able to sell their furs to the highest bidder (often Pedersen). This situation was entirely different from the one in eastern Arctic Canada, where either the HBC or Revillon Frères maintained a monopoly in most settlements.

Unable to counter the successes of Pedersen and the independent traders, the HBC responded by lobbying the Canadian government for protection. In 1924 the government enacted legislation preventing foreign vessels from participating in the coastal trade east of Herschel. In response Pedersen bought a much larger vessel, the *Patterson* (Fig. 9), in 1925 and created a Canadian corporation, the Canalaska Trading Company. To comply with the new regulations, he also built a bonded warehouse and store at Herschel Island (Fig. 10), and used two smaller Canadian-flagged schooners, the *Nigalik* and the *Emma*, to supply the Canalaska posts in the east, where the schooners overwintered. Every summer, from 1925 through 1936, the *Patterson* arrived at Pauline Cove to meet the Canalaska schooners

as they arrived with furs from the Canalaska posts on Victoria Island, King William Island, and in Coronation Gulf. The *Patterson* also traded directly with many Inuvialuit and independent traders who travelled to meet Pedersen.

Hudson's Bay Company at Herschel Island

In the first decade of the twentieth century, the HBC began planning to advance north from its posts on the Mackenzie River. The company sensed the opportunity for a fur trade on the Arctic coast and figured that supplies would be less expensive to deliver by sea. The cost of ocean freight from Vancouver to Herschel Island would be a maximum of $35 per ton, against $160 or more for the same tonnage carried via HBC's Mackenzie

Fig. 9 Capt. C.T. Pederson's *Patterson* at Herschel Island in August 1930. Pederson had a number of schooners built in San Francisco and transported them to Herschel Island on board the *Patterson*. This one is almost certainly *Our Lady of Lourdes*, built for the Roman Catholic mission. Others were purchased by Inuvialuit trappers.
Photo courtesy of Library and Archives Canada, R.S. Finnie fonds, C 66709.

Fig. 10 Northern Whaling and Trading Company store and Canada Customs warehouse, formerly a warehouse of the Northern Whaling and Trading Company, in 2010. *Photo by Christopher Burn.*

transportation system. In 1912 the company set up posts at Aklavik and Kittigazuit and decided to buy a coastal schooner, the *Fort MacPherson*, to help reorganize the trade in the western Arctic and Mackenzie River District. The plan was to establish a post at Herschel in the summer of 1913, but the HBC was unable to find a suitable freighting vessel for charter. In 1914 exceptionally heavy ice forced both the *Fort MacPherson* and the chartered supply ship *Ruby* to turn back. The next year, however, they reached Pauline Cove, where, with the help of Inuvialuit labour, the HBC men quickly put up a store, a dwelling house, and outbuildings (Fig. 11). Later a 40-foot x 80-foot (12-metre x 24-metre) warehouse was added (Fig. 7).

The company was hampered, however, by its own procedures and by its attitude toward its customers. Because of its bureaucratic command structure and clumsy organizational directives, it was unable to meet the higher fur prices that its competitors offered. To make matters worse, in autumn 1914 the company stopped buying furs with the outbreak of the First World War, because the London fur auctions were temporarily cancelled. When Archdeacon Hudson Stuck visited the island in spring 1918, he observed:

> *The Hudson's Bay method of business is primitive beyond what would be tolerated anywhere in Alaska. The shop or store is wholly unwarmed—for fear of fire.... This, I was informed, is the custom at every Hudson's Bay post. No trader who had a competitor could afford to treat his customers in such a way.... The last reports from the fur market received at Point Barrow quoted white foxes at thirty dollars.... Mr. Brower [at Barrow] was paying twenty for foxes; at Demarcation Point Mr. Gordon was paying fifteen, and here at Herschel the Hudson's Bay agent was paying twelve...'in trade' of course, so that*

Fig. 11 The newly built HBC store at Herschel Island with post manager Mr. Christy Harding, 1916. *Photo courtesy of Library and Archives Canada, Royal Canadian Mounted Police fonds, e003525182.*

there was the large profit on goods sold as well as the profit on the furs.

Not surprisingly, the Herschel Island post acquired very little fur in the winter of 1915–16.

From the company's point of view, Herschel was mainly a centre for distributing supplies to the mouth of the Mackenzie and to posts as far east as King William Island. The HBC's presence primarily established Herschel as the supply hub for

the western Arctic. Nevertheless, a combination of severe ice years, bad luck, and questionable planning impeded the company's plans for sea-borne resupply in the western Arctic. The HBC never realized its projections of $35 per ton for the cost of ocean freight. Between 1915 and 1918 its costs varied from $75 to $85 per ton, which contributed to the company's decision to build its own ship to carry the cargo.

The ice-strengthened three-masted auxiliary schooner *Lady Kindersley* was launched in Vancouver in March 1921. The ship was to carry four small schooners on deck to assist with transfers for supplying posts in the shallow waters of the western Arctic. In 1922 *Lady Kindersley* was ordered to visit posts as far east as Coronation Gulf, but that year heavy ice prevented travel beyond Herschel. As a result some of the eastern posts ran very low on supplies, and one ran out entirely.

Two years later the ship was immediately slowed by engine problems when it left Vancouver, arriving at Point Barrow, Alaska, eleven days behind schedule. There it encountered extremely heavy pack ice, which closed in and disabled the rudder. The ice then carried the ship northeast into the Beaufort Sea, where it was abandoned on August 31. Without supplies, the HBC was forced to temporarily close the Herschel Island and Cambridge Bay posts.

The *Lady Kindersley's* replacement, the much-larger steamer *Baychimo*, was likewise abandoned in the ice 60 miles from Point Barrow in October 1931.

The following year the company chartered another ship, the *Karise*, which proved unsatisfactory for the task. In 1933 the *Anyox* was sent to resupply the Herschel Island post, but it too was crushed in the ice and succeeded only in limping back to Vancouver with much of its cargo spoiled. After that the company gave up its sea-borne cargo plans, sending the western Arctic goods down the Mackenzie River to Tuktoyaktuk and trans-shipping them onward.

GWICH'IN TRADERS

According to oral history, the early relations between Gwich'in and Inuit people, whom Gwich'in called Ch'ineekaii, were hostile. By the time of Franklin's journey along the coast in 1826, however, Gwich'in people were regularly travelling north to trade for Russian metal goods that Qikiqtaryungmiut had brought back from Barter Island. After the HBC opened its post at Fort McPherson in 1840, its operations were expanded into northern Yukon, with posts at Lapierre House, just over the mountains, and, in 1870, at Rampart House near the Alaskan border. Both of these posts were closed in 1893, a sign that Gwich'in people now preferred the more favourable trade with the whalemen at Herschel Island, which they called Chuu Choo Vee.

Gwich'in people travelled to Herschel Island by dog team in winter and on foot in summer, with the dogs packing supplies.

They brought furs and meat to trade for tobacco, guns, ammunition, and tents, as well as tea and other groceries. In winter they could sell frozen meat to the whalemen, but in summer they traded with Inuvialuit for dry meat and bone grease. Myra Moses recalled that *"that's how it became good for the people, you know, [because of] the American people [traders]."* As the trade developed, Gwich'in people brought beaded mitts and moccasins, using beads originally traded for at Herschel Island. They continued to travel to Chuu Choo Vee as whaling gave way to the fur trade, mainly because the HBC at Fort McPherson and other independent traders paid such frugal amounts. They also considered American goods superior to the English items traded by the HBC.

The trade declined in the 1930s, but the contact was renewed after the RCMP detachment was reopened at Herschel Island in 1948. Gwich'in men guided the winter police patrols through the mountains between Old Crow and Herschel Island, often using the Firth River to descend to the coast. People also climbed up to the headwaters of the Babbage and Blow rivers as traditional routes to reach the country of the Ch'ineekaii.

Gwich'in caribou skin jacket acquired in trading at Herschel Island by Capt. Albert C. Sherman of the *Beluga*. *Photo courtesy of New Bedford Whaling Museum, New Bedford, MA.*

Fig. 12 Taking on bales of white fox skins at Herschel Island. Each bale held an average of 100 furs and, in 1930, was worth about $4,000. *Photo courtesy of Yukon Archives, Finnie family fonds, 81/21 #207.*

Twilight of the Fur Trade at Herschel Island

The boom years of the western Arctic fur trade were brief (Fig. 12). The stock market crash, followed by the Great Depression of the 1930s, caused a drastic slump in fur prices. When the *Patterson* reached San Francisco in September 1930, Pedersen found the market stagnant. The following summer at Herschel Island he bid against the HBC for a collection of 1,500 white fox skins, offering $40 per skin to the HBC's $39.50, but when he returned south the market price had fallen to only $12 per skin. This decline was particularly hard on the Inuvialuit trappers. "During the whole spring season of 1931 I made only $600 on furs," wrote Nuligak (Bill Cockney). "The year 1932 was worse still. I made only $70. White fox had practically no value."

The *Patterson's* last voyage to Herschel took place in 1936. The poor market for furs, along with labour chaos in the west coast ports, made it impossible for Pedersen to continue. In 1938 he sold the Canalaska Company and its assets to his former rival, the HBC. The HBC, meanwhile, had decided

that it made little sense to keep its Herschel Island post, having established Tuktoyaktuk as its transportation hub for the western Arctic. By 1938 its trading operation had been moved to Shingle Point. The company loaned one building at Pauline Cove to the Anglican Church, dismantled the others, and rebuilt them at Tuktoyaktuk.

The fur trade on the island had a short and minor revival after the Second World War. As a relief measure for the few Inuvialuit families living on the Yukon North Slope, the RCMP opened a small trading post (Fig. 13). Aklavik, however, had become the major settlement and the productive fur harvests were in the Mackenzie Delta.

Fig. 13 Old Irish Kegoyook, Cst. Bill McFarland, and Neil Allen at the RCMP detachment, Herschel Island, early 1950s. *Photo courtesy of Parks Canada, Jim Hickling Herschel Island 1953–56 Collection, #001.*

THE HUDSON'S BAY COMPANY SHIPS

The establishment of the Hudson's Bay Company post on Herschel Island was key to the development of the company's fur trade along the western Arctic coast. HBC employees from Fort McPherson were in charge of building the new post, using materials and supplies that had been shipped to the western Arctic down the Mackenzie River. The goods were transported along the coast in the schooner *Fort MacPherson*, which then spent the winter of 1915–16 at Herschel Island. The HBC's trade goods were also shipped to the western Arctic via the Mackenzie River, incurring transportation costs much higher than those paid by the independent traders who sailed in annually from the west coast of the United States. In response, the HBC built the *Lady Kindersley*, a 57.5-metre-long, 700-ton, three-masted schooner with auxiliary steam power.

The *Lady Kindersley*'s wooden hull was nearly two feet (0.6 metres) thick and was reinforced in the bow with steel to help protect the schooner from the ice. Its first annual Arctic voyage was in 1921. After reaching Herschel Island, the schooner continued eastward to the trading posts in Dolphin and Union Strait and Coronation Gulf. It carried boats as deck cargo, including small schooners for use in the shallow waters of the Mackenzie Delta area.

In 1924 the *Lady Kindersley* left Vancouver on June 27, but because of mechanical trouble only reached the Arctic Ocean a month later. The schooner arrived off Point Barrow on August 2 and became stuck in the pack ice, which damaged its rudder and propeller. It drifted eastward with the ice, then northwestward, further into the Arctic Ocean. On August 31, in desperation, Capt. Gus Foellmer reluctantly abandoned his ship about 40 kilometres (22 miles) northeast of Point Barrow. Dragging small boats from the ship, the crew walked several kilometres to the edge of the ice.

Here they launched the boats and rowed to the U.S. government vessel *Boxer*, which was waiting nearby. On September 2, near Point Barrow, they transferred to the HBC ship *Baychimo*, which had been sent to help them. The *Baychimo* took them back to the edge of the ice to search for the *Lady Kindersley* and salvage some of the cargo, but they saw no trace of the ship. On September 15 they gave up and sailed for Vancouver. The *Lady Kindersley* was not seen again, and none of the western Arctic coastal posts received their supplies that year.

The next year, the HBC assigned the *Baychimo* to its western Arctic operations. The ship had been built in Sweden and was designed to cope with the ice in the Baltic Sea. Bought in the aftermath of the First World War, it had been renamed and registered in London. During most of its time in the company's service, the ship returned to Scotland each winter, travelling to and fro through

The *Baychimo* at Herschel Island. *Photo courtesy of Yukon Archives, Derek Parkes fonds, 95/53 #4.*

The *Lady Kindersley* at Herschel Island. *Photo courtesy of Library and Archives Canada, Royal Canadian Mounted Police fonds, e010836738.*

The schooner *Fort MacPherson* hauled out for the winter at Herschel Island. *Photo courtesy of Library and Archives Canada, Royal Canadian Mounted Police fonds, e010836733.*

the Panama Canal. It was the first steel ship in the western Canadian Arctic, causing some consternation among people who wondered how it stayed afloat.

The *Baychimo* left Vancouver around the end of June each year, aiming to reach Herschel Island in about a month. It then usually travelled as far as Cambridge Bay, stopping at posts along the way for a few days at most—often only for a few hours. The nagging fear that the ship would be trapped in the ice north of Alaska on its way out of the Arctic drove the haste. In fact, on the first voyage to the western Arctic posts, the *Baychimo* was detained at Herschel Island until September 29 by the ice conditions and was fortunate to get out in the next two weeks.

The *Baychimo*'s inbound cargo consisted of supplies for the HBC posts and freight ordered by other parties. Outbound, it carried fur.

Although the ship was not licensed to carry passengers, people would often be signed on as temporary crew members to bypass the regulations, and in the Arctic there were no inspectors. Many agencies and companies came to rely on the ship to transport staff along the coast.

The *Baychimo*'s last voyage was in 1931, a year of severe ice off Alaska, which delayed progress so that the ship only reached Herschel Island on August 26. At that point, Capt. Sydney Cornwell wanted to discharge his cargo and have it taken onward by schooner, with the *Baychimo* returning to Vancouver while ice conditions permitted. Instead, two HBC officers, Commissioner Ralph Parsons and regional manager Richard Bonnycastle, who were waiting at Herschel Island for transport to more easterly posts, urged him to continue, partly because it would be more comfortable and

efficient for them to travel by ship. As a result, the *Baychimo* left for Coppermine (Kugluktuk) on August 30, after two false starts. Parsons left the ship there and travelled south by aircraft.

The *Baychimo* returned to Herschel Island on September 12. There then followed a desperate and ultimately futile attempt to reach the Pacific. In mid-October, almost out of fuel and stuck in the ice pack, the *Baychimo* was abandoned north of Wainwright, Alaska. Some passengers and officials were airlifted out on October 15. The rest of the crew built a cabin on shore, surviving until they were rescued on February 20. By then the drifting ice had taken the ship away. For several years it simply floated, locked in the ice. It was sighted and boarded several times in the 1930s and some of its cargo and equipment salvaged. The ship's final resting place is unknown.

—*Christopher Burn*

POLICE

David Neufeld

The North-West Mounted Police (NWMP), as they were originally known, represented Canada's interests in the country's extreme northwestern corner (Fig. 1). Their duties included establishing a national presence through the enforcement of Canadian law, protecting the country's commercial interests, extending state services to the region, and transforming hunters into citizens. They served at Herschel Island and along the North Slope between 1903 and 1964, and were intermediaries in the complex cultural relations between the aboriginal inhabitants of the North Slope and southern whalemen, fur traders, gold miners, and missionaries. For the inexperienced young Mounties posted to Herschel Island, these challenges were compounded by isolation and the demanding climate. Yet for some of them the experience was to be one of the most interesting and exciting of their lives.

Establishing a Detachment at Herschel Island

Despite their different purposes, both missionaries and whalemen had an interest in the arrival of a state authority. In the 1890s, Bishop Bompas of Selkirk (Yukon) Diocese and Inspector Constantine of the NWMP, both then living in Dawson City, often wrote to Ottawa asking for a police presence to control contact between the aboriginal inhabitants and the whalemen at Herschel Island. At the same time the whaling fleet, overwintering at Herschel Island, wanted a neutral and level-headed third party to settle disputes between the ships' captains and their often restive crews. The Hudson's Bay Company (HBC) also complained to Ottawa because the whalemen brought in much cheaper trade goods directly from San Francisco, initially avoiding customs duties. That meant stiff competition in the regional fur trade.

There was little appetite in the 1890s for the dispatch of a police force to the western Arctic. An economic depression had emptied government coffers, and a commitment to police the Klondike gold rush pushed the capacity of the NWMP to its limits. The petitions from Bompas and Constantine were ignored. Then, in late 1903, the unsatisfactory settlement of the Alaska boundary dispute caused a nationalist furor and the Dominion government quickly responded.

A small and poorly equipped detachment was sent to the western Arctic before the final boundary agreement was completed. They arrived at Herschel Island in late summer 1903 and camped there into the fall. The next year a permanent detachment was established, connected mainly to

Fig. 1   Two members of the RNWMP, identified as "Paddy" and "Walker," in the mission at Herschel Island, late winter 1906. They had arrived on the patrol from Dawson City. Walker, on the right, was Cst. Robert Henry Walker. The identity of Paddy is not clear. *Photo courtesy of Anglican Church of Canada, General Synod Archives, C.E. Whittaker Album, P9901-B6-155.*

The Royal Canadian Mounted Police detachment at Herschel Island, around 1930. *Photo courtesy of Library and Archives Canada, Royal Canadian Mounted Police fonds, e010836723.*

Fig. 2 Police dog team departing Herschel Island, 1923. *Photo courtesy of Yukon Archives, Ernest Pasley fonds, #9243.*

Fort McPherson but also to the Yukon detachment at Dawson City. Early police work focused on monitoring the whaling and trading activity and meeting the aboriginal people in the region.

In 1910 Herschel Island was made the subdistrict headquarters for the RNWMP in the western Arctic. It became the base for regular patrols along the North Slope to the Mackenzie Delta and south to the Porcupine River and Old Crow (Fig. 2). The same year, Inspector G.L. Jennings undertook one of the earliest of the long dog-team patrols. His diary records the difficulties of travel, regional place names, and the presence of aboriginal people. Curiously, when his account was published in the RNWMP report to Parliament for 1911, much of the geographic description was retained but most of the references to people he met were omitted. The land was emptied of people and its potential as territory highlighted.

This interpretation held true only for people far away. Two years earlier, in 1909, the Herschel Island police had hired their first special constable, recognizing that the knowledge and skills of aboriginal people were crucial for their survival (Fig. 3).

Like the Inuvialuit around them, the police appear to have spent most of their time working to stay where they were. They caught fish for the dogs' winter diet, cut ice for the summer water supply, and kept the buildings from collapsing (at least once spending several days looking for their outhouse when it blew away in a gale). They also spent time travelling on patrol in the region by dog team or boat. It was the

co-operation of the Inuvialuit—both the special constables and the local population—that made effective police work possible on the North Slope. In these early years, the police were more of a federal presence than a force for change. Gradually, however, they began asserting Canadian law and extending government services as the local population grew accustomed to the cultural and social changes.

Fig. 3 RCMP patrol in spring at an Inuvialuit camp on the Yukon North Slope, 1954. *From left to right:* Lucy Cockney and Special Constable Bill Cockney, Kitty and Roland Saɼuaq. *Photo courtesy of Parks Canada, Jim Hickling Herschel Island 1953–56 Collection, #153, reproduced with kind permission of Bill and Lucy Cockney.*

Enforcing the Law

The application of the law and the reach of British justice had its most serious consequences in cases of suspected murder. Courts in southern Canada were lenient in early murder trials involving Inuit, recognizing the awkward cultural context of the justice system. From the perspective of the police, however, who were anxious to establish order and end "savagery," these judgements set dangerous precedents. In the early 1920s the police investigated a number of such

Fig. 4 Inuvialuit schooners at Herschel Island, 1930. *Photo courtesy of Library and Archives Canada, R.S. Finnie fonds, PA 100699.*

cases in a growing determination to demonstrate the meaning of the law to Inuit. In 1923 several murder trials were held at Herschel Island. Two men from the central Arctic, Tatamigana and Alikomiak, were convicted of killings at Tree River to the east and hanged at Herschel Island in February 1924.

The intended lesson, however, was misconstrued by people in the area. Interviews with elderly Inuvialuit women who would have been young girls at the time of the trial revealed a conflation of these cases with a later infanticide conviction. These women recalled their mothers' warning them that the white men at Herschel Island often took Inuvialuit girlfriends but dropped them when they became pregnant. In their stories they recalled the police would threaten to put the pregnant young women in jail and hang them unless they married an Inuvialuit man. The exercise of Canadian law at Herschel Island was apparently sometimes misunderstood.

Regulating the Fur Trade

As the whaling industry declined in the 1910s and 1920s, the fur trade and the establishment of national sovereignty by the police became intertwined. A plentiful population of white fox or **tiriganniaq** in the region, along with high fur prices, drew American traders into the area, operating out of ships that sailed north annually from San Francisco. These traders continued to

buy Canadian furs until regulations were tightened to prohibit ship-borne trade. In 1915 the HBC established trading posts on Herschel Island and, briefly, at Clarence Lagoon, very near the international boundary. The fur trade at Herschel Island was extremely successful in the 1920s. In summer, Inuvialuit would gather at Pauline Cove from throughout the western Arctic to trade their skins. They travelled in schooners they bought with revenue from their furs (Fig. 4).

The collapse of fur prices with the Great Depression and the loss of the HBC ship *Baychimo* wrecked the economic sustainability of the trade in the early 1930s. Inuvialuit trappers gradually retreated to the trading posts at Barter Island and in the Mackenzie Delta, and as a result the importance of the police post at Herschel Island diminished. In 1931 the subdistrict headquarters was transferred from Herschel Island to Aklavik and the island detachment was closed two years later. In 1936 Capt. C.T. Pedersen, the last of the ship traders, made his final voyage to Herschel Island. In 1938 he sold up to the HBC, and the company abandoned its post on Herschel Island the same year.

RCMP Schooner *St. Roch*

St. Roch was built specifically for the RCMP to patrol the Arctic and enhance Canada's sovereignty in the region. Constructed in 1928 in the North Vancouver shipyards, the schooner

The two RNWMP graves overlooking Thetis Bay. *Photo by Fritz Mueller.*

POLICE GRAVES

Two of the RNWMP officers stationed at Herschel Island died there and were buried overlooking Thetis Bay. Sgt. Stafford Eardley Aubyn Selig fell ill toward the end of January 1911 and died of an internal sickness during the night of January 28–29. The cause was described in the annual report from the detachment as "bladder trouble." Cst. Alexander Lamont caught typhoid in January 1918 while nursing Vilhjalmur Stefansson in the police barracks. Lamont died the next month, in the room next to Stefansson. Stefansson was sent out by sled to St. Stephen's Mission Hospital at Fort Yukon in April and made a full recovery.

Fig. 5 RCMP schooner *St. Roch* in Pauline Cove, 1947–48. *Photo courtesy of Vancouver Maritime Museum, HSDO-40-16.*

Fig. 6 Old Irish Kegoyook and Cst. Jim Hickling trading white fox. *Photo courtesy of Parks Canada, Jim Hickling Herschel Island 1953–56 Collection, #164.*

patrolled widely in the western and central Arctic for twenty years. In 1940–1942 *St. Roch* was the first vessel to travel the entire Northwest Passage in a west to east direction. This voyage, interestingly enough, had a top secret mission. As part of securing the North Atlantic from Nazi control, the British had invaded Iceland in early 1940. In Europe, Denmark fell to Germany and Britain then asked Canada to protect strategic mineral deposits (cryolite, used in the production of aluminum) in Greenland, Denmark's colony. A small occupying force was proposed, to be deployed from the east coast in the HBC ship *Nascopie*. *St. Roch*, then in Vancouver, was to be the support ship and patrol vessel once the force had been deployed. Although the Canadian occupation of Greenland was strenuously opposed by the United States on the basis of the Monroe Doctrine, *St. Roch* continued on its journey through the Northwest Passage and made history.

Postwar Re-establishment of the Detachment

In the late 1940s, when the Canadian government introduced family allowance and old age pension programs, there were unexpected effects in the western Arctic. Inuvialuit families who had settled at Barter Island, Alaska, in the 1930s now decided to move east to join their relatives in Canada. The migration of these families prompted the re-opening of the police

detachment at Herschel Island in 1948, after the *St. Roch* had coincidentally spent the previous winter in Pauline Cove (Fig. 5). Shortly after the detachment was re-established, both the value and number of white fox on the North Slope collapsed, complicating police work there over the next fifteen years.

As the only representatives of the Crown stationed on the western Arctic coast, the Herschel Island detachment had, before the Second World War, registered traders coming into the region and investigated criminal acts. After the war, the detachment was called on to enforce hunting and trapping seasons with increasing rigour, and to deal with various other tasks. For a short period around 1949, the detachment was the Mining Recorder for prospectors on the Firth River during a minor gold rush, and provided relief supplies to the aged or sick as necessary from 1948 to 1964. Perhaps the most important activity for Canada was the police attention to local trends and activities submitted in the annual report on the "Conditions of the Eskimo."

Traditionally the fur trade companies had extended credit to Inuvialuit trappers for the next year's outfit. However, with the poor business outlook for fur, traders began refusing further credit to trappers already deeply in debt. A large proportion of the Inuvialuit now living along the

North Slope were refused such credit. People coming from Alaska had also been left out of the allocation of registered trap lines in the Mackenzie Delta and were not allowed to share trapping privileges there. Further, Aklavik had little room for new residents, while both the Catholic and Anglican schools were packed and unable to accept new students.

Despite protests by both the Herschel Island detachment and RCMP headquarters about the resulting hardship for these people, the traders argued that the issue was one of relief and therefore a government responsibility. The Herschel Island detachment was instructed to keep the people on the land while alternatives were considered. As a temporary response, the detachment established a trading store in 1950 (Fig. 6). In 1951, eleven families with 37 children (a total of 85 people) collected family allowance as rations from the detachment. Relief rations distributed that year included flour, sugar, milk powder, matches, tea, baking powder, lard, ammunition (30/30 and .22), coal oil, macaroni, tinned tomatoes, rolled oats, prunes, rice, beans, and salt. In January 1951 the store obtained six white fox skins, two pairs of caribou mitts, a pair of caribou boots, a pair of seal skin slippers, and two pairs of seal skin mitts. Poor hunting conditions persisted until 1953, making many people dependent on the store.

Fig. 7 Constables McFarland and Hickling intercept the first truck train to the Stokes Point DEW Line site near Herschel Island. *Photo courtesy of Parks Canada, William McFarland Herschel Island 1953–55 Collection, #074.*

Fig. 8 Assembling two RCMP dog teams at Herschel Island in 1957. *Photo by Morley Riske, courtesy of Alan and Marilyn Fehr.*

Cst. Jim Hickling recalled the store during his posting at Herschel Island in the mid-1950s:

> [W]e realized that there were enough people living on the coast, trapping, that we could handle a small store, so Northern Affairs put in a bunch of supplies at Herschel Island, staples ... and then they [Inuvialuit people] caught fox or wolverine or whatever and brought it to Herschel. They would ... trade for staples.... [In] 1956, we thought we'd increase things a little bit and we got some traps and all kinds of ammunition and I think we even got some clothing—some heavy wool shirts and ... the big things—tea, sugar, flour, lard. I think we even got a case of butter.... [T]he butter was a real treat. [T]here would hardly be a week go by that somebody wouldn't drop in, either one of the Allens or the Meyooks. The Meyooks used to come out and trap and then they'd catch a few fox and then bring them in and trade them to us for flour, tea, lard, so on. Oh, yeah, as the store grew, of course,

and the price of fox was pretty good ... it would bring more people out of the delta to the coast to trap.

In searching for a permanent solution, in 1951 Northern Affairs proposed to relocate a large portion of the Inuvialuit population from the North Slope and the delta to Holman Island, where game was reported to be plentiful. The Inuvialuit politely declined, confident in their ability to make a living on familiar ground. However, even though trapping and prices improved in 1954, a major storm in August the following year wiped out many of their outfits. Hickling, who sat out "a terrific storm" with northwest winds of up to 75 mph and a great rise in water level near Shingle Point, reported that Gus Tardiff's family nearby suffered a lot of damage, "losing their entire summer fish catch, meat cache, food stuffs, and dog equipment." The family moved their tent into the hills behind Shingle Point and hunted the numerous caribou in order to survive until freeze-up. The schooner *Red Mountain* was washed up on shore at King Point, and while it

appeared undamaged, many others lost fish nets and dog equipment. For many families the losses wiped out the last remains of white fox wealth from the halcyon days of the 1920s. Nevertheless, by the mid-1950s many Inuvialuit were employed as construction workers on the DEW (Distant Early Warning) Line across the whole of the Arctic (Fig. 7).

The possibility of more jobs, and the development of the town of Inuvik, drew more of the Inuvialuit into the Mackenzie Delta. As a result the North Slope gradually lost most of its already limited population. By the early 1960s, the Herschel Island detachment's responsibilities had shrunk to occasional patrols to the DEW Line stations and the maintenance of a yard for breeding sled dogs (Fig. 8). With the onset of more reliable aircraft travel and the replacement of dogs with snowmobiles, even those functions disappeared. In 1964 the Herschel Island detachment was closed for the last time.

STAMP DUTY

The Herschel Island Post Office, initially operated by the RCMP, was open from April 17, 1925, to September 14, 1938. In the early years the mail arrived five times a year by boat or dog team from Aklavik. Insp. Vernon Kemp was postmaster from 1927–29. In his memoirs he complained about

the volume of mail sent by stamp collectors asking him to cancel stamped, addressed envelopes and dispatch them southward. In 1930 mail began to be delivered to the island by aircraft.

The first mail plane at Herschel Island in 1930. *Photo courtesy of Library and Archives Canada, R.S. Finnie fonds, PA 100756.*

RCMP jolly boat. *Photo courtesy of Parks Canada, William McFarland Herschel Island 1953–55 Collection, #026.*

Dog team hauling up the jolly boat to the warehouse on Herschel Island for winter storage. *Photo courtesy of Parks Canada, Jim Hickling Herschel Island 1953–56 Collection, #022.*

PATROL REPORT
Nov. 18, 1954, Cst. W.L. McFarland

September 11: Heavy overcast, strong NW wind. Departed Herschel Island at 2:30 P.M. Pack ice very thick from Herschel Island to about three miles offshore from the mainland. Seas were very heavy and patrol forced to put into Sadyook's River and travel one mile inland to camp of Rowland Sadyook (Roland Saŕuaq). Arrived 5:30 P.M., camp made there for the night. Sadyook had a very good fishing season and has already shot a good supply of caribou this fall. Although close to 70 years of age, he and his family will have plenty of food, clothing and dog feed this winter.

September 12: Clear, strong N/W wind in A.M., calmer in P.M. Forced to remain at Sadyook camp until 4:30 P.M. due to high winds. Large herds of caribou seen south of camp along the Buckland Range. Proceeded back to the coast and then towards King Point. Pack ice was right into shore from Kay Point eastward and travelling very slow. Near King Point Jolly Boat 7284 broke down and it was necessary to tow it into King Point harbour with canoe and outboard motor. Arrived at 11:10 P.M. Native schooners *Bonnie Belle* and *Shamrock* anchored in the harbour.

September 13: Clear and calm. A.M. issuing game licences to natives. Left on native schooner *Bonnie Belle* at 11 A.M. travelling along coast to Shingle Point. Arrived at 4 P.M.

Heavy pack ice encountered and travelling very slow. Caribou herds noted all along the coast. Native camps visited at Shingle Point and three Eskimo girls previously reported ill found to have completely recovered. Yukon game licences issued to two natives. Camp made at Shingle Point for the night.

September 14: Overcast, light snow, strong east wind. Remained at Shingle Point due to weather.

September 15: Clear and calm. Left Shingle Point at 7 A.M. and arrived back at King Point at 11:45 A.M. Ice conditions much improved due to strong east wind of previous day. *Bonnie Belle* left immediately, bound for Herschel Island. P.M. spent repairing police cabin at King Point, removing fishnets, and preparing to move fish camp equipment aboard Cargo Boat 7311. Cargo Boat 7311 arrived King Point at 8:30 P.M. and anchored there for the night.

September 16: Overcast and stormy, strong east wind. Remained at King Point due to weather. Cargo boat moved to the south end of the harbour as it was dragging its anchor in high winds. P.M. working on Jolly Boat 7284 but unable to start same.

September 17: Overcast, snowing, very strong west wind. Remained at King Point all day due to weather. Fish loaded into barrels and fish camp dismantled and taken aboard

cargo boat. Walked to high bluff above west of harbour and noted that old ice was packed in along the shore from King Point to Kay Point and as far out to sea as the eye could see. Young ice was also forming between the old ice and along the shore of the harbour. As it was impossible to return to Herschel Island and there was a danger of being frozen in at King Point if the patrol remained there longer, the jolly boat and canoe were beached at King Point for the winter and S/Cst. Cockney and the writer proceeded to Aklavik with Cargo Boat Code 7311.

September 18: Clear and cold, turning to overcast with strong N/W winds. Left King Point at 6:30 A.M. travelling south-east to Shingle Point. Anchored at Shingle Point at 9:30 A.M. because of steadily rising winds. Left Shingle at 12:45 P.M. travelling inside Escape Reef. Water very high due to storms. Arrived to Tiktaluk River at 4:30 P.M. and anchored for the night.

September 19: Overcast, snowing in A.M. clearing in P.M. Departed mouth of the Tiktaluk River at 8:30 A.M., arrived Aklavik at 4:30 P.M.

September 20 to November 9, 1954: Working in Aklavik office and region.

November 10: Clear, calm and cool -20 Deg. Departed Aklavik via Aklavik Flying Services Aircraft CF-GSG at 11:15 A.M. and arrived Herschel Island 12:15 P.M.

SCIENTISTS AND EXPLORERS

Christopher Burn
and Stuart E. Jenness

Fig. 1 Thomas Simpson, Arctic explorer (1811–1840). *Image courtesy of Royal Geographical Society, S002201.*

Schooners of the Canadian Arctic Expedition in Pauline Cove, August 10, 1914. The *Alaska* is in the foreground, in front of the *Mary Sachs*. The *North Star* is furthest from the camera. *Photo courtesy of Canadian Museum of Civilization, John Johnston O'Neill, 38668.*

Europeans and North American settlers first learned of Herschel Island after July 15, 1826, when Capt. John Franklin (1786–1847) saw and named it from Kay Point on the mainland coast. Franklin landed on the north side of Workboat Passage two days later, where he met three groups of Qikiqtaryungmiut. He and his party probably camped near Lopez Point. Franklin saw numerous caribou on the island and learned that fish were abundant in the surrounding waters.

A series of explorers and scientists, most of whom are described in this chapter, have visited the island since then. The visits were occasional until the whaling period, but since the late nineteenth century, researchers have studied much of the natural and cultural environment.

Thomas Simpson and Peter Dease

Thomas Simpson (1811–1840) and Peter Dease (1788–1863), both of the Hudson's Bay Company, travelled along the Yukon and Alaskan coasts in 1837. Their purpose was to map the coastline, extending Franklin's survey. They reached Herschel Island on July 14 during their journey westward, when they sailed through Workboat Passage and landed on Avadlek Spit. They met several people hunting caribou and found part of the skeleton of a bowhead whale. They also noticed that baleen was used to make fish nets.

On the return journey, when they reached Herschel Island on August 15, they did not land, but reported that many people were on the island.

Lt. William Pullen

In 1849 Lt. William Pullen (1813–1887) of the British Royal Navy was sent to search the coast eastward to the Mackenzie Delta for Franklin's lost third Arctic expedition. He travelled with four small boats from HMS *Plover* and HMS *Herald*, which were stationed in the Bering Sea. Together with William Hooper (1827–1854), mate of the *Plover*, and 23 other men, Pullen began his search on July 27. They reached Herschel Island on August 21 and camped on Avadlek Spit, where the crew stayed in an "Esquimaux hut." The next day they sailed through Workboat Passage, camping to the east of Calton Point, and carried on to Fort McPherson, where they arrived on September 5.

Capt. Richard Collinson

Two years after Pullen's expedition, HMS *Enterprise*, commanded by Capt. Richard Collinson (1811–1883), travelled eastward from Bering Strait, again searching for Franklin's lost expedition. Collinson saw Herschel Island on August 14, 1851, and spent a few days nearby. When the ship tacked north of the island, Collinson noted the sudden deepening of the ocean as *Enterprise* crossed the edge of the continental shelf.

The crew saw several Qikiqtaryung-miut from the ship and made the first estimate of the position of Qikiqtaryuk's north point (69°40' N, 139° 0' W). On the return journey, *Enterprise* passed the island on September 5, 1853, but was blown back to Kay Point by September 8. Several people came out to the ship in kayaks and asked for tobacco. A day later the wind changed and Collinson left Herschel Island behind.

Lt. Cdr. Charles Stockton

USS *Thetis*, commanded by Lt. Cdr. Stockton (1845–1924), was a steam bark assigned to assist the western Arctic whaling fleet. *Thetis* was in the eastern Alaskan sector when Joseph Tuckfield returned from the Mackenzie Delta area in the summer of 1889 with news of many bowheads and a good harbour at Herschel Island. On August 15 *Thetis* sailed to the island, where Stockton carried out a survey, reporting that the ocean was clear of ice to the north and east as far as he could see. He correctly attributed the distinctly different sea ice conditions east and west of the island to the influence of the Mackenzie River. His survey led to the first chart of Herschel Island, published in March 1890 (see page 21).

Frank Russell

Frank Russell (1868–1903), an ethnologist from the Univerity of Iowa, spent the summer of 1894 on and near Herschel Island, collecting materials that were sent to the museum at his university. He first reached the coast at the beginning of July and was immediately struck by the better material conditions of the Inuit people he met compared to those of the First Nations people. In particular, he appreciated the abundance of food—coffee, syrup, and flour—all part of the trade goods brought by the whalemen. When Russell arrived at Phillips Bay, he found the goods were "used by every family." He crossed to Herschel Island on July 8, 1894, before the whaling fleet could leave the

harbour, and remained in the area until August 30, when he left for the south on the *Jeanette*, captained by E.W. Newth. He took with him an extensive collection of artifacts, described in his book *Explorations in the Far North*.

Alvin Seale

Alvin Seale (1871–1958), a student of natural history at Stanford University, travelled to the western Arctic in summer 1896, courtesy of the Pacific Steam Whaling Company. At Qikiqtaryuk he sighted and reported on Long-tailed Jaegers, Snow geese, and Black Brant geese.

Andrew Jackson Stone

In 1896 the American Museum of Natural History sponsored a series of expeditions by Andrew Jackson Stone (1859–1918) to northwest North America, including a journey in 1897–99 to the western Arctic coast. Stone reached Fort McPherson in October 1898 and travelled by dog team out to Herschel Island, beginning his return

from the island just before Christmas. He wrote:

> In November I traversed the Mackenzie Delta [from Fort McPherson], and the Arctic coast westward for 250 miles, as far as Herschel Island, returning in December. ... Anthropometric measurements were taken of quite a number of the Noonitagmioots at Herschel Island. During the entire journey not the fluttering of a bird, the hoot of an owl, or the cry of a wolf could be heard. We were completely enveloped in the pervading stillness of Arctic night.

Alfred Harrison

An independent British traveller and surveyor, Alfred Harrison (1865–1933) arrived at Herschel Island on February 22, 1906. He intended to acquire supplies and assistants and to search for land in the Arctic Ocean. What he found were five stranded whaling ships, a population short

AN EARLY REPORT ON LEMMINGS

Andrew Jackson Stone, who visited Herschel Island from November to December 1898, provided one of the first accounts of lemmings from Qikiqtaryuk:

A small rodent, brownish gray in summer and white in winter, I found on the Arctic coast, was a peculiarly interesting little animal. The whalers universally claim that they never find them except just after a storm, and that when they find them on top of the hard snow, appearances indicate that they have dropped on the snow from the clouds, and that after running around in a small circuit, they keel over and die. It is probable that they may come

up to the surface of the snow during wind storms and are then blown from the ridges for some distance, and falling on the hard snow or ice they die. One secured at Herschel Island and placed on a sheet of sensitized paper spread on a table gave a very clever exhibition of the manner in which it must dig through snow or earth. It would not try to get away but would double up, with its feet seemingly all in a bunch, and then move therein with such rapidity as to create a buzzing noise, in its attempt to make a hole through the paper. The movement of its feet was astonishingly rapid.

Fig. 2 Amundsen's *Gjøa* at King Point, winter 1905–06. The photograph was taken in moonlight. *Photo courtesy of National Library of Norway, NPRA 1174.*

Fig. 3 The grave marker of Gustav Wiik, erected at King Point in 1906. The marker was moved back from the eroding coast several times and is now kept in Whitehorse. *Photograph taken in 1957 by J. Ross Mackay.*

of food, and no enthusiasm among the aboriginal people to head north. Harrison spent the rest of the winter and spring on Qikiqtaryuk and the mainland, joining in hunting, and surveyed the island on foot in early summer.

On August 14 he met Vilhjalmur Stefansson, who had recently arrived on the island. Harrison hoped to acquire supplies from the whaling company's tender that summer, but the ship never arrived. Instead, he and Stefansson travelled locally along the coast. Harrison subsequently published a map of Herschel Island, marking a fish camp on Avadlek Spit as well as the board and observation spot of USS *Thetis*. His book, *In Search of a Polar Continent 1905–07*, published in 1908, contains detailed impressions of "Kogmolik" and "Nunatama" life at the time. Harrison noted that Nunatarmiut people had taken advantage of the whalemen's presence by working for them, and had acquired whaleboats and other goods.

Roald Amundsen

The *Gjøa* spent the last winter of her transit through the Northwest Passage at King Point, where she was impounded by ice in early September 1905 (Fig. 2). Roald Amundsen (1876–1928) made his first visit to Herschel Island two weeks later to collect mail, arriving on September 25,

and staying for four days with Capt. James Tilton on board the whaling ship *Alexander*. He met and formed a good impression of the Anglican missionary, Rev. Charles Whittaker, then living in the community house. Amundsen returned to the island on October 21 to join the small party departing for Fort Yukon, in order to inform the outside world of his progress. He returned to the *Gjøa* on March 12, 1906, and spent the rest of the winter at King Point, where the ship's second engineer, Gustav Wiik, died of an undiagnosed illness and was buried (Fig. 3).

On July 10 the *Gjøa* left King Point and anchored in Pauline Cove three days later. For the next month or so Amundsen remained near Herschel Island, confined by the ice to the west. He observed various aspects of life including diet, clothing, Sunday services, the prevalence of syphilis, and the graveyard. Tragically, on July 21 the *Gjøa* lost Manni, her Inuit hand, who drowned in the harbour while shooting ducks from a small boat. Amundsen met Vilhjalmur Stefansson, who arrived on August 9 with the mail from Edmonton and Fort McPherson. The *Gjøa* finally left Pauline Cove on August 10, with Amundsen "being rather tired of Herschel," and reached Cape Prince of Wales 20 days later to complete the transit of the Northwest Passage.

Ejnar Mikkelsen

Ejnar Mikkelsen (1880–1971) was a celebrated Danish Arctic explorer. In 1906 he set out from Victoria, BC, in the *Duchess of Bedford*, a schooner named after his patron, aiming to winter at Herschel Island. His expedition partner was Ernest Leffingwell (1875–1971), the American geologist. Together with Stefansson they were to explore the Arctic Ocean north of Alaska, searching for land as the Anglo-American Polar Expedition. Unfortunately the *Duchess of Bedford* drew too much water to sail between the ice and the coast, and Mikkelsen only reached Flaxman Island before winter set in. In March he travelled with Leffingwell out from the coast by sled, but found no land.

When they returned to shore, Mikkelsen headed for Herschel Island, where he was extremely disappointed that the aboriginal ways had been modified—he thought corrupted—by the whalemen and missionaries. In particular he was disturbed by the number of children of mixed race on Qikiqtaryuk (Fig. 4), the attitude of Europeans to the treatment of aboriginal people, the growing dependence of aboriginal people on material goods brought in from "outside," and the loss of traditional skills. He walked out of the Arctic along the coast of Alaska.

Fig. 4 Three Inuvialuit children at Herschel Island. The photo was taken to show that over a hundred years ago some of the children living on the island had aboriginal parents (boy on the left), some had a Portuguese father (girl in the middle), and some an Afro-American father (boy on the right). Unfortunately, the names of these children are not recorded. *Photo courtesy of Anglican Church of Canada, General Synod Archives, C.E. Whittaker Album, P9901-B7-21.*

Vilhjalmur Stefansson

Vilhjalmur Stefansson (1879–1962) joined the Anglo-American Polar Expedition as an anthropologist while he was a graduate student at Harvard University (Fig. 5). He reached Herschel Island on August 9, 1906, where he expected to meet Mikkelsen and Leffingwell. While waiting there he met Christian (Charlie) Klengenberg, who had encountered Inuit with apparently Nordic features the previous winter on the south coast of Victoria Island. These people had not seen non-aboriginals before.

When Mikkelsen and Leffingwell failed to reach Herschel Island, Stefansson wintered at Shingle Point with Roxy Memoganna (Fig. 6) and his family, studying fishing and hunting methods and learning Siglitun.

Early in 1907 Stefansson travelled west by dog team, seeking news of his expedition. At Flaxman Island he learned that the expedition's schooner, the *Duchess of Bedford*, was ice-bound and badly damaged, and that Mikkelsen and Leffingwell had led a party north in search of land. After they returned safely, Stefansson made

his way east to Herschel Island and then left the Arctic, going overland by way of the Firth, Porcupine, and Yukon rivers.

Stefansson–Anderson Expedition 1908–1912

Stefansson returned to the western Arctic in summer 1908, accompanied by the American zoologist Dr. Rudolph M. Anderson (1876–1961) (Fig. 7). They were sponsored by the American Museum of Natural History and the Geological Survey of Canada. Their expedition was to

Fig. 5 Vilhjalmur Stefansson at Herschel Island. *Photo courtesy of Canadian Museum of Civilization, Storker Storkerson, 50669.*

Fig. 6 Roxy (Roksi) Memoganna and whaleman Christian Sten at King Point, 1905–06. *Photo courtesy of National Library of Norway, NPRA2016.*

Fig. 7 Dr. R.M. Anderson. *Photo courtesy of Anglican Church of Canada, General Synod Archives, C.E. Whittaker Album, P9901-B6-267.*

Fig. 8 Fanny Pannigabluk and Alex Stefansson at Herschel Island. *Photo courtesy of Anglican Church of Canada, General Synod Archives, Stringer family collection, P7517-384.*

Fig. 9 Some of the members of the Canadian Arctic Expedition at Herschel Island, August 7, 1914. *Photo courtesy of Canadian Museum of Civilization, George Hubert Wilkins, 51435.*

explore the central Arctic, visit and study the native people Stefansson had heard Klengenberg speak of in 1906, and collect anthropological and zoological specimens.

Travelling north down the Mackenzie River, they reached Herschel Island late in July. Stefansson, who intended to live off the land and sea, had brought few provisions with him and had to ask RNWMP Sgt. Francis Fitzgerald for more matches. Fitzgerald, however, refused, evidently to prevent the two men from proceeding east without adequate provisions. Stefansson then went west to Point Barrow on the whaler *Karluk* to obtain the matches he needed. Anderson, meanwhile, proceeded west by whaleboat with a small party of Nunatarmiut, including Ilavinirk and his family, to hunt in the mountains south of Barter Island.

Stefansson and Anderson spent the next three years east and south of Cape Bathurst, working separately much of the time. Stefansson's remarkable linguistic abilities enabled him to learn about and document the life of the Inuit in the central Arctic for the first time, while his marksmanship proved a great asset for his survival. He and Anderson were accompanied and greatly assisted by three Nunatarmiut: Natkusiak, Ilavinirk, and Pannigabluk. Pannigabluk provided Stefansson

with much folklore and she also gave birth to their son, Alex (Fig. 8), though Stefansson carefully avoided any public mention of his close relationship with her and Alex during her lifetime.

Stefansson subsequently publicized his exploration and anthropological accomplishments in his popular book *My Life with the Eskimo,* in articles in *Harper's Magazine*, in a formal report for the American Museum of Natural History, and in numerous public lectures on both sides of the Atlantic. His revelation that some people living on Victoria Island had Nordic features (the "Blond Eskimos") created widespread interest. Anderson's zoological collections from the regions of Langton Bay and western Coronation Gulf received far less publicity, largely because of his limited writing about his Arctic activities.

Canadian Arctic Expedition 1913–1918

Stefansson and Anderson returned to the Arctic in 1913 with a larger expedition (Fig. 9), sponsored this time entirely by the Canadian government. The expedition had a dual format and purpose. A northern party, led by Stefansson, was to explore for land northwest of Banks Island. A southern party, under Anderson's direction, was to map the coast for 600 miles

from Cape Bathurst east to the Kent Peninsula, and conduct geological studies of known native copper occurrences. They were also to carry out ethnographical studies of the "Blond Eskimos" (today the Copper Inuit) in the Coronation Gulf region, and biological studies and collections of mammals, birds, fish, and plants in the same area.

The expedition's flagship, *Karluk*, was crushed by the Arctic ice shortly after leaving Nome for Herschel Island, and later sank off the Siberian coast. On board were all the members of Stefansson's northern party as well as their provisions and equipment. No one perished at the time, but 11 of the 25 survivors died within the next few months. The loss of his northern party severely crippled Stefansson's plans, but he quickly found replacement supplies, personnel, dogs, and ships along the northern Alaskan coast.

Stefansson recommenced his Arctic exploration by striking north from Martin Point, Alaska, in March 1914. He suddenly appeared at Herschel Island in August 1915, having chartered Capt. Louis Lane's schooner *Polar Bear* when they met by chance on the south coast of Banks Island. In the next two weeks Stefansson spent government money buying the *Polar Bear* and provisions for the expedition, as well as hiring numerous Inuit both for his own further explorations and to assist Anderson.

In the spring of 1915, the Canadian government sent instructions to all members of the expedition to return from the Arctic no later than the summer of 1916, which the men on the southern party dutifully did. Stefansson, however, continued exploring until the summer of 1917. The following January, he reached Herschel Island seriously ill with pneumonia. He was nursed initially by the police stationed there, then by the Rev. W.H. Fry, but subsequently developed pleurisy and typhoid fever and was not expected to live. On his insistence, however, he was bundled onto a sled in April and taken south over the mountains to St. Stephen's Mission Hospital at Fort Yukon, where he slowly recovered.

Anderson and the southern party had spent the 1913–1914 winter icebound at Camden Bay in northern Alaska, far west of their intended investigation area. In March 1914 one of the members of the party, the geologist John J. O'Neill, travelled east to Herschel Island by dog sled and examined the sediments exposed in the cliffs. He and his colleague, geographer John Cox, then mapped the nearby Firth River to the Alaskan boundary before joining geographer

Kenneth Chipman to map the major branches of the Mackenzie Delta. In early August, after arriving with Anderson, his ships, and their crews, the naturalist Fritz Johansen studied the plants and insects on Herschel Island.

On August 6, Chipman, Cox, and O'Neill returned to Herschel Island with mail that had been shipped down the Mackenzie River. Included were government instructions to Anderson to send a search party and ship for Stefansson and his two companions, who had failed to return from their exploration trip over the Arctic ice. Three days later the steam whaler *Herman* (Capt. C.T. Pedersen) reached Herschel Island with news of the loss of the *Karluk* and several of its personnel, and of attempts being made to rescue the survivors on Wrangel Island. Faced with changed circumstances, and the new government orders, Anderson placed George H. Wilkins, the expedition's photographer, in charge of the schooner *Mary Sachs* (instead of the smaller schooner *North Star*, as Stefansson had instructed), and had him sail from Herschel Island with two years of supplies and added personnel to establish a base on Banks Island and search for the missing men.

The southern party then headed east and established a base northwest of Coronation Gulf, from which they

completed their tasks during the next two years. In July 1916 they sailed west from Bernard Harbour, stopping briefly at Herschel Island to let off assorted non-expedition personnel and some leftover supplies for Stefansson before continuing on out of the Arctic.

Diamond Jenness, the ethnographer, and other members of Anderson's southern party wrote thirteen of the fourteen published scientific volumes detailing the expedition's findings. Stefansson's account of the expedition, *The Friendly Arctic,* written for the general public, proved immensely popular when published in 1921, although it contained many inaccuracies.

Erling Porsild

Erling Porsild (1901–1977), a Danish botanist living in Greenland, and his brother Robert (Bob) were hired by the federal government to survey the vegetation in northern Alaska and Canada's western Arctic to determine if it would support a reindeer herd. Porsild visited Herschel Island several times during his ten summers and eight winters in the western Arctic. His first visit took place between March 30 and April 4, 1927, shortly after he arrived from Alaska. He stayed with the RCMP then and on later occasions (Fig. 10). In 1932, when he spent six weeks on the island between January 30 and March 12,

Fig. 10 **RCMP buildings at Herschel Island in March 1933.** *Photo courtesy of Library and Archives Canada, A.E. Porsild fonds, PA 101095.*

he was relieved to arrive because there was little food available along the coast. Porsild's surveys led to the 1929–35 reindeer drive. His field surveys were summarized in a number of publications that are still in use, including the standard text *Vascular Plants of Continental Northwest Territories, Canada*, published posthumously in 1980 with W.J. Cody.

J. Ross Mackay

In the 1950s the Geographical Branch of the federal Department of Mines and Technical Resources sent several field parties along the Yukon coast, led by geographer J. Ross Mackay (b. 1915). These field investigations produced two major insights. First, Qikiqtaryuk is a glacially ice-thrust feature, pushed up from Herschel Basin during the last ice age. Second, the ice sheet overrode the coastal plain, leaving behind sediments brought up by ice from ground that is now below sea level. The second point enabled archaeologists to develop a sensible time scale for the occupation of the Engigtsciak archaeological site, a bedrock knoll near the Firth River that had been used by hunters for millennia.

Paul Fenimore Cooper, Jr.

In the early 1970s, Herschel Island was the location of a series of experiments by Paul Fenimore Cooper, Jr. (1930–1988), a wealthy, independent scientist. Cooper sometimes chartered an aircraft to take him directly to the western Arctic, and then flew on to Herschel Island using an aircraft company he had bought into for this purpose. He built a wind turbine at Pauline Cove to develop a source of power and investigated how sea ice expanded and contracted according to the temperature.

John R. Bockstoce

In 1973, John Bockstoce (b. 1944) was asked by Paul Fenimore Cooper, Jr. to excavate two mounds at Pauline Cove thought to have been Inuvialuit houses. The investigations went well until the authorities realized that Cooper had no archaeological permit and ordered the research to stop. Bockstoce was told to store the artifacts he had found in the Newport house, close to the traders' warehouses toward the west end of the settlement. Unfortunately, many drums of fuel were also stored in the building. When

the Newport house burned down on August 23, 1973, all the artifacts were lost (Fig. 11).

Research in the Park

After Herschel Island became a territorial park in 1987 as a result of the Inuvialuit Final Agreement, a number of studies began to document conditions on the island. A detailed inventory of terrain conditions led to the classification and mapping of all the island's landscape units. Between 1990–93, elders who had spent significant time in the region contributed to the main account of Inuvialuit oral history of Herschel Island and the Yukon North Slope (Fig. 12). As a result, considerable material was published about social and environmental conditions during the twentieth century.

During the most recent International Polar Year, 2007–09, the island was a focus for research projects on its ecosystem (summarized in earlier chapters), permafrost and climate change, and the temperatures in the ice house. Other long-running projects continued to study coastal erosion and the nature of ground ice on the island.

Fig. 11 Fire consuming the Newport house in 1974. *Photo taken by Sven Johansen from the* North Star of Herschel Island, *courtesy of John Bockstoce.*

Monitoring of the biophysical environment is integral to park operations at Qikiqtaryuk. Some of the measurements are of annual totals, such as late-winter snow depth, but other measurements, as with ground temperatures or thaw slump development, are made monthly. Plants and raptor nests are measured toward the beginning of summer. Throughout the season park staff record the numbers of caribou, muskox, and bear sightings. Some park staff and biologists visit the island to make annual population estimates, as with studies of Black Guillemots. Within the next decade, these data will be among the most detailed, informative, and consistent environmental records in the western Arctic. Along with the logistical support that the park facilities offer, the monitoring capability and the accumulating record from Qikiqtaryuk ensure that Herschel Island will remain a centre for scientific research for a long time to come.

Fig. 12 Herschel Island Cultural Study, summer 1990. *Left to right:* Renie Arey, Murielle Nagy, Dora Malegana, Jean Tardiff, and Kathleen Hansen, with Sarah Meyook in front, Herschel Island. *Photo by John Tousignant, reproduced with permission of the Inuvialuit Cultural Research Centre, and courtesy of Yukon Heritage Branch and Inuvialuit Social Development Program.*

WHERE ARE THE ARTIFACTS?

Archaeological, cultural, and other artifacts collected at Qikiqtaryuk have found their way to museums throughout North America. The principal collections of archeological materials are at the Canadian Museum of Civilization in Gatineau, QC; the Prince of Wales Northern Heritage Centre in Yellowknife, NT; and Heritage Resources Unit, Department of Tourism and Culture, Government of Yukon, in Whitehorse, YT. The original gravemarkers of the whalemen are also housed in Whitehorse.

The largest collections of animal specimens were taken to the American Museum of Natural History in New York, NY, where some cultural artifacts are also stored. The University of Iowa in Iowa City, IA, acquired a substantial collection of cultural material from Frank Russell. Gwich'in caribou clothing acquired in trade by Capt. Albert Sherman of the *Beluga* is held at the New Bedford Whaling Museum, New Bedford, MA. Ancient bones are now collected and studied by the staff of the Heritage Resources Unit in Whitehorse.

Artifacts collected on Herschel Island and held by the Heritage Resources Unit in Whitehorse. *Photo courtesy of Government of Yukon.*

CONSERVATION AND GOVERNANCE

conservation and governance

BUILDINGS

Doug Olynyk

About a dozen historic buildings stand in the settlement at Pauline Cove (Fig. 1). The community house, erected by the Pacific Steam Whaling Company (PSWC) in 1893, is the oldest frame building in the Yukon. Other structures include subterranean ice cellars, whalemen's quarters, dog kennels, grave markers, and the buried remains of ancient Inuit dwellings (Fig. 2). These structural remains not only provide tangible evidence of a wide cross section of the people who lived and worked here, but also offer insights into both Inuvialuit and Euro-American culture along Yukon's Arctic coast.

Both prehistoric and historic Inuvialuit built some of the structures on Herschel Island, but the whalemen, missionaries, traders, and police who arrived later erected the majority that stand today. The wood frame buildings are the only historic examples of such construction along Yukon's North Slope. Some were made of so-called "Oregon pine" (actually fir) and redwood brought in by American whalemen, pre-cut and labelled for assembly. Today, Inuvialuit travellers, park staff, researchers, and other visitors use these buildings.

After contact, and particularly from about 1890 to 1920, when the whalemen introduced foreign materials and technologies, the Inuvialuit began to modify their traditional dwellings. Their houses, and the temporary houses put up by visitors, still used sod for cladding, but eliminated the subterranean interior floor and used glass instead of seal gut for the windows (Fig. 3). None of these sod houses are left, but the archaeological evidence indicates that they had one storey and were aligned in a series of rows from east to west, with sheltered entrances mainly oriented to the south. The houses were likely on beach ridges, where the ground was relatively dry. The frame buildings still standing follow the same orientation and pattern. Most of their doors are on the south side for shelter from winter storms.

Whaling Industry Buildings

The settlement area at Pauline Cove was developed to support whaling ships overwintering in the southeastern Beaufort Sea. The extant historic buildings are rectangular and most are relatively small. They were built at grade with rudimentary wall sills, floor beams, and floor joists resting directly on the frozen ground. The roofs are typically low-to-medium-pitch gables with minimal eaves, clad in wood shingles, sheet metal, or simply roll asphalt roofing.

The community house and bone house at Pauline Cove. *Photo by Cameron Eckert.*

Fig. 1 Aerial view of the buildings on the spit at Pauline Cove. *Photo by Doug Olynyk.*

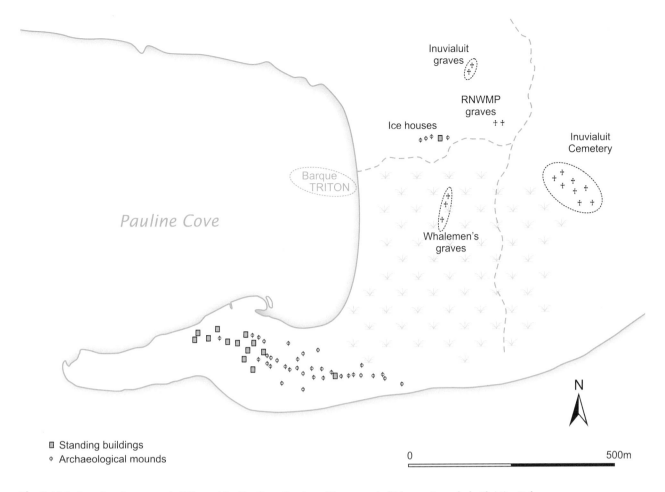

Inuvialuit graves

RNWMP graves

Ice houses

Inuvialuit Cemetery

Barque TRITON

Pauline Cove

Whalemen's graves

N

■ Standing buildings
φ Archaeological mounds

0   500m

Fig. 2 Historic and contemporary buildings at Pauline Cove. *Courtesy of Government of Yukon; cartography by Christine Earl.*

The exterior wall claddings are usually horizontal wood siding, with some using vertical board and batten, sheet metal, or wood shingle. Trims are simple, with plain door and window casings and corner boards. Windows, which are small and usually square, were placed high on the walls because snow is often driven up to and over

roof eaves by high winds. Interior wall finishes are spare—bare or painted wood or wood sheathing with paper lining. The floors, walls, and ceilings were not insulated.

The oldest extant building in the settlement area is the Pacific Steam Whaling Company's community house.

It was offered to Rev. Isaac Stringer as a residence and mission in 1897, and was used by the Anglican Church until 1906. The first building built by the company, in 1890, was a warehouse on Avadlek Spit, but it was soon dismantled and rebuilt at Pauline Cove. This warehouse has since disappeared, possibly dismantled and reused by

Fig. 3 Royal North-West Mounted Police Sergeant F.J. Fitzgerald *left* and Constable F.D. Sutherland *right* in front of sod house rented from the Anglican mission for their first winter at Herschel Island, 1904–05. *Photo courtesy of The Mariners' Museum, Newport News, VA.*

Fig. 4 The bone house and other buildings at Pauline Cove in 1913–16. The small blubber house is partially obscured by the structure closest to the camera. *Photo courtesy of Canadian Museum of Civilization, George Hubert Wilkins, 1916, 51360.*

Fig. 5 The community house and bone house. *Photo by Cameron Eckert.*

the Royal Northwest Mounted Police (RNWMP) after they acquired the company's assets for $1,500 in 1911.

Other PSWC buildings from the 1890s, including the bone house and the smaller blubber house, still stand at Pauline Cove (Fig. 4). The bone house was originally a warehouse used to store baleen (whalebone), but it also functioned as a gathering hall (Fig. 5). The community house measures 9.3 x 17.7 metres, while the bone house is 10.4 x 12.4 metres. The two Inuit hanged for murder in 1924, Alikomiak and Tatamigana, were executed in the bone house, where a roof tie-beam served as the gallows.

The beam was removed from the island and burned before the RCMP detachment closed in 1964. The small blubber house, only 8.5 x 4.9 metres, is now the park workshop (Fig. 6), but may have been used to store whale meat and blubber for dog food. Unlike the whaling stations of the eastern Arctic, Herschel Island had no land-based tryworks to render blubber into oil because the industry was focused on baleen.

Three other small buildings, constructed around 1893, are still standing. One was apparently a home for James McKenna, the captain of a whaling ship (Fig. 7). It is a small

building, only 3.7 x 5.6 metres, and its redwood siding is now covered by cedar shingles, but the words *R.E. Byrne May 7/94 Str Grampus* were carved into one exposed board. (The *Grampus* was a PSWC steam bark). The names of the occupants of the other two dwellings have been lost.

A number of other PSWC buildings, ranging in size from 3.7 x 5.5 metres to 7.6 x 12.2 metres, were dismantled over the years. One of the company's buildings, the Newport house, named for a whaling ship, burned down in 1973.

Fig. 8 St. Patrick's Anglican Mission, now abandoned, with nesting boxes for Black Guillemots on the roof. *Photo by Louis Schilder.*

Fig. 6 The white blubber house, now a workshop. *Photo by Cameron Eckert.*

Fig. 7 The McKenna house.
Photo by Cameron Eckert.

Mission House

The Anglican Church spent a decade trying to build a church and mission on Herschel Island. Rev. Isaac Stringer ordered building materials in 1895, but when they arrived they were used by the PSWC. This was part of the reason the company offered Stringer the community house in 1897 when he came to live on the island. The mission continued to own a sod house, which they rented to the police in 1904.

After the establishment of the Hudson's Bay Company (HBC) post in 1915, when the island appeared to have a secure economic future, Stringer (who by then was Bishop of Yukon) reordered building supplies. These reached the island the following year, but the HBC trader sold a portion of the lumber to another customer. Despite this loss, Rev. Charles Whittaker and a group of men from Fort McPherson hastily completed St. Patrick's Anglican Mission (Fig. 8). The building, 6.1 x 9.1 metres, was occupied year-round until 1919. After the focus for mission work switched to Shingle Point in 1922, the one-and-a-half-storey building was used intermittently until the mid-1930s. It is now gutted and abandoned except for a colony of Black Guillemots.

Northern Whaling & Trading Company Buildings

Three of the buildings still standing at Qikiqtaryuk—a store, a shed, and a warehouse—were constructed by Capt. C.T. Pederson of the Northern Whaling & Trading Company (NWTC) in 1926 (Fig. 9). All three have exterior cladding of galvanized sheet steel except for the store's front wall, which has diagonal tongue-and-groove siding. The store, 6.2 x 16.8 metres, was the first building wired for electricity on the island, powered by a generator on Pederson's trading ship, the *Patterson*. The warehouse was a bonded customs shed, 7.6 x 12.2 metres in size, with two padlock hasps. The keys to one of the locks were held by the police as customs agents and the other keys were kept by Capt. Pederson. This arrangement allowed Pederson only to pay duty on goods he brought out of the warehouse to trade. The framework of the small shed, measuring 4.7 x 2.4 metres, was originally part of a ship's deck cabin. These well-built structures were used mainly for the fur trade.

Fig. 9 Northern Whaling & Trading Company store and Canada Customs warehouse, formerly a warehouse of the Northern Whaling & Trading Company. *Photo by Doug Olynyk.*

Fig. 10 Royal Canadian Corps of Signals building, shortly after it was erected in 1930. The Signals building has recently been used as a residence by the park rangers. *Photo courtesy of Library and Archives Canada, R.F. Finnie fonds, PA 100701.*

Hudson's Bay Company Buildings

Although no longer standing, a number of buildings in the settlement area were owned by the Hudson's Bay Company. The four largest were a house, a store, and two warehouses, one built in 1915 and the other in 1922. These were each one storey except for the house, which was one-and-a-half storeys, and ranged in size from 5.1 x 6.3 metres (the store) to 10.3 x 37.6 metres (the second warehouse). All were of frame construction and had gable roofs covered with roll roofing. Smaller structures served as coal, oil, and storage sheds. The HBC buildings disappeared soon after the post was closed in 1938. They were dismantled and the materials used at Tuktoyaktuk.

Royal Canadian Corps of Signals Building

In 1924 the government of Canada shipped materials for construction of a wireless signal station at Herschel Island on the *Lady Kindersley*. These materials were lost with the ship off the northern coast of Alaska. Six years later, in 1930, the Royal Canadian Corps of Signals (RCCS) constructed a building of 6.5 x 7.1 metres with the only hip roof in the settlement to house a wireless transmitter and personnel (Fig. 10).

The RCCS used the building until 1938, when it became a residence for the RCMP's special constables until the detachment closed. It formed a part of the Northwest Territories and Yukon Radio System, now commemorated as a National Historic Event of Canada. Today, park rangers use the building when in residence on the island.

Royal Canadian Mounted Police Dog Kennels

The RCMP constructed dog kennels with a wire-fenced dog yard in order to run a sled dog breeding program in the 1950s and 1960s (Fig. 11). The availability of seal meat made the island an ideal location for the program.

Fig. 11 Dog kennel and enclosure at Pauline Cove. *Photo by Sara Nielsen.*

Fig. 12 View of Pauline Cove showing the wreck of the whaling bark *Triton*. *Photo courtesy of Library and Archives Canada, Royal Canadian Mounted Police fonds, e010836725.*

Fig. 13 Doorway of the southern cabin at Lopez Point, showing the entranceway posts (see page 117). *Photo by Doug Olynyk.*

Ice Cellars

The remains of at least five subterranean ice cellars are at the north end of the historic settlement area. Most are completely collapsed and two are currently unsafe to enter. The whalemen learned to freeze and store fresh supplies such as caribou and seal meat from the Inuvialuit, who traditionally used shallow pits in the permafrost for food preservation. The whalemen's "ice houses" were created by blasting holes roughly two metres deep with dynamite, squaring up the resulting hole in the ground, and placing driftwood logs on top for a roof. Sod was then piled on the roof for insulation. The entrance vestibules typically faced south, with the main structure backed into the hill behind.

Cemeteries

Four areas containing graves exist north of the settlement. One contains two fenced-in grave markers for RNWMP officers, while another consists of a row of 24 grave markers for whalemen. The other two are distinct Inuvialuit graveyards, including a grouping of about 10 graves on a hilltop near the police graves and another containing approximately 100 graves. The larger cemetery was used between 1895 and 1930, with many of the deaths occurring during epidemics of various diseases. A large number of the coffins were placed above ground, as was the Inuvialuit custom. The hilltop graves were dug

in the 1950s. Many of the wooden markers have deteriorated, collapsed, or disappeared.

The original police grave markers have been replaced with granite stones inscribed with the names of Sgt. Stafford Eardley Aubyn Selig, who died in 1911, and Cst. Alexander Lamont, in 1918. The RCMP maintain these graves. The whalemen's headboards, marking deaths between 1890 and 1916, were replicated and re-installed in 1986. One additional marker pays respect to the bark *Triton* that was condemned, stripped, and abandoned in Pauline Cove in 1895 (Fig. 12).

Other Buildings in the Settlement Area

There are several non-historic buildings in the historic settlement area. One is a driftwood log cabin owned by Elizabeth (Kowana) Mackenzie and her daughters, who return annually from Kaktovik (Barter Island) in Alaska to live seasonally in their family home. Another, the hunters' and travellers' cabin, built on the site of the former Newport house in the same style and scale, is used by visitors staying over on the island. A sauna and wash house have been constructed for park staff and visitors as well as a number of other structures such as outhouses, fuel storage sheds, and wind shelters for campers.

Buildings Elsewhere on the Island

Archaeological evidence of sod dwellings exists on Avadlek Spit, but the only other standing structures on the island are two small cabins at Lopez Point, possibly related to the Reindeer Drive of 1929–35 (see page 117). Made of round driftwood logs, joined with saddle notches and shaped by axe and saw, they display a vernacular architecture unique in the Yukon. Two unusual parallel rows of vertical posts lead to the entrances in the south-facing gable end (Fig. 13). We do not know whether this corridor was once roofed. Framed openings in the east slopes of the sodded log roofs resemble the roof vents of a traditional Lapland *pirtii*, a type of cabin used by the Sami people.

Preservation of the Built Heritage

Soon after the signing of the Inuvialuit Final Agreement (IFA) in 1984, conservation efforts began on structures at Pauline Cove. In 1985 Parks Canada helped the Yukon government to record and document the buildings, leading to emergency stabilization work. The government appointed a full-time restoration planner in 1987 to carry out historic research on structures, produce detailed as-found records, and develop specific conservation plans for each building based upon the *Standards and Guidelines for the Conservation*

Fig. 14 The settlement area at Pauline Cove inundated by a storm surge in August 2008.
Photo courtesy of Government of Yukon.

of Historic Places in Canada. In 1988 a government restoration work crew, dedicated solely to Herschel Island, began annual work onsite. The initial stabilization work focused on building foundations and weather sealing, including roofs, door and window openings, and exterior painting. Most of the major work was completed by the mid-1990s. In the past decade, buildings have been moved and raised because of shoreline erosion and flooding.

Present Uses

Seven of the historic buildings at Pauline Cove are now used seasonally by parks operations, including the McKenna house, the bone house, the blubber house, and two NWTC buildings. The community house is now an interpretive centre, while the RCCS building serves as the rangers' quarters. Both the hunters' and travellers' cabin and the community house are used as residences for visiting scientists and government staff. The Anglican mission house has been adapted to provide for a nesting colony of Black Guillemots, the most westerly in Canada. Nesting boxes have been fastened to the roof for this purpose.

Fig. 15 The Northern Whaling & Trading Company store, lifted, braced, and prepared for the move back from receding shoreline, July 2003. *Photo courtesy of Government of Yukon.*

Threats to Buildings

Wooden structures on Herschel Island have suffered greatly from the ravages of time and the harsh arctic climate. In winter the persistent winds snow-blast the paint and scour the lignin from exposed wood, raising the grain dramatically. Newly observed changes in climate may be taking an additional toll.

Given the low elevation of the spit on which the settlement lies (less than 75 centimetres above sea level), erosion and flooding can be destructive and even catastrophic for heritage resources. High tides and storm surges have regularly flooded Simpson Point spit in the last 10 years (Fig. 14)

because of higher average annual air temperatures and a significantly smaller area of permanent sea ice in the Beaufort Sea. The reduction in sea ice also means greater fetch on the ocean (a larger area where waves are generated by wind), while the longer season of open water means a higher probability of flooding from a big storm each year. In combination, these factors appear to be affecting the rate and pattern of shoreline erosion.

In the 1980s archaeologists raced to excavate Thule dwellings at the Washout site, east of Pauline Cove. Sea surges and wave action began undermining the foundation of the NWTC store in the 1990s. In 1998

Fig. 16. Inuvialuit coffins that have been exposed by ground movement. *Photo by Fritz Mueller.*

Fig. 17 Inuvialuit grave. The dry grass was caught by the fence during spring snowmelt. *Photo by Fritz Mueller.*

large neoprene sandbags were placed along the shore in front of the store in a futile attempt to stabilize the shore there. In fall 2000 storm surges rammed sea ice into the shed attached to the store, damaging it so badly that it had to be dismantled. The wooden foundation was left in place in another attempt to stabilize the shoreline. With continuing degradation of the shore and the building foundation, in 2003 the store and the neighbouring Canada Customs warehouse were moved back about five metres until they abutted the hunters' and travellers' cabin (Fig. 15). Both buildings, along with the cabin, were moved another five metres in 2004.

As of summer 2009 the buildings had remained relatively dry, with no more apparent erosion of the shoreline. However, the NWTC shed was moved to re-establish its relationship with the other company buildings. Future building moves will consider the historic context of the settlement area as well as the practical needs of park operations.

There are signs that the seasonally thawed active layer is deepening and may lead to soil instability and moisture damage to wooden foundations. At the main Inuvialuit cemetery, movement on south-facing slopes has led to displacement of caskets downslope along with the soil.

Some of the coffins have been pushed up to the surface and broken open (Fig. 16). The park rangers monitor these changes and cover any newly exposed graves with soil. The site is on an alluvial fan where the graveyard is now flooded annually during spring snowmelt because of changes to the surface drainage pattern (Fig. 17).

With the shrinkage of permanent sea ice in the Arctic, increased shipping along with its accompanying threats to the environment is likely. Over the past decade two cruise ships per year have been stopping at Herschel Island (Fig. 18). Park staff carefully manage and monitor cruise ship visitors to ensure protection of park resources. Visitors must use established paths to limit damage to sensitive ground and to bird nesting areas. As visitor numbers grow, the result will be more wear and tear on buildings, particularly flooring, and increased demand for building maintenance, security, and site interpretation services.

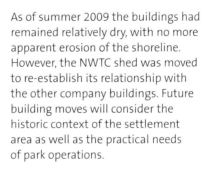

Fig. 18 MV *Hanseatic* at Herschel Island in August 2005. *Photo courtesy of Government of Yukon.*

PARK HISTORY

Gordon MacRae and
Sara Nielsen

Fig. 1 Richard Gordon is Senior Park Ranger of Herschel Island–Qikiqtaruk Territorial Park.
Photo by Cameron Eckert.

The settlement at Herschel.
Photo by Cameron Eckert.

Richard Gordon has been a Herschel Island ambassador and park ranger all his working life (Fig. 1). For generations his family has hunted, fished, and gathered on the island. This is his understanding of how Qikiqtaryuk became a territorial park.

Here is my recollection as to why the park was created by the Inuvialuit from Aklavik. Before any land claims were in place, many things happened without any consultation with the Inuvialuit, like ice roads, seismic lines, dynamite, industrial camps, visits by researchers, and harvesting by other people. The whaling period was one that stood out in the elders' memories; they didn't have control in their homeland with other people coming in and taking over. The Inuvialuit didn't want to see this happen again, so during the land claim negotiations they asked if certain land could be set aside for protection from any development. Because of the long history of Qikiqtaryuk, they felt that it should be protected under their land claim. The other reason for creating the park was researchers. Over the years many elders saw these people coming into the area and taking artifacts, saying that they would return them and never did. The elders asked if these historical sites and graves could be protected under a park. It was explained to them that, if they wanted certain land to be protected, it would have to be transferred to the government to ensure protection under the Parks Act.

They agreed to this condition, but also asked that the Inuvialuit would still have their right to continue to harvest and practise their traditional and cultural lifestyle within the park.

Still today Inuvialuit are concerned about certain land areas, especially bird nesting grounds and wildlife habitat. They will continue to observe these lands, and if they feel that an area should be protected under a park status, they maybe will give up the lands for protection as long as they keep the harvesting, traditions, and cultural lifestyle.

Yukon's First Territorial Park

Herschel Island, known in the Siglitun dialect as Qikiqtaryuk, has a long history of occupation and use by Inuvialuit. Since 1890 it has also been used by other groups of people such as commercial whalemen, police, Anglican missionaries, and the Hudson's Bay Company and other traders (Fig. 2). Because of its location, Herschel was used to assert Canada's sovereignty in the western Arctic and was the first port of call for vessels leaving American waters. In the mid-twentieth century the principal agency operating at Herschel Island was the RCMP, but after the detachment closed in 1964, the Polar Continental Shelf Project (PCSP) of Energy, Mines and Resources Canada assumed control of the police buildings in 1968. In turn, PCSP handed them over to Parks Canada in 1977.

Fig. 3 The most important reason for setting aside Qikiqtaryuk as a protected area is to help sustain Inuvialuit culture by preserving a place that has been in use for centuries. *Photo by Richard Gordon.*

Fig. 2 The heritage buildings at Pauline Cove, reminders of their occupation by whalemen, police, and the Royal Canadian Corps of Signals. *Photo by Louis Schilder.*

On ratification of the Inuvialuit Final Agreement (IFA) on June 5, 1984, it was agreed that Herschel Island–Qikiqtaryuk would be established as a Yukon territorial park in accordance with the IFA and its guiding principles. The park assists in the preservation of Inuvialuit cultural identity and values within a changing northern society (Fig. 3), and the protection and preservation of Arctic wildlife, environment, and biological productivity.

In order to help create the park, the federal Department of Indian Affairs and Northern Development transferred control and administration of lands to the Yukon government on January 31, 1985. The island was withdrawn from staking under the Territorial Lands (Yukon) Act and Order-in-Council 2003/148 under the Placer Mining Act. The historic buildings had already been transferred to the Yukon from Parks Canada in 1983. On July 30, 1987, Herschel Island was established as a territorial park with the classification of "nature preserve" through Order-in-Council 1987/148 (Fig. 4). The first formal monument placed in the park was a plaque, erected in 1988 at Pauline Cove, which recognizes the national historic significance of the intercultural contact at Herschel Island, the whaling industry in the southeastern Beaufort Sea, and Canadian sovereignty in the western Arctic.

Planning for the park included archaeological, palaeontological, and natural resource inventories, which were conducted in the latter half of the 1980s and in the 1990s. This work included archival documentation and an extensive oral history project, as well as investigations into the physical historic resources. The information collected provided benchmark materials for the future management of the park, with much of the park's interpretation based on this work. The research is continuing in several areas.

QIKIQTARUK OR QIKIQTARYUK?

Herschel Island–Qikiqtaruk Territorial Park is the working name for the administration of Herschel Island. The park was originally named Herschel Island Territorial Park. Inuvialuit heritage and use of the park, and its creation through the Inuvialuit Final Agreement, are recognized by the name Qikiqtaruk.

The precise pronunciation of the Inuvialuktun word varies among dialects. In this book we have used the Siglitun pronunciation, Qikiqtaryuk. Siglitun is the closest current dialect to the language spoken by Qikiqtaryungmiut before the arrival of whalemen in 1889.

Fig. 4 The "foundation stone" of Herschel Island–Qikiqtaruk Territorial Park, established in 1987. *Photo by Cameron Eckert.*

Fig. 5 Jonas Brower out hunting on Qikiqtaryuk. The island is a place where traditional skills may be passed on to young Inuvialuit. *Photo by Richard Gordon.*

Fig. 6 Senior Park Ranger Richard Gordon models an Inuvialuit parka as Ranger Edward McLeod watches. *Photo by Sara Nielsen.*

Full of sand in this area

Started back from here working west

Working this area

900 ft to here

Fig. 7 After storms in summer or autumn, the beach landing area often requires maintenance. A significant storm in autumn 2006 led to realignment of the landing area during the 2007 operating season. *Photo by Richard Gordon.*

Park Zoning and Classification

In 1987 Herschel Island was classified as a nature preserve under the Yukon Parks Act. In order to accommodate the new Parks and Land Certainty Act, the park was reclassified as a "natural environment park" on December 3, 2001. This designation meets the criteria set out in the IFA and is compatible with the original purpose, objectives, and intent of the previous nature preserve designation. Under the Act, a natural environment park means a park established to protect representative or unique landscapes that display ecological characteristics or features of one or more of the Yukon's ecoregions. The designation is the most compatible with the park's intended function because it allows for traditional aboriginal use while protecting the park's resources in accordance with the underlying

principles of the IFA (Fig. 5). If any inconsistencies or conflicts over aboriginal use of the park occur, the IFA prevails over the Parks and Land Certainty Act.

The IFA sets out the overall management regime and identifies two different regimes based on the National Parks System that apply to Qikiqtaryuk. The first is a wilderness regime, which applies to most of the island. In these areas, the park regime is no less stringent than that of a wilderness national park. Under the Yukon government park system, a wilderness zone land-use designation meets the intent of the IFA. The second regime is a historic zone for the lands adjacent to Pauline Cove, where the historic resources are protected no less stringently than in a national historic park.

Safeguarding an Arctic Island Park

Since 1987, Yukon government's Parks Branch (Yukon Parks) has operated Herschel Island–Qikiqtaruk Territorial Park during the summer season. Four park rangers, in shifts of two, are stationed on the island from April through September to accommodate visitors and maintain the cultural, historic, and ecological values of the island. The rangers provide a diverse range of visitor services and maintain park facilities (Fig. 6). These facilities include the historic community house, which serves as a heated gathering place with a seating area and small library for visitors. It contains displays of local flora and fauna, research activities, and cultural artifacts. A heated hunters and travellers cabin provides shelter upon request throughout the year. A boat dock and helicopter pad are maintained by hand and shovel, while an area on the beach is used by Twin Otter aircraft (Fig. 7). There are campsites in driftwood windbreaks (Fig. 8), public outhouses, fire pits, and signed trails. The rangers collect ice blocks from small interior lakes by snow machine in April and May for the summer drinking water supply (Fig. 9), and cut and collect driftwood on the mainland to preserve the experience and ecology of Pauline Cove. They keep daily records of visitors, weather, wildlife, and other observations, and provide park and safety information to the public (Fig. 10). The rangers also play an essential role in the inventory, monitoring, and research activities on Herschel Island. This work has increased as the island has become a focal point for arctic and climate change studies, with researchers from universities and government institutes coming to the island from all over North America and Europe. Much of this work would not be possible without the dedicated support of the rangers and Yukon Parks.

Park rangers offer the warmth and comfort of human welcome at all hours of the day or night. Hosts and stewards of Herschel Island, their warm smiles, dedication, and patience reflect the special energy of this little haven in the Arctic, a gathering place for hundreds of years.

Elder/Youth Host Program

As part of the park's ongoing interpretive programs, an elder/youth host program has been developed jointly with Inuvialuit and their agencies from Aklavik, Northwest Territories. The program was initiated in the mid-1990s with the assistance of the Aklavik Hunters and Trappers Committee and the Aklavik Community Corporation. It is designed to give elders and youth an opportunity to return to part of their homeland and connect with their

Fig. 8 Driftwood windbreaks shelter campsites from arctic storms. *Photo by Louis Schilder.*

Fig. 9 Ice blocks are cut and brought from an inland lake for the summer drinking water supply. *Photo by Lee John Meyook.*

Fig. 10 Jonas Meyook surveying snow conditions on the mainland. Park staff act as environmental monitors and assist the programs of Yukon government scientists and other researchers. *Photo by Lee John Meyook.*

Fig 11 Inuvialuit elders and youth butcher a caribou harvested on the island.
Photo by Richard Gordon.

Fig 12 Scientists and others bringing freight to Qikiqtaryuk usually arrive at Pauline Cove by Twin Otter from Inuvik. *Photo by Cameron Eckert.*

past while allowing youth to learn the "old" ways.

Generally four elders, four youth, and two camp managers/assistants are flown to Herschel for two weeks. On the island they interact with park visitors and carry on their traditional activities. Activities include big and small game hunting, fishing, food preparation and preservation, and camping and travelling on the land, along with the telling of traditional stories. The elders help educate visitors about their subsistence lifestyle and provide a direct perspective on why they continue to hunt, fish, and live at Qikiqtaryuk in a sustainable manner. This perspective has minimized conflicts between southern visitors and Inuvialuit hunters, especially during harvesting of caribou or other animals in the park.

Transportation to Herschel Island

Visitors to Herschel Island arrive by various means, but always on or over the water. The most frequent visits to the island are made by Twin Otter aircraft, which land either on the beach or on ice in Pauline Cove. This is the mode of transport preferred by scientific and park maintenance parties and for hauling equipment and supplies to the island. During the oil boom of the 1980s, an airstrip was built on the sea ice in Thetis Bay to handle large transport aircraft.

Tourists commonly arrive by float plane in summer and also touch down in the cove. The largest daily numbers of visitors to Qikiqtaryuk arrive on cruise ships, when over a hundred people may disembark at Simpson Point. The steady arrival throughout the summer of Inuvialuit from the Mackenzie Delta or Iñupiat from Kaktovik, Alaska, is characteristically by small boat. There are also a few international visitors each summer, usually Europeans, who are attempting to make the Northwest Passage either in sailing or motor vessels. In winter, Inuvialuit hunters travel by snow machine to the island, and others make similar journeys in the spring.

Fig. 13 Qikiqtaryuk has relatively few visitors until a cruise ship arrives, and then for a few hours there are people everywhere. *Photo by Cameron Eckert.*

HERSCHEL ISLAND'S BLACK GUILLEMOTS

For many visitors to Herschel Island, the chance of seeing nesting Black Guillemots is a highlight of their trip. This charismatic seabird of the alcid family has a circumpolar distribution, but the Yukon's only nesting colony (and one of very few in the western Arctic) is on Qikiqtaryuk. Here the guillemots lay their eggs in nest boxes and crevices in the historic Anglican mission house at Pauline Cove. The colony has been monitored for population and nesting productivity since the mid-1980s. The continuation of this work is identified as a high priority in the park management plan and the Yukon North Slope Long Term Research and Monitoring Plan. This species' position at the top of the food chain makes it a valuable indicator of the ecological integrity of the park environment.

Heightened concern about the health of the colony arose after very poor nesting success in 2003 (two chicks) and 2004 (no chicks). The nearest Black Guillemot colony to Herschel Island, located at Point Barrow, Alaska (650 kilometres northwest of Herschel), which has about 150 breeding pairs, also had poor productivity in 2003 and 2004. Researchers at Point Barrow have found that nesting productivity is influenced by nearshore sea ice conditions, with poor nesting success observed when the ice moves out early. The warming climate in the Arctic may well affect the long-term health of Black Guillemot populations.

In 2006, the monitoring program at Herschel Island was expanded to include colour-banding of chicks. A small numbered metal band and a coloured plastic band are attached to a bird's leg, a safe method of individually marking birds.

Merran Smith and Cameron Eckert banding a Black Guillemot chick. *Photo by Jukka Jantunen.*

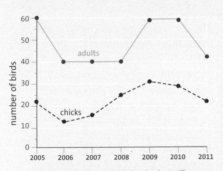

The population of adult Black Guillemots and chicks at Herschel Island, 2005–2011.

The former St. Patrick's Anglican mission at Pauline Cove, used today by a colony of nesting guillemots. *Photo by Sara Nielsen.*

This technique enables tracking of yearly survival and dispersal, and enhances our understanding of factors associated with population changes. A key aspect of this monitoring is to determine if guillemots hatched on Herschel return there to breed. In other words, is the colony's population health dependent on its own nesting success? Guillemots do not generally breed in their first three to four years of life, so the first return of adult guillemots banded as chicks at Herschel in 2009 was right on schedule. In 2011, an adult guillemot born on the island in 2006 returned and successfully nested—and so the cycle continues. These results are exciting as they do indicate that the Black Guillemot population at Herschel depends to some extent on its own productivity. Observations over the coming years will determine the rate of return and nesting activity of the island's hatchlings. Our hope is that the Black Guillemots that occupy the mission house, whose construction in 1916 was organized by Bishop Isaac Stringer, himself a birdwatcher, will continue to delight visitors to the island.

—*Cameron D. Eckert*

INUVIALUIT FINAL AGREEMENT AND CO-MANAGEMENT

Lindsay Staples

Fig. 1 Andy Carpenter, Sr., and Charlie Haogak sign the Inuvialuit Final Agreement in Tuktoyaktuk, June 5, 1984. *Photo courtesy of Inuvialuit Regional Corporation.*

View near sunset over the buildings at Pauline Cove. *Photo by Cameron Eckert.*

In 1984, the Committee for Original People's Entitlement, representing the Inuvialuit, agreed to a settlement of Inuvialuit land claims against Canada. The settlement was expressed in the Inuvialuit Final Agreement (IFA), which established the Inuvialuit Settlement Region (ISR), an area covering 906,430 square kilometres mostly north of the tree line (Fig. 1). It includes the Canadian Beaufort Sea and western Arctic islands, the Mackenzie Delta, the portion of the Yukon known as the "North Slope," and the northwestern corner of the mainland Northwest Territories. The ISR includes both public, or Crown, lands and Inuvialuit private lands.

The IFA was made law through the (Inuvialuit) Western Arctic Claims Settlement Act and is protected by Section 35 of the Canadian constitution. The IFA extinguished aboriginal title and all other aboriginal claims, rights, and interests of Inuvialuit in the Northwest Territories, the Yukon, and adjacent areas offshore. In exchange, the Inuvialuit retained absolute ownership to about 91,000 square kilometres of land (surface and subsurface), secured harvesting and management rights, and received guaranteed economic benefits and financial compensation. The IFA also established specified territorial and national parks and other protected areas.

The Final Agreement was the first modern land claims settlement in the Northwest Territories, and it has become an exemplar for subsequent settlements in the remainder of the Northwest Territories, the Yukon, and British Columbia. It introduced new arrangements that dramatically changed the face of wildlife and park management in western Arctic Canada. The management goals and arrangements that apply on Herschel Island derive from core features of the IFA, particularly Inuvialuit harvesting rights; management rights and arrangements for traditional use and conservation of wildlife and habitat; development impact assessments; and worst-case scenarios and wildlife compensation.

Inuvialuit now have exclusive or preferential rights to harvest wildlife, to trade and barter, and to establish camps on the land. Harvesting rights are subject to the requirements of conservation, but the overriding intent of the IFA is to ensure that Inuvialuit can maintain an active way of life on the land. However, harvesting rights mean little if wildlife and other resources are insufficient or scarce. The Agreement therefore established a new system for federal and territorial governments and Inuvialuit to work collaboratively in the co-management of wildlife, parks, and protected areas; in the

Fig. 2 Fishing at Pauline Cove. Inuvialuit may harvest renewable resources on Herschel Island and the Yukon North Slope throughout the year. *Photo by Lee John Meyook.*

Fig. 3 The Wildlife Management Advisory Council (North Slope), July 2011. Danny C. Gordon, Rob Florkiewicz, and Christian Bucher behind, Lindsay Staples and Ernest Pokiak in front. *Photo by Jennifer Smith.*

review of development proposals; and in establishing priorities for wildlife research programs as well as their design and implementation. This system has enabled co-management decisions to be based on the best available contemporary science as well as Inuvialuit traditional and local knowledge. Hunters and Trappers Committees (HTCs) in each community, together with the Inuvialuit Game Council, self-manage and self-regulate harvesting. The Game Council is the umbrella body representing the collective rights and interests of the Inuvialuit in wildlife. Together with the HTCs, it has broad and exclusive law-making and regulatory-like powers over harvesting.

Hydrocarbon exploration in the Beaufort Sea and Mackenzie Delta during the 1970s and 1980s was a major factor leading Canada to settle the Inuvialuit land claims. The interest in hydrocarbon development continues, almost three decades after the signing of the IFA. The IFA established the Environmental Impact Screening Committee (EISC) and the Environmental Impact Review Board (EIRB) as joint bodies of federal and territorial governments and the Inuvialuit to screen and review development proposals. All development projects are initially examined by the EISC and, if necessary, referred to the Board for a full environmental review.

Offshore development is subject to provisions of the IFA that are designed to recognize the importance of the marine and coastal environment in the ISR. Other provisions in the Agreement prevent damage to wildlife and habitat as well as disruption of Inuvialuit harvesting activities, and calculate and cost the risks associated with allowing development to proceed in the area. The IFA requires the EIRB to estimate the total liability of a developer for damages if a worst-case event, such as a pipeline rupture or blowout, were to occur. The liability for the developer is absolute. It includes the costs associated with wildlife and habitat restoration to an original or near-original state, and compensation to Inuvialuit for lost harvesting opportunities.

Establishment of the Park

Within this framework, the IFA recognizes that the Yukon North Slope and Herschel Island are special places that require unique protection and innovative management. The Agreement established a special conservation regime for the entire Yukon North Slope—the area between the Alaska–Yukon and Yukon–Northwest Territories borders, extending from the height of land in the British Mountains northward across the coastal plain to the nearshore and offshore waters of the Beaufort Sea. Ivvavik National

Park covers the area westward from the Babbage River to the international border. Inuvialuit negotiators also proposed that Herschel Island be a territorial park, to protect a place of cultural, historic, geographical, and ecological significance (Fig. 2). The formal vision for the park captures the thinking of the negotiators and still rings true today:

Herschel Island is a unique arctic island, special for its role as a meeting place, as a place of traditional use, and as a place for learning and the maintenance of culture. Its wildlife, wilderness and history should be protected and used sustainably for generations to come.

Herschel Island became the Yukon's first territorial park with full wilderness status. No development is permitted in the park. Inuvialuit have full and exclusive harvesting rights on Qikiqtaryuk, and the IFA provides special economic and employment benefits associated with the park's operation. Park management issues are addressed by the Inuvialuit and territorial and federal governments at the Wildlife Management Advisory Council (North Slope), known as WMAC(NS), and commonly pronounced Y-MAC (Fig. 3).

Fig. 4 Lee John Meyook has been a park ranger at Qikiqtaryuk since 1989. *Photo courtesy of Herschel Island– Qikiqtaruk Territorial Park.*

Fig. 5 Park ranger Sam McLeod takes measurements of permafrost temperature on Collinson Head. *Photo by Lee John Meyook.*

These aspects of the park's operational framework were innovative developments in the co-management of wildlife and parks in northern Canada. The management regime established for Herschel Island has become a standard for the growing number of parks, protected areas, and wildlife management arrangements established by land claims agreements in the Yukon and other parts of Canada. Vuntut National Park, which extends the protected area of the North Slope southward from Ivvavik National Park into the Old Crow Flats, operates under a similar regime.

The management of Herschel Island has evolved since its formal establishment in 1987. The park is focused today on several important areas that are set out in a management plan and in other administrative arrangements.

Park Management Arrangements

Environment Yukon has overall management authority for Qikiqtaryuk, while the Yukon Parks Branch has responsibility for day-to-day operations on the island. The Parks Branch works closely with WMAC(NS) and the Aklavik HTC in the development of policies and plans affecting most park activities, from wildlife research and environmental monitoring to site and interpretation plans and waste management. Richard Gordon, an Inuvialuk from Aklavik, is the senior

park ranger and plays a key role in onsite operations as well as offsite planning and public consultation.

WMAC(NS) consists of an equal number of Inuvialuit and government members and an independent chair (Fig. 3). The Council has broad responsibilities for advising the appropriate federal and territorial ministers on all matters related to wildlife management, habitat, and harvesting on the Yukon North Slope. The Council also provides advice on matters related to park management and planning for Herschel Island and Ivvavik National Park. The Council facilitates cooperative management arrangements between the governments of Yukon and Canada and the Inuvialuit Game Council in these areas. Regular meetings are held with these and other interested parties. The Council also attends national, circumpolar, and international forums where matters affecting environment and development on the North Slope and adjacent areas are discussed. Through the Council, Inuvialuit have played a central role for over two decades in the development and implementation of the management plan, and the wildlife research, management, and monitoring programs for Herschel Island.

Within the structure of Inuvialuit organizations, the Aklavik HTC represents the collective interests of Aklavik Inuvialuit in wildlife and park management. Inuvialuit from Aklavik

are the most frequent users of park facilities at Pauline Cove and are the most active harvesters on the island. The Aklavik HTC advises on operational plans and other matters that affect Inuvialuit harvesters and users of Qikiqtaryuk. These matters include the application of harvest quotas, use of park facilities, employment of local people, and the participation of Inuvialuit elders and youth in park programs.

Inuvialuit Employment and Preferential Hire

The IFA provides that the majority of those working in the park should be Inuvialuit (Fig. 4). Since the park's establishment, the Yukon Parks Branch has met this obligation through a preferential hiring policy. The majority of park rangers, who are responsible for day-to-day operations at the park, have been Inuvialuit from Aklavik. Through the opportunities presented by regular employment from April to September each year, the park rangers have grown to assume a critical role in many of the park's research and monitoring programs. In particular, they are actively involved in field monitoring programs as diverse as breeding and nesting bird surveys, vegetation phenology studies, and climate change research projects (Fig. 5).

In addition, the rangers are the *de facto* cultural ambassadors of the Inuvialuit, receiving hundreds of visitors annually by cruise ship and air charter from

Fig. 6 Frank Pokiak, Larry Carpenter, and Lindsay Staples, chairs of the Inuvialuit Game Council, WMAC(NWT), and WMAC(NS), respectively, confer at a meeting in September 2008. *Photo by Jennifer Smith.*

Canada and the rest of the world. Each year a number of visitors stop off at Pauline Cove on their way back to Inuvik after paddling the Firth River. The rangers are also on-the-ground protectors of traditional Inuvialuit rights to hunt and fish on the island.

Wildlife Management

A large focus of the Council's work is wildlife management as it affects the conservation of wildlife and habitat and harvesting by Inuvialuit. The Council has developed a wildlife conservation and management plan for the Yukon North Slope that establishes conservation requirements and conditions for development in the area. The Council has also prepared a long-term research plan to provide guidance for all researchers with an interest in the area.

The Council is committed to providing equal consideration to the application of traditional Inuvialuit knowledge and contemporary science in wildlife management decisions. The Council has initiated and facilitated traditional knowledge studies for many species of wildlife on Herschel Island, including shorebirds, Porcupine caribou, grizzly bears and, most recently, polar bears.

An important aspect of the Council's work concerns the setting of harvestable quotas for wildlife. The quotas must be based on the best available information and be fully justified. The setting of these quotas and other forms of harvest restriction requires the Council to work closely with the Inuvialuit Game Council, the Aklavik HTC, Parks Canada, and Environment Yukon (Fig. 6). This task has proven to be challenging for harvest of caribou on the North Slope, for these animals are shared between Inuvialuit harvesters, harvesters from the Gwich'in Settlement Region in the Northwest Territories, and Vuntut Gwitchin, Tr'ondëk Hwëch'in, and Na-Cho Nyak Dun harvesters in the Yukon. The total harvest is managed by a number of different federal and territorial departments and the Porcupine Caribou Management Board. Management also requires cooperation with the Alaskan Department of Fish and Game because the Porcupine Caribou Herd migrates across the US–Canada border.

On Herschel Island, Inuvialuit have exclusive rights to harvest wildlife. Herschel remains a place where Inuvialuit harvesters of all ages come to enjoy time on the land, hunting, and fishing. The interests of visitors to the park are also given consideration by the Council, which recognizes that visitors travel to Herschel Island from around the world to experience its unique setting and wildlife. Some restrictions have been accepted by Inuvialuit harvesters to enhance wildlife viewing by visitors at certain times of the year. In addition, for safety reasons, shooting is prohibited within a kilometre of the settlement.

Research and Monitoring

Today Qikiqtaryuk is both the site of intensive ecological monitoring programs and a support base for field research on the island, in the nearshore Beaufort Sea, and on the Yukon Coastal Plain. The management plan recognizes the unique role that the park plays in scientific research in western Arctic Canada. It encourages and facilitates use of park facilities as a staging area for regional population surveys of polar bear, grizzly bear, barren-ground caribou, and muskox, and as a centre for research on coastal erosion, permafrost, and vegetation (Fig. 7). Funds associated with the implementation of the IFA directly support several of these programs. Herschel Island's place as an important and remote centre for documenting certain long-term environmental effects of climate change has brought it membership in Canada's Ecological Monitoring and Assessment Network (EMAN).

Fig. 7 Water-jet drilling on Collinson Head to install equipment to monitor permafrost temperature. *Photo by Christopher Burn.*

Safe Moorage

Pauline Cove offers a safe haven from extreme marine weather throughout the open water season. The harbour has been used for as long as Inuvialuit and Iñupiat families have travelled the coast between the Mackenzie Delta and the communities of the Alaska North Slope, and while whalemen overwintered there. The buildings and infrastructure in the settlement at Pauline Cove are managed to provide shelter and safety for those who require it at any time of the year (Fig. 8), either when hunting on the land or in transit by snow machine or boat to visit relatives in Aklavik or Kaktovik (Barter Island), Alaska.

Future Challenges: Herschel Marine Industrial Park?

Herschel's strategic location in the Beaufort Sea and on the Yukon's north coast has made it attractive for more than park purposes. In the late 1980s, Canada's Department of National Defense (DND) decided to upgrade the Distant Early Warning (DEW) Line, a system of radar stations. At the time, Herschel Island was considered a potential site for a short-range radar installation. The strength of the IFA and the purposes for which the park was established were quickly accepted as incompatible with DND's requirements, especially given the availability of alternative sites on the mainland and the ability to upgrade existing facilities. The same concerns may emerge for other related uses of the land, perhaps in the case of an emergency search and rescue depot, for example. The nature of Canada's military presence in the Arctic will likely evolve in the next decade or two, but decisions regarding the North Slope are expected to be taken within the framework of the IFA.

The greatest future management challenges for Herschel Island may have less to do with changes on the island and more with what might occur in adjacent waters. In the 1960s, when it was anticipated that there

Fig. 8 The buildings at Herschel Island provide logistical support for scientific research and government patrols, and offer shelter for hunters and travellers. *Photo by Donald Reid.*

Fig. 9 The drilling platform *Kulluk* and oil tanker *Gulf Beaufort* in Thetis Bay. *Photo courtesy of Bharat Dixit.*

Fig. 10 Concrete caissons in Thetis Bay. *Photo by Michael Kawerninski.*

might be oil production in the Beaufort Sea, Herschel Island was considered as a site for a potential tanker terminal. The deep water in Herschel Basin was the principal attraction, but the water above Herschel Sill is too shallow

for loaded, deep-draught tankers on departure. However, in the 1970s and 1980s Thetis Bay was identified and used as a safe anchorage for drill platforms, an oil tanker, support ships, and caissons operated by Gulf Oil and

Dome Petroleum (Fig. 9). There are few protected and accessible anchorages along the western Arctic coast, and Thetis Bay is the only area of historic use on the Yukon coast. Recently, this interest in offshore drilling has returned, along with the mobile platforms that are used in exploration. However, one set of caissons, used as a foundation for an artificial island, was placed in Thetis Bay in the 1980s and has remained there ever since (Fig. 10).

The significance of the value placed on the park's visual integrity is difficult to quantify, but the public concern with industrial structures adjacent to the park is real and ongoing. Of more direct impact, increased levels of offshore activity near Herschel will increase the aircraft and ship traffic in the area, affecting terrestrial and marine wildlife. Potential oil spills from ships, or through the development of

oil and gas wells near the island, may all have direct and indirect negative effects. The park management plan recognizes that, even though these structures would be located outside the park, they would be inconsistent with the values of the park protected under the plan. To date no alternative moorages have been identified along the Yukon coast and adjacent areas, although there have been recommendations by WMAC(NS), the EISC, and the Beaufort Sea Strategic Regional Plan of Action to do so.

Meeting Future Challenges

The management challenges that represent the greatest potential threats to the vision and purposes established for Qikiqtaryuk are climate change, marine industrial activity, and the risk of oil spills from offshore drilling in the Arctic Ocean. The park's management regime has

little ability to change these threats, but the management plan and associated ecological monitoring and research offer the means to study, learn, and understand the environmental changes that are occurring on the island.

Just as future offshore drilling, marine activity, and moorage fall outside the park's jurisdiction, even though the resulting effects may not, so the management regime that may most effectively address these threats also lies outside Qikiqtaryuk. The park management regime for Herschel Island is a component of a broader environmental management regime for the Yukon North Slope and the Inuvialuit Settlement Region.

The 1989 *Exxon Valdez* oil spill in Prince William Sound, Alaska, and the 2010 Deepwater Horizon oil spill in the Gulf of Mexico, are forceful reminders of the potentially catastrophic risks to wildlife and environmental values posed by offshore development. It is almost always difficult to quantify the value of places like Herschel Island when it comes to weighing the benefits of future developments. The IFA provides a framework for making sound decisions and evaluating the risks of future offshore development that will also affect the future of Herschel Island. Ultimately, however, it is federal and territorial ministers who will determine what is in the best interests of Canadians, balanced against Inuvialuit rights and interests in the region as well as the goals for Herschel Island and the rest of the Yukon North Slope established in the IFA.

Inuvialuit elders at a special meeting in Aklavik, December 2007, to celebrate their contributions of traditional knowledge to WMAC(NS). *Photo by Michelle Christensen.*

COMMUNITY CONSULTATION

The Wildlife Management Advisory Council (North Slope) holds meetings from time to time with Inuvialuit who use the area. The views and knowledge of elders are important

contributions to these discussions. These meetings are often held in Aklavik, where many of the people who used to live on the North Slope now reside.

IN CONCLUSION

in conclusion

A FINAL WORD

This book is a multifaceted account of Qikiqtaryuk, presented in a way that we hope has been accessible and visually engaging. It has an unprecedented diversity of authors for a study of northern Canada, especially as it concentrates on a relatively small, remote island. Although the project began as a review of current knowledge, there were surprises of discovery as well (Fig. 1). Some of these were the result of active research that was implicitly interdisciplinary, particularly where historical documents were examined for environmental information rather than the record of sovereignty or social development. Reports that lay dormant have been read in a new light.

In the last 20 years, a fundamental evolution has begun to take place in the practice of northern research. These changes have been stimulated by land claim agreements that incorporate the values of aboriginal peoples toward activities within their traditional territories, and that also recognize the importance of traditional knowledge and aboriginal participation in research and environmental management. Such changes are not simply the result of altered attitudes but are based on fundamental rights, protected in the Canadian constitution.

Justice Thomas Berger summarized opposing views of the North in his report on the Mackenzie Valley Pipeline Inquiry in the 1970s. Entitled *Northern Frontier, Northern Homeland*, the report argued that "frontier" and "homeland" must accommodate each other for social and economic development beneficial to all. Industry has grasped this position through the collaboration and consultation that are legal requirements of the Inuvialuit Final Agreement as well as functions of an evolving social, economic, and political relationship with the Inuvialuit. The Canadian research community is not far behind, but our concerns often bemuse colleagues in other countries, who have little experience of the North as a home.

Fig. 1. Decaying landfast sea ice in Thetis Bay, early June 2010. The ocean farther out has already broken up. A comparison of freeze-up in the whaling era with conditions in the last 20 years (see page 53) has supplied new data that documents the impact of climate change on one aspect of the environment at Qikiqtaryuk. *Photo by Cameron Eckert.*

Fig 2. Visitors to Herschel Island at St Patrick's Mission, now nesting habitat for Black Guillemots, August 2009. *Photo by Cameron Eckert.*

Fig. 3 Bob (Nuligak) and Margaret (Panigak) Cockney with four of their grandchildren. From left to right: James Cockney, Lily (Cockney) Gruben, Jane (Cockney) Gordon, and Lily (Elias) Taotuk, at the RCMP detachment for Christmas, early 1950s. *Photo courtesy of Parks Canada, Jim Hickling Herschel Island 1953–56 Collection, #173. Reproduced by kind permission of Bill and Lucy Cockney.*

In the North, for the North, and by the North is the vision of northern institutions carrying out northern research. It may be counterproductive to interpret the preposition *by* in an exclusive way. Instead, we need to recognize the usefulness of collaboration so that northern research may be enriched, on the one hand, by the contribution of people from "outside." They will normally bring formal aspects of research activity to a project, and have often clearly identified motivating questions.

Northerners, on the other hand, bring two principal capacities. The first is local knowledge—sometimes intimate traditional knowledge—grounded in observations made over time and passed on from one generation to another. Projects thus necessarily acquire a historical dimension beyond the knowledge of outsiders, as well as a more detailed set of observations. More subtle, however, is the second capacity: the engagement with a project that is about a northern home. Northerners cannot help but bring an interdisciplinary awareness of the North, with the multitude of perspectives that we all have of our own homes and homelands.

Interdisciplinary approaches to research are currently fashionable, but few genuinely interdisciplinary projects stand out as exemplars to northern researchers. Although we have not presented an explicitly interdisciplinary account of Herschel Island in this book, we have included contributors who bring varying perspectives to the understanding of the natural and social environment at Qikiqtaryuk. We can also claim that we have presented a northern story by northerners. Twenty-four of the book's 43 authors live north of 60°N, and most of this book's production has been in the North, especially in Whitehorse, the home of many of the authors as well as our copy editor, the production team, and the publisher. Most of the articles, 21 out of 35, have been written by northern authors. Nevertheless, the book is not exclusively for the North, although the financial support for the project has come mostly from northern agencies. It is, instead, for anyone interested in the North.

Many visitors to Herschel Island can glimpse elements of the island's story as they explore the built structures (Fig. 2) and view the wildlife living there. For almost all the authors of this book, the time they spend at Qikiqtaryuk is a precious part of their lives. The unhurried days, the opportunities to think, read, and talk without interference from electronic communication, the unlimited views, the warmth of wood stoves, the fresh char sizzling in the pan, the chance to study the Arctic environment in relative safety, the uniformly friendly welcome of the rangers and other residents, the mewing of hawks, the blowing of belugas out in the bay—some or all of these experiences draw us back again and again, creating a special space in memory for Herschel Island Qikiqtaryuk, a land where it is, indeed, as Nuligak said, good to live.

—Christopher Burn and Patricia Robertson

ABOUT THE AUTHORS

John R. Bockstoce, historian and archaeologist, received his B.A. from Yale and his doctorate from Oxford. He has been working in the North since 1962 and has traversed the Northwest Passage twice by boat. He also served for ten seasons with an Inuit whaling crew at Point Hope, Alaska. He is the author of the award-winning *Whales, Ice, and Men* and *Furs and Frontiers in the Far North*.

Christopher Burn is Professor of Geography and holds the Natural Sciences and Engineering Research Council of Canada (NSERC) Northern Research Chair in permafrost science at Carleton University in Ottawa. He has been conducting research on permafrost in the Yukon continuously since 1982 and in the western Arctic since 1987.

Eddy Carmack works as an oceanographer for the Department of Fisheries and Oceans in Sidney, British Columbia. He has participated in over 80 field investigations in rivers, lakes, and seas from the Antarctic to the Arctic and from the Yukon to Siberia. He has published over 150 scientific articles on circulation and water mass formation in oceans and lakes.

Dorothy Cooley was born and raised in the Yukon. She has worked for the Government of Yukon as the North Regional Biologist since 1991. Helping the Herschel Island rangers with their monitoring program has been one of her most memorable and rewarding experiences during those 20 years.

Nicole Couture is a permafrost geomorphologist with the Geological Survey of Canada. Her doctorate research focused on erosion of permafrost along the Yukon coast and the subsequent flux of organic carbon to the Arctic Ocean. She has been involved in international coastal science activities since 1999, and is co-leader of the multi-national research group Arctic Coastal Dynamics.

Andrew E. Derocher is Professor of Biological Sciences at the University of Alberta in Edmonton. Dr. Derocher joined the university in 2002 after spending seven years at the Norwegian Polar Institute as a research scientist studying polar bears in Svalbard and western Russia. His research over the last 28 years has focused on the ecology, behaviour, population dynamics, conservation, management of, and effects of pollution on, polar bears.

Helene Dobrowolsky is an author and historian based in Whitehorse. She and her partner, Rob Ingram, operate Midnight Arts, a heritage resource consulting business. They have over thirty years' experience in planning, researching, and interpreting the Yukon's history and heritage resources.

Cameron Eckert has studied the birds, wildlife, and ecosystems of the Yukon's North Slope and Herschel Island for the past twenty years. As Conservation Biologist with Yukon Parks, he works with the senior park ranger and regional biologist to coordinate Herschel Island's ecological monitoring program. He has come to know Qikiqtaryuk as a very special place with a rich culture and remarkable natural history.

Tiffani Fraser is a petroleum assessment geologist with the Yukon Geological Survey. Whitehorse has been her home since 2006, but she has been working in the Yukon and Alaska since the middle 1990s.

Max Friesen is Professor of Anthropology at the University of Toronto. Since 1986 he has conducted archaeological fieldwork in Yukon, Northwest Territories, and Nunavut. He has a particular interest in the history of Inuvialuit culture and worked at Herschel for three summers from 1990 to 1992.

Daniel Gallant studies biology at Université du Quebec à Rimouski. His research focuses on the role played by climate in the northern expansion of the red fox in the North American Arctic and on the interaction between red and arctic foxes in tundra habitats of northern Yukon.

Scott Gilbert came to the Yukon as a summer student and never left. He now teaches in the Renewable Resources Management Program at Yukon College and still looks forward to getting out in the field. He has trapped small mammals along the coast of the Yukon and Northwest Territories since 1990 and treasures his memories of visiting Herschel Island.

Danny C. Gordon, respected elder, was born at Barter Island, Alaska, and travelled to Canada by dog team with his family when he was ten years old. They stayed at a number of places along the coast, including Herschel Island, for almost two years, living off the land, and arrived in Aklavik in 1947. Danny has lived in Aklavik ever since, where he has served on the Inuvialuit Game Council and is currently a member of WMAC(NS) and the Aklavik Hunters and Trappers Committee.

Richard Gordon is Senior Park Ranger of Herschel Island–Qikiqtaruk Territorial Park. He was born and raised in Aklavik, Northwest Territories. He has worked for the park for 12 years. His efforts have been fundamental in promoting and maintaining Inuvialuit culture at Qikiqtaryuk, both through youth and elder camps and as a mentor for new park rangers.

Lois Harwood is a stock assessment biologist with the Department of Fisheries and Oceans. She has lived and worked in the North for over thirty years, working closely with resource harvesters in the delivery of community-based research and monitoring programs focusing on Beaufort Sea fish and marine mammals. She lives in Yellowknife with her family.

John B. Hattendorf is the Ernest J. King Professor of Maritime History and Director, Naval War College Museum, at the U.S. Naval War College, Newport, Rhode Island. He holds degrees in history from Brown University and a doctorate from Oxford University. He is the author or editor of more than 40 books on naval and maritime history, including the *Oxford Encyclopedia of Maritime History*.

Michael Hoskin taught history of science at Cambridge University throughout his career. He has written five books and numerous articles on the Herschel family. He is an Honorary Fellow of the Royal Astronomical Society, and has had an asteroid named Minor Planet Hoskin after him by the International Astronomical Union.

Glenn Iceton began work in the heritage field in 2003 at the Old Log Church Museum in Whitehorse, where he was involved with *The Bishop Who Ate His Boots* travelling exhibit. After completing a master's degree in history at the University of Calgary, Glenn returned to Whitehorse, where he works at the Yukon Archives.

Rob Ingram has multiple interests in graphic, fine, and martial arts, but his greatest love is the history and heritage of the Yukon. Rob spent time on Herschel Island in the early 1980s as the Yukon's Historic Resources Officer. After Herschel Island was designated a territorial park in 1987, Rob and Helene Dobrowolsky prepared an interpretive history of Herschel Island, *Waves Upon the Shore*.

Stuart E. Jenness is the second son of Diamond Jenness, one of two ethnologists on the Canadian Arctic Expedition, 1913–1916. He has published four books about the expedition, most recently *Stefansson, Dr. Anderson and the Canadian Arctic Expedition, 1913–1918,* which appeared in 2011. He retired in 1985 after a career in geology and scientific editing with the Geological Survey of Canada and the National Research Council of Canada.

Jim Johnson has been an Arctic fisheries research biologist with the Department of Fisheries and Oceans for the past 22 years. His studies have focused on fish populations of the nearshore southern Beaufort Sea, as well as on populations in the central and high Arctic. Along with his wife and two sons, he presently resides in Winnipeg, Manitoba, but spends as much time as possible at his cottage on Lake Winnipeg.

Catherine Kennedy has studied vegetation in permafrost environments throughout the Yukon as vegetation ecologist for the Government of Yukon. Her work has included vegetation inventories of parks and protected areas such as Herschel Island and Ivvavik, and monitoring vegetation and climate change on the Yukon North Slope. Recently she led an International Polar Year project to develop an arctic vegetation database and classification as an extension to the Canadian National Vegetation Classification.

Alice Kenney is an ecologist with thirty years' experience working in boreal forest and tundra ecosystems of northern Canada. She has worked largely with snowshoe hares, lemmings, and other small mammals.

Charles Krebs is Emeritus Professor of Zoology at the University of British Columbia. He has studied the population and community ecology of vertebrates in the boreal forest and tundra ecosystems of northern Canada for 41 years, concentrating on voles, lemmings, and snowshoe hares.

Larry Lane is a specialist in geological mapping, rock deformation, and plate tectonics at the Geological Survey of Canada. He has published geological maps of western and northern Canada since the mid-1970s, and has studied the geological history of northern Yukon and the Beaufort Sea region since 1986.

Hugues Lantuit is a postdoctoral researcher at the Alfred Wegener Institute for Polar and Marine Research in Potsdam, Germany, and the Executive Director of the International Permafrost Association. He has been studying coastal erosion on Herschel Island since 2001.

Maria Leung is a wildlife biologist with degrees from the universities of Guelph and British Columbia. She lives in Whitehorse, where she pursues the conservation biology of mammals, birds, fish, and invertebrates. She took part in the International Polar Year project Arctic Wildlife Observatories Linking Vulnerable EcoSystems (ArcticWOLVES) on Herschel Island from 2007 to 2009.

Gordon MacRae worked in provincial parks in British Columbia for 22 years, managing several different wilderness areas including Tatshenshini–Alsek Provincial Park. He joined Yukon Parks in 2001 as Klondike Regional Superintendent. Herschel Island Park is the most northerly protected area within his region.

Ramona Maraj completed her doctorate on grizzly bear ecology at the University of Calgary. She has studied grizzly bear populations in Canada's north since 1997, including the grizzlies of Herschel Island and the Yukon North Slope. She is currently the carnivore biologist for Yukon.

Lee John Meyook was born at Komakuk Beach in the Yukon and raised in Aklavik, Northwest Territories. He has worked as a Ranger at Herschel Island—Qikiqtaruk Territorial Park for the past 22 years. His warm welcome and knowledge of island culture and wildlife help create a memorable experience for many visitors to Herschel Island.

Dave Mossop first visited Herschel Island in 1973 when he instantly developed an abiding interest in the birds of the place. His prime interest is in tracking the long-term fortunes of bird species and trying to understand their dynamics. He visited the island annually for 16 years as a government biologist and still returns to survey the raptors.

Murielle Nagy is a consultant in anthropology. She has been editor of the journal *Études/Inuit/Studies* since 2002. She received a master's degree in archaeology from Simon Fraser University and a doctorate in anthropology from the University of Alberta. From 1990 to 2000 she coordinated three major oral history projects for the Inuvialuit.

David Neufeld has been Parks Canada's historian for the Yukon and western Arctic since 1986. He worked on the Inuvialuit North Slope oral history project in the early 1990s and was part of the Distant Early Warning (DEW) Line research project jointly funded by the United States Air Force and Parks Canada. He has been swimming (very briefly) in Pauline Cove.

Sara Nielsen is Environment Yukon's parks interpretive planner. She trained as a biologist in Alaska and is currently studying nature and culture at the University of Copenhagen. She has been particularly involved in the development of the Tombstone Park Interpretive Centre. Her work on the island reflects a place rich in story and experience.

Doug Olynyk has recently retired from his position as Manager of Historic Sites for the Government of Yukon. He has over 35 years of experience in architectural conservation and heritage resource management. He was responsible for managing the research, documentation, planning, conservation, management, operation, and interpretation of historic places in Yukon.

Wayne Pollard is a Professor of Geography at McGill University and began work on Herschel Island in the 1980s. His research focuses on the evolution of polar landscapes, with a particular interest in the analysis of dynamic relationships between climate and terrestrial systems, including permafrost and ground ice. He has conducted research throughout northern Canada and in Antarctica.

Donald Reid is an Associate Conservation Zoologist with Wildlife Conservation Society Canada, based in Whitehorse. From 2006 to 2010 he was a lead investigator on the International Polar Year project Arctic Wildlife Observatories Linking Vulnerable Eco-Systems (ArcticWOLVES) and organized ecological fieldwork on Herschel Island and the Yukon North Slope. He works on wildlife conservation issues in Yukon's land use planning, and wetland conservation in the northern boreal mountains.

Patricia Robertson is a freelance writer and editor whose work often involves editing scientific and technical material for general audiences. She is also a writer of fiction and a creative writing instructor at Yukon College in Whitehorse. She has published two collections of short stories, has co-edited an anthology of Yukon writers, and is a contributing editor for *CNQ (Canadian Notes and Queries)*.

Charlie Roots studies rocks and investigates ancient geological processes through the creation and interpretation of bedrock geological maps. As a regional mapper he is familiar with many parts of southern Yukon but still looks forward to visiting Herschel Island. He lives in Whitehorse and works for the Geological Survey of Canada.

Martin Rose, currently Director of the British Council in Morocco, was Director of the British Council in Canada (2006–10) and has also served in Iraq, Italy, and Belgium. Educated at Oxford University in history and later Middle Eastern Studies, he is a fellow of the Royal Canadian Geographical Society and a member of the Church Monuments Society. He visited Herschel Island in 2009.

Lindsay Staples is a Whitehorse-based resource management consultant. He has over 25 years of experience in land claims, self-government negotiations, and settlement implementation in the Yukon, Northwest Territories, and British Columbia. He is chair of the Wildlife Management Advisory Council (North Slope).

Bill Williams has visited Herschel Island and the ocean surrounding it several times aboard the CCGS *Nahidik* as part of the Northern Coastal Marine Ecosystem Study. He is a scientist with the Department of Fisheries and Oceans.

Grant Zazula is the Yukon Palaeontologist with the Department of Tourism and Culture, Government of Yukon. His research interests include Pleistocene palaeoecology, mammalogy, and glacial history of northern North America. Grant completed his doctorate in biology at Simon Fraser University in 2006 and has since called Whitehorse his home.

SOURCES AND FURTHER READING

Yukon's Arctic Island

Bockstoce, J.R. 1986 and 1995. *Whales, ice and men: The history of whaling in the western Arctic*. Seattle, WA: University of Washington Press.

Burn, C.R., and Y. Zhang. 2009. Permafrost and climate change at Herschel Island (Qikiqtaruq), Yukon Territory, Canada. *Journal of Geophysical Research* 114: F02001. doi:10.1029/2008JF001087.

Coates, K.S., and W.R. Morrison. 1998. "To make these tribes understand": The trial of Alikomiak and Tatamigana. *Arctic* 51: 220–230.

Lantuit, H., and W.H. Pollard. 2008. Fifty years of coastal erosion and retrogressive thaw slump activity on Herschel Island, southern Beaufort Sea, Yukon Territory, Canada. *Geomorphology* 95: 84–102.

Nagy, M.I. 1994. Yukon North Slope Inuvialuit oral history. Hudç Hudän Series. Occasional Papers in Yukon History No 1. Whitehorse, YT: Heritage Branch, Government of Yukon.

Pálsson, G., ed. 2001. *Writing on ice: The ethnographic notebooks of Vilhjalmur Stefansson*. Hanover, NH: University Press of New England.

Peake, F.A. 2001. *The bishop who ate his boots: A biography of Isaac O. Stringer*. Whitehorse, YT: Yukon Church Heritage Society. (Orig. pub. 1966, Don Mills, ON: The Anglican Church of Canada).

Morrison, W.R. 1985. *Showing the flag: The mounted police and Canadian sovereignty in the north, 1894–1925*. Vancouver, BC: University of British Columbia Press.

Nuligak (Bob Cockney). 1975. *I, Nuligak*. Edited and translated by Maurice Metayer. Markham, ON: Pocket Book. (Orig. pub. 1966, Peter Martin Associates).

Whittaker, C.E. 1937. *Arctic Eskimo*. London: Seeley, Service & Co.

Yorga, B. 1980. Washout: A western Thule site on Herschel Island, Yukon Territory. Ottawa, ON: National Museum of Man, Mercury Series, Archaeological Survey of Canada Paper 98.

The Herschel Family

Burn, C.R. 2009. After whom is Herschel Island named? *Arctic* 62: 317–323.

Crowe, M.J. 2004. Herschel, Sir John Frederick William. In *Oxford dictionary of national biography*, eds. H.C.G. Matthew and B. Harrison, 26: 825–831. Oxford: Oxford University Press.

Hoskin, M.A. 2003. *The Herschel partnership, as viewed by Caroline*. Cambridge: Science History Publications.

Hoskin, M.A. 2004a. Herschel, Sir William. In *Oxford dictionary of national biography*, eds. H.C.G. Matthew and B. Harrison, 26: 831–837. Oxford: Oxford University Press.

Hoskin, M.A. 2004b. Herschel, Caroline Lucretia. In *Oxford dictionary of national biography*, eds. H.C.G. Matthew and B. Harrison, 26: 822–825. Oxford: Oxford University Press.

Place Names

Bockstoce, J.R. 1977. *Steam whaling in the western Arctic*. New Bedford, MA: Old Dartmouth Historical Society.

Burn, C.R. 2009. After whom is Herschel Island named? *Arctic* 62: 317–323.

Burn, C.R., and J.B. Hattendorf. 2011. Toponymy of Herschel Island (Qikiqtaryuk), western Arctic coast, Canada. *Arctic* 64: 459–464.

Franklin, J. 1971. *Narrative of a second expedition to the shores of the polar sea in the years 1825, 1826, and 1827*. Edmonton, AB: M.G. Hurtig Ltd. (Orig. pub. 1828, London: John Murray).

Stockton, C.H. 1890. The Arctic cruise of the U.S.S. *Thetis* in the summer and autumn of 1889. *National Geographic Magazine* 2: 171–198.

Physical Setting

Lantuit, H., and W.H. Pollard. 2008. Fifty years of coastal erosion and retrogressive thaw slump activity on Herschel Island, southern Beaufort Sea, Yukon Territory, Canada. *Geomorphology* 95: 84–102.

Mackay, J.R. 1959. Glacier ice-thrust features of the Yukon coast. *Geographical Bulletin* 13: 5–21.

Norris, D.K., ed. 1997. The geology, mineral and hydrocarbon potential of northern Yukon Territory and northwestern District of Mackenzie. Ottawa, ON: Geological Survey of Canada, Bulletin 422.

O'Neill, J.J. 1921. The geology of the Arctic coast of Canada, west of Kent Peninsula. In *Report of the Canadian Arctic Expedition 1913–18*, vol. XI, Geology and Geography, Part A. Ottawa, ON: King's Printer.

Rampton, V.N. 1982. Quaternary geology of the Yukon Coastal Plain. Ottawa, ON: Geological Survey of Canada, Bulletin 317.

Smith, C.A.S., J.C. Meikle, and C.F. Roots. 2004. Ecoregions of the Yukon Territory: Biophysical properties of Yukon landscapes. Summerland, BC: Agriculture and Agri-Food Canada, PARC Technical Bulletin 04–01.

Geology

Dixon, J. 1996. Geological atlas of the Beaufort–Mackenzie area. Ottawa, ON: Geological Survey of Canada, Miscellaneous Report 59.

Dixon, J., J.R. Dietrich, L.S. Lane, and D.H. McNeil. 2008. Geology of the Late Cretaceous to Cenozoic Beaufort-Mackenzie Basin, Canada. In *Sedimentary Basins of the World*, ed. A.D. Miall, vol. 5, chap. 16. Amsterdam: Elsevier B.V. Press.

Hannigan, P.K. 2001. Petroleum resource assessment of the Yukon north coast, Yukon Territory, Canada. Whitehorse, YT: Oil and Gas Resources Branch, Department of Economic Development, Government of Yukon.

Issler, D.R., K. Hu, L.S. Lane, and J.R. Dietrich. 2011. GIS compilations of depth to overpressure, permafrost distribution, geothermal gradient and regional geology, Beaufort Mackenzie basin, northern Canada. Ottawa, ON: Geological Survey of Canada, Open File 5689; scale 1:1,000,000.

Lane, L.S. 2002. Tectonic evolution of the Canadian Beaufort Sea–Mackenzie delta region: A brief review. *Canadian Society of Exploration Geophysicists Recorder* 27: 49–56.

Norris, D.K., ed. 1997. The geology, mineral and hydrocarbon potential of northern Yukon Territory and northwestern District of Mackenzie. Ottawa, ON: Geological Survey of Canada, Bulletin 422.

Climate

Bodfish, H.H. 1936. *Chasing the bowhead*. Cambridge, MA: Harvard University Press.

Burn, C.R., and Y. Zhang. 2009. Permafrost and climate change at Herschel Island (Qikiqtaruq), Yukon Territory, Canada. *Journal of Geophysical Research* 114. F02001. doi:10.1029/2008JF001087.

Climate Normals are available at: www.climate.weatheroffice.gc.ca/climate_normals/index_e.html

Herschel Island weather records are available at: www.climate.weatheroffice.gc.ca/advanceSearch/searchHistoricData_e.html

Ritchie, J.C. 1984. *Past and present vegetation of the far northwest of Canada*. Toronto, ON: University of Toronto Press.

Wahl, H.E., D.B. Fraser, R.C. Harvey, and J.B. Maxwell. 1987. Climate of Yukon. Ottawa, ON: Atmospheric Environment Service, Environment Canada, Climatological Studies No. 40.

Ocean Water and Sea Ice

Aagaard, K., and E.C. Carmack. 1989. The role of sea ice and other fresh water in the Arctic Ocean circulation. *Journal of Geophysical Research* 94: 14485–14498.

Carmack, E.C. 2000. The Arctic Ocean's freshwater budget: Sources, storage and export. In *The freshwater budget of the Arctic Ocean*, eds. E.L. Lewis, E.P. Jones, P. Lemke, T.D. Prowse, and P. Wadhams, pp. 91–126. Dordrecht: Kluwer Academic.

Carmack, E.C., and R.W. Macdonald. 2002. Oceanography of the Canadian Shelf of the Beaufort Sea: A setting for marine life. *Arctic* 55 (Supp. 1): 29–45.

Macdonald, R.W., D.W. Paton, E.C. Carmack, and A. Omstedt. 1995. The freshwater budget and under-ice spreading of Mackenzie River water in the Canadian Beaufort Sea based on salinity and $^{18}O/^{16}O$ measurements in water and ice. *Journal of Geophysical Research* 100: 895–919.

Milliman, J.D., and R.H. Meade. 1983. Worldwide delivery of river sediment to the oceans. *Journal of Geology* 91: 1–21.

Ice Age

Guthrie, R.D. 1990. *Frozen fauna of the mammoth steppe: The story of Blue Babe*. Chicago, IL: University of Chicago Press.

Harington, C.R. 2003. *Annotated bibliography of Quaternary vertebrates of northern North America with radiocarbon dates*. Toronto, ON: University of Toronto Press.

Mackay, J.R. 1959. Glacier ice-thrust features of the Yukon coast. *Geographical Bulletin* 13: 5–21.

Rampton, V.N. 1982. Quaternary geology of the Yukon Coastal Plain. Ottawa, ON: Geological Survey of Canada, Bulletin 317.

Zazula, G.D., P.G. Hare, and J.E. Storer. 2009. New radiocarbon-dated vertebrate fossils from Herschel Island: Implications for the palaeoenvironments and glacial chronology of the Beaufort Sea coastlands. *Arctic* 62: 273–280.

Permafrost

Burn, C.R., and Y. Zhang. 2009. Permafrost and climate change at Herschel Island (Qikiqtaruq), Yukon Territory, Canada. *Journal of Geophysical Research* 114: F02001. doi:10.1029/2008JF001087.

Fritz, M., S. Wetterich, H. Meyer, L. Schirrmeister, H. Lantuit, and W.H. Pollard. 2011. Origin and characteristics of massive ground ice on Herschel Island (western Canadian Arctic) as revealed by stable water isotope and hydrochemical signatures. *Permafrost and Periglacial Processes* 22: 26–38.

Kokelj, S.V., C.A.S. Smith, and C.R. Burn. 2002. Physical and chemical characteristics of the active layer and permafrost, Herschel Island, western Arctic coast, Canada. *Permafrost and Periglacial Processes* 13: 171–185.

Lantuit, H., and W.H. Pollard. 2008. Fifty years of coastal erosion and retrogressive thaw slump activity on Herschel Island, southern Beaufort Sea, Yukon Territory, Canada. *Geomorphology* 95: 84–102.

Pollard, W.H. 1990. The nature and origin of ground ice in the Herschel Island area, Yukon Territory. Proceedings of the Fifth Canadian Permafrost Conference, pp. 23–30. Ottawa, ON: National Research Council of Canada; Québec City, QC: Centre d'études nordiques, Université Laval.

Rampton, V.N. 1982. Quaternary geology of the Yukon Coastal Plain. Ottawa, ON: Geological Survey of Canada, Bulletin 317.

Coastal Environment

Couture, N., M. Hoque, and W.H. Pollard. 2008. Modeling the erosion of ice-rich deposits along the Yukon Coastal Plain. Proceedings of the Ninth International Conference on Permafrost, vol. 1, pp. 303–308. Fairbanks, AK: Institute of Northern Engineering, University of Alaska Fairbanks.

De Krom, V., and W.H. Pollard. 1989. The occurrence of ground ice slumps on Herschel Island, Yukon Territory. *Musk-Ox* 37: 1–7.

Lantuit, H., and W.H. Pollard. 2008. Fifty years of coastal erosion and retrogressive thaw slump activity on Herschel Island, southern Beaufort Sea, Yukon Territory, Canada. *Geomorphology* 95: 84–102.

Pollard, W.H. 2005. Herschel Island. In *Encyclopaedia of the Arctic*, ed. M. Nuttall, pp. 860–861. London: Fitzroy Dearborn Publishing Company.

Pollard, W.H. 2010. Northern Canada. In *Encyclopaedia of the world's coastal landforms*, ed. Eric Bird, pp. 169–177. Dordrecht: Springer Science + Business Media B.V.

Vegetation

Burt, P. 1991. *Barrenland beauties: Showy plants of the Canadian Arctic*. Yellowknife, NT: Outcrop Publishing.

Cody, W.J. 1996. *Flora of the Yukon Territory*. Ottawa, ON: NRC Research Press.

Inuvialuit elders with R.W. Bandringa. 2010. *Inuvialuit Nautchiangit: Relationships between people and plants*. Inuvik, NT: Inuvialuit Cultural Resource Centre, Aurora Research Institute, and Parks Canada.

Myers-Smith, I.H., D.S. Hik, C. Kennedy, D. Cooley, J. F. Johnstone, A.J. Kenney, and C.J. Krebs. 2011. Expansion of canopy-forming willows over the twentieth century on Herschel Island, Yukon Territory, Canada. *Ambio* 40: 610–623.

Ritchie, J.C. 1984. *Past and present vegetation of the far northwest of Canada*. Toronto, ON: University of Toronto Press.

Smith, C.A.S., C.E. Kennedy, A.E. Hargrave, and K.M. McKenna. 1989. Soil and vegetation survey of Herschel Island, Yukon Territory. Whitehorse, YT: Research Branch, Agriculture Canada, Yukon Soil Survey Report 1.

Insects and Spiders

Bale, J.S., I.D. Hodkinson, W. Block, N.R. Webb, S.C. Coulson, and A.T. Strathdee. 1997. Life strategies of arctic terrestrial arthropods. In *Ecology of arctic environments*, eds. S.J. Woodin and M. Marquiss. Special Publication No. 13 of the British Ecological Society, pp. 137–165. Oxford: Blackwell Science.

Danks, H.V., and J.A. Downes. 1997. *Insects of the Yukon*. Biological Survey of Canada (Terrestrial Arthropods) Monograph Series No. 2. Ottawa, ON: Canadian Museum of Nature.

Korczynski, R.E. 1985. An enigmatic protozoan infection in the isopod *Mesidotea (=Saduria) sibirica* from Herschel Island. *Arctic* 38: 336–337.

Butterflies

Lafontaine, J.D., and D.M. Wood. 1997. Butterflies and moths (Lepidoptera) of the Yukon. In *Insects of the Yukon*, Biological Survey of Canada (Terrestrial Arthropods) Monograph Series No. 2, pp. 723–785. Ottawa, ON: Canadian Museum of Nature.

Layberry, R.A., P.W. Hall, and J.D. Lafontaine. 1998. *The butterflies of Canada*. Toronto, ON: University of Toronto Press.

Scott, J.A. 1986. *The butterflies of North America: A natural history and field guide*. Stanford, CA: Stanford University Press.

Birds

Eckert, C.D. 1996. Wood Sandpiper a Yukon first at Herschel Island. *Birders Journal* 5: 247–251.

Eckert, C.D., P.H. Sinclair, and H. Grünberg. 2000. Checklist of the birds of Herschel Island. Whitehorse, YT: Yukon Bird Club.

Eckert, C.D., D. Cooley, and R.R. Gordon. 2006. Monitoring Black Guillemot population and nesting success at Herschel Island, Yukon Territory, 2005. Whitehorse, YT: Department of Environment, Government of Yukon. Technical Report Series TR-06-01.

Johnson, S.R., and D.R. Herter. 1989. *The birds of the Beaufort Sea*. Anchorage, AK: BP Exploration (Alaska) Inc.

Sinclair, P.H., W.A. Nixon, C.D. Eckert, and N.L. Hughes, eds. 2003. *Birds of the Yukon Territory*. Vancouver, BC: University of British Columbia Press.

Small Mammals

Chitty, D. 1996. *Do lemmings commit suicide? Beautiful hypotheses and ugly facts*. New York, NY: Oxford University Press.

Gruyer, N., G. Gauthier, and D. Berteaux. 2009. Demography of two lemming species on Bylot Island, Nunavut, Canada. *Polar Biology* 33: 725–736.

Reid, D.G., and C.J. Krebs. 1996. Limitations to collared lemming population growth in winter. *Canadian Journal of Zoology* 74: 1284–1291.

Stenseth, N.C., and R.A. Ims, eds. 1993. *The biology of lemmings*. London: Academic Press.

Caribou and Muskoxen

Bockstoce, J.R. 1980. The consumption of caribou by whalemen at Herschel Island, Yukon Territory, 1890 to 1908. *Arctic and Alpine Research* 12: 381–384.

Kennedy, C.E., C.A.S. Smith, and D.A. Cooley. 2001. Observations of change in the cover of Polargrass, *Arctagrostis latifolia*, and Arctic Lupine, *Lupinus arcticus*, in upland tundra on Herschel Island, Yukon Territory. *Canadian Field-Naturalist* 115: 323–238.

Gunn, A., and J. Adamczewski. 2003. Muskox. In *Wild mammals of North America*, eds. G.A. Feldhamer, B.C. Thompson, and J.A. Chapman, pp. 1076–1094. Baltimore, MD: The Johns Hopkins University Press.

Russell, D.E., and P. McNeil. 2005. Summer ecology of the Porcupine caribou herd. Whitehorse, YT: Porcupine Caribou Management Board. Available at: www.taiga.net/pcmb/summer_ecology/index.html.

Hummel, M., and J. Ray. 2008. *Caribou and the north: A shared future*. Toronto, ON: Dundurn Press.

Wildlife Management Advisory Council (North Slope). 2009. Aklavik local and traditional knowledge about Porcupine Caribou. Whitehorse, YT: Wildlife Management Advisory Council (North Slope). Available at: www.wmacns.ca/pdfs/287_WMAC_rpt_pcbou_knwldg_web.pdf.

Small Carnivores

Copeland, J.P., and J.S. Whitman. 2003. Wolverine. In *Wild mammals of North America: Biology, management and economics*, eds. G.A. Feldhamer, B.C. Thompson, and J.A. Chapman, pp. 672–682. Baltimore, MD: The Johns Hopkins University Press.

Eberhardt, L.E., and W.C. Hanson. 1978. Long distance movements of arctic foxes tagged in northern Alaska. *Canadian Field-Naturalist* 92: 386–389.

King, C.M., and R.A. Powell. 2007. *The natural history of weasels and stoats: Ecology, behaviour and management*. New York, NY: Oxford University Press.

Pamperin, N.J., E.H. Follman, and B.T. Person. 2008. Sea-ice use by arctic foxes in northern Alaska. *Polar Biology* 31: 1421–1426.

Pamperin, N.J., E.H. Follmann, and B. Petersen. 2006. Interspecific killing of an arctic fox by a red fox at Prudhoe Bay, Alaska. *Arctic* 59: 361–364.

Smits, C.M.M., B.G. Slough, and A. Angerbjörn. 1989. Abundance and summer occupancy of arctic fox dens in northern Yukon Territory, 1984–1988. Whitehorse, YT: Yukon Fish and Wildlife Branch, Department of Environment, Government of Yukon. Unpubl. report.

Grizzly Bears

MacHutchon, A.G. 2001. Grizzly bear activity budget and pattern in the Firth River Valley, Yukon. *Ursus* 12: 189–198.

Nagy, J.A., R.H. Russell, A.M. Pearson, M.C.S. Kingsley, and B.C. Goski. 1983. Ecological studies of grizzly bears in the Arctic Mountains, northern Yukon Territory, 1972 to 1975. Edmonton, AB: Canadian Wildlife Service.

Wildlife Management Advisory Council (North Slope). 2008. Aklavik local and traditional knowledge about grizzly bears of the Yukon North Slope. Whitehorse, YT: Wildlife Management Advisory Council (North Slope).

Polar Bears

Brower, C.D., A. Carpenter, M.L. Branigan, W. Calvert, T. Evans, A.S. Fischbach, J.A. Nagy, S. Schliebe, and I. Stirling. 2002. The polar bear management agreement for the southern Beaufort Sea: An evaluation of the first ten years of a unique conservation agreement. *Arctic* 55: 362–372.

Derocher, A.E. 2012. *Polar bears: A complete guide to their biology and behavior*. Baltimore, MD: The Johns Hopkins University Press.

Ellis, R. 2009. *On thin ice: The changing world of the polar bear*. New York, NY: Knopf.

Fischbach, A.S., S.C. Amstrup, and D.C. Douglas. 2007. Landward and eastward shift of Alaskan polar bear denning associated with recent sea ice changes. *Polar Biology* 30: 1395–1405.

Monnett, C., and J.S. Gleason. 2006. Observations of mortality associated with extended open-water swimming by polar bears in the Alaskan Beaufort Sea. *Polar Biology* 29: 681–687.

Stirling, I. 2002. Polar bears and seals in the eastern Beaufort Sea and Amundsen Gulf: A synthesis of population trends and ecological relationships over three decades. *Arctic* 55 (Supp. 1): 59–76.

Marine Mammals

Adams, M., K.J. Frost, and L.A. Harwood. 1993. Alaska and Inuvialuit Beluga Whale Committee (AIBWC): An initiative in "at home management." *Arctic* 46: 134–137.

Harwood, L.A., and T.G. Smith. 2002. Whales of the Inuvialuit Settlement Region in Canada's western Arctic: An overview and outlook. *Arctic* 55 (Supp. 1): 77–93.

Harwood, L.A., P. Norton, B. Day, and P. Hall. 2002. The harvest of beluga whales in Canada's western Arctic: hunter-based monitoring of the size and composition of the catch. *Arctic* 55:10–20.

Richard, P.R., A.R. Martin, and J.R. Orr. 2001. Summer and autumn movements of belugas of the eastern Beaufort Sea stock. *Arctic* 54: 223–236.

Smith, T.G. 1987. The ringed seal (*Phoca hispida*) of the Canadian western Arctic. *Canadian Bulletin of Fisheries and Aquatic Sciences* 216. 81p.

Stirling, I., and N.A. Øritsland. 1995. Relationships between estimates of ringed seal (*Phoca hispida*) and polar bear (*Ursus maritimus*) populations in the Canadian Arctic. *Canadian Journal of Fisheries and Aquatic Sciences* 52: 2594–2612.

Fishes

Baker, R.F. 1985. A fisheries survey of Herschel Island, Yukon Territory, from 9 July to 12 August 1985. Prepared by North/South Consultants Ltd., Winnipeg, MB. Available from Department of Fisheries and Oceans Canada, WAVES Cat. No. 231981.

Bond, W.A., and R.N. Erickson. 1997. Coastal migrations of Arctic Ciscoes in the eastern Beaufort Sea. In *Fish ecology in Arctic North America*, pp. 155–164. American Fisheries Society Symposium 19, Fairbanks, Alaska, 19–21 May 1992. Bethesda, MD: American Fisheries Society.

Bradstreet, M.S.W., K.J. Finely, A.D. Sekerak, W.B. Griffiths, C.R. Evans, M.F. Fabjian, and H.E. Stallard. 1986. Aspects of the biology of Arctic Cod (*Boreogadus saida*) and its importance in Arctic marine food chains. Canadian Technical Report of Fisheries and Aquatic Sciences 1491. Central and Arctic Region, Fisheries and Oceans Canada.

Kendal, R.E., R.A.C. Johnston, U. Lobsiger, and M.D. Kozak. 1975. Fishes of the Yukon coast. Beaufort Sea Technical Report No. 6, Beaufort Sea Project. Victoria, BC: Northern Operations Branch, Fisheries and Marine Service, Department of the Environment.

Majewski, A.R., M.K. Lowdon, J.D. Reist, and B.J. Park. 2011. Fish catch data from Herschel Island, Yukon Territory, and other offshore sites in the Canadian Beaufort Sea, July and August 2007, aboard the CCGS *Nahidik*. Canadian Data Report of Fisheries and Aquatic Sciences 1231. Central and Arctic Region, Fisheries and Oceans Canada.

McAllister, D.E. 1962. Fishes of the 1960 "Salvelinus" program from western Arctic Canada. National Museum of Canada, Bulletin No. 185, Contributions to Zoology. Ottawa, ON: Department of Northern Affairs and Natural Resources.

Inuvialuit Archaeology

Alunik, I., E.D. Kolausok, and D. Morrison. 2003. *Across time and tundra: The Inuvialuit of the western Arctic*. Vancouver, BC: Raincoast Books.

Bockstoce, J.R. 2009. *Furs and frontiers in the far North: The contest among native and foreign nations for the Bering Strait fur trade*. New Haven, CT: Yale University Press.

Friesen, T. M. 1994. The Qikiqtaruk archaeology project 1990–92: Preliminary results of archaeological investigations on Herschel Island, northern Yukon Territory. In *Bridges across time: The NOGAP archaeology project*, ed. J.-L. Pilon, pp. 61–83. Canadian Archaeological Association Occasional Paper No. 2. Victoria, BC: Canadian Archaeological Association.

Friesen, T.M. 2009. Event or conjuncture? Searching for the material record of Inuvialuit-Euroamerican whaler interaction on Herschel Island, northern Yukon. *Alaska Journal of Anthropology* 7: 45–61.

McGhee, R. 1988. Beluga hunters: An archeological reconstruction of the history and culture of the Mackenzie Delta Kittegaryumiut. 2nd ed. Newfoundland Social and Economic Studies No. 13. St. John's, NL: Memorial University of Newfoundland.

Yorga, B.W.D. 1980. Washout: A Western Thule site on Herschel Island, Yukon Territory. Mercury Series, Archaeological Survey of Canada Paper 98. Ottawa, ON: National Museum of Man.

Inuvialuit Ancestors

Alunik, I., E.D. Kolausok, and D. Morrison. 2003. *Across time and tundra: The Inuvialuit of the western Arctic*. Vancouver, BC: Raincoast Books.

McGhee, R. 1988. Beluga hunters: An archeological reconstruction of the history and culture of the Mackenzie Delta Kittegaryumiut. 2nd ed. Newfoundland Social and Economic Studies No. 13. St. John's, NL: Memorial University of Newfoundland.

Nagy, M.I. 1994. Yukon North Slope Inuvialuit oral history. Hudç Hudän Series. Occasional Papers in Yukon History No 1. Whitehorse, YT: Heritage Branch, Government of Yukon.

Nuligak (Bob Cockney). 1975. *I, Nuligak*. Edited and translated by Maurice Metayer. Markham, ON: Pocket Book. (Orig. pub. 1966, Peter Martin Associates).

Petitot, É. 1999. *Among the Chiglit Eskimo*. 2nd ed. Translated by Otto Hahn. Edmonton, AB: Canadian Circumpolar Institute (orig. pub. 1887).

Stefansson, V. 1919. The Stefansson-Anderson Arctic expedition of the American Museum: Preliminary ethnological report. *Anthropological Papers of the American Museum of Natural History* 14: 1–395.

Whaling

Bockstoce, J.R. 1977. *Steam whaling in the western Arctic*. New Bedford, MA: Old Dartmouth Historical Society.

Bockstoce, J.R. 1986 and 1995. *Whales, ice and men: The history of whaling in the western Arctic*. Seattle, WA: University of Washington Press.

Bockstoce, J.R. 2009. *Furs and frontiers in the far north: The contest among native and foreign nations for the Bering Strait fur trade*. New Haven, CT: Yale University Press.

Bodfish, H.H. 1936. *Chasing the bowhead*. Cambridge, MA: Harvard University Press.

Cook, J.A. 1926. *Pursuing the whale: A quarter century of whaling in the Arctic*. Boston, MA, and New York, NY: Houghton Mifflin Co.

Missionaries

Alunik, I., E.D. Kolausok, and D. Morrison. 2003. *Across time and tundra: The Inuvialuit of the western Arctic*. Vancouver, BC: Raincoast Books.

Cody, H.A. 2002. *An apostle of the north: Memoirs of the Right Reverend William Carpenter Bompas*. Edmonton, AB: University of Alberta Press.

Coates, K.S., and W.R. Morrison. 2005. *Land of the midnight sun: A history of the Yukon*. 2nd ed. Montreal, QC, and Kingston, ON: McGill-Queen's University Press.

Nagy, M.I. 1994. Yukon North Slope Inuvialuit oral history. Hudç Hudän Series. Occasional Papers in Yukon History No 1. Whitehorse, YT: Heritage Branch, Government of Yukon.

Peake, F.A. 2001. *The bishop who ate his boots: A biography of Isaac O. Stringer*. Whitehorse, YT: Yukon Church Heritage Society. (Orig. pub. 1966, Don Mills, ON: The Anglican Church of Canada).

Stuck, H. 1920. *A winter circuit of our Arctic coast: A narrative of a journey with dog-sleds around the entire Arctic coast of Alaska*. New York, NY: Charles Scribner's Sons.

Fur Traders

Bockstoce, J.R. 1980. The consumption of caribou by whalemen at Herschel Island, Yukon Territory. *Arctic and Alpine Research* 12: 381–384.

Bockstoce, J.R. and C.F. Batchelder. 1978. A chronological list of commercial wintering voyages to the Bering Strait region and western Arctic of North America. *American Neptune* 38: 81–91.

Dalton, A. 2006. *Baychimo: Arctic ghost ship*. Victoria, BC: Heritage House.

Gillingham, D.W. 1955. *Umiak!* London: Museum Press.

Nuligak (Bob Cockney). 1975. *I, Nuligak*. Edited and translated by Maurice Metayer. Markham, ON: Pocket Book. (Orig. pub. 1966, Peter Martin Associates).

Robertson, H. 1984. *A gentleman adventurer: The Arctic diaries of Richard Bonnycastle*. Toronto, ON: Lester and Orpen Dennys.

Usher, P. 1975. The growth and decay of the trading and trapping frontiers in the western Canadian Arctic. *The Canadian Geographer* 19: 308–320.

Vuntut Gwitchin First Nation and S. Smith. 2009. People of the Lakes: Stories of our Van Tat Gwich'in elders/Googwandak Nakhwach'ànjòo Van Tat Gwich'in. Edmonton, AB: University of Alberta Press.

Police

Coates, K.S., and W.R. Morrison. 2004. *Strange things done: Murder in Yukon history*. Montreal, QC, and Kingston, ON: McGill-Queen's University Press.

Dobrowolsky, H. 1995. *Law of the Yukon: A pictorial history of the mounted police in the Yukon*. Whitehorse, YT: Lost Moose Publishers.

Grant, S.D. 1993. Why the St. Roch? Why the Northwest Passage? Why 1940? New answers to old questions. *Arctic* 46: 82–87.

Nagy, M.I. 1994. Yukon North Slope Inuvialuit oral history. Hudç Hudän Series. Occasional Papers in Yukon History No 1. Whitehorse, YT: Heritage Branch, Government of Yukon.

Morrison, W.R. 1985. *Showing the flag: The mounted police and Canadian sovereignty in the North, 1894–1925*. Vancouver, BC: University of British Columbia Press.

Zaslow, M. 1988. *The northward expansion of Canada, 1914–1967*. Toronto, ON: McClelland and Stewart.

Scientists and Explorers

Amundsen, R. 1908. *The North West Passage: Being the record of a voyage of exploration of the ship Gjøa, 1903–1907*, vol. 2. New York, NY: E.P. Dutton; London: Constable.

Anderson, R.M. 1917. Recent explorations on the Canadian Arctic coast. *Geographical Review* 4: 241–266.

Jenness, S.E. 2011. *Stefansson, Dr. Anderson and the Canadian Arctic Expedition, 1913–1918: A story of exploration, science and sovereignty*. Mercury Series History Paper 56. Gatineau, QC: Canadian Museum of Civilization.

Russell, F. 1898. *Explorations in the far north*. Iowa City, IA: University of Iowa.

Stefansson, V. 1913. *My life with the Eskimo*. New York, NY: Macmillan.

Stefansson, V. 1921. *The friendly Arctic*. London: Macmillan.

Stone, A.J. 1900. Some results of a natural history journey to northern British Columbia, Alaska and the Northwest Territory, in the interest of the American Museum of Natural History. *Bulletin of the American Museum of Natural History* 13, 31–62.

Buildings

Bockstoce, J.R. 1986 and 1995. *Whales, ice and men: The history of whaling in the western Arctic*. Seattle, WA: University of Washington Press.

Bodfish, H.H. 1936. *Chasing the bowhead*. Cambridge, MA: Harvard University Press.

Kemp, V. 1958. *Without fear, favour or affection: Thirty-five years with the RCMP*. Toronto, ON: Longmans, Green and Co.

Godsell, Philip H. 1951. *Arctic trader*. London: Robert Hale.

Park History

Martin, B. 2011. Negotiating a partnership of interests: Inuvialuit land claims and the establishment of Northern Yukon (Ivvavik) National Park. In *A century of Parks Canada*, 1911–2011, ed. C. Campbell. Calgary, AB: University of Calgary Press.

The web site for Herschel Island Territorial Park is at: www.env.gov.yk.ca/parksconservation/HerschelIslandQikiqtaruk.php

The Herschel Island Territorial Park Management Plan is at: www.env.gov.yk.ca/pdf/Final_version.pdf

Inuvialuit Final Agreement and Co-management

Inuvialuit Regional Corporation. 2009. Inuvialuit Final Agreement: Celebrating 25 years. Inuvik, NT: Inuvialuit Regional Corporation.

Staples, Lindsay. 1996. The Inuvialuit Final Agreement: Implementing its land, resource and environmental regimes, vol. 5, Appendix D. Research study prepared for the Royal Commission on Aboriginal Peoples.

The web site of the Wildlife Management Advisory Council (North Slope) is at: www.wmacns.ca

The Ivvavik Park Management Plan can be found at: www.pc.gc.ca/~/media/pn-np/yt/ivvavik/pdfs/pd-mp_e.ashx

A Final Word

Burn, C.R. 2008. Science in the changing North. *The Northern Review* 29: 7–20

INDEX

A

active layer, 13, 33–35, 65–70, 76, 80–81, 84, 209

air temperature, 34, 49–53, 66, 76, 94, 116

aiviq, 37, 132–133, see also walrus

akłaq, 123, 127, see also bear, grizzly

Aklavik xii, 5–6, 9, 21, 53, 116–117, 127, 131, 133–134, 139, 143, 153, 157, 173, 178, 181, 183, 188–191, 210, 213, 218–221

Aklavik Hunters and Trappers Committee, 126, 213, 218–219

Alces alces, 114, see also moose

alcohol, 6, 8–9, 162–163, 170, 174, 176

Alexander, 25, 167–169, 188, 194, 207

Alikomiak, 11, 188, 204

alluvial fan, 36–37, 67–69, 83, 209

Amaolik, 95, see also Eider, Common

amaruq, 118, 122, see also wolf, tundra

Amundsen Gulf, 132–134

Amundsen, Roald, 10, 53, 55, 168, 172, 194

Anaakliq, 142, see also Whitefish, Broad

anadromous, 5, 56, 59, 137–140, 142

Anahluk, 142, see also Whitefish, Round

Anaqkiq, 138, 142–143, see also Whitefish, Broad

Anderson, Dr. R.M., 13, 195–197

Anglican Church, 7, 157, 169–175, 183, 186, 195–196, 203, 205, 215

Aqidjigiq, see Ptarmigan, Willow

Aquila chrysaetos, 106, see also Eagle, Golden

Arctic Ocean, 26, 42, 44, 48, 55–56, 59, 76, 101, 131, 137, 184, 193–194, 221

artificial island, 47, 221

arvak, 132, see also whale, bowhead

arviq, 25, 59, 132, 158, see also whale, bowhead

Asio flammeus, 105–106, see also Owl, Short-eared

Atoogaok, Susie, 172

Atpa, 95, 99, see also Guillemot, Black

Atumiksana, 157, 171–174

aukpilaqtaq, 120, see also fox, red

Avadlek Spit, viii, 5, 22, 24–25, 36, 73–75, 84, 98, 136, 139, 143, 149–150, 159, 192, 194, 203, 207

Avaliq, 22, see also Avadlek Spit

avingaq, 107–108, 125, see also lemming

Avumnuk, 154

B

Babbage River, 22, 25, 27, 114, 133, 140, 146, 150, 217

Balaena, 166, 168

Balaena mysticetus, 59, 132, 158, see also whale, bowhead

baleen, 6, 9, 132, 147–148, 158–160, 192, 204

Banks Island, 23, 105, 121–122, 128–129, 131, 136, 153, 179, 196–197

Barter Island, xii, 150–154, 158, 182, 188–189, 196, 207, 220

Baychimo, 182, 184–185, 188

bear
  black, 37, 125
  grizzly, 109, 113, 121, 123–127, 219
  polar, 4–6, 12, 53, 59, 64, 121, 124–125, 128–131, 135, 156, 219

Beaufort Sea 2, 5, 7, 14, 22–25, 30, 32, 37–38, 42–48, 50–51, 53–56, 59, 61–64, 72, 75–76, 85, 87, 90, 95–96, 101, 105, 121, 128–136, 140–141, 143, 148, 151–152, 158, 165, 182, 202, 208, 211, 216–217, 219–221

Bell Bluff, 22–23, 37, 66, 73, 76, 103

Beluga, 26, 158, 160, 165, 170, 182, 199

Belvedere, 7, 157, 178

Beringia, 60–62, 64, 80, 85, 88, 124

Bering Sea, 14, 23, 97, 101, 133–134, 136, 192

Binder, Otto, 11

birds, table of, 101–102

blizzard, 35, 50

Bodfish, Capt. Hartson, 21, 164, 166–168, 177

Bompas, Bishop William, 8, 186

bone house, 202, 204, 208

Boreogadus saida, 139–140, 142, see also Cod, Arctic

break-up, 12, 52, 135

British Mountains, 30, 32–33, 38, 40–41, 43, 46, 49–50, 84, 106, 114–116, 149, 176, 217

Bubo scandiaca, 13, 103, 105, see also Owl, Snowy

Buckland Hills, 30, 38, 41–42, 44, 191

Buteo lagopus, 104, see also Hawk, Rough-legged

butterflies, table of, 94

C

Calcarius lapponicus, 98, see also Longspur, Lapland

Calton Point, 22–23, 36, 58, 140, 143, 192

Cambridge Bay, 182, 185

Canadian Arctic Expedition, 13, 22, 117, 173, 192, 196

Canis lupus, 118, see also wolf, tundra

Cape Bathurst, 6, 129, 153, 160–161, 165, 172, 196

Cape Parry, 136, 151, 160

caribou, barren-ground, 3, 6, 13, 37, 62–64, 81, 106, 112–116, 121–127, 147–150, 153–156, 161–162, 176, 182, 190–192, 207, 214, 219

Carter, Cst. Samuel, 10–11, 175

Cepphus grylle, 95, see also Guillemot, Black

Charadrius semipalmatus, 13, 97, see also Plover, Semipalmated

Char, Dolly Varden, 56, 59, 90, 135, 137–143

Mackenzie Mountains, 46, 89

Mackenzie, Mrs. Elizabeth, 6, 142, 207

Mackenzie River, 6, 8, 10, 26–27, 32, 36–37, 49, 53, 55–56, 59, 67, 74–75, 134, 139–141, 151, 154–155, 169, 180–182, 184, 193, 196–197, 216

Mackenzie Trough, 5, 32, 37, 54–59

Malcolm River, 15, 39, 43, 122–123

mammals, table of, 37

mammoth, 62–64

Mary D. Hume, 165, 168–169

mastodon, 63–64, 84

McFarland, Cst. William, 179, 183, 190–191

meltwater, 33, 56, 61–62, 95, 111

Merlin, 101, 106

Microtus oeconomus, 108, see also vole, tundra

moose, 6, 37, 62, 114, 116, 149, 176

mosquito, 50, 87, 89–90

mountain avens, 81–83, 107–109, 114

Mountain Indian River, 6, 23

Mount Sedgwick, 41

muskox, 15, 33, 37, 39-41, 49, 62–64, 112–117, 121–122, 199, 219

Mustela erminea, 118, see also ermine

Mustela nivalis, 118, see also weasel, least

Mysosotis alpestris ssp. *Asiatica*, see forget-me-not, alpine

N

Nahidik, 37, 59

Nanuk, 9–10, 180

nanuq, 59, 124, 128, see also bear, polar

Narwhal, 165, 168

Nasugaluak, Hanna, 157, 171–173

Nataarnaq, 142, see also Flounder, Arctic

Natarinaq, 137, 139, 141–142, see also Flounder, Arctic

natchiq, 32, 130, 132, 135, see also seal, ringed

Natchuk, 147

nauřiaq, see lupine, arctic

nautchiaq, see lupine, arctic

Neruokpuk Formation, 40–41

Newth, Capt. E.W., 193

Nicoline, 169

Nikhaaktungiq, 95, see also Ptarmigan, Rock

Nipaiłuktaq, 105–106, see also Owl, Short-eared

niutiuyiq, see lynx

Northern Whaling and Trading Company, 180–181

North-West Mounted Police, 8, 10, 23, 163, 172, 186, 203–204

Northwest Passage, 10, 13, 53, 189, 194, 214

Notik, Gareth, see Nutik, Garrett

Nuligak (Bob Cockney), 2–3, 8–9, 132, 173, 183, 225

Nunaluk Spit, 24, 36, 41, 135, 139–140, 143, 154–155

Nunatarmiut, 3, 7, 9, 21, 153–154, 169, 171, 194, 196

Nutik, Garrett, 7, 174

O

Odobenus rosmarus, 132–133, see also walrus

oil and gas exploration, 37, 43–45, 47, 131, 136

oil and gas reserves, 38, 43–45, 221

Okpik, 170–171, see also Owl, Snowy

Old Crow, 33, 49–50, 63, 156, 182, 187

Old Crow Flats, 7, 25, 106, 153–154, 218

oral history project, 13, 211

Orca, 24–26, 158

Orca Cove, 24, 74

Osborn Point, 24–25, 36, 58, 73, 116, 143, 149

Ovibos moschatus, 112, 115, see also muskox

Owl
Short-eared, 105–106, 109
Snowy, 13, 95, 101, 103, 109

P

Pacific Steam Whaling Company, 2, 9, 21, 25, 159–160, 163, 170, 193, 202–203

Pannigabluk, Fanny, 8, 171, 196

Patterson, 178–180, 183, 205

Paulatuk, 21, 128, 131, 135, 153

Pauline Cove, viii, 2–13, 20–21, 23–26, 30, 34–38, 47–48, 50–53, 59, 63–64, 67–69, 71, 73–75, 83, 85, 87, 90, 96–101, 104, 106–108, 111, 113–114, 118–120, 123, 127, 132, 137–140, 142–143, 146–150, 155–161, 163, 165–166, 169–171, 176–181, 183, 188–189, 192, 194, 198, 202–204, 206–208, 211–220

Pedersen, Capt. C.T. 9, 117, 179–180, 183, 188, 197

permafrost, 4–5, 13, 33–36, 51, 59, 65–73, 76, 80–82, 84, 88, 115, 159, 166, 198, 207, 218–219

Phillips Bay, 2, 22, 24, 140, 193

Phoca hispida, 130, 132, 135, see also seal, ringed

Piqquaqtitaq, 142, see also Cisco, Arctic

plants, table of, 86

Pleistocene, 60, 62–64

Plover, Semipalmated, 13, 96–98, 100

Pluvialis dominica, 97, see also Golden-Plover, American

pneumonia, 8, 197

Point Barrow, 26, 121, 128–129, 139–140, 152, 158, 181–182, 184, 196, 215

Polar Bear, 178, 196–197

Polar Bear Management Agreement, 131

Porcupine Caribou Herd, 6, 12, 112, 114, 123–124, 162, 219

Porsild, Erling, 101, 117, 197–198

Ptarmigan
Rock, 90, 95, 98
Willow, 25, 156

Ptarmigan Bay, 25, 111, 134–135, 139–140, 143, 155

Pullen, Lt. William, 23, 192

Putukeluk, 97–98, see also Longspur, Lapland